Post-medieval archaeology in Britain

Post-medieval archaeology in Britain

David Crossley

Leicester University Press
(a division of Pinter Publishers Ltd)
London, Leicester and New York

© David Crossley 1990
First published in Great Britain in 1990 by Leicester University Press
(a division of Pinter Publishers)

Paperback edition first published in 1994

Editorial offices
Fielding Johnson Building, University of Leicester, University Road
Leicester, LE1 7RH, England

Trade and other enquiries
25 Floral Street, London, WC2E 9DS, England

British Library Cataloguing in Publication Data

A CIP catalogue record for this book is available from the British Library.

ISBN 0–7185–1285–5
ISBN 0–7185–1937–X pbk

Library of Congress Cataloging in Publication Data
Crossley, David W.
    Post medieval archaeology in Britain / Brian Crossley.
        p.   cm.
    Includes bibliographical references.
    ISBN 0–7185–1285–5
    1. Great BritainĀntiquities.   2. Historical sites—Great Britain.
    3. Excavations (Archaeology)—Great Britain.   4. Great Britain—
    History—Tudors, 1485–1603.   5. Great Britain—History—Stuarts.
    1603–1714.   I. Title.
    DA90.C93   1990
    942.05—dc20   89–29601 CIP

Typeset by CG Graphic Services, Tring, Herts
Printed and bound in Great Britain by
Biddles Ltd, Guildford and King's Lynn

Contents

List of illustrations

Introduction

The archaeology of the centuries after 1500 has attracted resources on a growing scale over the past 30 years. Excavation and fieldwork have been published in many national and county journals, as well as in *Post-Medieval Archaeology*, whose foundation, as the journal of the society of that name, was a recognition of the amount of work for which, in the mid-1960s, it was difficult to find an outlet. That other journals now frequently include post-medieval material is a measure of the acceptance that an archaeological approach to the history of the years after 1500 is no less valid than it is to earlier periods. Indeed the continuity of so many economic indicators between the Middle Ages and the early-modern period makes a former tendency to treat late deposits with scant regard as incomprehensible as it is regrettable. Not that the excavators of the 1950s or before were always as guilty of unrecorded destruction of late deposits as some have argued: due to the vulnerability of these later levels, the more recent the evidence the less the chance of survival. In theory there is compensation from standing structures, but demolition, particularly during urban redevelopment, has made major inroads into the stock of surviving buildings.

So how far have we come, in three decades of intensive work in post-medieval archaeology? A good deal of the essential data are now in place. Artefact sequences, notably of pottery, clay tobacco pipes and glass, enable the dating of excavated deposits to be established in most parts of Britain, with important benefits to those working in North America and on the Continent of Europe. Data from dendrochronology are well established for much of Britain and western Europe; dating by thermo-remanent magnetism has been an important source, for the period in which the earliest observations of magnetic north were made. Post-medieval building types, particularly in the vernacular, have been researched in many districts, if not always fully published. The archaeology of post-medieval industry has produced at least a framework into which more detailed assessments of technical change can be placed. Research into relict landscapes with dominant post-medieval features has shown how changes in the intensity of agriculture and the development of industry can be demonstrated on the ground.

But has the published archaeological record added greatly to the mainstream literature of British economic history? Much work in, for example, rural landscape studies, or the archaeology of towns or of industry, receives little mention, and the archive-based information and arguments remain dominant. This is not always the economic historians' fault: although some move easily between archive and physical sources, many have yet to be persuaded of the contribution of the study of the physical remains, finding too few archaeological publications in which detailed results are discussed in any breadth of context or with a real attempt to integrate physical and written evidence. Archaeologists must bear a good deal of the responsibility for this, even if they have suffered from the reluctance of the major funding bodies for rescue excavation to foster the documentary research which would round out the reports which they sponsor. Had more resources been available for such work, the results would be of greater interest and value to the historical community as a whole, at a time when an underfunded archaeology needs all the friends it can find.

Further, archaeology, medieval and post-medieval, has done itself a disservice by compartmentalized specialization which needs imaginative leaps to overcome. It is all too easy, as the chapters which follow illustrate, to split the archaeology of the historic periods into close, all but self-sufficient sections, whose inter-relationships, in the totality of the economy, are apt to be obscured. Prehistorians see communities and their activities in broader terms, even if some might suggest that this can be due to a relative paucity of evidence or simplicity of economic structures. The attempt to fit the archaeological information into the wider economic development of post-1500 Britain is vital, not only to enrich the historiography of the period but to demonstrate the relationships between specialisms within archaeology itself.

What are the priorities for archaeology, in making an effective contribution to the historical record after the end of the Middle Ages? To complement the written archive by concentration on topics for which archives are sparse is one strategy, for despite the growth in record keeping in the sixteenth century and after, there remained activities which generated few written archives. As an example, the contrast might be cited between the extent of documentation for the lands and activities of large estates and for those of their tenants, often leaving the latter best investigated through physical traces. Even where archives are at first sight substantial, they are often quantitative, and rarely contain description or comment, apart from those contained in surveys, or in depositions in courts of law. Where the qualitative written record is lacking, it is to structures, standing or buried, to the plots or fields which surrounded them, or to the products or residues of industries or crafts that we turn. If, to take a rare example, the ironmasters, John Fuller father and son, had been typical in leaving vivid descriptions of their activities and their operating problems in their letters, archaeology might have less to contribute, from the physical evidence either for success or for difficulties encountered in an industrial process.

As it is, the lives of the majority of the population living in sixteenth-, seventeenth-and early-eighteenth-century Britain are barely touched upon by the written word, and even then only at the major occasions or crises of life. But where the exception does occur, where, for example, inventories or building accounts survive for modest domestic or industrial buildings, correlation with the structures to which they relate has a high priority. The author has long argued that at the outset of any programme of historical research where much of the evidence is likely to be archaeological rather than written, it is vital to set up an initial measure, by the examination or excavation of the buildings or the sites for which the best archives survive, and where these and the archaeological sources are mutually illuminating. We need to see the relationship between, for example, building costs and the structures on which they were incurred, between recorded profitability on the one hand and, on the other, product quality and process efficency as shown by artefacts and residues. This juxtaposition of the written and physical evidence is a keystone of work throughout the historic periods; it is the basis for interpretation by historian and archaeologist of, respectively, records without related structures and artefacts or, on the other hand, sites for which no records have been found. In addition, extending the latter point, the evidence of place and time provided by field survey or excavation can give a new focus for documentary research, in which the significance of scattered references may be recognized.

What is the overall framework in which post-medieval archaeological research should be placed? Without doubt, the economic history of the three centuries from 1450 is dominated by demographic recovery after the late-medieval epidemics, to which changes in agriculture, industry and trade as well as in individual wealth and status are related. The archaeological record provides ample material evidence for these developments.

The field archaeology of the period is dominated by landscape changes which accompanied the response of agriculture and industry to the demands of the growing population: the British landscape, although a palimpsest deriving from all periods from prehistoric to present, owes most to the years from the end of the Middle Ages to the onset of agricultural depression late in the nineteenth century. Despite the unprecedented extent of change since the 1960s, the features which developed during the post-medieval centuries still remain prominent, and in large areas dominant. They comprise a historical document, particularly of the history of British agriculture as it emerged from the restraints of medieval custom and took the shape which made it possible to feed the great growth in population of the industrial revolution. The signs of this development in the landscape are still relatively fresh, comprising a series of overlays which are readily distinguishable. They are indeed overlays which the archaeologist whose interest lies mainly in earlier periods needs to recognize, when identifying the landscapes of previous ages. The approach owes a great deal to the work of William Hoskins, whose *Making of the English Landscape* (1955) awakened so many to those wider aspects of historical archaeology to which less than due attention had previously been given. What Hoskins wrote in the 1950s may now seem to have stated the obvious; but the archaeological literature of the time shows that few had his width of vision; indeed, it is a mark of Hoskins' achievement that his approach is now accepted, if implicitly, by so many.

An important aspect of landscape archaeology, which has received increasing recognition since Hoskins wrote, is the inter-relationship of relict agrarian and industrial features. It is a mistake to treat pre-nineteenth-century industrial features in the landscape in isolation, for the connections with the agrarian sector are important in terms of complementary or competing land use. They also reflect the mixture of occupations within rural communities, and within the lives of individuals, for many people divided their time between work in farming and woodland, textile workshop, mining or some branch of the metal trades. Studies of the archaeology of, for example, iron or lead production have been apt to concentrate on structures and earthwork features demonstrably specific to the processes. Extension is important, to show how industry was integrated into the rural landscape, before the dominance of coal and of steam power led to concentration and urbanization. It is desirable that programmes to give protection to relict landscapes, under consideration at the time of writing, should recognize that in many districts there can be no separation of the industrial from the agrarian, so interlinked were these in the rural economy.

An example, for which evidence appears in several of the succeeding chapters, is the supply of fuel: the importance of coppice woodland for a range of industries before the mid-eighteenth century. Coppice was often a factor in estate land use, integrated into management and amenity patterns which also included timber woodland and parks. The relationship with farming lay in the relative profitability of alternative forms of land use over the medium term. In few cases has evidence for this supply of wood fuel been incorporated into field-surveys of industrial sites. Other complex relationships may be interpreted from the landscape in the case of coal and ore mining, where the gains from mineral exploitation had to be weighed against agriculture or amenity.

The current interest in the interpretation of historic landscapes is welcome for its interdisciplinary potential, and particularly for the extent to which specialists are seeing the wider significance of their research, in a way which may overcome the limitations referred to earlier. To take one example, work in vernacular building studies is becoming an important contributor: although frequently, and rightly, concerned with typology, notably of the development of structural carpentry, the wider significance of improved building to landscape archaeology has to be stressed. This is not new, for nearly 40 years ago Hoskins was emphasizing the relationship between improved standards of accommodation, visible in surviving sixteenth-and seventeenth-century houses, changes in agricultural wealth and practice, and developments in markets for agricultural produce consequent on the rise in population of urban or specialist-industrial communities. As will be indicated in Chapter 1, there remain districts where these relationships have yet to be fully explored. Where vernacular building studies have been particularly significant is in the use of archives relevant to individual houses. This can be seen with probate inventories which, used with discretion, have a potential for the confirmation of house size and room use, and in relating the size of a building to other aspects of the wealth of the occupier.

One matter which has received insufficient study, and whose importance needs emphasis in this introduction as well as in more detail in the chapter which follows, is the need to link the improved post-medieval house with evidence from its surroundings, in determining the sources of income which made its construction possible; it is not enough to assume a general development in commercial farming in the locality. It is necessary to establish the sources of income of the occupant, whether the size and contemporary character of the farm, or complementary industrial occupations, or sources even harder to define, such as moorland or fenland grazing. Some of this information must be sought in archive sources, but much may be derived from study of the historic landscape.

Just as standing buildings must be related to other field and archive evidence for the wealth of their owners, so there is a need for greater attention to be paid to comparable implications of assemblages of excavated artefacts. The problem is how far such residues can inform us about the wealth and the conventions of consumption of their former owners. There have been few cases where excavated finds-groups have come from contexts associated with documented individuals, and research on such associations poses great difficulties in both rural and urban contexts. This is particularly the case with rescue excavation, but there are arguments for giving priority to sites where former buildings and their occupants are well documented. The excavations in St Ebbes, Oxford are an example of the benefits of research to fit material from excavated contexts to their former owners: one such case is illustrated in fig. 12.1 (p. 244).

The study of such artefacts has aroused interest in standards of quality which industrial and craft production could achieve before the industrial revolution. In particular, evidence from excavations and from the examination of artefacts is increasingly seen as of value for assessing the problems faced in manufacture, and showing how these were overcome empirically, rather than on any scientific basis. In the study of ceramics, such questions have long been of interest: the presence of wasters is an obvious key to kiln location, as is the distribution of the second-quality wares sold in local markets. Experimental firings of replica kilns, including post-medieval types such as the Potterton replica included in the Leeds experiments of 1967, showed some of the problems which the pre-industrial potter encountered in minimizing losses and costs through waste. Residues from other industries have received scientific examination on an increasingly sophisticated level. For many years, metallurgical slags and cinders were analysed, but it is now accepted that well-sampled deposits can present, in microcosm, an account of the methods of the smelter and the problems he encountered. This is true for the post-medieval period as much as for any other, and is particularly significant in complementing early descriptions of processes, and explaining in scientific terms the difficulties to which commentators refer. The potential has been shown with particular clarity in the case of glass production, where scientific examination of the product, of reject glass, and the various forms of process wastes has demonstrated the consistency with which the glassmaker overcame obstacles presented by the available materials, by fuel characteristics, by refractories and by empirical traditions of furnace design. These examples emphasize a direction which research projects into post-medieval industry should take, and the import-ance of establishing collaborative ventures in this area of science-related archaeology.

To attempt an overview of post-medieval archaeology involves not only a review of published work but, within this, more detailed surveys where publication is scattered or syntheses are lacking. Coverage and accessibility are variable: recent interest in certain aspects of the rural landscape has led to publication on a scale which makes a detailed examination unnecessary here, and suggests the need for an overview, with a reminder of problems yet unsolved or neglected. Publication in urban archaeology has suffered serious problems: a great deal of excavation has been done, but much has been of a complexity whose implications for post-excavation work have been underestimated. In many cases only brief summaries are yet available in print, many in the 'Post-Medieval Britain ...' section of *Post-Medieval Archaeology*. The reactive nature of much urban archaeology has worsened the position, not only adding to delays in the publication of past excavations, but hindering the creation or operation of any strategy for problem-oriented deployment of resources. This weakness is likely to become even more serious as locally negotiated developer funding comes to provide an increasing proportion of the resource for excavation.

It is particularly for those aspects of the archaeology of industry for which published syntheses are not yet available that detailed surveys need to be set out in this book. There need be no apology for a relatively close examination of, for example, the archaeological evidence for power sources, a subject which, for Britain, has received insufficient coverage in print. Some detail is also justified in the coverage of industries such as glass, where the archaeological evidence for the important post-medieval changes has only recently become available, for iron, where syntheses are apt to separate the metallurgical from the wider archaeological results, and for non-ferrous metals, a topic where archaeological coverage is still inadequate.

Many friends have helped with the development of this book. Substantial parts have been read and commented upon by Jonathan Coad, Peter Davey, David Hey, David Higgins, John Hurst, John Kenyon, Stephen Moorhouse, David Palliser and Stuart Wrathmell. I hope I have done justice to their suggestions. In particular I thank John Hurst, who has not only been my guide to the pottery of the period, but has to a large extent been responsible for fostering the development of post-medieval archaeology in Britain over the last 30 years.

I am grateful to the following, who have advised me on illustrations or who have provided photographs or plans:

F.G. Aldsworth, Denis Ashurst, Owen Bedwin, Robert Bell, Guy Beresford, Pauline Beswick, David Butler, Lawrence Butler, David Caldwell, the late Alan Carter, Faith Cleverdon, David Cranstone, Peter Crew, Carol Cunningham, Joan Day, Philip Dixon, Christopher Drage, Paul Drury, John Earnshaw, Geoff Egan, Russell Fox, Sandy Gerrard, Christopher Green, Tom Greeves, John Harvey, Tom Hassall, John and Julia Hatfield, Colin Hayfield, Hilary Healey, John Hedges, Chris Henderson, Cecil Hewett, David Hey, David Higgins, Jennifer Hillam, Felix Holling, John Hume, Derek Hurst, Ruth Hurst Vose, Keith Jarvis, Barry Johnson, David Kiernan, John Lewis, Andrew Marvell, Robina McNeil, Stephen Moorhouse, Dennis Mynard, N.E.S. Norris, John Pickin, Chris Place, Michael Ponsford, Derrick Riley, Peter Ryder, John Schofield, Michael Shaw, Chris Tabraham, Barrie Trinder, Rick Turner, A.H. Ward, Martin Watts, John Weaver, Rosemary Weinstein, Christopher Whittick, David R Wilson, Stuart Wrathmell.

The assistance of the following bodies in providing illustrations is acknowledged:

Bath Archaeological Trust, Bristol City Museum, Cambridge University Collection of Aerial Photographs, Centre of East Anglian Studies: University of East Anglia, East Sussex County Record Office, English Heritage, Exeter Museum, Glamorgan and Gwent Archaeological Trust, Hereford and Worcester County Museum, Department of Greater London Archaeology and Department of Urban Archaeology: Museum of London, Milton Keynes Archaeological Unit, Newport Museum, Northamptonshire Archaeological Unit, Oxford Architectural and Historical Society, Borough of Poole Museum, Royal Archaeological Institute, Royal Commission on the Ancient and Historical Monuments of Scotland, Scottish Development Department, Sheffield City Museum, Sheffield Record Office, Society for Post-Medieval Archaeology, Sussex Archaeological Field Unit, West Yorkshire Archaeology Service.

I apologize to any individual or organization whose material has been mistakenly attributed or has passed unacknowledged. I and the publishers would wish to remedy such error in any subsequent edition.

Chapter 1

The archaeology of the post-medieval rural landscape

Agricultural improvement and the landscape

The archaeology of the post-medieval landscape of Britain is the visible record of a period when agriculture recovered from the consequences of the demographic setback of the later Middle Ages, and developed to supply successive increases in population. There was an approximate doubling of numbers over the country as a whole between late in the fifteenth century and the middle of the seventeenth, although in many places the increase was a good deal greater. In these two centuries the market for grain and livestock changed not only in scale but in form, as urban demand affected the farming pattern of increasingly distant areas. London was outstanding in the effect it had on districts whence grain could be economically carried or livestock sent on the hoof, but there were regions dependent on towns such as Bristol, Norwich or York, over which commercial farming also became significant. Although overall population growth eased for a century from about 1640, the momentum of change in agrarian life was maintained: arable farms were rationalized into larger holdings as urban markets continued to develop, particularly those of industrial areas whose growth foreshadowed the headlong development of the second half of the eighteenth century. There was in particular a continued expansion of livestock production, a response, it might be argued, to dietary change among those urban consumers who benefited from the development of commerce in the century after the Restoration.

The written record is a copious source for many of these changes, but it is uneven: the bias is in part due to the records of those larger estates which generated consistent archives and were, in turn, more likely to preserve them. Also emphasized are particular events and problems, which overshadow gradual change. In the case of enclosure, sixteenth-century litigation and commissions of enquiry concentrated on hard cases, and in the eighteenth century many Parliamentary Enclosure Acts reflected contemporary changes in local landed political power and in perception of new market opportunities. Just as these records understate the long-term changes such as piecemeal enclosure by agreement, so other aspects of improvement are distorted: in marshland reclamation, for example, evidence for the great fenland schemes overshadows the widespread work of individuals or work which can only be discovered by painstaking research on records of Commissioners of Sewers, for which survivals on the ground often provide a good focus.

An informed interpretation of the landscape produces a picture of post-medieval agrarian development which goes well beyond mere confirmation of what can be learned from the archives. There are of course many imperfections in the visual record, which is often confused by subsequent events, but there are numerous districts where a chronology of agrarian change is plain to see and where written evidence is lacking. Perhaps the most fruitful cases are those where ample written records and the physical survivals can be juxtaposed: only by such matching will yardsticks be established, vital for archaeologist and local historian alike.

Over the last 20 years there has been development in the specialisms which, placed together, build an archaeology of the post-medieval countryside. Yet, despite the emphasis which the pioneer work of Fox and Hoskins placed on the relationship of local and field studies to wider economic developments, compart-mentalization and its pitfalls are still plain to see. Work on vernacular building, on changes in field systems, on woodlands, parks or great houses, needs to be placed squarely in the wider context of economic change, if the results of fieldwork are in turn to enhance the understanding of that change among historians in general. Also, we have seen too little interrelation of specialisms. How many post-medieval farmhouses, for example, have been placed in the context of the entire holding, and related to the signs of improvement of the land whose productivity enabled these buildings to be constructed or extended? There are some admirable exceptions: Cunliffe's study of the post-medieval farm at Chalton (1973) demonstrates an awareness of the economic connections between agrarian change and the wealth which gave rise to building. Airs' work (1975) on great houses sees construction in a wider light, emphasizing, for example, the effect on local and distant communities in terms of short-and long-term employment. Several of the contributors to the 'English Landscape' series recognized the width of their brief, relating archive to archaeological material and placing regional features in the context of national change.

Emphasis in the archaeology of the post-medieval landscape has been on field survey and the recording of standing structures. Indeed the returns from excavation have perhaps been rather understated: it can be shown how work on sites abandoned during our period can give a valuable view of structures free of later accretion and alteration. Also, it has been demonstrated that constant archaeological observation of buildings during maintenance work and minor alterations can generate a valuable store of information.

PRE-PARLIAMENTARY ENCLOSURE

The arable fields

Change in the post-medieval landscape is linked with the movement towards systems of farming which could increase yields and incomes at a time of demographic growth, but there was a great variety of response, before enclosure by Act of Parliament and the construction of new planned farmsteads brought a greater visual uniformity. This is a topic which lacks comprehensive documentary sources: much enclosure was piecemeal, at best recorded through legal cases or in estate archives, but there is a significant proportion which has left no explicit written evidence. The difficulty of identifying the date or circumstances of pre-parliamentary enclosure resulted in its neglect, to which Taylor's *Fields in the English Landscape* (C.C. Taylor 1975) provided a remedy. But at present we have only a scatter of well-researched cases, which archaeologist and local historian alike could well enlarge. Any examination of an area where pre-parliamentary enclosure is apparent must be combined firstly with research into other aspects of contemporary settlement, notably the relationship between enclosures and the building or rebuilding of farms, and also with archive research, not only on the occupants of farms, but on the extent to which commercial food marketing was entering the local economy and providing the incentive for the improvements visible on the ground.

As a starting point in the field investigation of enclosure, it can be useful to seek out landscapes where the process was never completed, where there has been some consolidation of strips but without permanent enclosure. In the south, fragments of open field can still be seen at Braunton in north Devon. On Portland strips are still visible over an area of 150 acres, and although common management ceased in the nineteenth century, many lands are still cultivated with boundaries only indicated by baulks and occasional mere-stones (RCHM 1970: 259). At Soham, Cambridgeshire (fig. 1.4), a considerable area survives without fenced boundaries and with intermingling of strips (C.C. Taylor 1973: 96). Open-field configuration survives round Haxey and Epworth, in the Isle of Axholme, Lincolnshire, and although there is no communal control of cropping, there are tracts of unfenced strips, consolidated to varying degrees. The undulating terrain shows this layout to advantage, and the practices of the area deserve more study than they have yet received. Laxton, Nottinghamshire, is the classic survivor: largely by chance, no Enclosure Act was ever secured for the main fields of the village, although the surrounding lands were enclosed, and eighteenth-and nineteenth-century farmsteads were built on the periphery much as around other midland villages. The inner fields are still operated under the control of the court leet, and are worked from farms on the village streets. Chambers' (1964) study of Laxton was important in amplifying the Orwins' references to the village fields (1938: later editions, 1954, 1967), and his film of practices as seen in the 1950s was a significant visual record; further films have been made by John Saville and by John Beckett, this last to accompany his book on the village (Beckett 1989). At Laxton we have a landscape in which, despite the part-consolidation of strips early in the present century and the ploughing down of the ridge and furrow, accelerated by the use of modern equipment, it is still possible to perceive many of the essentials of open-field farming; this is particularly apparent on the spring-sown field, where Laxton farmers have customarily planted a diversity of crops.

Such survivals are quite exceptional, for consolidation and enclosure of open-field strips began well before the end of the Middle Ages: during and after the period of epidemics there were opportunities for farmers to rationalize, as manorial restraints slackened, to the point of offering incentives to tenants to take vacant lands. Thus consolidation is not just a post-medieval phenomenon, although it continued in the sixteenth and seventeenth centuries as farmers encountered developing markets. This is the background to a great diversity. In some cases there was agreement to rationalize lands on some scale: Butlin's work on Northumberland coastal villages (1967) showed a practice of concentrating tenants' lands in a part of the arable, wherein some farmers fenced off their holdings. Study of

Northumberland villages from the air and from maps shows that some of the sixteenth-century boundaries survived the parliamentary enclosure procedures. Enclosure agreements in many parts of the country were formalized by decrees in Chancery, as indicated by Beresford's sampling of this important source (1961; 1979). In some cases this meant only that the participants preferred to have public legal proof of their arrangements, but the practice can also indicate opposition, against which the stronger parties to an agreement wished to be prepared.

In many villages the process of enclosing the open fields consisted of a gradual accumulation of convenient blocks of land over several generations, which can only be followed in the rare cases of the survival of successive and sufficiently detailed leases, or where there is a succession of estate maps. This has been done in Derbyshire with the aid of William Senior's early-seventeenth-century maps of the Chatsworth estates (Fowkes and Potter 1988); similarly in Buckinghamshire, maps of Great Linford made in 1641 and 1678 show the fields and roads of the parish before and after the enclosure agreement of 1658 (Reed 1984). In the absence of earlier sources, maps drawn during planning for parliamentary enclosure can show field patterns typical of gradual consolidation, reflecting former furlongs and strips. What is no longer in doubt is the scale of the alteration to the landscape over the period. It has been calculated that in Leicestershire, Lincolnshire, Nottinghamshire and Buckinghamshire, considerably less than half of the land remained to be enclosed by Act of Parliament, the rest having changed before the middle of the eighteenth century (Reed 1981). What we cannot yet say for certain is what proportions of, for example, the 56 per cent of Leicestershire enclosed before the eighteenth century were fenced off before or after 1500.

In many parts of the country there are examples of walls and hedges which enclose blocks of former arable strips: these frequently show the curve typical of medieval ploughing, fossilized in the boundary lines. Air photography has shown many fine examples which have not previously been recognized. The photograph of Wardlow, Derbyshire (fig. 1.1), provides a spectacular case, paralleled in several villages in the Peak and further north in the Yorkshire Pennines. The map of Mexborough, Yorkshire (fig. 1.2) shows an exceptionally late case, of eighteenth-century consolidation encouraged by the landowner (Harvey 1974).

The dating of consolidation may be difficult in areas of stone walling, but elsewhere the study of the age of hedges might be expected to be of assistance. The theory of hedgerow dating is by now well known, resting on Hooper's perception that species counts show an increase with the age of the hedge (Pollard *et al.* 1974). The enthusiasm with which the concept was originally grasped led to suggestions that hedges could be dated in isolation, on rules of thumb which equated the number of species with the centuries of age of a hedge. What has become clear from several careful local studies, in parts of East Sussex (Maloney and Howard 1986) and Norfolk (Tillyard 1976; Addington 1978, 1982; Johnson 1982), is that in a locality where growing conditions are uniform, the rate of plant colonization in hedgerows over several centuries can enable broad distinctions to be made between boundaries of different periods, usually between medieval and eighteenth/nineteenth century hedges, with some measure of success in detecting those laid out in the interim. However, anyone who seeks to use this method in the absence of cartographic or archive sources, or as a back-up to them, has to remember the distorting factors, such as the proximity of woodland or former waste whence invasive species may have come. It is also significant that sixteenth-century land

Fig. 1.1 Consolidated and enclosed strips, formerly open-field arable, at Wardlow, Derbyshire. William Senior's survey of 1617 (Fowkes and Potter 1988: 130–33) indicates that the fields of the village were yet to be enclosed (Cambridge University Collection).

surveyors advised the planting of trees in hedges: Fitzherbert advocated increasing the supply of hardwoods thereby, and Norden recommended planting fruit trees. Such additions give a misleading impression of age to a boundary.

Upland and forest enclosure

There are parts of upland Britain where open-field husbandry was either not practised at all or was limited to land immediately adjacent to the village. In many pastoral districts the significant post-medieval changes are the increases in enclosure around the fringes, which can be very hard to date, and even where estate or manorial records survive, are often particularly difficult to identify. Expansion and encroachment on the waste was frequently carried out on an individual basis over lengthy periods, and even when done by a township, with some degree of co-ordination, the result was usually a division into individual land parcels.

The significant concept behind any archaeological appreciation of the upland landscape is what constituted viable or marginal grazing land at a particular time. Late in the Middle Ages the influences are complex and virtually impossible to quantify. In straight demographic terms, we would expect there to have been a

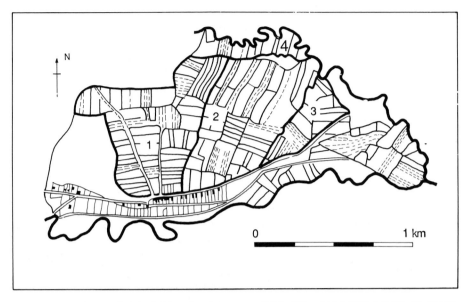

Fig. 1.2 Mexborough, Yorkshire: the three open fields, Wood Field [1], Middle Field [2], and Low Field [3], and pasture to the north and east [4], were shown on a map of 1700 and are here indicated by thick lines; by the time of the map of 1839 they had been divided into these small enclosed fields, comprising consolidated strips. This is an exceptionally late case of consolidation, rather than radical enclosure by private Act of Parliament (after John Harvey).

retreat from land used at the end of the thirteenth century. Not only would reduced demand, and hence prices, make the poorer and more distant grazing grounds uneconomic, but the conversion of lowland arable to good-quality pasture would add to the problems of the upland farmer in the fifteenth century. But his position was alleviated in one, perhaps two respects. The English textile industry grew during the period, at the expense of continental rivals, and the wool market was correspondingly buoyant in the fifteenth century. While this also benefited lowland pasture farmers, by the middle of the sixteenth century the textile industries of the north were emerging from their traditional status of local suppliers, and provided an increasing market for Pennine sheep farmers. The other point is more speculative; in the fifteenth century higher per capita incomes among the surviving population may have led to a greater consumption of meat, further questioning the assumption that retreat from traditional pasture lands would have been in proportion to demographic decline.

This background is significant in explaining post-medieval changes in the pastoral economy. If grazing land colonized in the pre-Black Death period had not all been abandoned, then, in the sixteenth century when population rose again, and particularly as lowland pasture was returned to arable, the pressures on old grazing grounds, on upland waste and on marsh would be the greater. And so it turned out, for in hill country, sixteenth-and seventeenth-century enclosure provided new improved grazing: the needs of the larger towns, pre-eminently London, were felt over increasing distances through well-organized droving trades. Hence what had hitherto been moorland was enclosed over the length of the Pennines from Northumberland to the Peak District, and in many areas of Wales.

There are examples of upland enclosure where archive material and field observation give mutual support. A much-quoted source is the Duchy of Lancaster petition and enquiry involving the agreement of villagers on the fringes of Bowland forest, to enclose their moorland grazing near Grindleton (Tawney and Power 1924; I, 81). This is a case where rising local population, to which the petition refers, led to a scheme for the improvement of moorland and presumably the release of valley-bottom pasture for improved meadow or for arable. The modern map and the present-day appearance of the land around Grindleton show where enclosures took place and where boundaries and farms were created. The research which has been published on the manor court rolls (Porter 1973) has shown the extent of building, and it is important to relate a source such as this to present-day topography. Elsewhere in the Lancashire Pennines the results are similar: this is illustrated by the programme of survey and excavation in the Watergrove valley, near Rochdale, where sixteenth-and seventeenth-century farm buildings are associated with boundaries of fields colonized early in the sixteenth century (*PMA* 1988: 222–3), and is also indicated by the pattern of building shown in the study of houses around Colne and Burnley (RCHM 1985b). In Northumberland the mid-sixteenth-century enclosure of Rothbury forest led to the creation of new farms and enclosures which can be identified on the ground; west Yorkshire was similarly affected, as were the valleys of the Lake District, areas where developing textile industries brought a further incentive to improve pasture by enclosure. A commission on encroachments in Westward Forest in the Lake District enquired in 1571 into 127 encroachments and found that 32 were new farms carved from the waste. A well-known west-Yorkshire parallel is the Act of 1555 which refers to 500 new households on the wastes around Halifax.

In the Midlands, there are good examples of upland encroachment and enclosure in Derbyshire (fig. 1.13), Northamptonshire, Staffordshire and Shropshire. North-east Staffordshire contains valleys where small hedged or walled fields create irregular boundaries with the unenclosed moor: many are undocumented, but form parts of farms whose buildings are of this period. In Shropshire there are notable examples of encroachment and the creation of smallholdings and farms on the fringes of the Clee hills, many on apparently inhospitable moorland (fig. 1.3). Less visually striking are the many small-scale extensions of farms in the southern parts of the county, dating from the sixteenth century and marked by small fields, and by thick hedges, some of which are relict fragments of woodland. In Rockingham Forest, Northamptonshire, there were numerous encroachments, well documented as a result of the observations of royal officials in the sixteenth century (Pettit 1968: 142–5; Porter 1974).

There are sometimes dangers in making firm visual distinctions between sixteenth-and seventeenth-century pastoral enclosure and the schemes brought about by private Acts of Parliament. This has been underlined by Taylor in his study of enclosure on the Dorset downlands, and can be backed up by examining boundaries in Somerset, Staffordshire and west Yorkshire. It is clear that on occasion large regular fields were laid out at an early date. On the downlands in Dorset there are documented cases of enclosure by agreement between the 1590s and the 1740s which can be related to large fields with hedges set on low banks.

Fig. 1.3 Oreton, Shropshire, showing cottages and enclosures taken in from the moor. Earthworks from shallow mining are also visible (see figs. 9.1 and 9.2) (Cambridge University Collection).

Adjacent, to the north, the lands around Gillingham, disafforested early in the seventeenth century, are divided into large fields around isolated farmsteads in a manner foreshadowing later procedures and giving an impression very different from the small enclosures which are apt to be regarded as typical of the period (C.C. Taylor 1970: 127–32). The stone walls of the Throwley valley in Staffordshire (fig. 1.22) could at first sight be taken for parliamentary-enclosure boundaries, but in fact seem to be the result of estate reorganization.

Upland expansion could go too far, leading to over-grazing of poor ground. In Derbyshire, the movement was as strong as elsewhere in the Pennines, and the disafforestation of the High Peak in the second half of the seventeenth century led not only to the improvement of former waste but to increases in stock densities on the open moors. Studies of the Edale moors indicate that over-stocking led to degeneration of vegetation, and hence erosion of the peat during the eighteenth century (Somerville 1977; Shimwell 1974).

It should not be assumed that upland improvement was universal, or that the margins of intensive land use which can be identified as of sixteenth- or seventeenth-century date were determined only by the quality of the ground and by market considerations. In some cases there was strong resistance to encroachment by holders of common rights, a resistance which also occurred in the lowlands. Where commoners' rights were strong, open grazing survived, and such rights were tenaciously held where farms were small and common grazing a vital supplement. This could also apply to the migratory summer grazing which was still practised in the more remote regions. Summer shielings were in use in northern England and in Wales and Scotland, and there are several case studies which indicate the growth of the practice. In Northumberland, surveys in Redesdale have recorded sites which correspond with sixteenth-and seventeenth-century references to shielings and grazing grounds, and which possess features such as stack-stand enclosures, which indicate the storage of hay and hence the occupation of upland outposts over extended seasons. In Scotland considerable field research has shown that summer grazing expanded, marked by the construction of shielings and bothies at a time when the market for livestock products became particularly buoyant. Similar patterns can be seen in Wales, with work in the north and in the Brecon Beacons showing how land hitherto little used for grazing was brought into the pattern of seasonal use (Miller 1967a, 1967b).

Marshland reclamation

Remarkable though the effect of medieval marsh and fen drainage had been, the schemes of the seventeenth and eighteenth centuries were on a still greater scale. They illustrate the worth of relating archive sources to field observation, for the latter demonstrates the problems which many schemes encountered, not only during the original work but in maintaining the new lands. In the Fens, the layout of the major seventeenth-century schemes associated with Cornelius Vermuyden is well known. Taylor (1973: 188ff.; RCHM 1972a: lxii) has shown how the lands of the Adventurers and Undertakers can be identified on the ground, in relation to the drainage channels cut before and, more successfully, after the Civil War. What he has also done is to draw attention to earlier schemes, the fifteenth-century work of Bishop Morton, and that of Popham in the first quarter of the seventeenth century. Thirsk (1957: 21, 97) has described the process of reclamation in the south Lincolnshire fens, around Sutterton, Fosdyke and Harlaxton. Ravensdale's study of Landbeach and its Cambridgeshire neighbours (1974) has illustrated the potential for research and identification of drainage measures undertaken before the great seventeenth-century schemes, using sixteenth-and seventeenth-century records of Commissioners of Sewers, a source also valuable in Sussex, notably for the Pevensey levels.

The Fens illustrate what can be done to interpret a reclaimed marshland landscape where ample documentation survives. The area also shows some of the problems: intermingled with some of the schemes are examples of small-scale encroachment by individuals (fig. 1.4), comparable with moor-edge colonization in the uplands. But of greatest significance is the alteration of the appearance of reclaimed marshlands due to the fall in levels caused by shrinkage of the peat and by the less serious lowering of the silt fenland. Thus we have to visualize a seventeenth-century scenery in which the new drainage channels formed less obvious topographical features than at present, their flood-banks less upstanding above the surrounding ground. In the eighteenth century the difference would appear more marked, with windmill drainage pumps a striking feature, and farmsteads built on the relatively stable roddons, the silt beds of former channels

Fig. 1.4 Soham, Cambridgeshire: encroachments on marshland commons. Strips of unenclosed land can be seen in the background (Cambridge University Collection).

and creeks. In the nineteenth century the difference in levels was approaching what can now be seen, with the fenlands only saved from inundation by changes in pumping technology and the use of steam engines. As a well-documented model, the Fens are valuable for interpreting the landscape archaeology of other marshlands. The results of peat shrinkage and the silting of outfalls can be seen elsewhere and, again, their effects make it difficult to imagine the immediate post-reclamation landscape. Important areas of peatland marsh drainage can be seen in the Somerset levels and in the lower Trent basin. The latter was the scene of Vermuyden's first project in England, started in the 1620s, which involved the drainage of the Hatfield marshes and the diversion of the river Idle. Although shrinkage and later drainage and pumping (fig. 1.5) on the fenland pattern have made the landscape as created by Vermuyden hard to distinguish over much of the area, there are parts of the fringes of the Isle of Axholme where something can be seen of the field layouts which developed in the seventeenth and eighteenth centuries, with an impression also of the pre-drainage landscape, whose resources were defended so vigorously by the marshland communities.

The other enemy of drainage schemes, the blocking of outfalls, also challenged the technology of the sixteenth-and seventeenth-century improver. Changes in the Sussex Ouse valley, between Lewes and Newhaven, are an apt illustration, where interpretation from topographical features would be difficult

Fig. 1.5 Stump of drainage windmill at Owston Ferry, Humberside, built to pump water to the Trent (right) from the marshland drainage channel adjacent to the mill. The chimney of the later steam pump can be seen in the left background.

without documentary support (Brandon 1971). The works of the sixteenth-century Commissioners of Sewers entailed moving the outfall of the Ouse and creating meadowland on what had in the early sixteenth century been inundated marsh. In the seventeenth and eighteenth centuries natural movements in the outfall caused repeated problems, and only towards the end of the eighteenth century was a radical scheme designed by Smeaton sufficient to reclaim the Lewes and Laughton levels. The drainage channels and field boundaries current-ly visible are an amalgam of various phases in the complex history of the levels, from medieval features around the villages on the west side of the valley through to the channels of the eighteenth century, created when the present line of the river was stabilized to allow the development of the port of Newhaven.

Pre-eighteenth-century improvement and the form of the village

An important question, which has recently attracted attention, is how far sixteenth-and seventeenth-century consolidation of holdings affected the plan of the village or hamlet. Later, as is shown below, rationalization during the enclosures typical of the eighteenth century, by Parliamentary Act or otherwise, was to lead to new farmsteads being built on the village periphery. Prior to this, we are seeking changes of a more subtle kind. The debate over the extent to which medieval villages had been deliberately planned need not detain us, but we do find that by the sixteenth century many villages possessed apparently coherent groups of houses and crofts. As piecemeal consolidation led to the concentration of the lands of a farm, hitherto scattered in the village fields and best worked from the centre, it is to be expected that farmers would construct new houses and farm buildings on more convenient sites. To what extent has this obscured the medieval layout of the village, and how far have earthworks of buildings which were abandoned due to such shifts been misinterpreted as signs of late-medieval shrinkage? This aspect of the 'Great Rebuilding', is hinted at by Roberts (1987: 214–5), and briefly considered by Meeson (1987: 89–90) in connection with the village earthworks at Wychnor, Staffordshire.

Excavation has begun to demonstrate and explain post-medieval changes to medieval village layouts. Cowlam, on the Yorkshire Wolds, is an example: two crofts, in a group whose original layout was medieval, had been amalgamated, probably in the sixteenth century, and a single farm (fig. 1.16) occupied the pair of plots until the village was abandoned in the early 1670s (Hayfield 1988). West Whelpington, Northumberland, is the only other post-medieval desertion where large-scale excavation has been possible, also demonstrating changes to the medieval plan. Such opportunities are rare, and the evidence for change usually has to come from the study of the morphology of the existing village, and the relationship of surviving post-medieval houses to an earlier plan.

A further question is whether sixteenth-and seventeenth-century landowners themselves laid out planned villages as an accompaniment to agricultural change on their estates, as well as during their own building or landscaping schemes. The deliberate planning of the post-medieval village is best known from cases where landscaping was the first concern, most commonly in association with the building of the country house (see p. 71), or, in the eighteenth and nineteenth centuries, as an accompaniment to industrial development. What is uncertain is how frequently landowners responded to the rise in population of the sixteenth and seventeenth centuries by planning extensions to the village core, leasing new house plots to immigrants or to new tenants from within the growing community. There would be an incentive to raise rental income in this way: to rely on housing a population increase by allowing uncontrolled squatter-development on the waste, even on land containing abandoned medieval house sites, could be a poor use of ground which had potential for improvement, as well as threatening the common-grazing rights of existing farms.

PARLIAMENTARY ENCLOSURE

The systematic enclosures, notably of eighteenth-century date, which used the procedure of private Acts of Parliament, have archaeological implications which are apt to be taken for granted. These changes, with the improvements in farming method which often accompanied or succeeded them, formed the last great change to the rural landscape before the revolution brought by mechanized farming after 1945. Despite the effects of the latter, in large parts of England, lowland and upland, it is the landscape of parliamentary enclosure which dominates features of all other periods. Again, we have a system of boundaries which has to be recognized and understood if it is to be satisfactorily distinguished from its predecessors.

The rationalization of holdings achieved by enclosure commissioners enabled large fields to be laid out. The extent to which enclosure awards secured such changes depended on the degree of agreement which could be reached and often on the extent to which small farmers' interests could be satisfied or overcome. Where the latter were strongly held, older enclosures were retained, indicated by small and often irregular fields; in addition, there are many cases where tofts in the centres of villages had been extended outwards to incorporate parts of the open field, and the closes and paddocks which had resulted often survived the general enclosure of the village. The remainder, the open field or the unenclosed upland, was set out in large parcels with regular boundaries (Turner 1980, 1984).

This overlay of new fields upon the ridge and furrow of open-field furlongs is repeated in parish after parish in lowland England, and often represents a comment on the longevity of the open-field system itself. Enclosure records have had an uneven survival. The most interesting are the surveys drawn as a preliminary to enclosure, showing extant boundaries and representing a last glimpse of the old system in operation. There are cases where the notebooks and drafts of the commissioners also survive, which often add details that never reached the finished maps. Comparison of these preliminary records with those which accompany enclosure awards provides the best guide to what actually took place, and such examples of comprehensive archives are of the greatest value for interpreting present-day boundaries. These sources show the great range in the effects of awards. At the extreme, enclosure by Act was merely a final stage, involving remnants of unenclosed land, or old enclosures which were too small to work as viable farms. In counties such as Dorset and Northumberland most enclosures involved such remnants, or dealt only with common land and waste. Similarly, in Somerset, much of the county had been enclosed piecemeal before the eighteenth century, and the emphasis was on action which improved upland and marshland pasture (M. Williams 1972).

Even where enclosure involved a large proportion of village ground, it would be wrong to assume that the landscape always underwent a rapid change after an award was made. In upland areas enclosure could be permissive, and it has been shown in a study of the north Yorkshire moors that fencing and reclamation took place over many decades, often retarded by landowners' protection of their shooting or mineral rights. Hence, boundaries in this area, as in parts of the Pennines, can be relatively recent (Chapman 1976). Conversely, where reclamation was put in hand quickly, if food prices were high, some lands were later allowed to revert to low-intensity moorland grazing, or abandoned altogether during the late-nineteenth-century agricultural recession. Such lands required high levels of investment to maintain acceptable yields, needing repeated ploughing and liming.

THE IMPROVEMENT OF ENCLOSED LAND

Enclosure is only one aspect of agrarian change, even if for the archaeologist, alert for the visual evidence of improvement, it is one of the most crucial. A theme which requires more attention is the improvement which followed enclosure: there is a strong argument for emphasizing not just the colonization and fencing which so altered the post-medieval landscape, and the new building and rebuilding of farms considered later, but also the development of drainage and irrigation, the improvement of local roads, and the strengthening of boundaries by hedging and walling after initial enclosure took place. Little, for example, has been written about the archaeology of drainage of enclosed lands, but this is important in a

Fig. 1.6 Water meadows in the valley of the Kennet at Kintbury, Berkshire (Cambridge University Collection).

number of respects. It has done much to alter and obliterate the earthworks of open-field farming, and is not just a twentieth-century phenomenon. As Phillips (1972) has shown for Yorkshire, such drainage was carried out on a large scale early in the nineteenth century as a follow-up to enclosure. The use of ceramic pipe-drains was preceded by the laying of brushwood, stone or rubble drains, which required considerable effort in trenching. Drains of this kind encountered during archaeological excavations (fig. 7.9) are particularly destructive of stratification, but deserve to be recorded as features important in their own right.

Improvement of lowland pasture resulted from the growing market for meat and particularly for dairy products. The returns from such investment were attractive and a cause of one of the more spectacular and long-lived developments, the construction of water-meadow systems. These are best known in Wiltshire and Dorset (Kerridge 1953; Bettey 1977), although examples can be found in Berkshire, Cambridgeshire (C.C. Taylor 1973: 175–7) and Herefordshire. The system developed during the seventeenth and eighteenth centuries, becoming an important, even indispensable part of the valley economy. Although Fitzherbert hinted at such a practice early in the sixteenth century, the true floating systems, using stream diversions (catchworks) and closely spaced channels which can superficially resemble ridge and furrow, are first described in 1610, by Rowland Vaughan for Herefordshire. Good surviving examples are in the Kennet valley in Berkshire (fig. 1.6), and in the Frome and Piddle valleys of Dorset, where catchworks, 'carriages' (channels) and sluices can be seen. An alternative system can be found in Cambridgeshire where a leat, taken off a stream at a weir, had traps to allow water to return to the stream through channels across the valley floor.

Woodlands

There are two aspects of the archaeology of woodlands which are of particular significance. First, features of existing or relict woods are closely bound up with agricultural change, for old-enclosed fields in forest areas frequently mark parcels of former woodland. Secondly, many woods had a clear economic function, where production of wood and wood products, particularly for industrial uses, was seen as an alternative to clearance for agriculture. The identification of maintained and coppiced woodlands is important in the archaeology of numerous industries, but is often difficult to achieve without cartographic and archive support (Rackham 1976, 1980).

Several studies have shown how Crown forests were reduced in size over the sixteenth and seventeenth centuries, either by encroachments which became accepted as tenanted holdings, or by deliberate disafforestation and large-scale clearance, to form new agricultural lands. Needwood Forest, Staffordshire, shows an interesting sequence: there is evidence of piecemeal fencing, some from late in the Middle Ages, when reduced population in surrounding villages allowed the creation of deer-parks with little opposition. Disafforestation and disparking occurred from early in the seventeenth century, and there is an overlay of early-nineteenth-century enclosure, not only on the fringes of Needwood, but also in the core, where entrenched common rights had previously prevented change (Nicholls 1972). There are a number of former forests where similar variables have left their mark, if with differences in detail and chronology. Bowland, Lancashire, is a case where over the sixteenth and seventeenth centuries encroachment and enclosure on its woods and moorlands was seen as a source of Crown revenue (Porter 1973). As noted earlier, many farms on the former forest date from this time, and form a pattern of dispersed settlement with small enclosed fields. Disparking and sales of land took place, and by the middle of the century the forest was much reduced; the remaining timber was of generally poor quality and attempts at forest management were at best sporadic.

Disafforestation did not always mean the end of woodlands, for it is a feature of many Crown forests in the seventeenth century that clearance and encroachment left a core which was coppiced, or which was disputed with holders of common-grazing or timber rights. There are numerous examples of Crown woods which were seen by contemporaries as badly managed, where over-grazing by commoners and the prevention of regeneration were the cause. Woods which are well documented as having diminishing timber stocks can be found in the Weald, where the forests of Ashdown and St Leonards (Cleere and Crossley 1985: 169), were victims of surrounding communities alert to their grazing rights. Much of Ashdown Forest was disafforested at the end of the seventeenth century and sold off: eighteenth-century maps and archive references can be related to existing boundaries, showing how the new owners either created or recreated coppice woods or, where appropriate, cleared the ground for new farms.

The key to the best use of woodlands lay in the market for their products. Some could never generate an income comparable with their potential under agriculture, however intensively they might be coppiced, and these were often cleared. However, there were many woods where good management could make coppicing attractive. This was the case in several iron-producing districts, and it was the availability of such coppice lands which went hand in hand with the growth or survival of the charcoal-iron industry (Hammersley 1973). In the Weald there are even cases of lands which had been cleared for agriculture but were replanted for coppice in the mid-seventeenth century, even though this was a time when the local iron industry was in overall decline. In the Lake counties, particularly in Furness, the coppices were intensively managed right through the eighteenth century, ensuring the late survival of charcoal-iron furnaces in the region, and producing wood for purposes such as bobbin making or ash burning (Davies-Shiel 1972).

Coppice woodlands of the sixteenth to nineteenth centuries have distinctive landscape features, recognizable even when this intensive use has long passed. Rackham has given excellent guidance to the appearance of such woods, although his examples are concentrated in parts of East Anglia and the east Midlands where the industrial uses of wood were limited (1976; 1980). There is a wide geographical spread of identifiable traces of woodlands managed for industrial markets, and much work remains to be done on recording these and demonstrating the methods by which they were marked out. There are sufficient examples, in Derbyshire, Shropshire, Sussex (fig. 1.7) and the Lake counties, to accept that it was common for woods to be divided into coppice areas, and boundary banks often survive

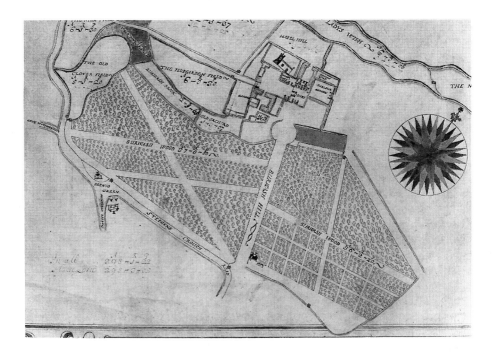

Fig. 1.7 Woodlands on the Ashburnham estate, Sussex, 1717. The south-east part of Burwash Wood (lower right) appears to be divided into coppice plots (East Sussex RO: ASH 4381).

Fig. 1.8   Kiln for drying wood (white-coal) adjacent to the lead-smelt (fig. 8.3) at Hoggett Gill, Cumbria. The air-intake passage is in the foreground.

which performed this function. On occasion such banks are survivors from the division of woods to control livestock, or relics of park boundaries. Those that are associated with coppicing can on occasion be confirmed on estate maps, particularly of the eighteenth century (Rowley 1972: 126).

Identification of old coppice by the characteristics of standing timber is risky. There are certainly some instances where former coppice can be recognized by trees with multiple boles, growing out of stools of considerable diameter. Where coppicing continued during the nineteenth century such relict trees can be found, particularly where trees of slow-growing species can date back to the coppicing period. In the Weald and parts of the west Midlands the market for hop poles was still active early in the present century; in the eastern Pennines there was a requirement for charcoal for the crucible steel industry until after the First World War; wooden pit props were also produced until quite recently from coppice. Woods which served these markets can still be identified, but many of the best-documented coppices of the sixteenth to eighteenth centuries were changed to timber-growing in the nineteenth century, and even where the woods survive, characteristic coppice trees are rare.

Woodlands also contain recognizable signs of activities carried on within them. Charcoal was burned as close to the coppices as possible, and platforms are frequently recognized, often with sites of the huts used by the burners. There are numerous examples in the Lake District and the Furness fells, and they can also be found in woods in Dean and on the fringes of the Peak District. Former burning platforms are also visible on long-cleared land, the patches of charcoal dust often identifiable on air photographs. More substantial are the kilns of the white-coal and ash burners. White-coal, or chop-wood, was kiln-dried wood, particularly used in the smelting of lead by the ore-hearth process. It was common in Derbyshire, the Yorkshire Dales and the Lake District to dig circular pits on sloping ground and to line these with stone. A flue admitted air from the down-slope side, to a fire set in the pit beneath wood which was stacked on bars of wood or stone. Recent work in Derbyshire has shown examples in the woodlands of the valleys of the gritstone, and the kiln adjacent to the lead-smelt at Hoggett Gill, near Ullswater (fig. 1.8), has been found to be of comparable design. The Lakeland ash-burners' pits are rather similar, but usually smaller in size.

Rural building in the sixteenth and seventeenth centuries

THE FARMHOUSE AND COTTAGE

The archaeological approach to post-medieval agrarian history has done much to strengthen the evidence for the growth in prosperity of the farming community, particularly by the study of domestic and farm buildings constructed or adapted between the later Middle Ages and the end of the eighteenth century. Work on vernacular architecture has developed over the past 30 years towards a national framework of information about the chronology, styles and techniques of building (Brunskill 1982a, 1985). Unfortunately, this archive reflects the pattern of survival of rural buildings: it emphasizes the houses of the better-off farmer, whose house could be both durable and worth adapting to changing standards and conventions, leading to its use up to the present day. Information at this level comes also from the study of probate inventories of moveable goods. These were frequently drawn up on a room-by-room basis, and despite certain pitfalls provide a guide to the layout of houses (for an urban study with rural implications, see Priestley *et al.* 1982). We know much less of the smaller dwellings, at husbandman, cottager and labourer levels, many of which were replaced in the late eighteenth and nineteenth centuries, leaving few survivals standing. The documentary record for such structures is also sparse, for many were occupied by people who died without a will, and hence no probate inventories would be made. Thus, with the small house there is a greater need for excavation, to fill out a record which at present depends on a very small number of surviving buildings.

Much of the research into post-medieval rural building has concentrated on vernacular style in a locality or as expressed in an individual structure. Wider issues, the relationship of buildings to the entire farm and to changes in the regional economy, are apt to be overlooked; this contrasts with the width of approach which characterized Hoskins' original exposition of the 'Great Rebuilding' (1953). His concept, subsequently refined, remains attractive as a measure of increasing agrarian wealth in the sixteenth and seventeenth centuries (Barley 1967; 1986, 239–63; Dyer 1986). Hoskins' overview placed rebuilding as one aspect of an improvement of living standards, paid for out of profits from market-directed farming. More recently, the case has been emphasized for examining the wider context, notably by Machin in his work on Dorset houses (1977; 1978), Harrison and Hutton (1984) in North Yorkshire, and the recent volume of the RCAHM Glamorgan county inventory (1988). The work of Alcock and Carson on houses

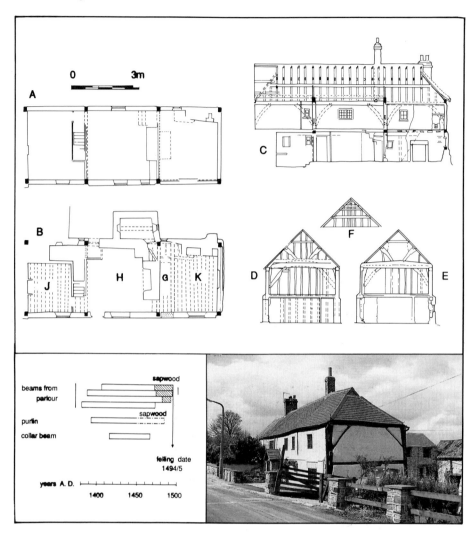

Fig. 1.9 Netherfold Farm, Rotherham, Yorkshire: plans and elevations (Peter Ryder) of the timber-framed house, built c.1500 and dated by dendrochronology (Jennifer Hillam).

described in estate surveys in south-west England is an important contribution not only to the recreation of house plans from documents but to placing these buildings in the context of the farm as a whole.

Nevertheless, there remains a need for a rigorous and comprehensive approach to individual buildings, although in large enough groups to provide a commentary on the prosperity of farming within a region. Assistance has come from the new precision (fig. 1.9) brought to the dating of timber-framed buildings by dendro-chronology (Morgan 1977, 1979, 1980; Hillam and Ryder 1980; Fletcher *et al.* 1981). This can assist the association of structures with those named persons who can be traced from written sources, not only from the probate inventories of former occupants of surviving houses, but from estate leases, maps and surveys. These last are important in detecting whether the policies of particular estates may have affected the extent of rebuilding, either by encouragement of tenants to rebuild or, conversely, by rent regimes which left tenants without the resources to do so. A recently noted eighteenth-century case, for which parallels might be sought, is on lands formerly belonging to the Duncombe estates in north Yorkshire, where contemporaries noted the poor standard of housing, and where there is still a greater survival of cruck-framed and thatched buildings than is usual in the area (RCHM 1987: 13).

An extension to these studies has been the interest in the development of non-domestic farm buildings, not only of the sixteenth and seventeenth centuries, but of the period after about 1750, over what may be called the period of the agrarian revolution. This latter period is characterized by construction of farmsteads with a certain uniformity of layout and appearance, many as new creations away from village centres and frequently accompanying the later phases of enclosure.

Rural housing: the study of standing buildings

The regional coverage of research into the development of styles and techniques in vernacular building leaves few large areas unexplored, but the extent and accessibility of publication is variable. An overview of work on standing buildings was set out by Mercer (1975), and subsequent surveys have filled some of the gaps implicit in the distribution of material used as examples in his book. Some impetus has recently been given by the accelerated resurvey of rural areas for the purposes of listing buildings for statutory protection. This has, of necessity, been a rapid process, but it has provided a reminder that there are significant districts where there has been scant detailed recording, let alone publication. This is not the place for a detailed résumé of research: more to review regional work in wider terms, to ask how far the chronology of improvement has been established, in relation to changes in local economies and to aspects of landscape archaeology. It should be stressed that we are dealing with the adaptation of medieval houses as well as with new building, and also with a range which at its upper end can embody aspects of polite architecture (Quiney 1984).

We now accept that the first appearance of what were to become characteristic post-medieval styles from the building types of the Middle Ages appears in the south of England before 1500. Rigold's brief pioneer essay (1963: 351–4) on the Wealden House pointed to areas in the south-east where farmers were able to invest in housing during the fifteenth century and at the beginning of the sixteenth (fig. 1.10): these were people for whom the priority was no longer always investment in land and equipment, but for whom the returns from sales into a developing London food market, and the tendency for rents to lag behind rising prices until late in the sixteenth century, allowed spending on enhanced standards of comfort. Awareness of the effects of the marketing pattern, which underwent great changes over the sixteenth century, is vital to the understanding of farmers' patterns of spending (Everitt 1967: 466–592). A telling example is the subject of a note by Rigold (1969) on Yardhurst, a late-fifteenth-century Wealden house near Ashford whose farm of only 80 acres was bringing its owners income sufficient to build and later to improve a house of some

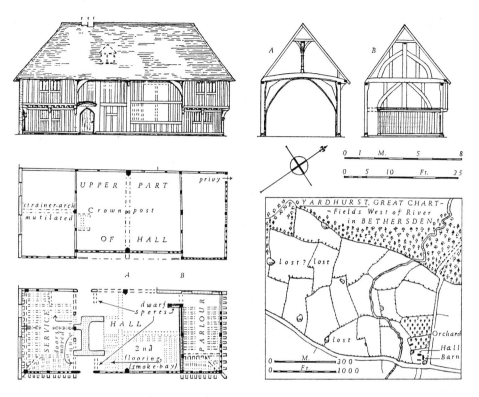

Fig. 1.10 Yardhurst, Kent: late-fifteenth-century Wealden house with first floor and chimney inserted in the sixteenth century. This drawing by the late Stuart Rigold (1969) is accompanied by his estimate of the lands of Yardhurst, comprising c.80 acres (32 ha) (Royal Archaeological Institute).

elegance. The Wealden House, with its jettied ends on either side of a hall, is now known to be much more widely spread than was originally suggested, for town houses of this type may be seen as far away as York; but the improvement in the buildings of the south-east which the original study suggested has been shown to hold good, and includes developments of a range of building types of which the Wealden House is just one (Barley 1967: 734ff.). The arable areas of Kent were among the first to see such improvements, but as the pressures of the food market increasingly affected the poorer lands of the Weald and the more distant coastlands of Sussex, so similar improvements can be seen there. The Martins' comprehensive and detailed surveys of the houses of the south-eastern Weald (D. and B. Martin 1987) have provided a wealth of information about an area where incomes came not just from agriculture but from woodland occupations and from the iron industry, and where it has been shown that lands abandoned in the Middle Ages were being reopened with new farms (Tebbutt 1981). The key signs of improvement in accommodation are all present: open halls were converted to two-storey structures; fireplaces were inserted, staircases built and extra rooms provided in out-shuts or cross-wings.

In East Anglia similar development can be seen, with farmers in arable Essex starting to build at much the same time as their counterparts in Kent, and improvement spreading as London wholesalers placed their contracts for grain and livestock further afield. This was the region well known to William Harrison when, in 1587, he described the 'great amendment of lodging' seen in the previous half-century. The area had also prospered with the supply of wool to the Essex-Suffolk textile trade, whose growth was demonstrated not only by improved housing but in early-sixteenth-century additions to churches. For sheep farmers who had gained from the wool trade, droving to London provided a second outlet, whose proceeds might be expected to have assisted the reconstruction of the more modest farmhouses along the Essex-Suffolk border. This research, however, would benefit from publication of material indicating more precisely the relationship of the improved houses with the sources of wealth of their owners, for we should be wary of too simple a model: in particular, there were variations in prosperity within the textile region, some localities gaining, others losing due to the arrival from the 1560s of immigrant producers of the 'New Draperies'. Rebuilding in Essex and parts of Suffolk is particularly characterized by changes in the use of timber and, in the seventeenth century, by the increasing use of brick in a region where building stone was scarce. Hewett's work on structural carpentry in Essex and Suffolk (1969, 1971, 1973) has generated a body of published information on the development of timber-building methods from medieval traditions, and has shown how even modest farmhouses benefited from skills in carpentry which enabled durable structures to be built with economy of materials (fig. 1.11).

A comparable case can be made for investigating the background to rebuilding in Norfolk: this was a county of diverse local economies, some more exposed to long-distance produce trades than others. The coastal ports were increasingly involved in the grain trade during the sixteenth century, and parts of central Norfolk became suppliers of sheep to London as well as wool to the Norwich and Suffolk textile industries. The question is how far local patterns of prosperity and hence building reflect these changes, and how far they are disguised by the diversity of local building traditions, strongly based on available materials, on timber in the south and east, and flints and clunch elsewhere, and with the increasing use of brick in the houses of the better off. A comprehensive guide to Norfolk vernacular building would be most welcome, particularly if related to the diversities of farming of the county.

Elsewhere in southern England, the availability of published material is uneven. Dorset is a well-researched county, as a result of work by RCHM and by Machin (1977, 1978). There are many contrasts amongst the surviving buildings: close to the coast, particularly in the east of the county, improvements are commonly seen, yet further inland many sixteenth-and seventeenth-century houses retain medieval features, and there is an impression that in areas north of the downlands farming was slow to be affected by distant trades. In Devon there have been significant publications on aspects of housing in the south of the county (Alcock 1969; Alcock and Laithwaite 1973). These have shown, as in south-east England, that improvement began before 1500, and raise questions about the late-medieval growth of prosperity among the pastoral farmers on the fringes of Dartmoor and in the valleys to the south and east.

In the west Midlands Alcock (1971–3) and Charles (1978–9) have produced

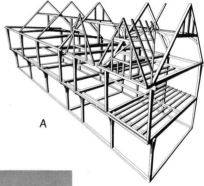

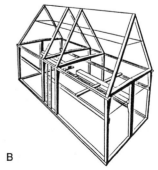

Fig. 1.11 Essex timber-framed houses:
(A) Bay Tree Farm, Stisted: sixteenth-century house
with added early-seventeenth-century bay in the foreground. (B) Tinkers Green, Finchingfield: early seventeenth-century house (Drawings by Cecil A. Hewett).

important work, particularly for Warwickshire, where Alcock's study of timber-framed buildings traces development from late-medieval cruck traditions through to typical post-medieval styles, in a district where farmers were benefiting from the food markets of towns with growing industrial populations. In Shropshire the pattern is similar, although in some areas later to develop. The box-framed timber houses so typical of the north of the county are generally of seventeenth-century date; they are obvious on the ground in villages such as Hodnet and Myddle, and in the latter have been placed in context by Hey (1974, 1981), drawing on inventory evidence and the early-eighteenth-century writings of Richard Gough. In southern Shropshire the varied local building stones were used in improved farmhouses on the fringes of the Clee hills from late in the sixteenth century, incorporated in a tradition of timber building based on the resources of Wyre Forest and the woodlands of the north of Herefordshire. There have been studies of inventories for both counties which demonstrate how standards of comfort changed between 1600 and 1750, although it is the east-Shropshire area of mixed agriculture and industry which has been most explored in this respect (Trinder and Cox 1980).

Staffordshire is one of the most difficult counties to sum up, for its buildings reflect a great diversity of materials and local economies, some more open to commercial development than others. The moorlands contain a range from marginal farmsteads on land colonized in the sixteenth and seventeenth centuries to ample stone houses built on the fortunes of dairying and stock rearing in the valleys. Least is known of the housing of the farmers of the growing industrial townships of the south of the county, where few examples survive: it is uncertain whether those involved in the metal trades were housed at husbandman standards of comfort, or if, at the level of chapman-entrepreneur, their houses were comparable with those of the yeoman farmer. Staffordshire's neighbour, Cheshire, also prospered from dairying; William Smith noted the changes to housing in the county between the 1540s and the 1580s, drawing attention, as did Harrison for East Anglia, to the building of chimneys and the improvement of fireplaces (Palliser 1983: 111).

For the rest of the Midlands, Barley's summary (1967: 742ff.) is still a useful introduction, and there are more recent local studies (Roberts 1974), but a comprehensive overview is still to come. This is ironic, in that it was the buildings of this region which contributed to Hoskins' interest in relationships between agrarian prosperity and increasing standards of domestic comfort. An indication does however come from Cambridgeshire, and the summary in the volume of the RCHM inventory for the north-east of the county (RCHM 1972a: pp. xliii–li) can be seen to hold good for districts to the north and west. It has been observed that in Cambridgeshire the hall house disappears early in the sixteenth century, as it became normal for two storeys to be built along the length of the structure. A large proportion of sixteenth-to eighteenth-century houses were built with central chimney stacks, many, but certainly not all with staircases adjacent. By the eighteenth century it was becoming normal to position chimney stacks on the end wall, allowing a greater flexibility of planning in the body of the house. All these points can be seen on the ground in Leicestershire, Lincolnshire and Northamptonshire, where pastoral farming was frequently the basis of prosperity, with the expansion of the area on which London drew for its meat (Armitage 1982: 94–106).

Further north, rebuilding tends to be rather later in date. Commercial arable farming developed in the sixteenth century in east Yorkshire and the Vale of York, but elsewhere was limited until the eighteenth century. Pastoral wealth, however, was strongly on the increase by the start of the seventeenth century, and building development reflects this. On the ground, the rebuilding in the Pennines is obvious enough, but many districts lack published studies. This is particularly so for Derbyshire: work is in progress on the buildings and related archives of the coal measures of the north of the county and in the valleys of the gritstone, but the limestone of the Peak District has only received sporadic attention. What is required is research into the relationship between rebuilding and a complex economy based on pastoral farming and the droving trade, and industries such as lead mining and smelting and stone quarrying. To the north, Ryder (1979) has produced an account of timber building in south Yorkshire, where there is an old-established tradition of vernacular building studies, dating back to work on cruck construction by Innocent (1916) and Addy (1933) in the early years of this century (fig. 1.12). Jones (1980) has outlined the developments in construction in stone, but a full-length study remains to be undertaken, again relating buildings to occupants in an area of mixed agriculture and industry. The three recent RCHM volumes, on the Lancashire Pennines, specifically the Colne area (1985b), the rural houses of West Yorkshire (1986a) and houses of the North Yorkshire Moors (1987) are major developments in the subject, the first two covering districts where domestic production of textiles was an important aspect of the upland economy. Previously, Hutton (1973) had examined the survival of medieval styles in the Vale of York, and Harrison and Hutton (1984) surveyed part of north Yorkshire with Cleveland, in a study which goes further than most in explaining the context of new building. For the northern Pennines and Lakeland, however, information is limited to small areas and to individual houses. It is only for inland Northumberland and the Scottish border that there is more detailed coverage in the pioneer RCHM volume on shielings and bastles (Ramm *et al.* 1970; cf. Dixon 1972a).

In the uplands, not only in the north, it is important to emphasize not just the rebuilding of medieval houses, but new building, on farms carved from the waste. This is particularly the case in the Pennines, where new houses can be found on the fringes of the old lands, surrounded by blocks of new fields, in areas where moorland was enclosed and divided by agreement. Where the documentary evidence for such division does not exist, topographical features are often useful. There are good examples in north Derbyshire of houses of late-sixteenth-and early-seventeenth-century type, surrounded by small fields, many of which are still of marginal quality for grazing (fig. 1.13). Buildings erected in these circumstances were often originally plainer than their lowland counterparts, improvements either awaiting the prosperity of later generations, or being incorporated in new houses built adjacent, leaving the dwellings of the original settlers to be converted for livestock. The construction of small farm-houses on the periphery continued throughout the period, and frequently took the form of the laithe-house, a distinctive Yorkshire style (Stell 1965; RCHM 1986a, 182–3). This is a dual-purpose structure with dwelling and byre or barn in one range, but without the common cross-passage entry of the longhouse and built as late as the nineteenth century.

For Wales, there is a wide spread of information, accumulated since the

Fig. 1.12 Stumperlowe, Sheffield: crucks exposed during rebuilding. The drawing (Peter Ryder) shows the components of a typical cruck structure.

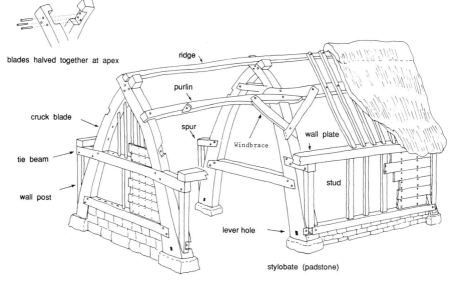

pioneer study of Monmouthshire houses by Fox and Raglan (1951, 1953). Wiliam (1986) has produced an overall survey and has covered the buildings of north-east Wales in more detail (1982). The work of RCAHM has accumulated a great deal of material for the whole of Wales, summarized by Smith (1988 edn); the work of the Commission is demonstrated in detail by the recent volume of the Glamorgan inventory, which in addition to a fine exposition of the architectural material, contains an important survey of the economic basis for rebuilding. In certain parts of Wales there is a wealth of material still to be surveyed and published; in

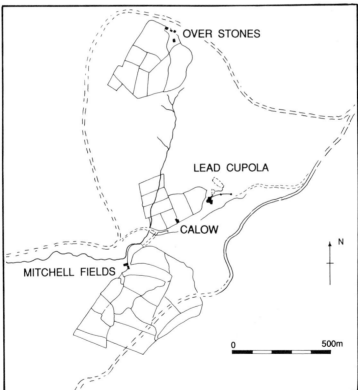

Fig. 1.13 Hathersage Dale, Derbyshire: The survey of old enclosures made at the time of parliamentary enclosure (1809) shows three farms, seen in the photograph, taken facing north with Mitchell Field (c.1600) in the left foreground, the now-abandoned Calow in the trees on the right, and Over Stones towards the skyline. Parliamentary enclosure modified the boundaries of the closes surrounding the farms, but many are still recognizable. The survey also shows the eighteenth-century cupola lead-smelt east of Calow (Chapter 8) (after a survey in Sheffield RO).

particular, the south-west, Dyfed, the old counties of Carmarthen, Cardigan and Pembroke, awaits detailed publication of its farmhouses.

In Scotland, Fenton and Walker (1981) have produced an overview of rural housing, but in general there has been less detailed recording on the ground than south of the border; in part this is a reflection of the smaller quantity of early post-medieval rural housing surviving. As a counterpart, there has been a significant start to field survey and excavation of sites of buildings which have been abandoned, work which will be noted later.

Excavations

Post-medieval house sites excavated over the past 20 years range from those of the substantial yeoman farm to the two-cell dwelling which inventories suggest is common among those of husbandman status. The total of such work is not great, due in part to a concentration of interest on excavations of medieval house sites, but also to a tendency to regard standing post-medieval buildings as a sufficient store of evidence. The latter is a standpoint which fails to recognize how few of the smaller houses of the period survive in anything like their original form.

Of excavations on and around the sites of the more substantial farms of the post-medieval period, the work at Manor Farm, Chalton, Hampshire, was of particular significance in showing the extent to which archaeological information can be gained from a working farm (Cunliffe 1973). Between 1966 and 1972, routine work requiring excavation or maintenance of structures was archaeologically observed and recorded. The result was to establish the sequence of development of the medieval farm into its present form, and to demonstrate how evidence from excavation could amplify the record derived from observation of the standing buildings and from archive research. In addition, it was important to relate the character and size of the farm buildings to the wider economy of the holding, particularly to its size and the levels of rents at various times in its history. An equally comprehensive approach has been adopted at Wharram Percy, Yorkshire, but on an abandoned farmstead. Excavation and field survey at Wharram is perhaps best known for the information on medieval settlement, but in the later years of the project much attention has been given to the post-medieval landscape. Excavations have now shown how a farmhouse was built near the vicarage at the beginning of the seventeenth century and how this farm developed. The house, whose footings survive, was originally a rectangular structure, one room wide, but in the eighteenth century was developed as part of a model farmstead (fig. 1.21), being rebuilt as a double-pile house which was demolished during the nineteenth century (*PMA* 1986: 350; 1987: 286–7).

Comparable in substance, but of varied fortune are the houses excavated at Caldecote, Herts (*MA* 1974: 216–7; *MVRG* 1974: 22–4). One, of fifteenth-century origin, is a valuable example of adaptation. Cob walls were replaced by poor-quality framing, and in turn by timberwork of a better standard. It was established that the house had a cross-passage, service rooms separate from the hall, a solar with fireplace and garderobe, and a hall heated from a central hearth until a corner fireplace was built contemporary with the insertion of a first floor, shortly before this part of the house was demolished. It is hoped that full publication will indicate the context for these changes. The other excavated house at Caldecote, the former rectory (fig. 1.14), was originally timber framed , but was encased in brick in the eighteenth century and abandoned about 1900. This was also an open hall which was later chambered over, and in addition the solar bay was replaced by cross-wings. A lowland farmstead abandoned in the seventeenth century has been excavated at Great Linford, Milton Keynes (noted in *PMA* 1975: 250–1, with subsequent interpretation prior to publication). This group (fig. 1.15) comprised two medieval houses (buildings 4 and 5), both extended during the seventeenth century, and a barn (building 7) of seventeenth-century build. The extension to building 5 comprised the north-west room shown in the site plan, and, immediately to the east, what was probably the base of an external stair. A new room was added to the north end of building 4 early in the seventeenth century, containing a substantial hearth and brick chimney stack, and probably roofed with tiles. The houses were marked on a map of 1641, but were omitted in 1678, and are hence likely to have been abandoned during an enclosure documented in 1658 (Reed 1984).

At Cowlam, on the Yorkshire Wolds (Hayfield 1988),is a contrasting case, a farmstead with medieval origins, which remained occupied until the village was depopulated between 1670 and 1674. It included a farmhouse, originally a longhouse with opposed doorways (fig. 1.16). The standard of construction of the house was poor; walls were of chalk and sandstone bonded with marl, and the floor was of earth with a slabbed central hearth. But this was more than a cottage property, for during the seventeenth century it formed part of a farmstead, which also included a byre and a barn, and was built over two medieval house plots. The presence of imported pottery, metalwork of good quality, and window-glass indicates a standard of comfort appropriate to the better-off husbandman, but the building itself was a traditional farmhouse in an upland area where improvement of dwellings appears to have been delayed until the consolidation of holdings in the eighteenth century. The small-scale excavations at Riplingham (Wacher 1966) and Lastingham (*PMA* 1972: 213) produced further examples of the abandonment of small Wolds farms at this time.

In order to establish the range of houses in a community, in terms of size and standard of construction, lengthy excavation programmes are necessary. This has been emphasized by experience at Wharram Percy where, despite 25 years work, only a small proportion of the medieval village has been examined. The most comprehensive work on a post-medieval deserted village site has been at West Whelpington, Northumberland, which disappeared about 1720 (Jarrett and Wrathmell 1977). Single-storey thatched stone houses (fig. 1.17) were grouped around a green, with typical living accommodation comprising a room of about 25 sq.m. The number of houses in the village declined during the seventeenth century, although glazed windows and metal locks and fittings suggest that the occupants of the remainder enjoyed certain comforts, if not those of the better-off lowland farmer. The village disappeared at a time when isolated farmsteads appear to have been built in the parish, reflecting a rationalization of land holdings.

It is hoped that work at two villages in Glamorgan, Llanmaes and Cosmeston, will also provide a range of house sizes. These are medieval villages which had shrunk in the classic manner, but instead of disappearing totally, were partially re-occupied in the seventeenth century, but went through a further process of decline during the nineteenth. Llanmaes (*PMA* 1986: 346) is important in that

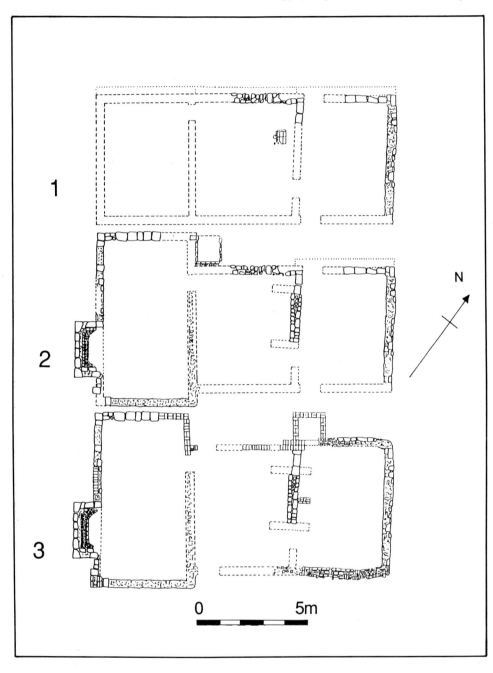

Fig. 1.14 Caldecote, Hertfordshire: the excavated rectory, c.1550–1920: 1. sixteenth century; 2. seventeenth/eighteenth century; 3. eighteenth/nineteenth century (Guy Beresford).

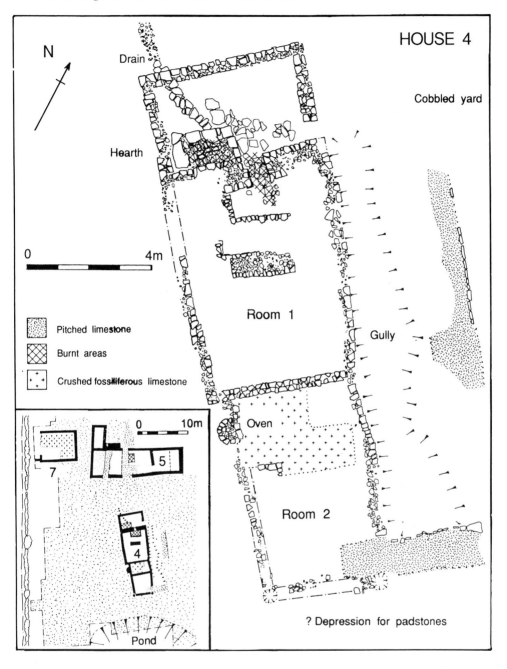

N

HOUSE 4

Cobbled yard

Drain

Hearth

0   4m

Pitched limestone

Burnt areas

Crushed fossiliferous limestone

Room 1

Gully

0   10m

5

7

Oven

4

Room 2

Pond

? Depression for padstones

Fig. 1.15 Great Linford, Buckinghamshire: building 4 of Croft B in its seventeenth-century form (phase 4 of the excavated complex) with (inset) buildings 5 (house) and 7 (barn) (Milton Keynes Archaeology Unit).

Fig. 1.16 Cowlam, Yorkshire: the excavated
post-medieval farmhouse (C) and farm
buildings (D, E, F) (Colin Hayfield, after
T.C.M.Brewster).

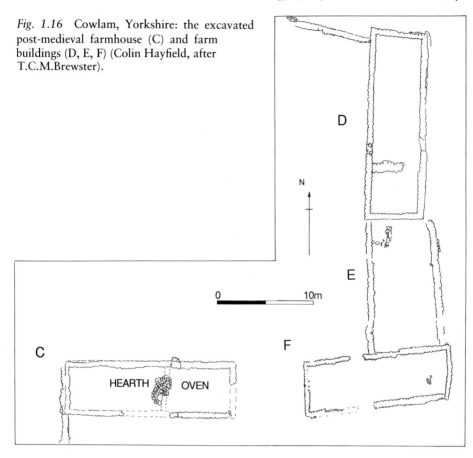

there were several seventeenth-century buildings, from a modest lobby–entrance
house to cottages at the smallholder level (fig. 1.18). At Cosmeston (*PMA 1985*:
169–70) it will be useful to compare the construction of the surviving seventeenth/
eighteenth-century two-roomed cottage with the excavated sixteenth or early
seventeenth-century foundations of a house put up after the abandonment of the
medieval village, but itself deserted at about the time the surviving cottage was
built.

In Scotland, a greater range of house sizes has been found by excavation, but
most are isolated examples. At the farmstead level, Smailcleugh, Roxburgh (*PMA
1983*: 197) had in its first phase a stone byre and possibly an adjoining timber
building, not yet proved to be the house; in the eighteenth century the byre was
extended, to form a two-cell house, one room being converted to a smithy before
abandonment by 1830. A farmhouse of bastle type was excavated at Glendorch,
Lanarkshire, the building having two rooms, one possibly a byre (*PMA 1986*: 349).
The desertions of the period 1750–1850 emptied many of the small post-medieval
houses built on marginal pastoral settlements. Work in the Western Isles has shown
examples of seventeenth and eighteenth-century date, although it is not always
clear whether these are remains of permanently occupied houses or of summer

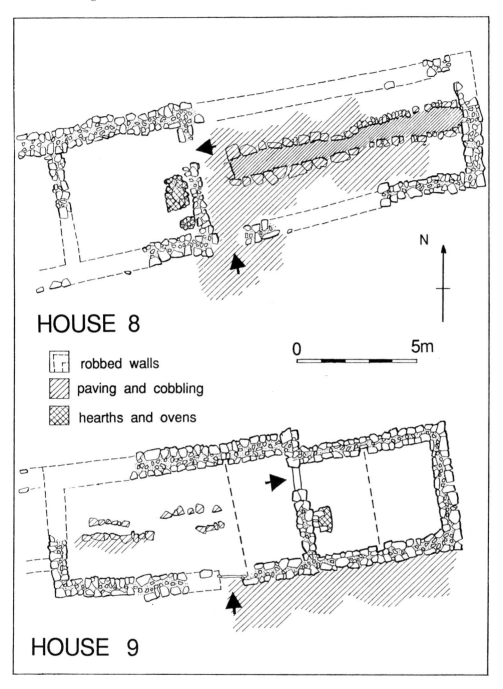

HOUSE 8

HOUSE 9

robbed walls

paving and cobbling

hearths and ovens

N

0   5m

Fig. 1.17 West Whelpington, Northumberland: excavated houses 8 and 9 in their final (seventeenth-century) form (Stuart Wrathmell).

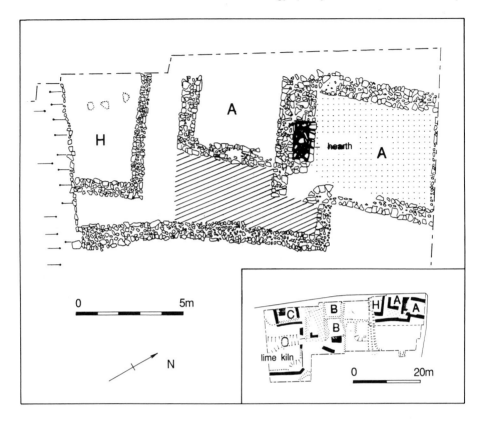

Fig. 1.18 Llanmaes, Glamorgan: excavated post-medieval buildings (A) and (H). In building (A) the room with the hearth was the main living and kitchen area; building (H) was an outhouse built into a boundary bank. The lime-kiln shown in the inset plan postdates the abandonment of the domestic buildings, and utilizes stone from them (Glamorgan and Gwent Archaeological Trust).

shielings. A series of surveys on Harris and North Uist were carried out in the 1960s (*PMA* 1967: 109–10; 1968: 183), and summary publication has recorded a range of examples of houses of seventeenth and eighteenth-century date. On the mainland, Fairhurst (1967–8; 1968–9) has published surveys of deserted settlements in Sutherland and Perthshire: in the former, in Strathnaver, three clusters vacated at the beginning of the nineteenth century comprised longhouses, byres and corn-drying kilns. Similarly, excavations at Lix, Perthshire showed an increase in settlement during the eighteenth century before shrinkage in the nineteenth: the eighteenth-century houses provide a useful guide to construction standards on the marginal lands. They succeeded documented seventeenth-century houses which have failed to leave any trace; these were built with byres adjoining, but fell into decay early in the nineteenth century when leases were not renewed.

The difficulty of distinguishing between shielings and permanently occupied houses also occurs in Wales; in a pioneer investigation in Glamorgan (Fox 1939), house platforms were excavated on Gelligaer Common which could not be proved to have been occupied permanently. In Carmarthenshire Crampton (1968) recorded hafod sites of uncertain date or permanency of occupation. The most comprehensive examination has been in the north, in the Brenig valley, where Allen (1979) excavated a set of seventeenth-century buildings which, although substantial, were considered to have been for summer occupation.

This leaves us with a lack of excavated post-medieval evidence for the cottages of the very poor in England. On the ground we cannot yet distinguish the property of the husbandman from that of the cottager, a distinction of which contemporaries were well aware: a division between, on the one hand, the yeoman and husbandman, able to varying degrees to spend on improved standards of comfort, and the cottager and labourer whose position ranged from the uncertain to the unfortunate. We have the occasional contemporary description, as by Plot who in 1686 wrote of cottages near Cheadle, Staffordshire, with their turf roofs (Palliser 1976: 100). Alcock and Carson have studied estate surveys in south-west England which contain evidence for labourers' cottages, some single-storeyed, with two bays, others with a single-room plan but with two floors. In some areas there is information about squatters, whose dwellings were of a poor standard: Bettey (1982) has examined documentary references to such buildings in the manor of Urchfont, Wiltshire, and Trinder (1981: 186ff.) has demonstrated material for eighteenth-century squatter settlement in Shropshire, and located plots and in a few cases the buildings mentioned (fig. 1.19). Such information about surviving structures is still limited; few cottages built before the middle of the eighteenth century remain in anything like their original form, although investigations have suggested that remnants lie hidden within later extensions. A significant survey made some years ago in Flintshire (Hayes 1967–8) disclosed a number of houses in the Hawarden area which were originally of cottager size, and the work by Pearson on the Colne and Burnley area (RCHM 1985b) has shown two-cell houses originally with very simple features, and has suggested that a search of apparently later buildings in the district would reveal more.

A related issue which requires more archaeological attention is how far the durability of the small house improved. There has long been a tendency to regard the medieval peasant house as an impermanent structure, frequently renewed. This view has been refined and a distinction made between the more substantial buildings, which could last several generations, as at West Whelpington, and those of poorer construction using, for example, earth-fast posts (Wrathmell 1984). The extent to which rural housing of poor durability was built in the post-medieval period is still uncertain; this is emphasized by the current discussion about the use of mud and clay lump (Harrison 1984; McCann 1987), which rarely survives except in farm buildings (fig. 1.20), and by seventeenth-and eighteenth-century references to small houses which could be moved from site to site (J.T. Smith 1985). These may indeed have been the hovels which contemporary records suggest as the common dwellings of the poor, but such references to portability need to be taken with caution, for substantial timber-framed buildings could be dismantled and the main frame or cruck members transported.

A category of village where small post-medieval houses might be found is the settlement abandoned for eighteenth-century or later emparking. So far, no examples have been excavated, but the potential is worth considering. In Northamptonshire, Brown and Taylor (1977) have drawn attention to villages such as Knuston and Overstone, of below-average size in the sixteenth and

Fig. 1.19 Documented smallholder houses in Shropshire: (1) Myddle: single-storey timber-framed cottage; (2) Upper Hayton: timber-framed cottage extended in brick, with the massive stone chimney typical of houses in the Clee hills. See also fig. 7.18.

Fig. 1.20 Welford, Northamptonshire: mud-walled farm building.

seventeenth centuries, whose sites were emparked in the second half of the eighteenth century. A well-known example is Nuneham Courtenay in Oxfordshire (Batey 1968), demolished and resited from 1760–1, and paralleled by cases such as Chippenham and Wimpole, Cambridgeshire, Henderskelfe (for Castle Howard), Yorkshire, or Gayhurst and Stowe (Buckinghamshire). The pattern continues into the nineteenth century, a late but spectacular example being the resiting of Edensor from Chatsworth Park to form Paxton's village of 1838–42.

FARM BUILDINGS

Work on vernacular building has been apt to concentrate on farmhouses, and, as part of the attempt to view farms as a whole, emphasis should be given to other buildings. There have been important movements in this direction. Wiliam's work in Wales has given priority to the complete farmstead, rather than just the house, and Brunskill's national guide (1982b) provides a succinct review of the main traditional types, amplifying the approach taken by Harvey (1970) in his brief but pioneering introduction.

Of regional work, Rigold's study of timber barns in Kent (1966) was also outstanding, emphasizing the continuity between the medieval and post-medieval: he identified important post-medieval barns, descendants of medieval traditions, but with features which only appear in the sixteenth century. Similar information has been accumulated for other areas, particularly the south-east. The Martins have recorded barns of the period in east Sussex; in the Greater London area a considerable record has been built up, and notes have been published for barns at Northolt (1595), two examples at Hillingdon, and others at Harrow and St Mary Cray (*PMA* 1975: 255, 256; 1974: 129–30). In Hertfordshire two seventeenth-century barns have been recorded on the site of the deserted settlement at Caldecote (*PMA* 1977: 95), and in Oxfordshire there has been a comprehensive survey of the seventeenth to twentieth-century farm buildings at Cogges Manor Farm near Eynsham (*PMA* 1975: 256). For Cambridgeshire, the RCHM inventories for the north-east and the west of the county give a useful overview, again emphasizing the continuity between medieval and sixteenth to seventeenth century forms of construction. In the north of England, there has been recording of farm buildings within the west Yorkshire conurbation, and in the Lake District Tyson (1980, 1981) has compared estate records with standing buildings at Rydal Hall, showing how a farm complex developed in the seventeenth century.

Little information about farm buildings of this period has come from excavation; one published case is a group occupying part of the site of the medieval village at Norton, Cheshire (*PMA* 1975: 252–3), where three structures have been excavated, one a probable barn, 7m.×17m long. At Abdon, Shropshire (*PMA* 1970: 178) a comparable re-occupation was recorded, comprising a barn or stock building, dated by pottery to the seventeenth or eighteenth centuries. Brewster's excavation of farm buildings on the seventeenth-century site at Cowlam has already been referred to (Hayfield 1988).

Two examples can be given of studies which put farm buildings in a wider context. Both cover parishes in Sussex, a county which has been well served over the years in the detailed recording of farmsteads. Caffyn (1983) has published an overview of the farm buildings of three geologically contrasting parishes near Brighton, in which she emphasizes the differences in materials, in density of farms according to soils, and in the local characteristics of structures. Farrant (1983) takes a neighbouring pair of parishes from a rather different angle, noting the relationship of farms to early enclosures, where possible relating structures to documented farmers, and tracing their development through to the changes of the nineteenth century. These two articles, brief as they are, indicate the kind of background work which would extend the utility of farm-building studies as historical material.

It is only in recent years that interest in farm buildings has extended to those of the century after c.1750. In all parts of the country there was significant rebuilding and new construction, which often accompanied the final and most radical phase of enclosure. Most significant in landscape terms are the new farmsteads built to work blocks of land enclosed from open fields distant from village centres. The study published by Peters (1970) of buildings in the lowlands of south-west Staffordshire was the first detailed contribution, and has an importance beyond the locality he surveyed. He showed how in the second half of the eighteenth century traditional designs of barn were adapted to cope with greater volumes of produce. Wagon entries and first-floor storage became standard, stock yards, stables and implement stores were built in compact groups, and farmhouses were incorporated in new courtyard layouts. Traditional materials frequently gave way to brick, which facilitated the incorporation of ventilation apertures in barn walls, and made for a uniformity of appearance which obscures the evolution from tradition. There are certainly areas where large new barns did perpetuate older styles. It has been noted that in Cambridgeshire aisled barns were still being erected in the nineteenth century, simplified softwood variants of their predecessors. Once the characteristic features are understood, farm complexes of this period can be recognized over most of the country. In Scotland, particularly the central lowlands, there are many examples: it is quite clear from the early-nineteenth-century sources, notably Loudon's *Encyclopedia*, that Scottish estates and their stewards were responsible for designs which were followed in England, particularly for farmsteads with sophisticated facilities for livestock. Estate archives are an important source: those for the Lowther lands in Cumbria include surveys and valuations which show developments ranging from piecemeal additions to completely new farms and village layouts (Brunskill 1967; Messenger 1975), and those of the Holkham estates in Norfolk show 30 farm rebuilding projects between 1790 and 1820 (Wade-Martins 1977).

Examples from different parts of England will illustrate the extent of new building of this kind. In north Nottinghamshire there are numerous fine farm complexes built in brick, which include well-ventilated barns, cartsheds incorporating stables, and farmhouses sited to give an overview of farm operations. In Shropshire the farms on the Sutherland estates follow similar patterns. There are good examples on the downlands of Hampshire and Dorset, in the Mendips, and on the chalklands of Cambridgeshire and east Yorkshire. Farms of this kind are usually to be found in areas where enclosure was late to take place, but many of the features are to be seen in rebuilt farms in earlier-enclosed districts. For example, wagon porches were added to medieval barns, stock yards and dairies were rebuilt, and farmhouses were replaced, the older buildings being used for farm storage. There are some areas where eighteenth-century ideas about improvements in access and storage were influential, but were incorporated in structures which used archaic features. In the southern Yorkshire Pennines, for example, existing and recently demolished barns of this period still incorporated raised crucks. Frequently such development can be identified from standing buildings, but subsequent changes can obscure the sequence. It has been shown at Wharram Percy that excavation has a function: the model farm built in the 1770s no longer stands, apart from a range rebuilt as cottages, but it is now known that the house of the seventeenth-century farm was rebuilt and extended, and that the courtyard was laid out adjacent (fig. 1.21). Two ranges have been excavated and their functions identified (annual entries in *PMA* 1983ff.).

A category of building on which little research has been done, but which is of considerable importance in the economy of upland districts, is the field barn. Many examples survive in the Pennines, Wales and Scotland. The landscape of the Peak District, for example, is dotted with such barns, and most appear to correspond with enclosure boundaries both of the eighteenth century and earlier. One example among many lies ruined to the west of Ilam, Staffordshire (fig. 1.22); it overlies ridge and furrow, and appears to have been sited to give

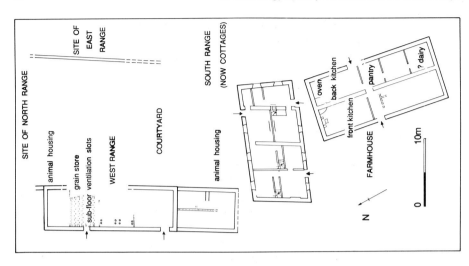

Fig. 1.21 Wharram Percy, Yorkshire: the farmstead built on the medieval village site in the 1770s. At the south end, a double-pile farmhouse, now under excavation, accommodated the tenant in the western rooms, with dairy and pantry, and facilities for farm-hands at the rear. This had replaced a seventeenth-century farmhouse, one room wide, on a slightly different alignment. To the north, there were four ranges of outbuildings around a yard: the south range was converted into cottages after the abandonment of the farm in the mid-nineteenth century; the other three ranges have been excavated, showing that the north and east buildings have been largely destroyed by gardening. Work on the west range shows three main structural phases within a century of use, as well as evidence for animal housing (post-holes for stalls and troughs) and for grain storage (sub-floor ventilation). The photograph is of the west range, taken from the south. The cobbled floor (lower left) with brick-edged drainage channels belongs to the final phase. An earlier east-west partition wall runs beneath. The stumps in the background postdate demolition of the range (Stuart Wrathmell).

access to a pair of fields enclosed in the seventeenth or eighteenth centuries. Such buildings are usually difficult to date, being simple structures bereft of significant architectural detail; nevertheless they repay attention, because their construction marks an extension of improved grazing, reflecting in turn the development of the livestock market.

LARGE HOUSES AND THEIR GROUNDS

The convention of the country house in its grounds, as it emerged before 1600 and developed in the seventeenth century and beyond, was shaped by a combination of influences, some new to England and fostered by their adoption in royal palaces, others traditional. Of the medieval legacy some aspects were in retreat, others were cherished. Apart from tower houses in the north, the incorporation of fortifications in sixteenth-century houses represented no more than a conceit. The discomfort, the lack of light, and the inaccessibility of rooms in the medieval castle had led many fifteenth-century landowners to develop the courtyard house, moated or not, as a set of buildings in which domestic facilities came first (Thompson 1987: 43ff.), and in the sixteenth century innovation in convenience and appearance gathered pace. Yet one aspect of medieval living found new favour. The surroundings of the

Fig. 1.22   Castern, Ilam, Staffordshire: ruined field barn and enclosure field wall overlying ridge and furrow.

house, its gardens, park and frequently the use of water, were of importance, and for some landowners the medieval moat and its associated waterworks could provide the basis for new designs. Amidst the sixteenth-century changes came a significant if fortuitous opportunity: the availability of ex-monastic land, buildings and materials. Of the aspects of country-house building which have claimed archaeological attention, this is one which features large in the literature.

Royal palaces and houses

The importance of archaeological research into the royal palaces rests in part on the disappearance of their structures, bringing a need to verify contemporary descriptions and views and to find out what the recorded expenditure on building could actually buy. It is also important in providing a background to the house-building activities of sixteenth and seventeenth-century landowners.

The first half of the sixteenth century was a remarkable period of building and rebuilding of houses for use by the Crown, and the results were significant for their influence on the way in which the greater landowners designed and built their houses and laid out gardens and parks in the next 100 years. The archaeology of the Henrician palaces has received considerable attention; much of the work of the past 30 years remains to be fully published, although the most significant points have been incorporated into the fourth volume of *The History of the Kings' Works* (Colvin 1982).

An explanation of the extent of royal building lies in part in the desire of Henry VIII to adopt continental styles in emulation of his contemporaries, but also in changing concepts of comfort. The rapidity with which new houses were built is matched only by the extent of their subsequent disappearance. Only Hampton Court remains sufficiently complete or original to give a fair impression of its original form. Of Nonsuch and Oatlands, nothing survives above ground; at Richmond there are fragments; and at Greenwich the standing structures are of the seventeenth century and later. Of the inherited medieval palaces, notably Clarendon, nothing survives above ground, and at the smaller houses which were acquired and adapted, such as Dartford, Eltham or Enfield, little sixteenth-century work can be seen.

A key theme is the shift from the use of the London palaces, Baynards and Bridewell, in favour of Whitehall Palace and of the houses built within reach of the capital. The change began with the favour with which Henry VII regarded Richmond and Greenwich, both within easy reach of London by river. Richmond was built early in his reign on the site of Sheen Manor. Neither the royal apartments adjacent to the Thames nor the Fountain Court, with its hall and chapel, survive, although part of the outer court and gatehouse can still be seen. A problem which has not been solved is whether a moat was retained from the layout of Sheen Manor, for one is mentioned in 1517 and 1534, and it has been suggested that the lack of substantial structures over a strip of ground to the north-east of the state apartments may represent its position. Excavations (Dixon 1975) have been possible to the west of the palace, but it was not clear whether the channel which was recorded there represents a late-medieval moat or part of an early-seventeenth-century system of waterworks. Richmond was not one of the residences reconstructed by Henry VIII, and although a good deal of work was done later in the sixteenth century, followed by development of the surrounding gardens and the laying out of Richmond Park in the reign of Charles I, the documentary record leaves unanswered questions about the palace buildings. Demolition and new building over the seventeenth and eighteenth centuries have left little opportunity for excavation on any scale, but there is a good case for observation should redevelopment take place.

The rebuilding by Henry VII of the medieval manor on the riverside at Greenwich provided a palace convenient for London and for the receipt of overseas visitors. An impression of the sixteenth-century buildings comes from excavations of the brick-built riverside range (fig. 1.23), which located the great tower and other features of the state apartments, begun in 1499 and demolished in the 1660s (Dixon 1972b). These can be related to the sixteenth-century sketches by Wyngaerde which are significant because of the scarcity of written accounts of the buildings and their construction, and also for their portrayal of the park to the south of the palace. Greenwich was well maintained during the sixteenth century, and was greatly developed in the seventeenth, with enlargement in a style similar to Somerset House, and the construction of the Queen's House to Inigo Jones' design.

Outstanding in terms of expenditure, architectural significance, and the interest taken by Henry VIII and his successors were the houses south-west of London: Hampton Court, Oatlands and Nonsuch. Hampton Court, built by Wolsey from 1514, was acquired by Henry VIII in 1529 and altered and enlarged up to the time of his death. Of the great houses of the period, Hampton Court stands as perhaps the finest English example of large-scale early-sixteenth-century building in brick: enough survived Wren's construction of Fountain Court, on the site of the state apartments of the 1530s, and the early-eighteenth-century remodelling of Clock Court for the original concept to be clearly perceived. Only limited excavation has been possible, but the alignment of the demolished Queen's Gallery, at the north-east corner of the original plan, has now been established (Batchelor 1977).

Hampton Court has to be seen as the centre of a much wider scheme, that was evolving during the 1530s and 1540s. The first extension was the acquisition of a moated house at Oatlands, across the Thames in Surrey, in 1537. The siting and layout of Oatlands have been established from excavations: despite the necessity for piecemeal work during redevelopment over a considerable period, it is now clear how the medieval house was enlarged to form the palace (Cook 1969; *PMA* 1984: 317; 1985: 172–3). A new range, with a gatehouse, was built within the moat in 1537–8, with bridge-wings which stood over the moat; this was filled in during the construction of an outer court, completed by 1545. The most recent excavations have shown that a polygonal building, perhaps a banqueting hall similar in plan to the example at Nonsuch, was erected in the second half of the sixteenth century. This does not appear in the lost Elizabethan drawing of the palace used by Manning and Bray in their *History of Surrey* published in 1801. Oatlands remained in use through to the Civil War, with a series of service buildings added outside the main court layout. In the seventeenth century the grounds were developed and a vineyard set out, but the house was demolished in the 1650s.

Thus there developed the scheme for Hampton Court Chase, a tract of country south of the river in which were to be two great houses. Oatlands was one, the other was to be built on the site of the manor of Cuddington, near Ewell, and came to be known as Nonsuch. The royal manor house at Woking, although maintained and

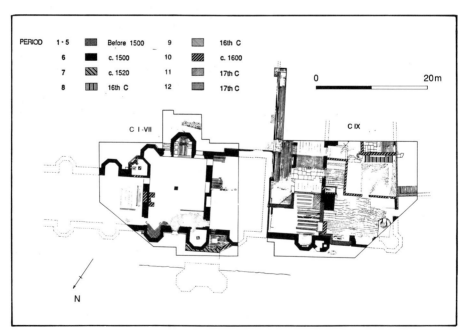

Fig. 1.23   Greenwich Palace: excavation of the river front, from the east, showing the state apartments, the great tower and the privy kitchen, with (below) the phase plan (Philip Dixon).

somewhat enlarged at this time, does not appear to have been part of the scheme. In the case of Nonsuch, there was to be no adaptation of a medieval building, but a fresh and grand design, to which building began in 1538 and was largely complete by the time of Henry's death in 1547. Nonsuch comprised two main courts, with a subsidiary kitchen court attached to the outer face of the east range. This information is largely derived from the excavations of 1959–60 (Biddle 1961), for Nonsuch lacks a contemporary birds-eye view or plan: surviving views show only outer facades, and the house had been demolished by the end of the seventeenth century. The excavations confirmed many of the items in the construction accounts. In order to build the house and lay out the park, the village of Cuddington, its manor and church had to be demolished. The foundations of the church were found during the excavation. Stone for the palace was brought from Merton Priory, and much of this was found in the foundations. Carved and gilded slate could be related to the decoration schemes of Nicholas Bellin of Modena (Biddle 1966). Full publication of this important excavation is awaited, but summaries show the extent to which the written sources have been clarified and amplified. Nonsuch was also significant for the development of its grounds, which contained a detached banqueting hall, referred to in the next section.

Less spectacular are a group of royal manors and houses in the south of England where, because of the lack of contemporary views or plans, archaeological research is the more necessary. To the south-east of London, there were royal residences at Eltham, Dartford and Otford. Eltham (*PMA* 1978: 116) was in royal hands at the beginning of the Tudor period, and was refurbished during the reign of Henry VIII, notably with the building of a new chapel. It was well maintained through to the end of the sixteenth century, and was considerably remodelled in the 1570s and 1580s, when the timber-framed building of Henry VII's time was faced with stone. Excavation has only been possible in a limited area, but has elucidated the construction of the chapel of 1528 over its medieval precursor and has shown that the plan made by John Thorpe in 1590 was largely accurate. Eltham was allowed to decay in the seventeenth century, and little now remains above ground.

Dartford was a post-dissolution development of a Dominican nunnery and was the subject of considerable expenditure towards the end of the reign of Henry VIII. Much of the site has been built over, but excavations (*PMA* 1978: 115) have recovered features which can be related to the gatehouse and a small part of the outer court, which survive among factory buildings. Further south, the former palace of the Archbishops of Canterbury at Otford, built by Archbishop Warham about 1518, was transferred to the Crown in 1537. Excavations (*PMA* 1975: 254) confirmed that Warham built on the site of a fourteenth-century manor house, and the extent of the palace has now been established. Although there are references to decay and repair at various times in the sixteenth century, it is not yet clear how significant these were, and detailed publication is awaited. Nor is it yet certain whether the subsequent owner, Sir Robert Sidney, who purchased the house in 1601, undertook any further building before the seventeenth-century decline of the property.

To the north of London, the Manor of the More, Rickmansworth, was taken over from Wolsey in 1530, and used as a royal residence into the 1550s. Excavations explained its medieval development, and how it was enlarged with new wings during Wolsey's use of the house. The dilapidation noted by Norden in 1598 was confirmed (Biddle *et al.* 1959). To the north-east of London, two royal properties have been excavated. At Enfield, convenient for Epping Forest, Henry VIII acquired Elsyngs from Sir Thomas Lovell in 1539. The fifteenth-century house was used and maintained for much of the sixteenth century, but allowed to fall into disrepair before its demolition in 1608 (*PMA* 1967: 113–4). Further from London, Hunsdon was acquired by Henry VIII in 1525, and enlarged with a range of royal lodgings in brick, added to the fifteenth-century house. Although rebuilt in the nineteenth century, recent excavation and survey (*PMA* 1986: 348) has shown that the Tudor cellars remain, and that moat and courtyard details survive from the time of Henry VIII. In particular, the moat bridge appears to be of this period, probably constructed in 1543.

Outside the home counties little building was done at royal houses in the Tudor or Stuart periods. Nothing which could be described as a palace was built north of London, and only Grafton, Northamptonshire and the King's Manor, York, received regular expenditure. No part of the house bought at Grafton in 1526 remains visible, although it was well liked by Henry VIII, used on occasion by Elizabeth, yet allowed to decay after 1600. At York, the surviving King's Manor was an administrative centre for the Council of the North rather than a place of residence.

Valuable though the archaeological coverage of royal houses has come to be, there remains considerable potential for further research. Only in the case of Nonsuch has a complete excavation taken place, and elsewhere work has been possible only during redevelopment. There are also sites where no recent excavation has been done, and three examples may be mentioned where important questions remain. Of the smaller Tudor houses, there are thought to have been early excavations at Woking manor, the record of which has not been traced; the house is of potential interest in view of the building undertaken there at the time when Oatlands and Nonsuch were being constructed. New Hall, Chelmsford, is also something of an enigma. It was purchased by Henry VIII in 1516, and a good deal of development took place during the reign. Indeed the published eighteenth-century plan shows a house of some size, but little sixteenth-century work remains, and no excavations are known to have taken place. On a different scale is Theobalds, Hertfordshire, the great house built by Burghley between 1564 and 1585, and acquired by the Crown in 1607. No excavations have been carried out, and despite survival of contemporary views and plans and the parliamentary survey of 1650, questions remain about the details of buildings erected between 1607 and 1610, of landscape features created then and in the 1620s, and of the new banqueting house of 1626.

The houses of the nobility and gentry

The study of the prodigy house has been more a matter for the architectural and art historian than for the archaeologist, due to the frequent survival of the above-ground fabric of the largest post-medieval houses, even if in altered form. Only recently has it been emphasized that rigorous archaeological examination of these large standing buildings has much to offer, by the detailed recording of structures, particularly when remedial or conversion work is taking place, using methods which owe something to the experience of the last 20 years in the archaeological examination of standing churches. Even without this development, the archaeological record does something to redress the historiographical balance, by observation of the less prestigious buildings. Although the residences of the greatest landowners have an importance in the economic history of the period, illustrating contemporary changes in the availability and disposal of wealth, the houses of smaller landowners also have a value, not only in demonstrating the changing fortunes of this numerically important group, but showing how, at this level of wealth, the improvement of standards of comfort generally involved an evolution of medieval building conventions rather than the radical changes which the greater landowners could, or perhaps felt obliged to, afford. It is at this level that one is aware of the indistinct boundary between polite and vernacular styles.

The re-use of monastic buildings

The release of monastic lands and buildings after the dissolution of the greater religious houses between 1536 and 1540 was of indisputable significance to English landowners. The injection of land into the market took place over a lengthy period and although many monastic estates were burdened with long leases, most were potentially attractive. Because of the time which it took for some ex-monastic lands to be disposed of, and for others to be managed to their full potential, the effect on landed incomes, and hence the ability to spend on the building of great houses, extended over much of the sixteenth century.

In the short term, the effect of the dissolution on house building was twofold: the availability of structures for conversion to residential use, and of materials which could be used elsewhere. Cases of the latter have been seen at royal houses: stone for Nonsuch came from Merton Priory, and Chertsey was used as a quarry for Oatlands. Parallels are the use by Sir Francis Willoughby of stone from Lenton Priory for Wollaton, or of materials from St Albans Abbey in Sir Nicholas Bacon's house at Gorhambury.

The availability of conventual buildings frequently determined the location and character of large houses built in the middle of the sixteenth century, for many were on a scale which might not otherwise have been within the means of their owners. Looked at in the longer term, expediency in the adaptation of monastic buildings is reflected in the frequent reconstruction which took place in the following century, as conventions moved away from the medieval style which many of the post-dissolution adaptations inevitably reflected. Numerous cases of such adaptations are known from documentary sources, and also from examination of examples where monastic features are easily recognizable. Dickinson (1968) has produced a useful guide to the post-dissolution history of former houses of the Augustinian Canons, amongst which are St Osyth, Essex, where the monastic gatehouse forms a prominent feature of Lord Darcy's house. A more precise view of how these adaptations were carried out has emerged from recent excavations and building surveys. Of particular significance is work done on the re-use of the buildings of the Benedictine Walden Abbey, the basis of the first phase of Audley End. Here Drury (1980; 1982) has demonstrated how the fragmentary records of past excavations, observations during more recent building and maintenance work on this guardianship monument, and modern small-scale excavations aimed at solving particular questions can build up a picture of the conversion of monastic buildings. It has been shown how the cloister was adapted by Sir Thomas Audeley between 1538 and 1544, and that an eighteenth-century copy of a lost sixteenth-century map does indeed show how this first house reflected the monastic plan.

A

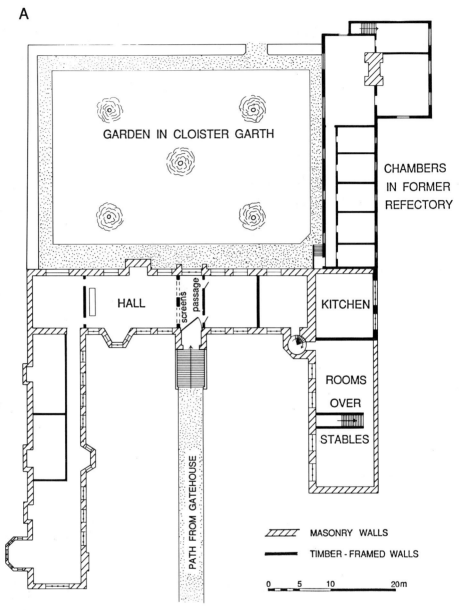

GARDEN IN CLOISTER GARTH

CHAMBERS
IN FORMER
REFECTORY

HALL

screens passage

KITCHEN

ROOMS

OVER

STABLES

PATH FROM GATEHOUSE

///// MASONRY WALLS

▬▬ TIMBER - FRAMED WALLS

0   5   10   20m

Fig. 1.24 Vale Royal, Cheshire: monastic features in the post-medieval house. (A) Suggested plan, at first-floor level, of Vale Royal House, c. 1616, based on evidence from prints and structural evidence. (B) (opposite) Isometric reconstruction of roofs of Vale Royal House derived from the claustral buildings of the Abbey (Rick Turner).

Further, it is now clear that the inner court of the seventeenth-century house also retained the outline of the cloister, even though no medieval structures are visible. An Essex parallel is Leez Priory, where Drury shows a comparable adaptation in the house built by Lord Rich immediately after the dissolution: it includes medieval

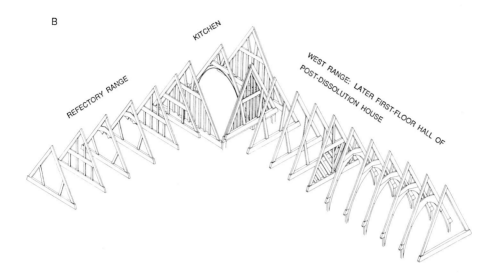

walling surviving to first-floor level within brickwork casings. A comparable approach to the development of standing buildings from monastic origins has been taken at Vale Royal Abbey (*PMA* 1985: 159–161). It has been shown how the church was demolished to its foundations soon after the dissolution, but that elements of the claustral buildings, to full gable height and including roof timbers, can be found incorporated in the present house (fig. 1.24). It should not be assumed that monastic buildings, when adapted, were in every case incorporated into large houses. Dickinson's research on Flitcham Priory, and the excavations at Denny Abbey, Cambridgeshire, have provided a reminder of farmhouses which have their origin in such re-use (Christie and Coad 1980).

Conversions of monastic buildings were not always as rapidly carried out as is often assumed: three recent excavations have shown that ruined buildings were used as the basis for houses for a century after 1540. At Waltham Abbey, Sir Edward Denny's house made use of the former chapter-house walls in the 1590s (A.E.S. Musty 1978); Sandwell Hall incorporated the lodgings of the prior of Sandwell at the beginning of the seventeenth century (*PMA* 1986: 348–9), and as late as the 1620s the remains of Elstow Abbey, Bedfordshire, were converted into a house (*PMA* 1968: 183). House building on monastic sites did not adhere as closely as is sometimes assumed to conventual plans: at Norton Priory, Cheshire, Greene's excavations have shown that Sir Richard Brooke's house of c.1545 was not built over the cloister, but further away from the church, making some use of the cellarer's range and of the abbot's lodgings, no doubt leaving the rest of the monastic complex for the quarrying of stone (*PMA* 1973: 108; 1974: 127; 1976: 168).

Excavations and surveys have confirmed that it was uncommon to adapt more than a small part of a monastic church for domestic purposes. One case of conversion is Warden Abbey, Bedfordshire, where it is probable that part of the nave was made into a three-storey building to form the north range of the sixteenth-century house. Calwich (Staffs) and Woodspring (Somerset) are ex-Augustinian examples. Mottisfont, Hampshire, and Haughmond, Shropshire, also employed fragments of church structures, in order to make use of the cloister as a courtyard.

ARCHAEOLOGICAL APPROACHES TO THE COUNTRY HOUSE

The development of domestic Tudor gothic from medieval origins, together with the late-sixteenth and early-seventeenth-century appearance of Continental-influenced renaissance styles in country-house building have been adequately described elsewhere, and a range of complete standing buildings which demonstrate these movements need hardly be illustrated here. Attention can however be drawn to houses which have been subject to detailed survey of phases and fabric and limited excavations addressed to the solution of key problems, as well as to abandoned house sites with or without above-ground remains, where excavation and survey has improved, or could improve our knowledge of structural sequences, or might portray original detail in structures free from later alteration and additions.

Few excavations have taken place on non-royal house sites which would complement the work done at Nonsuch and show how the styles developing there were used in less exalted contexts. Of the two cases in Essex, Copped Hall, built by Sir Thomas Heneage after 1564, has yielded a ground plan, but floor levels had been removed in the course of eighteenth-century landscaping (Andrews 1986). The other Essex house, the fire-gutted Hill Hall, is more rewarding: it was built by Sir Thomas Smith between 1557 and 1581, and altered and enlarged between the seventeenth and the nineteenth centuries. Excavations have shown that a fifteenth-century timber-framed building had occupied part of the site, but that its plan was not incorporated into the sixteenth-century design. The sixteenth-century house demonstrated changes of style within a short time span: the initial work of 1557–8 was typical of the Tudor gothic tradition, but in the late 1560s elements of classical design were incorporated, with French influence visible in fragments of interior decoration dating from the 1570s (Drury 1983; *PMA* 1982: 220–1; 1983: 194; 1985: 171). The only other example of excavation at a house of this period, apart from Audley End referred to earlier, is at Sheffield Manor (fig. 1.25), where work has taken place in and around the shell of the house which was built in the 1520s and enlarged in the 1570s to replace the medieval hunting lodge (*PMA* 1969 ff.). The full report on this work has yet to be published, but the plan of the wing which survives above ground has been clarified, together with features until recently buried.

There are other shells of houses of this period where there survive sufficient above-ground remains of largely original build to suggest that fresh attempts at structural recording and analysis would be worth while. Four of these may be cited by way of illustration. One is the early-sixteenth-century Cowdray House, Sussex, burnt out in 1793, but previously largely unaltered from the form in which it was completed before 1548, after a series of building phases over the previous three or four decades (fig..1.26) Another is the early house at Hardwick, the Old Hall, a shell (fig. 1.27) where further work is required to clarify the documented changes made by Bess of Hardwick before she had Robert Smythson design the adjacent New Hall in 1590 (Durant and Riden 1980). Not far to the north is Thorpe Salvin (fig. 1.28), built by Henry Sandford by 1582, abandoned at the end of the

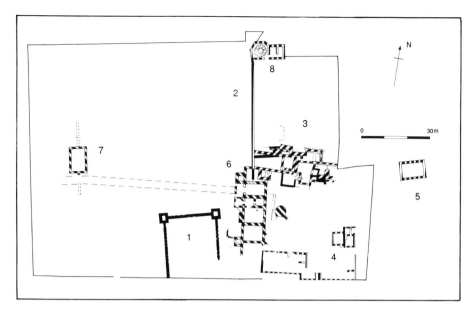

Fig. 1.25 Sheffield Manor: provisional plan of excavations. (1) pre-1500; (2) early-sixteenth-century standing walls on pre-1500 footings; (3) sixteenth century; (4) standing walls of sixteenth-century apartments, with earlier features beneath; (5) standing building with pre-1500 cruck framing, encased in sixteenth-century stonework; (6) 1574; (7) 1574 (turret house: fig. 1.37); (8) eighteenth-century pottery kiln built within turret (Sheffield City Museums).

Fig. 1.26 Cowdray House, Sussex: the sixteenth-century house destroyed by fire in 1793 (Cambridge University Collection).

Fig. 1.27 Hardwick, Derbyshire: the ruined Old Hall (left), with the New Hall built in the 1590s (right) (APS[UK]).

Fig. 1.28 Thorpe Salvin, Yorkshire, built for Sir Henry Sandford c. 1582.

seventeenth century, and so far archaeologically neglected. In Shropshire, there survives the spectacular south range of Moreton Corbet, (fig. 1.29) built adjacent to a medieval castle. The house was probably begun in the 1560s with the east range, and continued in magnificently extravagant classical style with the south wing of c.1579. The relationship between the medieval and sixteenth-century structures has been the subject of a brief exploratory excavation, but the problem of whether the second range embodies elements later than 1580 justifies further work: as the house was burnt out in 1644, to be repaired rather than rebuilt, and was derelict by the mid-eighteenth century, there are few problems caused by later development.

An important category of house, with archaeological potential, is the sixteenth-century structure later rebuilt but containing original elements. Current survey work at Sutton Scarsdale, Derbyshire, provides a good illustration: the house built at the end of the sixteenth century was radically reconstructed in 1724. The facades are of the latter date, and the extent of the sixteenth-century survival has not, until recently, been fully appreciated. The house was abandoned and gutted in the 1920s, and subsequent deterioration has exposed much of the early work. It is now thought that much of the plan of the west side (fig. 1.30), incorporating the entrance, follows the Elizabethan outline.

The archaeology of the gentry house

At the manorial level, it would be wrong to think of rapid and radical change in building styles in the sixteenth century. Changes there certainly were, which can be

Fig. 1.29   Moreton Corbet, Shropshire: the late-sixteenth-century house abandoned in the eighteenth century.

Fig. 1.30 Sutton Scarsdale, Derbyshire: the late-sixteenth-century house was incorporated in the building of 1724.

demonstrated by the examination of standing buildings and by excavation, but there were many routes to the changed aspect presented by the seventeenth-century house, compared with its fifteenth-century forebear. Some sixteenth-century landowners continued in a conservative style, building hall houses with screens-passages still separating the hall from the domestic offices. But, as in the yeoman house, halls were now rarely open to the roof, upper halls being placed at first-floor level. The excavation of the manor house at Wickham Glebe, Hampshire (*MSRG* 1980: 9), has shown how a medieval hall house could be improved: it comprised a thirteenth-century aisled hall with cross-wing in which the hall was rebuilt with a fireplace and a wooden floor, a conversion which was to survive into the seventeenth century, when an entirely new house was built in brick. Even in the early seventeenth century, when houses were rebuilt in brick, the hall and cross-wing plan frequently persisted. Acton Court, Gloucestershire (fig. 1.31), is a significant case where the sequence of rebuilding is being established by survey and excavation (*PMA* 1986: 346–7). The house was reconstructed in stages during the 20 years after about 1535: two ranges (south and east) were built in the 1530s,

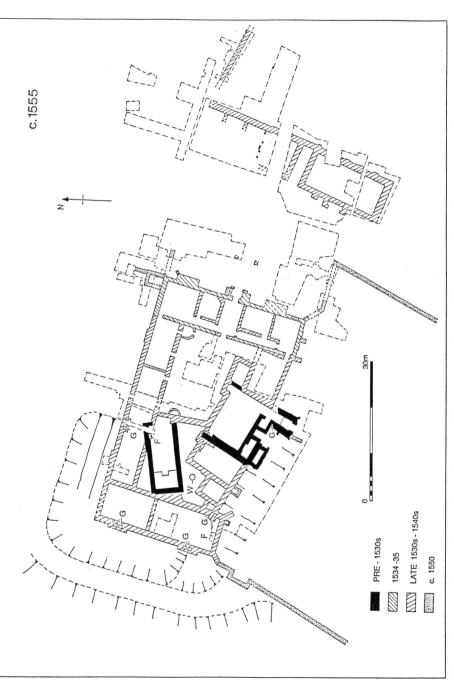

Fig. 1.31 Acton Court, Avon: plan of excavated features and the standing east and north-east ranges, incorporating medieval and sixteenth-century phases. (F) fireplace; (G) garderobe; (W) well (Bath Archaeological Trust).

joined to the earlier house by a narrow north range. Subsequently, most of the medieval house was demolished, to make way for new west and north ranges. The retention of a hall in the scheme is notable: this was linked to private rooms in the opposite range by a long gallery. Although reconstruction and detailed remodelling took place at the end of the sixteenth century, the layout remained much the same until the buildings came to be used as a farm 100 years later.

A frequent means of improving the appearance and the comfort of a house was to encase a timber-framed structure in brick or stone. Many cases can be cited, from most parts of the country: in Shropshire well-known examples are Upton Cressett, near Bridgnorth, where brick was used to encase a timber house in the sixteenth century, and New Earnstrey Park, a contemporary conversion of the same kind. In Lancashire, Ordsall Hall, Salford, is comparable, clad in brick early in the seventeenth century.

In the north of England and in Scotland, medieval conventions lasted longer, particularly in the incorporation of features with some defensive purpose. In Cumberland, the hall at Clifton, near Penrith, had a tower added in the early part of the sixteenth century, replacing a cross-wing (Fairclough 1980), while in Scotland the larger forms of bastle, and houses within barmkin walls were being built and rebuilt until the seventeenth century. Several examples have recently been noted in the Lanark area, part of a developing interest in the post-medieval domestic buildings of southern Scotland: an example is Halltown of Nemphlar, which a recent survey showed to be a sixteenth/seventeenth-century house in the bastle tradition where much masonry of the period survives (*PMA* 1987: 285) Comprehensive investigations have taken place at Smailholm Tower, near Galashiels (fig. 1.32): the medieval tower and the excavated outer hall range were adapted to new standards of comfort in the middle of the seventeenth century, when the hall was rebuilt to relieve overcrowding in the tower, and to bring the kitchen, formerly housed in a separate building in the courtyard, into the main house (Tabraham 1987: 227–238). Houses such as these can be hard to categorize, the difficulty being whether to regard them as farms or as houses of gentry status. Many were built to a standard and hence at a cost which places them above the status of the upland farm, although in the case of Smailholm the occupants moved early in the eighteenth century to a new building, Sandyknowe, which is comparable in size and character with the larger farmhouses of the district.

MOATS

Continuity is well demonstrated by the use of medieval moated sites for sixteenth-and seventeenth-century houses. Research on moats has emphasized their medieval use, studying their origins and typology. More emphasis could well be given to the extent to which moats remained occupied in the sixteenth century, how houses built within them were developed, and how moats could provide a basis for landscape schemes. Moated sites demonstrate how contemporaries were still attracted by archaic appearances of strength in a sixteenth-century house complex, a convention which was valued provided it was not accompanied by the discomforts of castle life. The facade-castle is a form admirably discussed by Rigold, and excavated examples can be added to those such as Hever and Scotney which he cited in his essay on buildings within moats (Rigold 1978: 29–36). Rochford, Essex (*PMA* 1986: 347), is an excavated sixteenth-century brick house

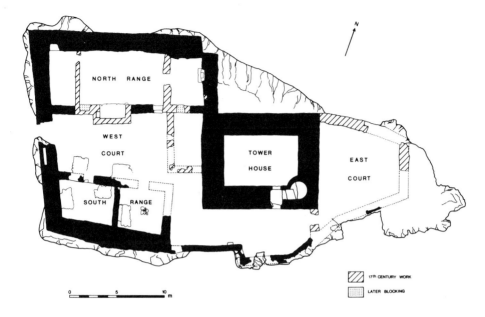

Fig. 1.32 Smailholm Tower, Borders (Roxburgh): plan of the tower with courtyard buildings as remodelled c.1645 (Historic Scotland).

with turrets, within a moat, while Laughton, Sussex, is another significant example, with an enclosing wall and towers (*PMA* 1985: 173–5). Particularly spectacular were buildings which rose directly from the island revetment, even if they were not specifically defensive in their details. Ightham Moat, Kent, for example, has densely packed buildings at the moat edge, of fourteenth-century origin but altered over a lengthy period. The sixteenth-century houses at Lullingstone, Kent, and Baconsthorpe, Norfolk must have presented much the same effect. Revetments were in any case important for stability. They were commonly built or rebuilt in brick or stone at the end of the Middle Ages, but Wickham Glebe is a case where timbers were used as late as the sixteenth century.

The hint of a defensive convention is at times present yet without a complete moat: the excavations at Acton Court (fig. 1.31) have shown how the outer court of the house was completed with imitation bastions, and it is known that the walls were crenellated in the sixteenth century. Similarly, at 'The Place', Uxbridge, Middlesex, the un-moated sixteenth-century house had hexagonal brick gate towers (*PMA* 1987: 283), and the rebuilding of Melbury Sampford House, Dorset, about 1540, incorporated an impressive crenellated tower over the entrance. Although such effects were enhanced by the gatehouse, over the sixteenth century the latter increasingly became a utility building, with the appearance less of fortification than of a domestic structure pierced by an entry. The gateway at Gedding Hall, Suffolk, though domestic in form, is still an imposing structure in the medieval tradition, but at Markenfield, Yorkshire, Little Moreton Hall, Cheshire, and Appleby Magna, Leicestershire, gatehouses have more mundane purposes. The often-illustrated Herefordshire example at Lower Brockhampton is a mere token, marking the position of the approach to the house.

Associated with moats and gatehouses were bridges. More is known about the structure of medieval timber bridges, but a few sixteenth-century examples have been recorded. Excavations at Hunsdon, Herts, have revealed details of the bridge possibly built for Henry VIII in 1543. At Baconsthorpe the bridge was remodelled about 1600 (*PMA* 1973: 101), approximately contemporary with the excavated example at Cheshunt (*PMA* 1970: 180–1). Stone bridges have been studied at Blickling, Norfolk, and at Eltham Palace. At Laughton, three bridges were identified, one medieval, the others apparently part of the sixteenth-century brick phase.

For the owner of a developing sixteenth-century estate, under some social pressure to elaborate and enlarge his house, the moat could be a constraint. Indeed many moated houses appear to have expanded to fill all the available ground. Ightham and Markenfield are well-known examples where most of the perimeter of the island was occupied, and where the internal courtyards were smaller than at non-moated counterparts. When insufficient space remained, various expedients were adopted: at Rochford sixteenth-century buildings appear to overlie the moat, and a new channel was dug around the extended house; the desire to maintain the feature value of the moat is significant. Similarly, excavations at Speke Hall, Liverpool, suggest the cutting of a new larger moat when building extension spilled over the filled-in original (*PMA* 1982: 221–2), and at Great Cressingham, Norfolk, the enlarged house was encircled on three sides by a new moat in the middle of the sixteenth century (*PMA* 1969: 196–7). One answer to the need for extra space was to abandon the complete circuit of the moat and, as seen at Oatlands and Richmond palaces, to construct an outer court across its line.

GARDENS AND PARKS

The past decade has seen growing interest in the surroundings of the post-medieval country house (C.C. Taylor 1983a). It is accepted that survey and excavation should have regard not only to the structures of houses themselves, but also to earthwork remains of gardens and parks, and the buildings which they contained. One result has been the creation of a register of gardens by English Heritage, to keep records not only of existing historic gardens, but also landscape evidence of gardens long abandoned.

It is in the post-medieval period that interest grew across Europe in the creation not only of parks but of formal gardens. This renaissance development, seen in Italy in the fifteenth century, and adopted in France early in the sixteenth, spread to England during the reign of Henry VIII. Hitherto, English gardens had been on a relatively small scale, reflecting limitations of space within the precincts of moats, fortifications and courtyards. Towards the more distant horizon, parks were developed in the sixteenth century which show a greater degree of planning than the deer-parks which are their medieval forebears. In both the garden and the park fashions were to change, and by the eighteenth century formality was in retreat, leading to a careful landscaping which tended to merge garden into park, providing a unified vista brought about by earth moving, tree planting and the construction of ornamental buildings.

Fig. 1.33 Lyveden, Northamptonshire: Sir Thomas Tresham's gardens, shown as crop-marks (left), and the New Bield, the viewing tower (upper right) (Cambridge University Collection).

Sixteenth-and seventeenth-century planned gardens

The archaeology of the post-medieval garden has been studied at two levels. There has been a widespread interest in the large garden projects of the century after 1550, many of which have left considerable earthwork remains. Secondly, it has been seen that excavation has a role in establishing the details of layout and even the planting schemes used.

The potential for research on garden earthworks has been demonstrated by the Royal Commission inventories for Northamptonshire, where significant remains are surveyed and described. A remarkable example was the garden laid out by Sir Thomas Tresham between 1597 and 1604 at Lyveden. His rebuilding of the manor house – the Old Bield – was accompanied by the planning of a garden scheme made up of terraces leading to a distant lodge, the New Bield. Thus the vista from the house was one of ordered gardens, a pattern of lawns and beds, with viewing mounds set at corners of the largest terrace. The garden remains at Lyveden are largely ploughed out (fig. 1.33), but those at Holdenby, also in Northamptonshire, survive with little disturbance. Laid out by Sir Christopher Hatton when building Holdenby House in the 1580s, the development of the garden earthworks can be understood by comparing the existing remains with Ralph Treswell's two plans, of

Fig. 1.34 Garden earthworks at Stainsfield, Lincolnshire (Cambridge University Collection).

1580 and 1587. Flights of terraces, a knot garden, the creation of pools and a prospect mound are all typical of the period and form a layout which impressed Norden in 1610 and the parliamentary commissioners who inspected the estate in 1651 shortly before the demolition of the house and the abandonment of the grounds.

A few examples will show how widespread the earthworks of gardens have proved to be: there are visible works of sixteenth-or seventeenth-century origin at Stainsfield, Lincolnshire (fig. 1.34), Ascott, Tackley and Walcott, Oxfordshire (Woodward 1982), Kenilworth castle (*PMA* 1976: 169), Driffield Manor, Gloucestershire (*PMA* 1979: 277), Bewsey Old Hall, Cheshire (*PMA* 1985: 170–1) and Iron Acton, Avon (*PMA* 1986: 346–7); recently discovered is the terraced garden-earthwork at Throwley Old Hall, of 16th-century date (fig.1.35). At Cranborne House, Dorset (C.C. Taylor 1970: 143) remains are visible of the Cecils' early-seventeenth-century layout, a walled garden containing nine rectangular units, accompanied by terraces and a mount.

The interest in landscaping led to the incorporation and adaptation of medieval moats and fishponds into garden schemes, and also to the creation of new moats which can be mistaken for works of medieval origin. Designs at Papley, Northamptonshire and Papworth St Agnes, Cambridgeshire, appear to have adapted medieval moats, whilst at Longford Hall, Shropshire, and at Grafton

Fig. 1.35 Throwley Old Hall, Staffordshire: the weathered earthworks of garden terraces lie to the right of the ruined sixteenth-century house.

Regis, Northamptonshire, fishponds were incorporated. By contrast, at Hamerton, Cambridgeshire, the moat is a seventeenth-century feature, and at Leighton Bromswold the three-sided moat adjacent to the gatehouse, the only standing part of the house complex, appears also to be a post-medieval creation. Similarly, in south Wales, where the gardens of Margam Park have been recorded (*PMA 1976:* 169–70), the ornamental ponds which correspond with seventeenth-century paintings appear not to have had medieval origins.

An overview of numerous examples around the country confirms that the form of the garden changed over the period. At Lamport, Le Notre was commissioned in 1660 to lay out gardens which, while retaining an element of formality in their rectangular lawns and beds, were more integrated with the park than in earlier practice, avenues radiating from the house towards the park boundaries. Newbottle, also in Northamptonshire, shows an interesting variation: a garden scheme was planned to accompany the rebuilding of the facade of Great Purston Manor, features stretching across the park to a prospect mount 600m distant. The plan seems never to have been finished, but forms a stage towards the eighteenth-century convention of emphasizing the park rather than the garden, as typified by Althorp, where after 1700 the formal elements were removed and a new landscape created, or Garendon, where Ambrose Phillips designed an integrated park and garden scene, with vistas of plantations and ornamental buildings. In conflict with such unity was the need to use parks for grazing: livestock were excluded from the garden by a ha-ha, a ditch with a hidden revetment wall which faced away from the house and garden. The significance of many of these changes for archaeological research is the extent to which earlier garden features were disguised or destroyed, as at Chatsworth, or at Bryanston, Dorset, where the eighteenth-century park largely destroyed the late-seventeenth-century garden, which is now visible only as earthworks.

Within the garden, the potential for archaeological research has been recognized as a means of finding out more about details of layout and planting. This has led to the possibility of recreating gardens of particular periods, complementing archive descriptions and plans with the results of excavation. There have been encouraging results from excavations of post-medieval gardens: at Chiswick House, London where budding trenches have been found in the Jacobean kitchen-garden levels (*PMA* 1984: 316); at Tatton Old Hall, Cheshire, channels presumed to be for tree planting have been recorded (*PMA* 1979: 277), and at Gawsworth Hall, Cheshire, geophysical survey has shown the geometric patterns of the garden layout (*PMA* 1988: 216). A more comprehensive view of an early garden arrangement has come from Hill Hall, Essex, where excavations have enabled a plan to be made of a layout of sunken gravelled paths enclosing deeply cultivated beds (*PMA* 1984: 315). As wet ditches survive at Hill Hall, containing organic material, there is potential for the recovery of environmental evidence as a guide to how gardens were stocked and maintained. A worthwhile aim would be to demonstrate, as in the Roman context at Fishbourne, the appearance of past gardens. Such is the plan at Audley End (Cunningham 1986; *PMA* 1988: 216–8), where the sequence of eighteenth-century alterations has been recorded, and the nineteenth-century layout of flower beds established with a precision which makes restoration possible (fig. 1.36).

The post-medieval park

Prospect mounds, set at the edges of sixteenth-and seventeenth-century gardens served not only to view the garden itself, but as a vantage point over the park beyond. Many survive, as at Holdenby, although there are cases where there has been confusion with windmill mounds or barrows. At Leighton Bromswold, Huntingdonshire, mounds were built at two corners of a rectangle which formed part of the grounds of the house built by Sir Gervase Clifton at the end of the sixteenth century (Brown and Taylor 1977); similarly, seventeenth-century landscaping at Childerley Hall, near Cambridge, incorporates mounds at the corners of a terrace. At Chatsworth, Queen Mary's Bower is a stone platform which is a development of the idea of the prospect mound, probably sited at the end of a formal garden obscured by later landscaping.

In addition to mounds, the view of the wider park was achieved by building towers, some at the end of the garden, as at Sheffield Manor (fig. 1.37), others further out into the park itself. At Nonsuch, there was an octagonal banqueting house which may well have marked a transition from garden to park in the same way as Tresham's cruciform viewing tower, the New Bield. An example of a more distant parkland tower is shown in Wyngaerde's drawing of Greenwich Palace, and a surviving example is the sixteenth-century Hunting Tower at Chatsworth, sited on the hill which overlooks the house and a great area of the park.

Fig. 1.36 Audley End, Essex: flower-garden layout of 1832 revealed during excavations (C. Cunningham; English Heritage).

The park itself is a subject less straightforward than might at first appear. It could be assumed that most of the lands which surrounded sixteenth to eighteenth-century houses were originally medieval deer-parks, developed according to changing convention. Some certainly were, but there are others which were laid out

Fig. 1.37   The Turret House at Sheffield Manor (see fig. 1.25).

from scratch in the sixteenth century, involving major alterations to the local economy; conversely, numerous medieval parks ceased to be used as such during the sixteenth and seventeenth centuries. What happened to these parks? There are several sources: maps, in particular those made by Saxton, give a good point of reference at the end of the sixteenth century, showing the extent to which parks known from medieval documentary sources had disappeared. An archaeological approach can be complementary: in several parts of the country most of the medieval deer-parks with surviving boundary banks are known; these can be checked for references to disparking, or failure to appear as parks on sixteenth-or seventeenth-century maps. The more recent RCHM county inventory volumes, for

Cambridgeshire, Dorset and Northamptonshire, have tackled the problem of listing such parks, and provide a sound basis for examining post-medieval changes. Northamptonshire provides a range of examples; there are a number which have clearly documented medieval origins and well-preserved boundary banks, but which were not associated with the country houses of the sixteenth or seventeenth centuries, and appear to have been gradually disparked as the agricultural land market revived. In the north-east of the county the parks at Wedenhoe and Oundle fall into this group, having thirteenth-and fourteenth-century origins, but of whose post-medieval history little or nothing is known. Some such parks, Gayton and Paulerspury for example, had been enlarged over ridge and furrow in the fifteenth century, at a time when arable areas were shrinking. Another profitable use for the park was the planting of coppice woods: in the sixteenth and seventeenth centuries this was common where wood was needed for industry, explaining the conversion of Derbyshire and Yorkshire parks such as Holmesfield, Ecclesall and Tinsley.

After 1600, medieval parks continued to disappear: food prices maintained their increase over the first half of the seventeenth century, and the attractions of an economic return from parks which did not contribute to country-house landscapes led to the formation of closes and farms, and the acceptance of encroachments. The process was a lengthy one, leaving some parks, even those where no house was developed during the period, recognizable as late as the mid-eighteenth century. In Yorkshire the old park at Wortley, reduced in area by encroachment and leasing, was still an entity during the eighteenth century, and although at nearby Tankersley the Old Hall had become overshadowed by Wentworth Woodhouse, its park was kept intact, even landscaped, after 1700 (Hey 1975).

Conversely, many parks were created or enlarged in the sixteenth century, attracting legislative attention at a time of concern over the problems of depopulating enclosure. This was the time when the medieval parks at Grafton Regis and Hartwell were enlarged, although neither were associated with any new building apart from the lodge erected at Hartwell. In Staffordshire, Sandon is an example of a sixteenth-century creation, as is Chettisham in Cambridgeshire. The effects were diverse: where land was of poor quality, park enlargement created fewest problems, and the land thus enclosed could be improved for grazing. Rowley (1972: 120) cites the example of Frodesley, near Wenlock Edge, where the park was thus improved early in the seventeenth century. There is no doubt that the enlargement of medieval parks frequently took place where villages had stood: for example, research in Hampshire has shown that within half the parks which can be identified there are village earthworks (M.F. Hughes 1982). The process was a lengthy one, and even if the date of depopulation can be established from the returns of 1515–17 or any other contemporary source, it is not always possible to establish how many people were displaced, or whether the village had been more than the remnant of a settlement weakened and dwindling over a lengthy period. Indeed, the number of cases where there is archaeological and archive evidence for sixteenth-century emparking depopulation of thriving villages is not large. Of the Northamptonshire cases, Holdenby is well documented, with the creation of the park at the time of the building of the house and the laying out of the gardens in the 1580s, but here it is known that new village houses were built. Elsewhere, the case of Nonsuch is well established, the village of Cuddington being demolished when the palace was built.

Despite the attractions of putting parks to economic use, the enlargement and landscaping of country-house parks continued through the seventeenth century and into the eighteenth: after 1700 new fashions in park landscaping led to the removal of a number of villages. Although the total is small, most are well documented, and the great houses to which they related in most cases survive, as do the estate villages which were created. Among the more noteworthy are Shugborough, Staffordshire, where Thomas Anson enlarged the hall and replaced most of the village with houses in Great Haywood, as part of the transformation of the park between 1720 and 1773. In Dorset, More Crichel was demolished, replaced by houses at Newtown from 1765, and at Milton Abbas the village was demolished and replaced as part of the Capability Brown landscaping scheme between 1771 and 1790. Humphry Repton's scheme for Herriard, near Basingstoke, involved the moving of the village, and, a late example, the houses of Middleton Stoney, Oxfordshire, were replaced at the beginning of the nineteenth century. Not all were so well documented: Rowley (1972: 133) has listed several Shropshire cases where there are surface indications but little documentary record of the removal of villages from land incorporated into eighteenth-century parks, and the construction of estate villages in their place.

The archaeological potential of the villages displaced by eighteenth-century emparking has not been tested. At Buxted, Sussex, an early-eighteenth-century example, the village site was observed during deep ploughing (*PMA* 1979: 276), but excavations were not possible. In many cases parkland has not yet been greatly disturbed, and the potential for gaining new information about village houses abandoned at this time should be emphasized in the event of threats to parkland sites.

Functional structures in the estate

Although the popular view of eighteenth-century estate building works might emphasize the picturesque, the planned village, the model farm or decorative follies and obelisks, a good deal of attention has been given to the archaeology of more practical estate works, in and beyond the park.

Ice-houses became common in the eighteenth century, although examples are documented from about 1660. Their function was to keep ice for domestic use, and there seems to have been no question of the storage of perishables. They have been surveyed and listed in many parts of the country, and the standard form of structure built in the eighteenth and nineteenth centuries is now well known. This comprised a cylindrical brick-lined chamber, often internally domed, usually set in the ground or with earth banked over the top. Access was normally from the side, by means of a passage which in the more complex examples such as at Wentworth Castle, Yorkshire (Ashurst, 1984), contained a series of doors (fig. 1.38). In some, a drain was incorporated, to remove melt-water, and there are examples with holes in the top of the dome through which extra ice could be added. Variations in form included structures of egg-shaped section, as at Croome Court, Worcestershire, and simple ice-wells without a side entrance (Yorke 1956). Near Darenth, Kent, there is an ice-house with two access doors, at different levels (Caiger 1965); a flight of steps from ground level reaches a landing whence leads the upper entrance to the ice chamber and a further flight to the lower door. A rare example of a rock-cut chamber is at Castle Semple, Renfrewshire (*PMA* 1970: 181), where a chamber has

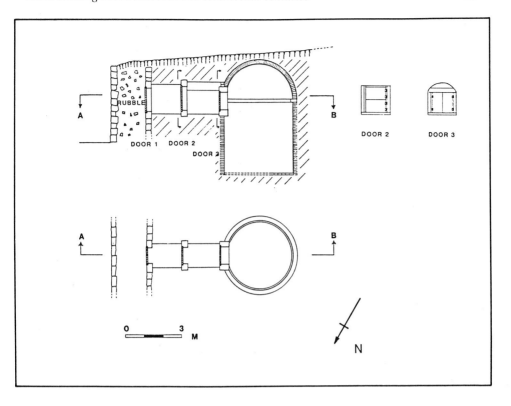

Fig. 1.38 Wentworth Castle, Yorkshire: eighteenth-century ice-house (Denis Ashurst).

been recorded close to a pond which could have formed a source of ice. There was a conventional brick ice-house near by, which is suggested as having succeeded the rock-cut chamber. An experimental filling at the Levens ice-house, Cumbria, has demonstrated a load of ice melting after 13 months, and that beneath the straw placed on the ice the temperature remained constant at +3°C, while in the dome above, the temperature varied with the outside level, to a summer maximum of +15°C (David 1982).

Not exclusively found in parks, but common among estate buildings are pigeon houses and bee-boles. Pigeon houses have been recorded in Glamorgan and in Devon and Flintshire, with individual examples published from elsewhere (Copeland 1967; J.D.K. Lloyd 1965–6). They are normally fairly easily identified, if difficult to date, either incorporated into agricultural buildings or free-standing square or circular structures, with pierced walls providing nesting holes accessible from the inside. An example published at Durleigh, Somerset (R.F. Taylor 1968), was built of cob, with a conical roof, and probably dates from the seventeenth century. There were 730 holes, in 13 tiers, each hole having a slate as a floor. In Kent, examples at Dartford and Leeds have been surveyed, of sixteenth-century build, the latter being modified to resemble a chapel as part of a Capability Brown landscaping scheme. Another estate structure which may be difficult to identify is the bee-bole of this period. These are recesses built into south-facing walls, in which straw skep-hives were placed, protected from rain. A number have been recorded in Glamorgan (RCAHM 1988), and a Staffordshire example has been published from Pipe Ridware (Whiston 1969–70).

Estate rabbit warrens are landscape features which are hard to date. The practice of warrening was common in the Middle Ages, but it is rarely possible to identify medieval banks as distinct from those of the seventeenth or eighteenth centuries. Information is more secure after 1700, and Harris (1970) has set out the evidence for East Yorkshire, where the majority of the references date from the eighteenth century and later, when improvement of farming led to antagonism against artificially high rabbit populations. In Yorkshire there are few surviving warren banks, in contrast with west Norfolk where a number can be seen in Breckland, with Sussex, where there are survivors on Ashdown Forest, and Devon, where warrens are recorded on Dartmoor. Rapid disappearance can be explained by the loss of profitability of rabbit production in Britain after 1800, partly due to changes in land use, but also to competition from imports and the freeing of trapping from legal restraints later in the nineteenth century (Sheail 1971). Hence many warrens disappeared, particularly as waste was enclosed for the improvement of pasture.

Chapter 2

The archaeology of the post-medieval town

The sources

As with urban archaeology in the medieval period, research on the topography and archaeology of post-medieval towns calls on a wide range of sources, physical and documentary. Indeed, as we come closer to the present day, the balance changes further, with the visible above-ground elements, whether standing buildings or obvious topographical features, making a contribution which can compensate for the relative scarcity of excavated data. The latter has been blamed on archaeologists' unwillingness to give to the more recent deposits the care and interest devoted to those below (Davey 1987: 70): there may once have been some truth in this, but the main reason for the scarcity of excavated information for the period must be the vulnerability of post-medieval levels to destruction, not only by modern urban building methods, but by cellars dug in the nineteenth century.

The balance is also shifted by the changing nature of the post-medieval documentary record, with its closer relationship to topographical features. Urban plans become an important source: Speed's series of 1610 covers many towns, and for London there are sources such as the views by Wyngaerde (c.1550), the plans of Leake and Hollar at the time of the Great Fire and the map by Ogilby and Morgan of 1677. This was a period of rapid development in surveying skills, seen by comparing the early and late work of Ralph Treswell, in which his panoramic representation of buildings in London gives way to scaled plans in the 30 years after 1580 (Schofield 1987). Sources which remain to be fully investigated are surveyors' own archives: the remarkable series of fieldbooks and draft maps by Fairbank of Sheffield which start in 1739 is an indication of the possibilities. In addition, the format of leases becomes more useful over the seventeenth century, with a greater precision in the description of boundaries and buildings, and the more frequent use of reference plans.

For the eighteenth century there are new sources: enclosure surveyors' maps portray the outskirts of many towns and show the progress of suburb development; the insurance of buildings became more frequent, for which the registers of the Sun and Royal Exchange companies are an important source; street and trade directories were published for many towns in the last quarter of the century; poor-rate books survive in increasing numbers. Some might argue that these eighteenth-century sources are merely a postscript to research into urban topography of the sixteenth or seventeenth centuries: in fact, they frequently present a view of a town before the period of radical alteration which in some cases accompanied and in others followed the industrial revolution, and often provide invaluable pointers to townscapes where change from an essentially medieval form was late to gather pace.

Unfortunately, the record of excavation on post-medieval town sites is difficult to view as a whole. Much of the work carried out over the last 20 years by urban arcchaeology units remains unpublished, except in summary in the annual 'Post-Medieval Britain' sections of *Post-Medieval Archaeology* or in a local journal. Where publication has taken place in multi-period monographs, it has to be disentangled from the earlier material; not that this is always a disadvantage, for it can emphasize continuity on either side of an arbitrary date. Significant self-contained reports on important post-medieval deposits are still fairly few. The St Ebbes excavations in Oxford (Hassall 1984) and the Moulsham Street site in Chelmsford (Cunningham and Drury 1985) are significant examples where the post-medieval material stands on its own. What are needed are more publications which bring together the results of watching briefs, small excavations and the relevant parts of larger campaigns: it is intended that the recently published survey of post-medieval work in Gloucester (Atkin 1987) should be the forerunner of a series of review–syntheses in *Post-Medieval Archaeology*.

The archaeology of urban change

POST-MEDIEVAL URBAN EXCAVATION

Despite the danger of generalization about excavated features from this period, it is true that a high proportion of the information about the use of properties on sixteenth to eighteenth-century urban sites has come from the fillings of pits and other features dug into lower levels, rather than from post-medieval surfaces and structural features. This is not only because of damage caused by the digging of cellars in the nineteenth century, but also because even the modest structures of the eighteenth century and onwards used more substantial foundations than their forebears, as well as better-constructed floors which required site levelling which could destroy earlier clay, tile or brick surfaces. In the larger towns in the nineteenth century damage to post-medieval stratification was very great, and evidence often has to come from strips of undisturbed ground between buildings or between cellars, or from the yards behind properties, where earlier occupiers had dug their rubbish pits, or where ancillary buildings had been sited.

There are numerous cases where the majority of material comes from pits and wells: their contents are valuable in the study of the date ranges and associations of artefacts, but are too frequently divorced from the buildings of the people who deposited them. Pit groups constitute a major part of the record in, for example, the excavations of sixteenth-century Southampton (Platt and Coleman-Smith 1975: 247ff.); they are significant in Stamford (*PMA* 1974: 124), and in the Bedern in York (*PMA* 1977: 93); even in smaller towns less affected by redevelopment, such as Newark (Fairclough 1976) and St Neots (Addyman and Marjoram 1972) the record is strongly biased to the contents of pits. The incidence and life of pits varied:

where soils were porous, they remained in use for a considerable time, but in towns such as Southampton where impervious clays prevented drainage into surrounding ground, pits had shorter lives, giving closer dating to the contents. In some towns pit digging became less common as a means of rubbish disposal, as has been observed in York, where it has been suggested (Schofield and Palliser 1981: 115) that epidemics in the sixteenth century encouraged the practice of carrying refuse to dumps outside the town, removing a source not only of dated artefacts but of environmental evidence.

There are, nevertheless, several important towns, such as Canterbury, Exeter and Norwich, where significant areas remained lightly built in the nineteenth century, assisting the correlation of rubbish deposits with adjacent structures. In Castle Street, Canterbury, for example, pits containing important groups of sixteenth to nineteenth-century pottery and glass were associated with the post-medieval buildings on the frontage. In Friernhay Street, Exeter (fig. 2.1) there have been excellent examples of tenements where a complete record of stratification has survived and where buildings can be related to features within the curtilages (*PMA* 1982: 218–20).

There have been few cases where such relationships can be amplified by surviving archives relating to the occupants of excavated sites. Twenty years ago, the results of seeking such a connection were demonstrated for a house at Waltham Abbey (Huggins 1969), which was occupied by a London mercer in the seventeenth century and whose standards of possessions were well illustrated by excavated pit groups. Subsequently, excavations in Chelmsford and Norwich have been related to written sources, but the opportunism of urban rescue archaeology will inevitably limit such examples, unless a deliberate policy can be fostered of confining resources to the excavation of the sites with the fullest range of complementary documentation.

In many towns, significant stratigraphical benchmarks are provided by fires. London is the outstanding example, for approximately 80 per cent of the area within the city walls was devastated by the Great Fire of 1666. The archaeological implications are enormous: where seventeenth-century levels exist, the characteristic fire debris can be seen: the New Fresh Wharf excavation provided a striking example, of a sixteenth-century house cellar whose wooden floor had been preserved by the collapse of the burning building (Schofield 1984: 9). Many City excavations have illustrated the rebuilding of London after the fire. In general the opportunity to replan was lost, and most of the new structures respected the property boundaries of their predecessors. Most churches were rebuilt on or close to the earlier foundations: Christchurch, Newgate Street, was built by Wren on the medieval footings, and at St Mildreds, Bread Street, he used part of the former plan, extending with poorly built foundations over earlier pits (*PMA* 1974: 120).

Although few large towns suffered fires as disastrous as that of London, many saw a number of serious outbreaks over the period. Nevertheless, it is important not to accept associations between signs of fire damage and documented conflagrations too readily, unless there is a corresponding sequence over several properties. The London evidence is usually clear, and in Norwich the destruction levels in the Pottergate excavation appear to represent the fire of 1507. Some well-documented outbreaks, on the other hand, have not been traced on the ground. The fire which destroyed over 300 houses in Oxford in 1644, in an area from George Street westwards to the river, covered ground where several

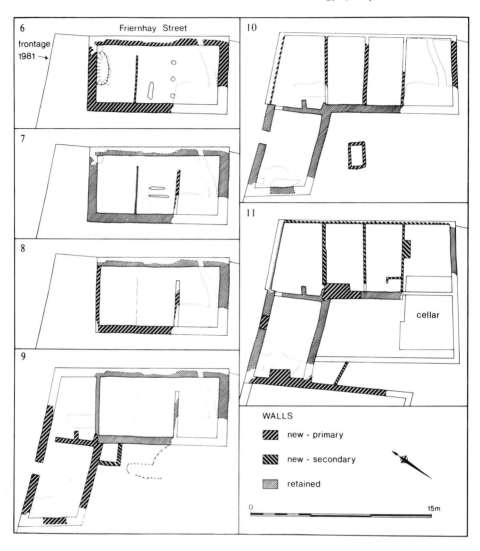

Fig. 2.1 Exeter, Friernhay Street: plans of the post-medieval phases (6–11) of excavated tenement C. (6) house of c.1500; (7) sixteenth-century alterations; (8) sixteenth-century rebuilding of north-west and south-west walls; (9) addition of west range, c.1600; (10) rebuilding of original range, c.1700; (11) rebuilding and infilling by 1900 (Exeter Museum).

excavations have taken place, but these have not produced firm indications of the event (Porter 1984: 289–300; Sturdy and Munby 1985). In other towns fires were well documented (E.L. Jones 1968), but excavation has not been possible. None, for example, has taken place in the centre of Blandford, where the fire of 1731 led to one of the most radical town-centre reconstructions of the period. Such rebuildings demonstrate, both through standing buildings and the record of excavations, the long-term effect of fire damage on building styles, with the use of brick increasingly laid down in by-laws, as in York in 1645 or London in the 1660s, and the continuation of the medieval trend towards the use of tile rather than thatch for roofing.

TOWN CENTRES AND THEIR SUBURBS

In virtually all towns in Britain the numbers of inhabitants grew between 1500 and 1750, the rate of increase varying widely. Built-up areas were enlarged, but within these there were wide variations in density, both between and within towns. The rate and timing of these changes varied, in some cases expansion being under way as early as 1500, while in others the late-medieval depression was prolonged well into the sixteenth century, with little sign of expansion appearing until after 1600. It will be shown later how the excavated evidence has demonstrated the mixed fortunes of towns in the sixteenth and seventeenth centuries. What stands out is the disproportionate growth of London, which absorbed a significant proportion of the population increase of the country as a whole, and grew to an extent which had a remarkable influence on the national economy.

Redevelopment of medieval towns

Urban growth can be seen on the ground in two ways: the infilling of underused land within old centres or suburbs, and the development of new suburbs. The late-medieval preface is important: by the middle of the fifteenth century much of the overcrowding of the pre-Black Death period had been relieved, and although it is the rural shake-out of land and population that is often stressed, the effects of demographic contraction had been important for many towns. The taxable population had dwindled, as many fifteenth-century urban authorities had found, even if some had complained too loudly to be entirely convincing. The results were dilapidation and empty plots, although many were in the medieval suburbs rather than in the old centres. Overall, in late-medieval towns it was possible for building densities to be reduced, and land which came to be used as gardens or for access space around the houses of the better off was not necessarily available for new housing when population began to recover.

Even so, much post-medieval urban building took place on land deserted during the fourteenth and fifteenth centuries. A pioneer archaeological illustration of the process of medieval desertion and later reoccupation came with the pre-war excavations on the site of the New Bodleian Library in Oxford (Bruce-Mitford 1939). These demonstrated that occupation ceased in the post-Black Death period, and that new buildings were not put up until the seventeenth century, using the old tenement boundaries. Recently, a similar pattern has been seen in a smaller town, Andover, where excavations in Winchester Street have shown seventeenth-century redevelopment of plots abandoned late in the Middle Ages (*PMA* 1985: 164). Expansion over the gardens and back-lands of medieval towns became common: in Oxford, the St Ebbes excavations have shown development after about 1570 on land hitherto used for gardens and scattered housing; in Bristol similar expansion has been seen, where plots which had been intensively occupied in the fourteenth and fifteenth centuries were built up along the frontages around 1600, to be infilled in the subsequent century (*PMA* 1977: 88).

Land became vacant as the result of religious change. After the dissolution, urban monastic lands became available, sometimes for grantees or well-to-do purchasers to build upon, sometimes being sold off piecemeal for development. Not only the sites of religious houses themselves, but their urban property entered the market, and to this was added possessions of the chantries dissolved in the reign of Edward VI. London changed considerably as a result. Excavation of the site of the church of Blackfriars has demonstrated how the area was redeveloped after demolition, stone from the church being found in the overlying seventeenth and eighteenth-century cellars (*PMA* 1986: 334–5). Among other examples recorded in City excavations is Holy Trinity, Leadenhall Street (*PMA* 1985: 165–6), where buildings were put up within the outline of the church, whose structure gradually disappeared over the three centuries following the dissolution. By contrast, some monastic buildings were attractive enough for conversion: the Charterhouse, whose lay brothers' court had been built early in the sixteenth century, was converted by Lord North and, later, by Thomas Howard into a town house incorporating many of the monastic structures (Schofield 1984: 141). By chance, London's land supply also benefited from the abandonment by the Crown of the two palaces at the western end of the City, Baynards Castle and Bridewell. Both have been partially excavated, showing the structure of the new Baynards Castle, built for Henry VII, abandoned during the sixteenth century and encroached upon up to the time of the Great Fire (Colvin 1982: 50–2). Bridewell (fig. 2.2), built between 1515 and 1523, and handed over to the City as poor-relief accommodation in 1552, was also partly built over by 1666, although parts were to survive until the nineteenth century (Gadd and Dyson 1981).

Outside London, the re-use of urban monastic sites was less rapid, emphasizing the contrast between the prosperity and physical growth of the capital and of the provincial towns. In the majority of excavations outside London it has been shown that demolition took place over decades rather than years, and that significant areas remained vacant. In Oxford sales of stone from the Dominican Priory are first recorded in 1557, but excavations have shown that the ground remained as gardens until the nineteenth century (Lambrick and Woods 1976). In Newcastle, the Carmelite Friary was being dismantled throughout the sixteenth century, and although one range was converted for domestic use in the seventeenth century and plots were created for development in the eighteenth, it was not until the nineteenth century that all the land was in use, despite the position close to the centre of the town (Harbottle 1968). In Bristol and Southampton excavations have also shown that re-use was slow. The Friary site at Lewins Mead in Bristol was occupied for clay-pipe manufacture in the 1620s (*PMA* 1974: 123), and in Southampton the Franciscan Friary underwent slow demolition late in the sixteenth century to be built over by short-life housing (Platt and Coleman-Smith 1975: I.218). By contrast, topographical and archive research on the re-use of monastic land in Worcester reflects the known sixteenth-century prosperity of the town, the more central properties being either converted for domestic or educational uses or redeveloped in the sixteenth and early seventeenth centuries (P.M. Hughes 1980).

The effect of infilling on the framework of urban boundaries was less striking than the changes in use might suggest. It is true that ground hitherto available for public access was frequently encroached upon: lanes and alleys were blocked up; market places were diminished in size where they lay in a part of a town where the pressure on space was greatest, and public buildings had outlying units let or sold

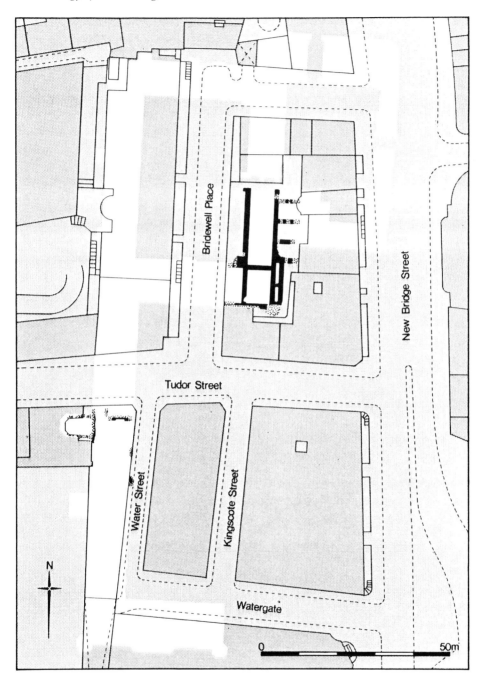

Fig. 2.2   London, Bridewell Palace: the features excavated in 1978 (bold) and the outline of the palace derived from Ogilby and Morgan's map of 1677, superimposed on the twentieth-century street plan. The palace layout is reflected by later property boundaries, particularly to the west of Water Street and Bridewell Place (Department of Urban Archaeology, Museum of London).

off. But this is in contrast with the permanence of boundaries between tenements: excavations in Norwich, Exeter and Canterbury have provided examples of such stability, and even in London the pre-and post-fire boundaries show a remarkable continuity, with houses built on the old plots and the walls of pre-fire house cellars being used as footings for their successors. Indeed many of these boundaries have survived the changes of the nineteenth and twentieth centuries.

Suburbs

A striking aspect of town growth was the development of suburbs. These are often indicated on Speed's early-seventeenth-century maps, compiled at a time when many towns were showing significant development of this kind. London was a prime example. The area between the Tower, the Thames and the river Lea had started to acquire urban characteristics in the Middle Ages, with villages such as Poplar and Stepney developing trades closely related to the needs of London, and with intensive farming and market gardening mingling with housing. In the sixteenth century this growth accelerated, and the same pattern can be seen around the city walls, differing in the north-west and the west to the extent that certain districts were developed for the houses of the well-to-do. Agas' view of the city shows buildings lining the roads outside the gates, in particular in those western areas around St Bartholomews, across the Fleet, around the Inns of Court and towards Westminster. London's defences, last refurbished in 1477, were obscured in the sixteenth century by buildings which encroached on the city ditch, creeping closer to the city wall which was eventually incorporated in buildings or demolished piecemeal.

Excavations off Aldgate have provided one of the rare impressions of the buildings and occupations of the London suburbs. Land which lay open until the early part of the seventeenth century was thereafter used for waste from a slaughterhouse and a glass factory, and finally for the construction of a terrace of slightly-built houses which lasted until the middle of the eighteenth century (fig. 2.3). Later, the site was saved from archaeologically destructive building by use as a railway yard. Occupants of the terrace made clay pipes, and there was also some indication of metal-using crafts. These were typical buildings and occupations of the areas behind the frontages of the roads radiating from the city: eighteenth-century maps show many such developments on comparable sites, and the Aldgate excavation must be regarded as one of the most valuable contributions to knowledge of this aspect of London's economy (Thompson *et al.* 1984). There have been further glimpses: marshes at Moorfields (*PMA* 1977: 90) were being reclaimed in the fifteenth and early sixteenth centuries prior to building; at Ratcliffe, close to the Thames, seventeenth-century building took place over the bed of a creek, traces being found beneath eighteenth-and nineteenth-century warehouse foundations (*PMA* 1976: 164–5). In Poplar High Street fragments of a timber-framed house have been examined, erected in the first half of the seventeenth century when the district was enjoying considerable prosperity (*PMA* 1973: 110). These indications parallel the map and archive material for East-end development, from which it is known that the east-London parishes at least quadrupled in population over the seventeenth century, bringing a new style of suburban building. Whereas the road layout of St Katherines parish, immediately

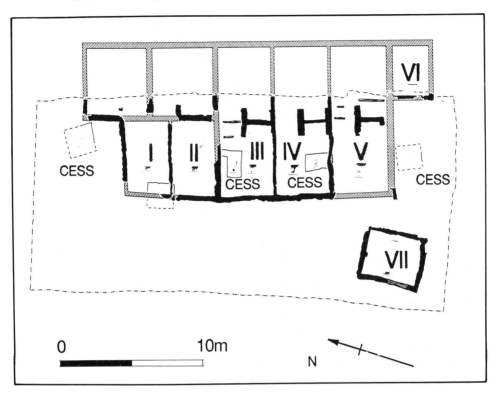

Fig. 2.3 Seven late-seventeenth-century houses south of Aldgate, with their cess-pits, excavated in 1974 (after Department of Urban Archaeology, Museum of London).

to the east of the Tower, is haphazard, further out towards Wapping marshes the development was more regular, with roads laid out between plots let on short leases specifically for building (Power 1972).

Suburban expansion has been demonstrated in several towns and has been shown to take many forms. In Oxford (Palmer 1980), excavations in the Hamel, to the west of the old town, indicate a continuity between medieval and post-medieval occupation of a suburb whose artisan housing was of late-medieval type, comparable with structures found in Norwich and Northampton. Similarly, in Worcester, excavations in the suburb of Sidbury have demonstrated continuity: bronze-workers' tenements were excavated, where buildings lasted from late in the fourteenth century to the middle of the seventeenth (Carver 1980). Often provincial suburban areas underwent rapid change as their relationship with old town centres developed. Many became integral parts of the parent town, vital to the housing of a population which had grown beyond the capacity of the medieval core: in the case of Exeter the suburban population had reached about one quarter of that of the town as early as the 1520s. Many suburbs were to be engulfed by commercial development: the modern centre of Leicester grew up on sixteenth/seventeenth-century suburbs rather than the medieval core; in Aberdeen the durable buildings of the nineteenth-century centre expanded over what had been new developments in the sixteenth and seventeenth centuries (D.H. Evans 1986). This is a pattern repeated in town after town, to the detriment of the archaeological record of the early poorly constructed phases, destroyed by the foundations or cellars of their successors.

The archaeology of urban trade and industry

THE PORTS

London

The written sources for the expansion of the trade of London in the sixteenth and seventeenth centuries are prodigious, and hardly require summary here. This growth is also reflected by the archaeology of London as a port. The London waterfront has been studied by means of a series of excavations along the north bank of the Thames, which show how the medieval shoreline had moved southwards by successive rebuildings and redevelopments (G. Milne 1979; G. and C. Milne 1979; G. Milne 1987). The excavations at Trig Lane, New Fresh Wharf and Seal House make this clear: the end of the advance of the waterfront by the building of the sixteenth/seventeenth-century river wall has been verified, shown also by observation at Bull Wharf (*PMA* 1980: 214) and excavations on Queen Victoria Street, where stairs from the medieval river wall to the foreshore were dismantled in the seventeenth century, and new quays built (*PMA* 1986: 342). The shoreline appears to have advanced as far as was possible, and its line is shown in Wyngaerde's mid-sixteenth-century view and in Hollar's map of 1647. At this time the pattern was one of consolidation and improvement of the permanent quays. Post-fire rebuilding further improved the port, not only by the replacement of warehouses but with facilities such as the new customs house, built by Wren in 1671 after the destruction of the medieval predecessor, which excavations confirm had itself been enlarged in 1544 (*PMA* 1974: 124–5). The really important developments at this time were the extension of the port by the building of new quays and docks outside the old city. In the seventeenth and eighteenth centuries the port expanded further down river, bringing about the housing developments of the eastern suburbs. This shoreline developed not just as an extension of the trading port but also for shipbuilding and maintenance, and attracted the trades on which such operations relied. It is, however, an area repeatedly redeveloped in subsequent centuries, and has limited archaeological potential. The south bank of the Thames was also built up, to form a river wall and a series of quays which provided a defence against flooding. Excavations at New Hibernia Wharf have revealed the eighteenth-century river wall and demonstrate the change of the area to commercial use (Milne 1981: 47).

The outports

The provincial ports in the sixteenth and seventeenth centuries demonstrate a paradox which the archaeologist may seek to resolve. On the one hand, a recurrent complaint from merchants and urban authorities in these ports, particularly in the sixteenth century, was that their overseas trade had dwindled as that of London had increased, the latter attracting merchants by its facilities and its proximity to the Continent. By contrast, we know that for many of these ports the period was one when the coasting trade developed at a remarkable rate, and it was to supply the needs of London and to redistribute imports that this took place.

To generalize about port-towns would be wrong, frequently though it has been done. In some cases the pull of London had little effect. Scotland's ports were largely protected from this tendency during the sixteenth century, and the French connection meant that Continental trades, which if at times hazardous, maintained mercantile traditions which some of the English ports lost. The English western ports, as in the case of Bristol, lost to London the export trade in cloth, but found new ventures in the Atlantic trade. By contrast, Newcastle took advantage of the rapid growth in the capital's needs for Tyne coal, while the ports further south – Lynn and later Hull – found rewards in the expansion of London's supply area for grain. An appreciation, therefore, of the archaeology of each port requires an understanding of movements in its staple trades and their effect on the ability of the inhabitants to improve standards of building and possessions.

Comprehensive examination of sixteenth-eighteenth-century deposits at ports has been rare, in face of the constraints typical of urban archaeology. A pioneer example of an urban research programme, where archaeological and documentary work proceeded together, was at Kings Lynn (Clarke and Carter 1977; Parker 1971). Medieval and later buildings were available for recording, and excavation was possible during redevelopment on sites which had been less damaged by nineteenth-century changes than in most port towns. Particularly striking was some of the sixteenth-century rebuilding on medieval plots, notably Clifton House, reconstructed above ground level at the end of the sixteenth century or early in the seventeenth. Warehouses in the curtilages of merchants' houses were extended towards the quayside, entire plots being covered in this way during the sixteenth century. This growth in the economy of Lynn was based on the food trade from the Wash hinterland, largely drawn by London.

Unfortunately, comparable programmes have not been possible elsewhere. At Ipswich, evidence is building up piecemeal for a growth in mercantile prosperity in the sixteenth and seventeenth centuries, and results from Hull reinforce our view of a port which if it had lost many traditional trades, prospered from coastal shipping and developed the export of lead at the end of the sixteenth century and through the seventeenth. Archaeological work on the Humber and Hull-river waterfronts, however, is hindered by the character of nineteenth-century development, which has left relatively small areas where post-medieval deposits are likely to be intact. Further from the water, the area of the sixteenth and seventeenth-century town, within the medieval walls, offers limited opportunity, partly due to postwar rebuilding, also because of the protection of areas of late-eighteenth-century development by building-listing and by conservation-area designation. Newcastle presents similar problems, for in contrast with the good preservation of sites along the town fortifications, elsewhere cellars, railway building and modern development have left limited scope for enquiry about how far improved building accompanied growth of the town's trade between 1550 and 1700.

The ports of the south and west have received considerable attention. The comprehensive publication of postwar excavations in Southampton has demonstrated that many of the medieval trading connections lasted into the sixteenth century, shown by the continuation of pottery imports. Thereafter, the view that the departure of the Italian merchants for London in the first half of the sixteenth century brought depression to the town is confirmed: several excavations in the town show the slow rate of redevelopment on ground where buildings had decayed in the fourteenth and fifteenth centuries. At Cuckoo Lane only slight structures were detected on such land, most of which remained empty or was used as gardens; at Winkle Street medieval buildings collapsed or were pulled down early in the sixteenth century and were not replaced until the middle of the seventeenth; and at Gloucester Square insubstantial houses built on the Friary site disappeared soon after 1600 (Platt and Coleman-Smith 1975: 247).

Further west, excavations at Poole have confirmed development of a small medieval port into a more important centre, particularly in the seventeenth and eighteenth centuries, when the town entered the Newfoundland trades. The medieval waterfront is marked by the present-day Strand Street (fig. 2.4), and the sixteenth/seventeenth-century development comprised the building of timber quays and jetties over the beach and mudflats. The major reclamation towards the present quay line came towards the end of the period (Milne 1981: 145–6). At Plymouth (*ibid.* 144) there has been sufficient excavation to show how the medieval layout of quays changed in the sixteenth century. This was caused by silting, and the quays were moved forward until the present line was reached in about 1700. In Bristol, numerous excavations have taken place in the area of the post-medieval town, many hindered by cellars and thus restricted to ground behind the sites of the buildings of the period. However, the sum of archaeological work confirms the seventeenth-century development of the town, when the Atlantic trade became a significant generator of wealth and employment. In the port area itself there has been good progress towards understanding how the docks grew, and excavations at the Narrow Quay have recorded a dry dock dated by pottery to the first quarter of the seventeenth century and built over by 1673, a facility designed for the construction of boats (Good 1987). This dock parallels the example found at the royal dockyard at Woolwich, but was less well built and is perhaps more typical of commercial practice.

It is at Exeter that one of the most comprehensive impressions of an out-port economy is emerging, of a town whose sources of wealth and employment were very wide. Exeter was the hub for a large agricultural area whose produce was increasingly sent to London; it was a distributor of imports whose range is indicated by port-books and as shown in chapter 10, there was a developing textile industry within and beyond the town. The archaeology of urban tenements reflects this spread: evidence of many trades has been found, and excavation and work on standing buildings have demonstrated the wealth of the post-medieval town. A key element in this prosperity was the development of the town docks, which began during the sixteenth century, and around which the south-western suburb expanded. The river Exe was canalized and a quay 70m long was opened in 1566, enabling boats of up to 16 tons to reach the town. A century later major improvements were made, and the sequence has been clarified by recent excavations and surveys (*PMA* 1986: 356–60). These have shown five phases of masonry in the structure of the dock, dating from the sixteenth century. The dock of 1676, of which much remains, had quays on three sides, with dock walls over 3m high by 1770, and usable by boats of up to 100 tons. There survives a remarkable 10-bay two-floor transit shed, the Quay House, which dates from the 1680s.

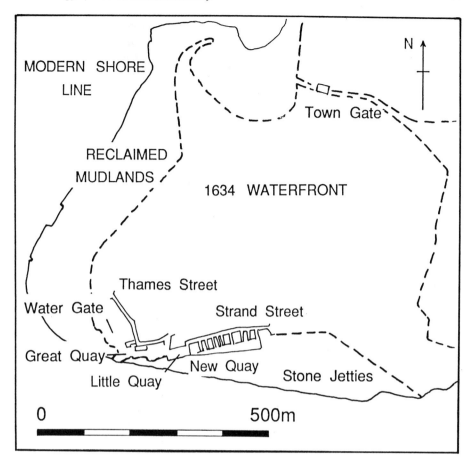

Fig. 2.4 Poole, Dorset: the waterfront of 1634 compared with the modern shore-line (Poole Museum Service).

The archaeology of the smaller harbours along the coasts of Britain has been little studied. An exception is the series of summaries of standing facilities compiled for the harbours of eastern Scotland and the Solway coast, which provide a framework for further investigation and include a particularly detailed description of the visible works at Dunbar (Graham 1966–7; 1968–9). Comparable scrutiny of early features at minor English and Welsh ports would be valuable, to establish the major periods of development.

THE HOME COUNTIES

A group of Home-Counties towns within the immediate trading area of the capital have a largely unappreciated archaeological potential, for gauging the effects of prosperity brought about by the relationship with London. Within a varying distance, governed by transport facilities, towns acted as collecting points for goods such as market-garden produce, grain, fruit, hops and malt, wood and wood products, as well as livestock brought long distances but fattened in the Home

Counties. In some cases their traditional markets performed the collecting function, but in others these were bypassed, and wholesalers and retailers from London, as well as merchants from these towns, controlled the trades. But even in these the indirect effects were considerable, the towns benefiting from the prosperity of local agriculture. What do we know of their growth and wealth? There are documentary outlines: towns in the Lea valley were increasingly the milling centres for London: the villages and small towns of Middlesex took part in the thriving market-garden trade; in Kent fruit and grain production for London brought urban prosperity, and the northern fringes of the Weald provided livestock and woodland products.

Outside the immediate suburbs, there were villages and small towns which were absorbed into the London conurbation only after the middle of the nineteenth century and where earlier buildings survive. Places such as Barnet, Edgware, Harrow-on-the-Hill, Kingston-upon-Thames and Uxbridge were on the main routes into London, and the development of inns reflects their position in the coaching trade: inns at Edgware and Uxbridge have been examined (*PMA* 1974: 129; 1984: 312), showing the enlargement and improvement which took place at the beginning of the eighteenth century. Recording of timber-framed buildings in Barnet and Harrow shows the growth of the housing stock in the middle of the seventeenth century (*PMA* 1975: 245) and at Kingston excavations have shown a merchant's house built about 1600, reflecting the growth and prosperity of the town and its market at this time (*PMA* 1972: 212).

Further out, few of the Home-Counties towns have yet received sufficient archaeological attention to show the effect of their trading location. In many cases the published record gives glimpses of individual buildings and sites rather than any impression of the developing post-medieval small town as a whole. One example where enough has been done for a picture to be emerging is Reigate, 20 miles south of London, in an area of mixed farming on the northern fringe of the Weald. A series of excavations has shown the importance of brewing and to a lesser extent oatmeal milling in the late seventeenth and early eighteenth centuries. Documentary evidence shows 20 mills, mostly manual and animal powered, supplying oatmeal for the navy via the London market (D.W. Williams 1984; *PMA* 1989, 46–7). Also on the fringe of the Weald is East Grinstead where, although no excavation has taken place, it can be seen from the examination of a mid-sixteenth-century survey in relation to surviving property boundaries, how consolidation was taking place within the medieval layout (P.W. Wood 1968). Another example, at a similar distance from London, is Waltham Abbey, a town at a focal point on the river Lea, in a district where both the through trade and milling were of importance. Houses excavated range from that of the London mercer mentioned earlier, to houses and cottages of varying standards which show the amount of construction which was taking place in the seventeenth century (*PMA* 1973: 104; 1974:122). A parallel can be seen at Faversham, which, although a port, shares the characteristics of inland neighbours thriving on similar trades. An important pioneering study of a town house showed construction covering an entire plot early in the seventeenth century, purchased by a shipmaster who owned a warehouse on the nearby quay (Laithwaite 1968). Inland, to the north-west of London, towns in the Chilterns show similar growth, piecemeal, over the two centuries from about 1550. Study of small houses in Chalfont St Peter (Stell 1969) illustrated the extent of building and rebuilding in towns of this kind. Such development continued in the eighteenth century, and in several cases markets survived, despite documentary signs that a good deal of trade bypassed them. Wide streets remained free of encroachment, as in Dorking and Maidstone, showing their continuing market function, and in several towns impressive new market halls were built in the streets traditionally used for open markets.

Forty and fifty miles from London, the capital's influence can still be seen, but archaeological evidence for urban prosperity has to be assessed more in the light of individual local economies. The important pioneer survey of the houses of Witham, Essex, showed phases of building which reflect a prosperity coming in part from the local textile industry but also from the position of the town on the road to London, which carried not only arable produce, but an important livestock trade (Wadhams 1972). Saffron Walden can be seen undergoing similar development (*PMA* 1985: 163), with old market areas in the town centre encroached upon and a new pig market being built over former gravel pits on the outskirts in the eighteenth century; here we have a town drawing on arable and pastoral country, yet its position on the western edge of the Essex textile area should not be forgotten.

PROVINCIAL MARKET TOWNS

Many towns continued as traditional market and crafts centres, others developed on the basis of a particular local product which could be gathered or processed for onward sale. They varied enormously in size, from provincial centres with an almost metropolitan function, through shire towns, to the market town whose significance was merely local. The pattern is a mixed one, of winners and losers in competition for dominance of local markets. In some cases physical growth during the period was slow: Gloucester was overshadowed by Bristol, Ripon by York and the growing West Riding towns; Canterbury suffered from its inability to supply London by sea. Archaeology in the widest sense draws attention to the slow physical expansion of such towns, and excavation has shown, in Canterbury for example, how long it took for medieval plots to be redeveloped. York is an example of a town acting as a regional capital, a centre of administration for much of the north, and commanding a market area which justified the existence of crafts so specialized and dealing in goods of such high value as to be second only to London in their range and wealth. Yet excavations have shown that the town was slow to regain its early-fourteenth-century density of occupation, and that although plots along the Ouse and the main roads were sought after, significant parts of the town, even within the walls, remained empty until the nineteenth century. The site of the church of St Helen-on-the-Walls, demolished as redundant in 1550, was left for garden use until the nineteenth century (Magilton 1980). Shrewsbury shows the same limitations. It too had a regional role, for the Welsh border, yet although tenements in the old town were built over in the sixteenth and seventeenth centuries, much of this expansion comprised piecemeal additions to medieval structures, and the development of suburbs on any scale had to wait until the eighteenth century when, for example, housing was developed in the area to the north of the Welsh Bridge. Towns on droving and coaching routes enjoyed a prosperity which can still be assessed from standing buildings. On the Great North Road, Stamford, Grantham, Newark and Bawtry are examples where the extent of seventeenth-century building can be seen, if often disguised by eighteenth-century facades which continue the story of pre-railway prosperity.

RIVERSIDE QUAYS AND WHARVES

The development of the coasting trade had a counterpart in the seventeenth-century improvement of river navigation, which connected numerous market towns with the coasting trades. This is a development which has received less than due attention, apart from Willan's pioneering documentary study (1936), in which he showed that seventeenth-century improvements to rivers enabled many farming districts to produce for distant markets. The excavation of the early-eighteenth-century timber quays at Reading is significant in this context, as part of the improvement of the river Kennet to Newbury (Fasham and Hawkes 1984). There are also examples of excavated riverside installations at Lincoln and York. In Lincoln, at Dickinsons Mill, a building of early-sixteenth-century date on timber piles appears to represent the contemporary wharf-side, built out into the river from the medieval line (*PMA* 1974: 124). In York, timber structures have been found along the Ouse river frontage, and the Skeldergate warehouses have been excavated, brick built in the sixteenth century over earlier stone foundations (*PMA* 1973: 106; 1986: 343). These are towns where most quays of the period before 1800 have suffered from redevelopment; more archaeologically promising are those smaller riverside towns which were bypassed by canals and later by railways. Bawtry is a good example, its overland trade from Derbyshire and Sheffield dwindling in the mid-eighteenth century, but where much of the street pattern and part of the wharf site survives from the time when the town was a busy port as well as a staging point on the Great North Road.

SPA TOWNS

Despite the growth of population in the sixteenth and seventeenth centuries, this was not an era of new-town foundation on the pattern of the twelfth or thirteenth centuries: most urban growth took the form of infilling and expansion of existing towns. There is however one particular group, the spa towns and certain seaside towns, which provides an exception. The seventeenth and eighteenth centuries saw the fashion of the visit to the spa grow to the point where certain villages became in effect new towns, and towards the end of the eighteenth century this enthusiasm spread, perhaps transferred, to seaside towns such as Scarborough or Brighton. The archaeology of the spa town is rarely a matter of excavation, rather one of recording standing buildings and disentangling the sequence of use. This is particularly appropriate to towns whose lives as spas were short and speculative, and whose buildings have passed into other uses.

There are several seventeenth-century examples of the recognition of the therapeutic value of springs. The earliest reference to the springs at Epsom, Surrey, comes in 1629, and they were mentioned by Sir Robert Boyle in 1684. Although there was some commercial exploitation in the early decades of the eighteenth century, as noted by Celia Fiennes and Defoe, it is uncertain exactly where the well of this period lay, or whether much building was associated with it (Lehmann 1973). At Tunbridge Wells the picture is clearer: the springs were an attraction by the end of the seventeenth century, for the Pantiles were paved about 1700, providing a focus for the eighteenth-century development of the town. At Scarborough the original Spa House dated from 1698, and in Scotland Moffat was attracting visitors from the 1660s. Bath was by far the most important eighteenth-century spa, with a scale of building development which eclipsed all the other spa towns and was to have an important influence on urban planning throughout the country. Others, such as Cheltenham, Buxton, Matlock and Leamington were to emulate Bath, but never with comparable success.

Urban housing

The key to the understanding of changes which took place in urban building is the need of contemporaries to make the best use of congested sites: to ensure sufficient floor space for shops and workshops and for domestic comfort within the constraints of frequently narrow or subdivided tenements.

Improvements in comfort and building standards in urban housing in the sixteenth and seventeenth centuries correspond in many respects with those seen in the countryside, and there are many parallels between the improved yeoman farmhouse and the town dwelling of the middling merchant. Typical late-medieval features, the open hall, the central fireplace, clay floors, all disappear, both in the course of modification of existing buildings and in new construction. There are numerous cases of excavated or recorded houses where such features were replaced during the sixteenth century. The examples recorded at Church Lane, Canterbury, are typical: houses with clay floors and central fireplaces, built in the later Middle Ages, gave way around the end of the sixteenth century to more modern, but still timber-framed houses with brick floors and back-to-back fireplaces (*PMA 1985*: 164–5). The classic survey of Exeter housing, carried out in the 1960s (Portman 1966), demonstrated the addition or original building of jettied upper floors, the use of brick chimney stacks, either on the side walls or axially placed. The gradual improvement of houses has been demonstrated by excavation: in Chelmsford, in Moulsham Street, an early-sixteenth-century timber-framed house had a brick chimney stack inserted towards 1600, extensions built early in the seventeenth century, followed in turn by insertion of a cellar, by rebuilding of the main structure on the same site before 1700 and by the underpinning of the timber frame in brick early in the eighteenth century. A more radical East Anglian example is published for Colchester, where Portreeve's House, a fifteenth-century hall house, had its open-hall range demolished about 1600 and a two-storey wing with chimneyed fireplace constructed in its place. As in the Essex and Suffolk countryside, houses in these and other East Anglian towns show how standards of structural carpentry improved and how brick was increasingly used for new floors and for chimney blocks built into new or existing ranges.

The use of more durable and fireproof materials is an important theme: brick was increasingly used for the main structure of the house, particularly in the seventeenth century in eastern England. A recently recorded example is the last house to survive in Hull of a type once common there, built in brick apart from timber framing on the frontage and part of one side (*PMA 1986*: 340). The survey of the buildings of Witham, Essex, shows the change to more durable materials over a whole town. Progress of this kind can also be demonstrated by excavation: at Alms Lane, Norwich, the late-medieval houses had cob walls, but were succeeded in the early part of the sixteenth century by structures with flint-rubble sills, later in the sixteenth century by flint-rubble walling to first-floor level, and in the seventeenth century by brick construction.

Even so, not all refurbished facades are what they seem: many hide timber framing, and facades in plasterwork, finished to resemble stone can be seen in many of the smaller towns of southern England, good examples being Petworth and New Alresford; even closer to London these features can still be seen: the examination of the White Hart at Edgware in the early 1970s showed just such a disguise on a sixteenth-century building. In the second half of the eighteenth century the fashion for brick-tiles (mathematical tiles) maintained this tradition: frontages of timber-framed buildings were commonly covered by tiles shaped to resemble brickwork in towns of south-east England, of which Lewes is a notable example.

The problem of the density of urban occupation has been approached from several directions. On the documentary side, probate inventories have been used as the basis of estimates of the numbers of floors and uses of rooms in houses. The most detailed published example of this approach is for Norwich, but a study which covers four towns (Birmingham, Coventry, Derby and Worcester) provides an important starting-point for the Midlands (Dyer 1981). The approach can provide a view of buildings which may either no longer exist or may have been subsequently modified. However, it is not always clear from inventories whether all the rooms of a house were occupied, or whether the appraisers of the property of a deceased person have only enumerated the rooms where goods lay, and whether items of small value have been listed without reference to their provenance. Further, a house as seen through an inventory may not be a structural entity, for the subdivision of properties was common and is hard to detect. These aspects particularly affect the housing of the elderly, who might occupy only a small proportion of their original accommodation, and who are inevitably prominent in this kind of record.

The Norwich study makes clear the tendency for the town's tenements and the housing stock within them to be increasingly intensively used during the period, a view supported by excavations. Some plots have been found to have been densely covered, either subdivided to accommodate extra houses or used for outbuildings connected with the textile and consumer trades. What the inventories tell us, and the archaeology of buildings no longer standing usually cannot, is the extent to which houses acquired more floors and how these floors were used. The excavations in Oak Street, Norwich have shown that although houses were subdivided to form smaller units, some late-medieval cottage properties in backyards went out of use. It has been assumed that to release this land for use as yards the houses on the street frontage were rebuilt with additional floors (fig. 2.5), an argument supported by inventories for houses elsewhere in the city, and paralleled by observation of buildings in York, whose side walls provided headroom sufficient for the roof-space to be used as attics (RCHM 1972b: lxiv).

In the towns of the Midlands, where the archaeological potential is often more limited than in Norwich, contrasts emerge from inventory studies, which reflect known differences in the growth of urban prosperity. For example, it is accepted that Coventry was particularly late in recovering from the early-sixteenth-century depression of its economy, and this is reflected in the relatively generous site areas of its housing. Worcester, by contrast, whose late-fifteenth-century revival is well known, had, by the end of the sixteenth century, many properties recorded as densely occupied, with cellars and attics in use.

These studies of the density of urban housing highlight the problem of assessing the accommodation standards of the artisan and poorer groups, amongst whom

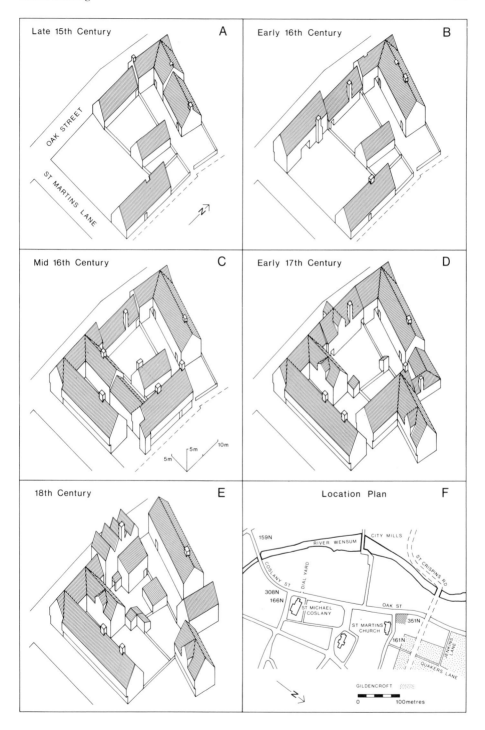

Fig. 2.5 Norwich. Estimated reconstructions of building phases of tenements on Oak Street and St Martins Lane (Centre of East Anglian Studies, University of East Anglia).

few left wills and, hence, probate inventories. It is important to bring together evidence for the smaller and less well-constructed houses, which inevitably had short lives. The survey of Exeter was significant in including examples of houses with single rooms on their two floors; the Norwich excavations have shown buildings similarly small, and excavations in St Peters Street, Northampton, and at the Hamel, Oxford, have added to a stock of information about buildings whose London counterparts are the houses excavated at Aldgate, and those planned by Ralph Treswell. His drawings show the frequency of houses comprising one room in plan, four or even five storeys high. After the 1666 fire a conventional terrace plan became common in London, covering a considerable range of sizes. At the larger end, the typical features were staircases placed between the front and rear rooms, opening from a corridor running the depth of the house. These were built in the city and in suburbs such as Islington, and in the seventeenth-century developments in Bloomsbury (Kelsall 1974). By contrast, smaller post-fire terraced survivors have been recorded; of two sets of particular interest in the City one was in Cock Lane, which had three storeys, attic and cellar, on a ground plan only 5m square, but with lean-to extensions. Another group, a row of six at Seal House, were correlated with a plan dating from 1686 (*PMA* 1976: 163–4). These dwellings were little different in size and quality from those excavated outside the City at Aldgate. At this level, the environmental evidence is also important, signposted by the illuminating comparison of animal bones from Aldgate with those excavated at Baynards Castle, showing the difference in the size and species of animal used for meat by the poorer and the richer citizens of London.

Examination on the ground shows how urban land values could affect the style as well as the size of houses. In certain towns it was normal practice to build the range of a house at right angles to a narrow street frontage, additional bays projecting further back along the tenement, with an internal side-passage extending for the full depth of the house. Space was saved by having chimneys along the side walls rather than along the axis of the building. This is a layout typical of but certainly not exclusive to West-Country towns. It was demonstrated by Pantin's pioneer work on housing in Oxford (1947), and more recently in studies of standing buildings in Exeter, Taunton (R. Taylor 1974) and Totnes. Excavations in Fore Street, Totnes, have complemented above-ground survey, providing an analysis of the development of a post-medieval tenement on which a detached house was put up early in the sixteenth century behind the medieval house on the street frontage. About 1600 the latter was demolished and replaced by a pair of houses packed into a space only 15m wide, yet also including a passage access to the house behind: the latter was extended further down the plot in the seventeenth century (*PMA* 1986: 337–9). This intensity of building in the back-lands of plots can be seen elsewhere in England. In the south-east there are many examples, a notable building recorded in High Street, Tonbridge having no less than seven bays running back at right angles to the road (*PMA* 1976: 162).

Where pressures on land had been less acute during the Middle Ages, houses had been built parallel with the street, but as plots became more scarce, projecting wings were frequently added at the rear, for domestic or trade use: a good example is a medieval house surveyed in the main street of Burford where a warehouse wing was added in the sixteenth or seventeenth centuries, later to be used as a domestic range (*PMA* 1972: 215–6). In less congested towns the Wealden House, with jettied end-bays, could still be used, similar in appearance to its better-known rural

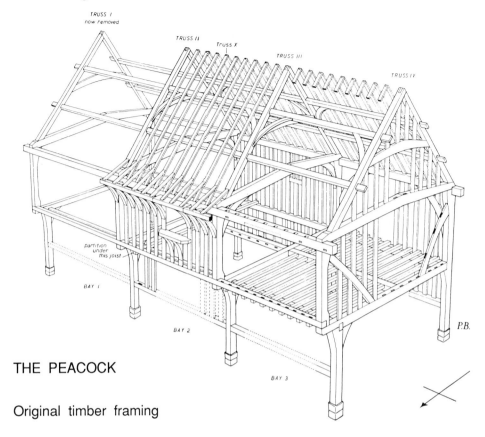

TRUSS I
now removed

TRUSS II
Truss X

TRUSS III

TRUSS IV

partition
under
this joist

BAY I

BAY 2

THE PEACOCK

BAY 3

Original timber framing

P.B.

Fig. 2.6 Chesterfield, Derbyshire: survey and reconstruction of the Peacock Inn (Philip Dixon).

counterparts. In many cases this type was modified to give continuous jettying, particularly if an open-hall central bay had a first floor inserted, the joists being carried forward to support the jettied frontage.

Work on timber-framed houses in towns has confirmed that apart from constraints imposed by siting, builders used methods little different from those found in rural areas. There are some excellent case studies of urban structures, one of the most interesting being 'Le Belle' Inn in Andover, carried out from the set of accounts for the rebuilding of 1534, rather than from the now-demolished fragments of the original building (Warmington 1976). There are numerous cases of timber-framed urban buildings being studied during demolition and adaptation. In southern England examples in small market towns are those in Alton, where sixteenth and seventeenth-century timber frames are recorded (*PMA* 1978: 112), Banbury, with several sixteenth and seventeenth-century examples (*PMA* 1974: 130) and in Burford (*PMA* 1972: 215–6). There are midland examples in Coventry and Worcester (Charles and Down 1970–2; Charles 1974), Loughborough (*PMA* 1976: 162) and Chesterfield, where the structure of the Peacock Inn (fig. 2.6) was thoroughly studied and the site excavated prior to refurbishment (Borne *et al.* 1978).

Towns and their utilities and facilities

Nineteenth-century commentators on urban living conditions stressed the inadequacy of inherited water supply, sewerage and burial facilities: these last are discussed in Chapter 3. Of water supply and sewerage, many industrial towns, which before the late-eighteenth century had been hardly more than villages, had little to inherit. In the seventeenth century there had been some attempts to provide water supply, particularly as streams were culverted and wells abandoned with the infilling of town plots. Several of these attempts have been recorded in the course of urban excavations, and in others the documentary and map evidence has been examined, providing an advance aid to the recognition of fragments of such schemes. In London an example is the Clerk's Well, a tank outside the Clerkenwell nunnery, which in the seventeenth and eighteenth centuries was successively enlarged as the local water table fell (*PMA* 1983: 191–2). In Hull excavations have shown evidence probably dating to the early years of the seventeenth century: the remains of an octagonal wooden pump were found, fed by a lead pipe: this appears to be the earliest evidence for a water supply in the town (*PMA* 1972: 213). Yet, overall, this is a neglected topic in the archaeology of the period, for of the more ambitious projects little has been found on the ground. At the start of the seventeenth century the New River scheme brought water to London from springs in Hertfordshire. A conduit which crossed the park at Theobalds fed a piped system in the city for which there appears as yet to be no archaeological evidence. A system of pipes served houses and colleges on the High Street in Oxford, fed via the Carfax conduit by a piped supply from Hinksey Hill: as yet this is known only from contemporary descriptions (Cole 1964–5), as are the systems used in eighteenth-century Newcastle and Gateshead, which have also been the subject of documentary rather than field investigation (Rennison 1977).

Early sewerage systems are rarely found, most refuse having been either buried, dumped in urban streams, or carried from towns and used by farmers and market gardeners outside. However, in London, a probable sixteenth-century sewer has been recorded running towards the Thames near Seal House, and the contents examined. In Canterbury, the cathedral sewer has been recorded, a timber-lined conduit dating in its excavated form to the seventeenth or eighteenth centuries (*PMA* 1978: 112), and in Edinburgh excavations within the Tron Kirk, built in 1637, have shown a sewer for the houses previously occupying the site and built within the preceding 50 years (Holmes 1975).

Excavations of institutional buildings such as almshouses, hospitals and schools have a valuable function, when contemporary descriptions are imprecise: their importance is to relate the sizes of buildings to the recorded numbers of inmates or pupils, as well as to the cost of upkeep or construction. In Bristol the medieval buildings of St Bartholomews Hospital became the first grammar school in the town in 1532, and although standing buildings date from the mid-eighteenth century, when Queen Elizabeth's Hospital School took over the site, the plan of the earlier structure has been recorded (*PMA* 1978: 111). An unusual case in a very small town is the school of c.1610 at Northop, Flint, which has been shown by excavation to have been built as a five-bay hall (*PMA* 1976: 171). Perhaps the most comprehensive results of excavation of a sixteenth-century school have come from the Whitefriars, Coventry, where the conversion of the monastic church to form the free grammar school took place in the middle of the sixteenth century: a large assemblage of closely dated finds illustrated the activities of the school and of the boys, their possessions lost beneath the pews giving a remarkable insight into recreational habits of the time (Woodfield 1981).

Chapter 3

Post-medieval church archaeology

The archaeology of churches has been a fast-growing specialism over the past 20 years: the detailed recording of standing structures, short of dismantling, coupled with excavation of available areas inside and outside the church, has provided evidence of an intensity which traditional architectural–historical studies have rarely approached. The number of churches for which this has been possible is small, and the results will have significance beyond the individual building or parish only when groups of churches can be examined, within a town or over a district.

This branch of archaeology has been preoccupied with questions about the origins and the medieval development of churches, and in particular how far there was a relationship with the growth of settlement and wealth in the twelfth and thirteenth centuries. After the epidemics of the fourteenth and early fifteenth centuries the picture becomes more complex and deserves further attention; in some places churches were reduced in size or pulled down, but in others they were maintained. After 1500, there are circumstantial reasons for expecting changes in the size of churches, with a near-doubling of population over the sixteenth century, but the response needs to be checked case by case. In many parishes, churches of a size sufficient for late-thirteenth-century numbers had survived intact, cherished by their communities over the later Middle Ages, and adequate for the needs of the sixteenth century. In parishes where churches had been reduced in size in the fifteenth century, when diminished congregations had failed to meet the costs of maintenance, we might expect aisles or chancels to be extended afresh in the sixteenth century; this is well illustrated at Hickleton, Yorkshire where, after the church was reduced in size in the fourteenth century, the tower and porch were built shortly before 1500, and new south and north aisles by 1600 (fig. 3.1). However, despite national growth in population, many villages which had declined in the fourteenth and fifteenth centuries failed to revive in the sixteenth: Morris (1983: 78) has noted churches abandoned in Norfolk, showing that 110 went out of use in the county in the sixteenth and seventeenth centuries, a delayed reflection of late-medieval population changes, as remnants of communities gave up trying to maintain the church fabric.

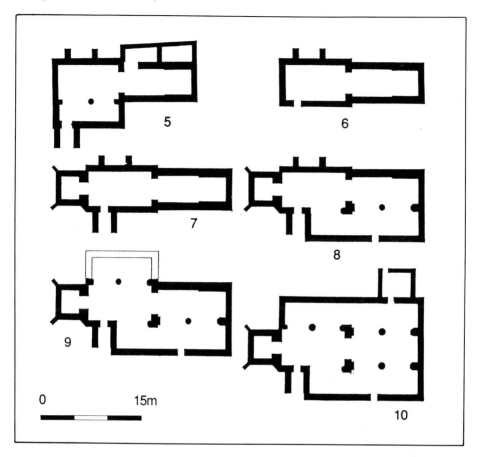

Fig. 3.1 Hickleton, Yorkshire: the later-medieval and post-medieval phases of the excavated church. (5) thirteenth century; (6) fourteenth century; (7) late-fifteenth century; (8) early-sixteenth century; (9) mid-sixteenth century; (10) nineteenth-century restoration and extension (1870–1880) (Sheffield City Museums).

Changes in the urban stock of churches

There was a great disparity in the fortunes of town churches during this period, with archaeological evidence indicating decay and development in adjacent parishes. In York, one third of the city parishes were united with their neighbours between 1547 and 1586: 14 of their churches were closed in 1549, including the excavated St Helen-on-the-Walls (Magilton 1980). Another, All Saints, Pease-holme, also recently excavated, went out of use in 1586 (Morris 1987: 179). In more fashionable quarters of the town, churches were well maintained, showing how charitable giving and guild activity could be concentrated and cumulative in certain urban parishes. Northampton is a case where a survey has been made of all the town churches, rather than relying on piecemeal or opportunistic work (RCHM 1985a: 64–5). This has been based on the examination of standing buildings and not upon excavation, and has also illustrated a variety of fortunes.

Northampton is a town where monastic churches were not converted for parochial use: the only survivor, as a building, was that of the hospital of St John, which was subdivided into almshouse accommodation. Of the four medieval parish churches, St Peters underwent a rebuilding in the seventeenth century which is architecturally important for its combination of medieval and contemporary styles, and All Saints was rebuilt in the manner of Wren after the town fire of 1675. In contrast, St Giles was rebuilt in medieval style after the collapse of the tower in 1613, but Holy Sepulchre, the circular twelfth-century church, is an example of post-medieval reduction in size: a chapel was demolished, and the chancel shortened. To take another case, Norwich gives the impression that most churches were rebuilt during the fifteenth and sixteenth centuries; there is however no accessible corpus of archaeological information for the churches of the city to show the balance between gains and losses; nor whether there is any contrast, in church upkeep or extension, between the years of depression in the traditional worsted trade and the late-sixteenth-century improvement in the town's fortunes after immigrants began to arrive from the Low Countries.

London churches show greater differences in fortune than might be expected at a time of spectacular growth in the population of the capital: the excavated church of St Nicholas in the Shambles was demolished between 1547 and 1552 (Thompson 1979), contrasting with other churches in the densely populated City or inner suburbs, such as St Andrew Undershaft, St Botolphs or St Giles Cripplegate which were rebuilt in the first half of the century. These cases again point to differences in the regard in which town parish churches could be held, and the extent to which they were the objects of charitable giving. London is a special case in two respects: the growth of its suburbs was remarkable, with new churches such as Inigo Jones' St Pauls, Covent Garden, accompanying development outside the walls. Secondly, the fire of 1666 gave a chance for rationalization, by renewal or abandonment among the 80 per cent of the medieval city churches which were destroyed. The extent of development in London since 1950 has given opportunities for archaeological examination of many of these, but a full assemblage of information about the post-medieval changes to London's stock of churches has yet to be published.

Ex-monastic churches provided extra accommodation for some of the reviving urban congregations, and those of the friars were frequently sited, as in the case of the Coventry Greyfriars, in the suburbs, where the need for new churches was greatest. It would be useful to assemble the archaeological information for monastic churches thus re-used, in a comprehensive and accessible form. A start was made by Dickinson (1968) for Augustinian houses, but there are many other cases where parochial worship had been catered for within monastic institutions, and whose churches were further adapted after the dissolution. A recently excavated example is St Botolphs Priory, Colchester, where the nave was blocked off for parish use (*PMA* 1987: 267).

A benefit of taking over monastic buildings for parochial use was the additional space for burial grounds. There is ample evidence for the shortage of graveyard space in post-medieval towns: in sixteenth-century London, city churches were increasingly confined by surrounding buildings, and in 1569 Sir Thomas Roe gave land for the New Church Yard, part of which has recently been excavated in advance of redevelopment at Broad Street (*PMA* 1986: 333–4). This has provided over 400 burials for examination, and as it is possible that many are those of inmates of the nearby Bethlehem Hospital, information on aspects of the health of the London poor may be forthcoming. There are examples of extreme congestion of vaults in urban churches, shown clearly in the examination of vaults below Christ Church, Spitalfields, London (Adams and Reeve 1987), and in St Augustine-the-Less in Bristol (fig. 3.2) At the latter, which has been completely excavated (*PMA* 1984: 307–9; 1985: 159) graves had been emptied in order to extend an aisle in the eighteenth century, and the church interior was completely filled with burial vaults in the eighteenth and nineteenth centuries.

Excavation of churches: post-medieval evidence

What have the results of excavations of churches to tell us about their history after 1500? Reports on which the latest survey (Morris 1983) is based form a small and disparate group, which rather support the impression that rebuilding and enlargement was less common after 1500 than before. Of 11 excavated churches which had survived to 1500, five went out of use by 1600. Of the other six, St Lawrence, Asheldham, Essex, underwent some contraction between 1400 and 1600, the two Lincoln churches, St Mark and St Paul, were little altered until their late-eighteenth-century rebuildings; St Bride, London was a Great Fire casualty rebuilt by Wren; St Mary, Rivenhall, Essex, was little altered in essentials between the fifteenth and the eighteenth centuries, apart from the construction of a new smaller tower c.1717. St Martin, Wharram Percy, Yorkshire, despite being left isolated by the abandonment of the village, survived in its late-medieval form, apart from a chancel shortened in the sixteenth century, until its dereliction in the present century and subsequent consolidation as a monument. This is an example of a church which remained viable on the tithe income from a widely scattered parochial population, for whom it was a convenient central point. The use of this church is confirmed by the maintenance of the adjacent post-medieval vicarage, recently excavated, and by the recasting of a bell in 1617, the casting pit and furnace base having been found in the nave of the church, and the bell itself in the church at Wharram-le-Street. This evidence for recasting bells inside a church is paralleled by excavation of two successive pits and a furnace base at Ilkley (*PMA* 1968: 175; 1983: 185–6). To this list of church excavations should be added St Peter, Barton-on-Humber, where a final phase of rebuilding, the extension of the chancel, may date from the end of the Middle Ages.

The excavations noted here have entailed the comprehensive recording of walls after the stripping of coverings, as well as major excavations within the churches. Where survey has necessarily been on a more limited scale it has been demonstrated that worthwhile information can still be recovered: work at St Michaels, Latchingdon, Essex, during conversion of a redundant church to domestic use, showed that post-medieval repairs could be identified and correlated with returns made during archdeacons' visitations, an important source of information on the condition of churches: in this case it was known that the church required repair late in the sixteenth century and that there was a wall collapse in 1618. The extent of this work was made clear by survey and excavation (Couchman 1979). Similarly, at Holton-le-Clay, Lincolnshire, it is known that the structure of the church was ruinous at the time of an archdeacon's visitation in 1519, and survey has shown that the chancel was rebuilt in the sixteenth century, although its condition was still poor in 1611 (Sills 1982).

Fig. 3.2 Bristol: St Augustine-the-Less. Eighteenth and nineteenth-century brick-lined burial vaults (Bristol City Museum).

Outstanding problems

The argument for relatively slight change to the fabric of church buildings after 1500 rests on the adequacy of many medieval structures for the needs of succeeding centuries, with expenditure more upon maintenance and detailed alteration than on radical renewal or enlargement. The difficulty about the latter point, as Butler (1983: 92–3) has argued, is that many changes made in the sixteenth-eighteenth centuries were lost during nineteenth-century restorations, which often left only slight indications of the prior appearance of a church interior. This may well apply to furnishings and memorials, but there are structural changes which did survive the Victorian era. Hewett (1971), in studying the carpentry of Essex churches, has found examples, such as the timber tower of St Andrews, Marks Tey, a well-built structure of the latter part of the sixteenth century, and the less well-conceived timber roof of St Martin, Chipping Ongar, built to replace medieval work in the middle of the seventeenth century.

A significant question must be how far existing churches could serve communities where there was exceptional growth in the sixteenth and seventeenth centuries, due to expansion of settlement into the uplands, to reclamation of marshes, the development of rural industries or the growth of suburbs. To assume a direct relationship is probably too simple: some existing medieval churches may always have been large for their surroundings, perhaps for reasons of landowner prestige or piety; ex-monastic buildings were in some cases available for parish use; and, of considerable significance, there was construction of Nonconformist chapels and meeting houses in fast-growing communities from late in the seventeenth century. Nevertheless, there is a case for research into the archaeology of parish churches in areas of colonization or developing industry, particularly in the sixteenth century, before the appearance of Nonconformist chapels, and before classical forms of church architecture make new places of worship more easily distinguishable. In short, in localities such as these, a critical eye should be cast on church buildings stylistically assumed to be late medieval in build, for possible sixteenth-century origins or reconstruction.

In such research it is important not only to gauge the size of parochial populations by the use of parish registers, but also to evaluate evidence from surveys of graveyards, recording evidence both from extensions and from memorials, where any quantity of early examples remain. Despite the interest in the recording of graveyards, supported by the CBA handbook on methods, there is a lack of published surveys, and a particular shortage of work on area-groups of cemeteries: Mytum's current work in south-west Wales (*PMA* 1986: 335–6), has demonstrated the potential of such an approach.

A number of churches in which post-medieval work is recognizable lie in parks revived or created in and after the sixteenth century. There are cases where the shrinkage or removal of villages left churches and country houses in close proximity, the church maintained virtually as an estate chapel as well as a landscape feature appropriate to the conventions of the time. In Staffordshire, Palliser (1976) has noted the extent of such rebuilding, and has contrasted the use of old and new styles of architecture in estate churches of the seventeenth century. Broughton, near Eccleshall, was a deserted medieval settlement where a church was built in the perpendicular style in the 1630s, at the same time as the Hall. Its relationship with the medieval church could well be investigated. By contrast,

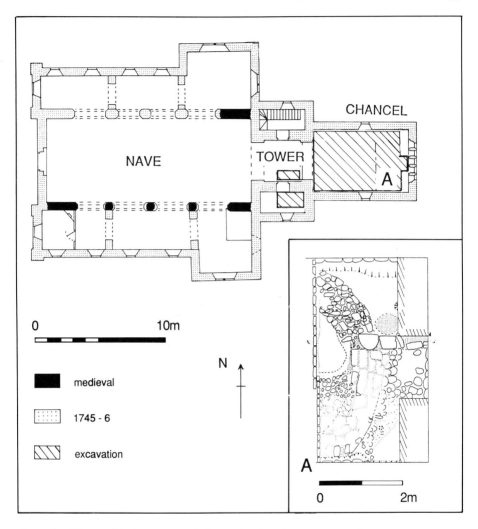

Fig. 3.3 Allerton Mauleverer, Yorkshire. The church reconstructed in 1745–6: excavations showing medieval features in the nave and (inset A) the chancel (L. A. S. Butler).

Ingestre was rebuilt in 1676 in classical style, probably by Wren. An excavation in which Butler (1978) has demonstrated the potential for study of such buildings has taken place at Allerton Mauleverer, Yorkshire. The medieval church, of which there survives a drawing made in 1734, was rebuilt in 1745 in classical style, using part of the fourteenth-century south wall and arcade, and reflecting the plan of the medieval building (fig. 3.3). Even where a church was less of an estate feature, and where the village community survived, patronage could still be strong. Taylor (1970) emphasized the extent of reconstruction in Dorset, citing as seventeenth-century examples Sir Thomas Freke's work at Iwerne Courtney and that of Robert Browne at Frampton.

The archaeological study of Nonconformist places of worship is a recent development. Meeting houses and chapels were built only from the second half of

Fig. 3.4 Goodshaw Chapel, Lancashire: the south front and west end of the Baptist chapel. The south front is an extension built about 1800 in water-shot stonework; the original roof-line (left) of c.1760, of the chapel and of an original minister's house to the west, is marked by rendering. To the right is a blocked door to the chapel gallery, at first reached from external stairs and after 1809 from the western bay, extended as a schoolhouse.

the seventeenth century, but the recording of their structures can show evidence of changes for which written records can be slight or non-existent. The CBA has produced a guide to recording, and a standard has been set by the RCHM inventory of Nonconformist places of worship in central England (1986b). Although not a comprehensive or detailed inventory, it is a good guide to the archive which is being assembled in the National Monuments Record. The worth of such an undertaking is confirmed by the information derived from the survey of the Baptist chapel at Goodshaw Chapel, Rawtenstall, Lancashire (fig. 3.4), essential detail for the elucidation of a monument which is now in guardianship (Brandon and Johnson 1986).

Chapter 4

Fortifications

In the archaeology of the fortifications of the sixteenth and seventeenth centuries can be seen the full effect of the development of artillery as a reliable weapon of war. Although in the fourteenth and fifteenth centuries there had been adaptations of medieval structures to accommodate and to counter artillery, it was only after 1500 that ordnance became a primary consideration. In the sixteenth and seventeenth centuries there were three particular occasions when new fortifications were built, the results differing in character and durability. The first was in the decade after 1538, when a massive programme of coastal defence was undertaken, with a deployment of resources on a scale not seen since the building of castles by Edward I in Wales. In contrast, during the Civil War many temporary fortifications were hurriedly built, which are of interest for their use of up-to-date ideas. Thirdly, existing fortifications were brought up to date during the reign of Charles II. This is not to say that construction ceased at other times: fortifications on the Scottish border and the sporadic preoccupation with the defences of Portsmouth and the Medway provide examples of changes in military thinking. At first sight, the ample documentary sources for the construction of fortifications by the Crown, with observation of surviving structures and earthworks, appears to leave little to be added from the results of excavation. In fact, the relation of ruined and surviving structures to excavated stratigraphy has given a new understanding of the written record.

Early artillery fortifications

The pre-Tudor development of artillery fortifications in Britain deserves a brief summary. The best-known examples of the incorporation of gun-ports in existing buildings are at Carisbrooke Castle, where they date from 1380, and in the town defences of Canterbury, Winchester and Southampton, where they were added at the end of the fourteenth century. God's House Tower, Southampton, is an early-fifteenth-century example of a structure where provision for artillery was made from the start, as was the case at Dartmouth in the castle built in 1481 and in the contemporary fortified house at Kirby Muxloe, Leicestershire (M.W. Thompson 1987: 91–6).

Between the accession of Henry VII and the middle of the 1530s there was sporadic construction of military works at key points which were to retain their defensive importance throughout the period. At Portsmouth, the seaward defences were improved by the construction of the Square Tower in 1494. This has recently been examined and the Tudor features were found to have survived later changes of use (*PMA* 1981: 226–7). This tower was intended to supplement the Round Tower, built between 1416 and 1422, and the later counterpart at Gosport, across the estuary. In 1512 the first tower was built at Camber, near Rye, and this has been shown by recent excavations to have been the basis for the Henrician artillery fort (Ames 1975). This tower was of a type also used at Dover and Hartlepool, and was similar in concept to those at Portsmouth. It was at Portsmouth that a major naval base was developed in the early years of the sixteenth century: a dry dock and two great storehouses were built, as part of the modernization of dockyard facilities at a time when the medieval provisioning quays, recorded in the Oyster Street excavations, were going out of use (Fox and Barton 1986). The new store at Portsmouth was built in 1514, and its plan has been recorded, measuring 70m × 9m. The second, within the curtain of Portchester Castle, was built at approximately the same time, and excavations have shown that its massive foundations supported a building of similar size to the Portsmouth store (Cunliffe 1971).

In the north, the incursion of the Scots in 1513 revealed the weakness of the border defences. The castles at Norham, Wark, Etal and Ford had been taken with apparent ease, and work was put in hand to improve the first two of these, on the banks of the Tweed. At Norham, the north curtain had been rebuilt with gun-ports in 1509, and the further strengthening of the defences is clearly visible. Kenyon (1977) has shown that the defences of Wark Castle were also improved in the years following the 1513 raid, with gun-ports incorporated in the reconstruction of the keep, which was able to withstand a brief siege in 1523. Throughout the sixteenth century the defences of Berwick-on-Tweed were a major preoccupation, and an early improvement was the incorporation of double-splayed gunports in the castle and the town defences at the beginning of the 1530s (MacIvor 1965).

The artillery forts of Henry VIII

By far the greatest expenditure on defensive works in the Tudor period was on the building of artillery forts and the enhancement of town defences undertaken towards the end of the reign of Henry VIII. Much is known about these works both from their physical survival and from the correspondence and accounts of the time. However, their significance goes beyond their form, important as this is in showing how ideas on fortification were changing. The need for a coastal defence policy resulted from the alliance between France, Spain and the Holy Roman Empire. Their unity, encouraged by the papacy, was seen as a means of reversing the changes in English Crown policy towards Rome and towards monasticism. The risk of an invasion was taken very seriously, but the interconnections between the events of the 1530s went further. It is doubtful whether the defence programme of the years after 1539 could have been carried out on such a scale without the resources derived from the disposal of monastic property.

The programme of coastal fortification began in 1539, with plans to construct a series of artillery forts and smaller blockhouses from the Thames estuary to Cornwall. Of particular interest is Camber, where excavations have demonstrated the evolution of the building (*MA* 1964: 259–60; Ames 1975; *PMA* 1983: 186; Colvin 1982: 415–447). In the first design, the tower built in 1512 was used as a basis, to be surrounded by a curtain wall of octagonal plan. A gatehouse, originally rectangular but soon given a circular end, was attached to the curtain, and four bastions were built into the curtain at alternate angles on the circumference. These were linked by walkways to the tower. It has been shown that the curtain wall was raised in height before later alterations took place. These elements of the design can still be seen, but excavations disclosed that each of the bastions originally had forward works of rectangular plan, with turrets at the outer corners. There was also a further octagonal-plan wall, outside the curtain, which has been suggested as designed to retain a shingle glacis. It is now clear how this design was modified, explaining the high total cost of the fort. In 1542–3 semi-circular bastions were built outside the originals, the early forward works being taken down and surviving only as footings beneath the new bastions. The curtain wall was increased in thickness, and the central tower had an extra floor added (fig. 4.1).

The importance of Camber, and the excavations carried out there, is that much of the fort survives, despite being abandoned in the seventeenth century, and that the Henrician works are not obscured by later adaptations. By contrast, at Sandgate, Kent, repairs and modifications, particularly in the eighteenth and nineteenth centuries, have greatly altered the appearance of the fort, which has also been undermined by erosion. Nevertheless, the form of the Tudor defences can be estimated, and it appears that the early design features at Camber were not repeated (E.C. Harris 1980). The fort was designed on the contemporary German principle of concentric circular masses: a central tower was surrounded by two concentric curtains, the inner incorporating three towers. The inner curtain curved between these towers, and the outer repeated these curves and was also concentric with the towers. There is a development of the idea of increasing the roofed area, as a platform for artillery, by covering some of the space between the tower and the inner curtain. The concept of ascending platforms was carried still further at St Mawes, where the circular central building was enclosed by three lower round towers, the roof-line of the seaward tower being lower than those of its neighbours, giving in all three levels on which guns could be mounted. The neighbouring fort, Pendennis, is of simpler design, comprising only a single tower. Although both these Cornish forts embody additions built later in the sixteenth century, their early form is clear. At other key points, around the Solent, on the Thames estuary and in the Downs of Kent, forts and blockhouses were built in groups: the Kent group, the forts at Deal, Sandown and Walmer, which covered the anchorage between the Kent coast and the Goodwin Sands, were built as a particularly close-knit system. Deal, whose plan is largely intact, was the centre of the scheme; Sandown, now almost entirely eroded by the sea, lay to the north, and Walmer, much changed by later rebuilding, to the south. These were linked by earthworks which incorporated four bulwarks, subsequently destroyed (Saunders 1969b: 215–9; Kenyon 1978).

In addition to the major forts, the building programme also included a series of smaller works. Excavations have been carried out on the sites of the blockhouses at Gravesend (D. Thompson and V. Smith 1977) and Milton (V.T.C. Smith 1980), on the south bank of the Thames estuary, both of which were built in 1539–40. The Milton structure had a short life, being demolished in 1558. It began as a simple D-shaped building, but about 1545 was enlarged with an angle-bastion facing inland. At Gravesend the original plan was similar, but was altered in 1588 and also at the time of the Dutch wars.

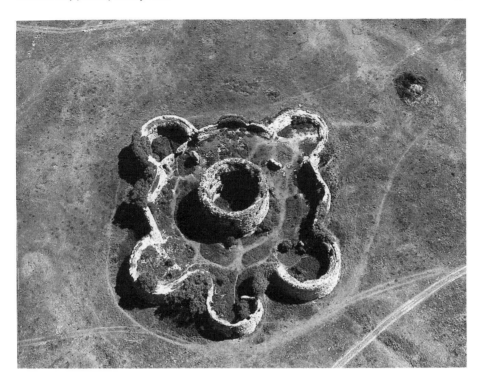

Fig. 4.1 Camber Castle, Sussex: the Henrician fort (Cambridge University Collection).

In the middle of the 1540s, the circular plan was largely abandoned in the last of this group of fortifications and in the refurbishing of the earlier structures of the series. It had for some time been obsolete on the Continent, and it has been suggested that the adherence to the circular plan in the designs of 1538–9 owed a good deal to the ideas of Henry VIII himself. By the mid-1540s the weakness of the circular fort against attackers in the immediate vicinity of the walls was appreciated, and the Italian development of the angle-bastion gave the close cover required. A variety of plans can be seen, starting with the documented rectangles of small forts on Southampton Water at St Andrews and Netley (Kenyon 1979). The fragment of St Andrews has been excavated (Aldsworth 1981), but too little survived to confirm the plan. A survey of 1623 suggests a rectangular tower with a round gun platform. The first certain example of an angle bastion was built at Sandown, Isle of Wight, in 1545, although this was not of the fully developed Italian plan, which is found at the Yarmouth blockhouse, also on the island, built in 1547, and is approximately contemporary with the first bastion to be added to the Portsmouth town defences (Saunders 1966: 141–2).

Outside this southern system there is a striking counterpart in the extension of the medieval defences of Hull, undertaken in 1542. It had been found during a visit by the king in 1539 that the town lacked any eastward defence, being open to attack from the river Hull. Originally a modest strengthening of existing defences was proposed, but the plans became more complex, and as well as protecting the mouth of the river with a chain, it was decided to construct a wall along the east bank, embodying three blockhouses, the central unit being named the 'castle'. Nothing can now be seen of these works, but their layout is known from contemporary maps (De Boer 1973) and from observation and excavations (*PMA* 1971: 198–201; 1977: 87; Colvin 1982: 472–7). The wall itself was of brick on a foundation of chalk blocks and survives in places to a height of 2.5m, buried in the nineteenth century. Of the blockhouses, the northern was surveyed before demolition in 1802, while the southern was largely demolished in 1864 but has been seen from observations in sewer trenches to be of identical form. Both had central square blocks with three semi-circular bastions, giving a trefoil plan: The 'castle' comprised a central rectangular structure larger than those of its neighbours, with two bastions of segmental plan. Construction appears to have been in full swing during 1542, supervised by John Rogers, who had been brought from France, and had much to do with the more ambitious design. His influence may be found in features such as the segmental bastions of the central blockhouse, a detail previously proposed at Guines.

The improvement of the defences of Hull was brought about as much by the threat from Scotland as by fear of direct attack from France. The attention given to protecting the Tyne can in part be similarly explained, although in 1545 there was thought to be some risk of a French landing in the north. Hence, the defences at Tynemouth were inspected in that year, and a scheme drawn up to strengthen them. Excavations at Tynemouth Castle and study of contemporary plans suggest that the works of 1545 were relatively modest: although a contemporary drawing shows two Italianate demi-bastions as part of a scheme linked to the castle, fieldwork has suggested that these were not built, and that work was concentrated on a lengthy rampart and wall enclosing part of the headland. It was perhaps realised that the castle lay too far along the coast for artillery mounted on the proposed bastions to be of much effect in preventing shipping from entering the Tyne (Jobey 1967; Colvin 1982: 682–8).

By the middle of the 1540s the main programme of building was complete and the forts were equipped. But despite the reduction in the French threat, certain longer-term preoccupations remained. There was concern about the security of the south-west, reflected in the improvement of the defences of the Isles of Scilly. On Tresco, 'King Charles Castle' was built between 1548 and 1554: excavations have shown that this was a blockhouse design similar to those of the Thames and resembling the small fortifications near Weymouth and on Brownsea Island, built at the beginning of the decade (Miles and Saunders 1970). Although this work contained no up-to-date features, there are signs that others on the islands did. A bastioned earthwork, thought to be contemporary, has been recorded nearby, and on St Mary's the fort known as Harry's Walls incorporated bastions in the Italian style, but was abandoned unfinished in 1551 (Colvin 1982: 588).

Other sixteenth-century works

The influence of Italian military engineering is first seen to any extent in the north. The English campaign into Scotland of 1547 led to the construction of earthwork fortifications at Broughty, Dunglass, Haddington and Lauder, and at all of these there were set out bastions designed on Italian principles, incorporating angular

Fig. 4.2 Eyemouth, Borders (Berwickshire): the 16th-century English and French fortifications. The English bastion is the prominent earthwork on the narrow neck of the peninsula, within the curve of the modern track; the ramparts and ditches are adjacent. The eroded French defences are to the right, towards the boundary of the caravan park.

(RCAHM Scotland)

plans giving better cover than those of the earlier English forts (Colvin 1982: 707–26). Of a more permanent character were the fortifications at Eyemouth (fig. 4.2), which have recently been the subject of survey and excavation (*PMA* 1983: 187; 1984: 310; 1986: 336; 1987: 271; 1988: 196). Works were begun by the English in 1547, confining a peninsula with a bastioned defence. After surrender to the Scots in 1551, an outer 'French' defence was built by 1557. The Scots were also actively using the new methods at Edinburgh, adding to existing defences in 1548–50, and at Stirling, where excavations have shown that the 'French Spur' is contemporary; this was an Italianate design of shallow bastion whose guns, at parapet level, covered the adjacent ditches (Ewart 1980).

In England, the most thorough applications of Italian principles were at Portsmouth and Berwick-on-Tweed. The defences of both towns were repeatedly revised, at each period of crisis (Saunders 1966: 142–3; Kenyon 1981; Colvin

1982: 490–527). The early-sixteenth-century additions to the defences at Portsmouth had been directed to securing the entrance to the inlet to the west of the town. This system was enhanced in 1544 by the construction of Southsea Castle, which extended the earlier series of towers towards the sea. It had a counterpart on the Gosport side of the water, at Hasleworth Fort. Southsea comprised a square central tower with gun-platforms on its north and west sides and triangular bastions to the east and west. An important modification revealed by excavations is the insertion of a flanker in the south platform, at its angle with the west bastion, giving cover along the bastion face. This corresponds with a plan of 1577 which shows pairs of flankers at each re-entrant angle.

The defence of the town itself had been put in hand in the 1520s, at a time when the dockyard was growing in importance and facilities. Earthwork defences were envisaged, and although a good deal of work was done, the complete circuit of the town was not completed until the early 1540s, when parts of the defence began to receive masonry additions. Later in the century there were two major phases of improvement. In the years 1560–3 the construction of angle-bastions went ahead, but much remained to be done at the time of the wars with Spain. The major remodelling took place in the 1580s, and the scheme then created survived until the rebuilding carried out under the direction of de Gomme in the reign of Charles II. The result of the remodelling of the 1580s is seen in a sketch of 1585–6, and is confirmed by an early-seventeenth-century description indicating that the town walls incorporated five bastions and a semi-bastion.

The Elizabethan works at Berwick-on-Tweed can be compared with those at Portsmouth: a sketch-view of 1570 shows three bastions around the northern perimeter with two half-bastions against the Tweed. They embodied a smaller perimeter than the medieval defence, about one third of the former area being excluded, together with the site of the castle. They also ignored the bastioned citadel, begun in 1551 on the east side of the town, traces of whose earthworks are still visible between the Windmill Bastion and the King's Mount. In contrast with Portsmouth, where little can be seen of the Elizabethan works, those at Berwick-on-Tweed are spectacular and explicit, and although subject to later modification, give an excellent impression of the achievements of the Tudor engineers (MacIvor 1965).

Along the rest of the English coast, only a small number of fortifications were improved during the wars with Spain. Overall, it seems that the Henrician designs were accepted as adequate, or at least that the cost of rebuilding was not worth while. There is no doubt that the condition of many of the forts was poor, and their equipment neglected. This indeed had been a consistent complaint, exemplified by the survey of the defences of the Isle of Wight in 1559 which sets out dilapidations and shortages (Kenyon 1979). Significant Elizabethan improvements took place at the Thames blockhouses, notably Gravesend, as well as at Pendennis and at Carisbrooke. Both of these were surrounded by bastioned defences, which are visible today. At Carisbrooke, there were two programmes: in 1585–6, two square towers along the south side of the bailey curtain were converted into angle-bastions, and an outwork was built near the gate. In 1597 a new bastioned trace was built to surround the castle, and new gun emplacements were constructed (Saunders 1966: 143). Excavations at Carisbrooke have added detailed information about the post-medieval works at the castle. A rather different case is Upnor, on the Medway. This fort had not been part of the Henrician system, for the first phase dates from the years 1559–67 (Saunders 1969c: 276–8). As originally built, an angle-bastion was placed on the Medway foreshore, backed by a rectangular blockhouse and flanked by towers. The fort was strengthened in 1599: although details were changed late in the seventeenth century on conversion of the fort into a store depot, examination of the fabric has shown that the appearance was not radically altered.

There are a number of small contemporary works about which less is known, but which call for further research. Earthwork defences set up in Norfolk in 1588 have been investigated, and the 'sconce' at Wootton Drift near Kings Lynn has been surveyed (*PMA* 1968: 176–7). The East Mount at Great Yarmouth, probably added to the town walls in 1588 has recently been surveyed during redevelopment, and the containing walls have been found to survive (*PMA* 1987: 269). Surveys on Lundy Island (*PMA* 1968: 175–6) suggest that there may have been some improvement of the fortifications at this time, prior to the better-known seventeenth-century developments.

As a counterpart to defensive works, the provisioning of the navy after the middle of the century has been illustrated by excavations on the Thames. At Woolwich, there have been major excavations on the site of the royal dockyard, which dates from 1512 and underwent repeated expansion between the 1540s and the 1580s and in the seventeenth century (Courtney 1974, 1975). Little evidence of the sixteenth-century slipways could be recovered, but the excavations provided considerable information about the seventeenth and eighteenth-century yard. In the middle of the sixteenth century the navy developed the former buildings of the Cistercian abbey of St Mary Graces, close to the Tower of London, and recent excavations (fig. 4.3) have shown how this victualling depot was used for the making of barrels and as a slaughterhouse and bakery (*PMA* 1987: 268).

The Irish-Sea coastlines contain a number of interesting post-medieval defensive works, notably those of the Isle of Man and the north Wales coast. The Manx fortifications erected by the third Earl of Derby between 1539 and 1551 parallel in style those of southern England, being built as defences against the Scots under the supervision of military architects. The Round Battery on the Horse Rock at Peel Castle is one of the best known of these works, and excavations have shown an adjacent contemporary earth bulwark, later occupied by the Half Moon Battery dated to 1595–6 (R.H. White 1986). The fort at St Michael's Isle, in the south of the Isle of Man, dates from 1539, and is circular in plan and well preserved. A series of look-out towers have been examined along the coast of north Wales: these are thought to have been built on the orders of the Sheriff of Flintshire, Caernarvon and Anglesey, Sir Thomas Mostyn, before 1618, as a system giving warning against pirates based in Ireland and the Isle of Man (Lloyd 1967).

Military works of the Civil War period

Forms of military architecture which evolved in Europe in the second half of the sixteenth century and during the Thirty Years War were employed during the English Civil War at times when defences had to be rapidly created. Most comprise earthworks, or additions or modifications to existing structures. Many have disapppeared due to erosion or subsequent development, but work in recent years has shown the typical forms that were used.

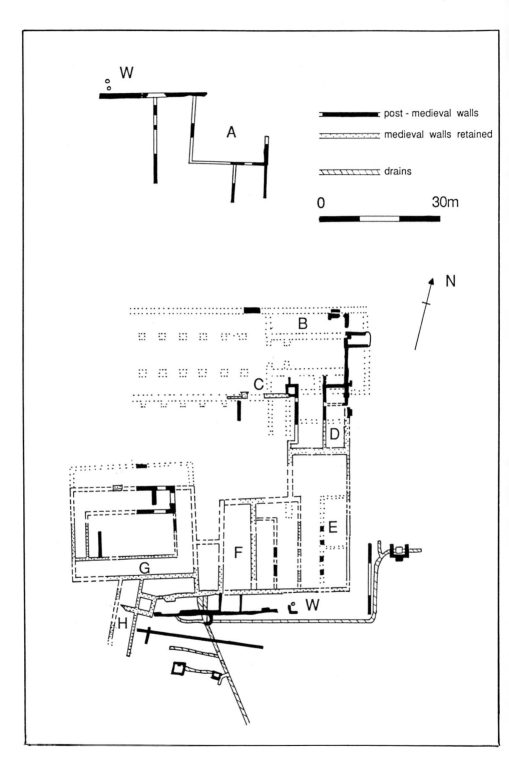

W

post - medieval walls

medieval walls retained

drains

0   30m

A

N

B

C

D

E

F

G

H

W

The defence of towns against siege did in certain cases employ existing medieval works, but frequently these had been made useless by suburban development, and it was necessary to place new lines further from town centres. The extent of the defences planned for London and Oxford underlines their importance. Stukeley's plan of the London defences shows a circuit of bank and ditch 11 miles long, with forts and batteries at intervals. No traces are visible, but approximate locations can be suggested for most of the defences, and the earthworks of the fort on the south side of Tavistock Square have been plotted from nineteenth-century maps (Sturdy 1975). How far Stukeley's drawing shows what was achieved rather than proposed is yet to be established. Similar difficulties apply to the royalist works around Oxford. These began with a short line of defences to the east of the town, from the Cherwell to the Isis, which were destroyed by the parliamentarians during 1642. The second phase comprised a northern line, beyond the town, stretching from St Giles to Holywell. As this was said to be equipped with ordnance in the summer of 1643, it seems likely that construction did take place. There are said to have been further works on the meadows to the south of the town, but the form of these is uncertain and any traces have disappeared. There was a proposal to add to the northern defences in 1645, but it is not certain if any work took place (Kemp 1977). An attempt has been made to plot the defence lines at Kings Lynn (*PMA 1968*: 177): the course of the earthworks and the position of bastions are approximately known, and a cannon has been recovered from the site of the bastion at Guanock.

The best guide to the form of earthworks used in these campaigns comes from Newark, (fig. 4.4) where there are notable survivals (RCHM 1964). The defence of the town was partly by lines of earthworks, for to the east there were no natural features which could be employed. A bank and ditch had to be created beyond the town's medieval wall due to suburban development; again, most traces have disappeared, apart from a short stretch of bank which has been traced in the north-east sector. The western approaches to the town were less vulnerable, for the two channels of the Trent gave a double defence. A line was created at the westerly arm, and batteries were set up at crossing points, most substantial of which were the Kings Sconce to the north-east of the town and the Queens Sconce to the south-west, of which the latter survives. Each had four bastions of typical seventeenth-century plan and an enclosing ditch. There were also smaller earthworks on the island between the channels of the river, the best preserved being a sconce close to the bridge at Muskham. In south Wales a similar style of earthwork plan can be seen at Caerphilly, adjacent to the castle (J.M. Lewis 1966). A flat-topped redoubt is visible, but only two of its bastions survive. It is assumed that there were originally four, which would give a plan resembling the Queen's Sconce at Newark.

In addition to defences, there also survive earthworks created by besiegers. At Newark traces of these are visible beyond the Trent, the work of the Scots army.

Fig. 4.3 London: the Cistercian abbey of St Mary Graces, part of the church site and the southern range converted to a navy victualling yard after 1565 and used as such until 1748. The range was a tobacco warehouse until demolition in 1808. (A) slaughterhouses; (B) 'long storehouse'; (C) salthouse and cutting house; (D) coopers' workhouse; (E) barrel store; (F) bakehouse; (G) former cloisters, used as stores; (H) salthouse; (W) wells (Department of Greater London Archaeology, Museum of London).

Fig. 4.4 Newark, Nottinghamshire: the Civil-War defences. (1) The Queen's Sconce, from the south-east. (2) Parliamentary redoubt at Hawton, adapted from a medieval moat (Cambridge University Collection).

Outside Kings Lynn an unfinished siegework made by the Earl of Manchester when besieging the royalist garrison has been recorded at Gaywood. At Raglan there is an interesting juxtaposition of earthworks of besiegers and besieged (Kenyon 1982): these were created during the siege of 1646 and there are traces of the royalist outworks and the parliamentary besiegers' positions. Comparable with the latter is the small semi-circular earthwork outside the defences at Basing House, Hampshire, probably dating from the siege of the royalist garrison in 1646 (Pike and Combley 1964).

Some town defences dating from the Middle Ages were restored during the Civil War. This has been recorded at Bristol (*PMA* 1970: 174), and was particularly frequent where castles could be refortified to contribute to urban defence. At Newcastle-upon-Tyne a bastion was added to the castle (Ellison and Harbottle 1983), and among others where extra works were added were Banbury, Oxford and Wallingford (Rodwell 1976; Hassall 1976; *PMA* 1973: 100). Particular details of adaptation for siege have been recorded during excavations at Pontefract Castle, where listening shafts were found, constructed as a defence against mining by besiegers (*PMA* 1983: 187).

A significant effect of the Civil War was the extent to which defences, particularly of castles, were slighted to render them unusable. This has been amply illustrated by Thompson (1987: 138–157, Appendix 3) who has listed parliamentary demolitions, proposed and implemented, of the years between 1642 and 1660. This shows that there are many towns, castles and large houses where significant deposits, closely dated to these two decades, may be expected. This has been effectively demonstrated at Pontefract and, nearby, at Sandal Castle, which was largely destroyed after its capture in 1646, medieval features having already been demolished by the besieged royalists to assist their use of artillery (Mayes and Butler 1983: 6–7).

The Dutch wars and after

Many military buildings of the late-seventeenth and eighteenth centuries survive, subsequently modified to a greater or lesser degree, and it is not proposed to provide an account of examples such as can be seen in Chatham or Portsmouth dockyards, or of the adaptations of Henrician forts, or castles such as Dover. There is however a period late in the seventeenth century when works were undertaken upon which field survey and excavation have proved to be of value. During and after the Dutch wars, principally as a result of the Dutch attack on the Medway in 1667, the defences of the Thames estuary and of Portsmouth were improved. The important figure was Sir Bernard de Gomme, under whose direction fortification took place. It was his work which was examined in excavations at Tilbury (Wilkinson 1983): the blockhouse built in the reign of Henry VIII (and demolished in the nineteenth century) had been surrounded in the 1670s and 1680s by a fort whose outline is typical of Continental practices of the age of Vauban. Although the complete design was not laid out, a bastion on the bank of the Thames being omitted, the excavation showed the extent of the landward features. These included a redan outside the main ditch, incorporating a triangular redoubt whose brick footings were recorded, and a covered way which allowed access from the fort to the redan. De Gomme was also responsible for the development of the defences of Portsmouth (Saunders 1966: 144–5) which involved the modernization of the sixteenth-century bastions, improvements to Southsea Castle, new batteries, and two new forts at the harbour entrance. The Medway examples of his work, the forts at Cockham Wood and Gillingham, have received brief notice (Saunders 1969a: 203), but nothing is visible on the ground and no excavations have taken place.

Chapter 5

The archaeology of shipwrecks

In bibliographical terms, the study of wrecks and their contents has been apt to stand somewhat apart from the main stream of archaeological publication. Further, the majority of ships and riverboats recorded over the last 20 years await detailed publication, and much information comes from summaries in *Post-Medieval Britain* and from progress reports published in the *International Journal of Nautical Archaeology*. This is, nevertheless, an important topic: the precision of dating of many wrecks can give to groups of artefacts a significance comparable with the rare instances of close association with known events, such as fires, on land. Secondly, structural remains of shipping should tell us about tradition and innovation in shipbuilding, and of the length of vessel life which shipowners could expect. Beyond, there is the wider question of how far the contents of a particular ship confirm or question assumptions about matters such as trade or armaments derived from documentary sources.

Underwater archaeology is hindered by the unsatisfactory state of British law regarding the protection of offshore wrecks: until 1973 there was no protection, a situation improved by the Protection of Wrecks Act of that year. This allows the Department of Transport to designate historic wrecks, which may only be explored under licence and are marked on Admiralty charts. This power has been sparingly used, and at the time of writing only 28 wrecks have been designated. Further, designation has been prompted by initiatives from exploring groups rather than resulting from a survey of academic priorities. A particularly unsatisfactory aspect of the current law is its relationship to traditional regulations for the disposal of material from wrecks: finds from underwater excavations must be delivered to the Receiver of Wreck, who is entitled to dispose of them, the proceeds going to the Crown, with some reward to the finder. The resulting dispersal of artefacts has serious consequences for the archaeology of any period due to the closed nature of groups from wreck contexts.

Numerous sea wrecks of the period 1500 to 1800 have been recorded, but the degree of preservation and the usefulness of artefacts and structural remains vary enormously. The pre-Armada period has provided relatively few examples, but three cases are of major importance. The wreck of a merchant ship currently under investigation in Studland Bay, Dorset (*PMA* 1985: 163; 1988: 197), is considered to date from the beginning of the sixteenth century, indicated by pottery which includes Spanish fine wares, notably lustrewares and Isabela polychromes, as well as Spanish coarse wares and a jug from Saintonge in western France. Approximately contemporary is the wreck of an armed merchantman investigated in the Cattewater, off Plymouth (Redknap 1984). The dating relies on early-sixteenth-century pottery, on three iron guns of composite construction which were being superseded by cast-iron pieces during the first half of the sixteenth century, and by structural features paralleled in the Bremen cog of c.1380, in the *Mary Rose*, and in the sixteenth-century Basque whaler at Red Bay, Labrador. The wreck of the *Mary Rose*, the warship which sank off Spithead in 1545, hardly requires detailed description here. Post-excavation work and publication of the structure of the ship, and its contents, will be a lengthy operation, but interim observations (Rule 1982) have shown the outstanding importance of the material, significant beyond the context of maritime archaeology, for the close dating of a wide range of artefacts.

Armada wrecks are known from the western coasts of Britain, although those on which most work has been done and publication begun are situated off the coasts of Ireland and Fair Isle, strictly outside the scope of this book. The two Irish wrecks, the *Trinidad Valencera* off Donegal (Martin 1979), and the *Santa Maria de la Rosa* in Blasket Sound, Co. Kerry (*PMA* 1969: 194; 1970: 175), as well as the *Gran Grifon* off Fair Isle (Martin 1972: 59–71; *PMA* 1978: 111) were wrecked in storms on exposed coasts; very little of the vessel structures have been found, and the contents are dispersed. In the main, the artefacts have comprised munitions, with little in the way of groups of domestic material or personal possessions. An interesting exception is the pewterware from the *Santa Maria de la Rosa*, which bears the initials of the commander of the infantry on board.

During the seventeenth and eighteenth centuries numerous ships of the Dutch East India Company fleet were lost off the coasts of Britain. These offer some potential for assisting the dating of Dutch ceramics, important for sites on land. However, the majority of these wrecks also took place in circumstances and places which made dispersal likely. An early case was the *Campen*, wrecked on the Needles in 1627 (Larn 1985). Material from the wreck has been affected by scouring and by early attempts at salvage, and the site is contaminated by artefacts from other wrecks.

Elsewhere the problems are similar: the *Kennermerland* [1664] (Price and Muckelroy 1979), *Der Liefde* [1711] (Bax and Martin 1974: 81–90; *PMA* 1975: 242), the *Curacao* [1729] (Stenuit 1977), the Dutch frigate *Wendela* [1737] (*PMA* 1973: 103), all off Shetland, the *Adelaar* [1728] (*PMA* 1973: 103; 1975: 242–3), off Barra, Hebrides, and the *Hollandia* [1743] (Cowan and Marsden 1972: 209–10), off the Scillies, have suffered dispersal of their cargoes, and there is thus a bias towards heavy material. Most were armed ships, and guns have been attractive to salvors. Ships outward bound from the Netherlands often carried bullion for trading, and hence have also attracted salvage attempts. Some occurred soon after ships were lost, as at the site of the *Liefde* wreck in 1712; but both there and in modern examples of coin searches, as in the case of the *Hollandia*, there has been dispersal of other artefacts, of less intrinsic value but of archaeological importance. Nevertheless, some significant material has been recovered. In several cases lead pigs have been found. Those from the *Kennermerland* have received particular study (Price *et al.* 1980): the shapes, weights and marks of the 119 ingots recovered have been recorded, and the sizes and weights suggest an origin in the northern Pennines. The ingots from the *Adelaar* are suggested as made in Derbyshire; those from the *Campen* have marks which have not yet been fitted to a known producer or area. The exceptional case among the East Indiamen is the *Amsterdam*, whose

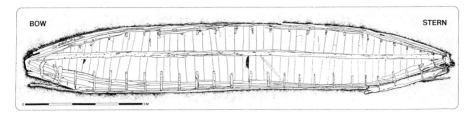

Fig. 5.1 Newbridge-on-Usk, Gwent: plan of post-medieval riverboat whose timbers are under conservation for reassembly and display at Newport Museum (Glamorgan-Gwent Archaeological Trust; Newport Museum).

wreck on the foreshore at Hastings survives in the sand to at least 7m above keel level (Marsden 1974). Despite the damage caused by non-archaeological exploration, this wreck has great potential, and has undergone initial excavation of which the outline results have been published. Questions of salvage and the destination of the hull and contents remain to be settled.

Much of the underwater archaeology of the last 20 years has been concerned with the identification of wrecks rather than detailed analysis of ships' contents or structures which, in the majority of cases, would present such physical problems as to render the expenditure and danger of questionable value for the archaeological return. In cases of outstanding preservation such as the *Mary Rose* or the *Amsterdam* an argument for research can be made, although instances such as the *Campen* and the Studland Bay wreck have also shown what can be achieved in apparently unfavourable conditions.

In addition to wrecks of sea-going ships, a small number of riverboats and inshore craft have been found. Their design is of interest, for this was a period of growing activity in the coasting and estuary trades and, in the seventeenth century and beyond, in the improvement of river navigation. So far, the indications are that traditional methods of construction persisted, although the sample is as yet far too small for any real conclusions to be drawn. The three best-preserved examples so far published are boats found in the Thames off Blackfriars, London, on the foreshore at West Mersea, Essex, and at Newbridge-on-Usk (fig. 5.1). The Blackfriars vessel (Marsden 1971) was a clinker-built flat-bottomed barge about 14m in length which had been carrying a cargo of bricks, and appears to have sunk in the second half of the seventeenth century, dated by clay pipes and pottery. The details of build showed the vessel as essentially of a medieval tradition of construction, and emphasize the need for further examples, to establish how eighteenth-and nineteenth-century designs evolved. The West Mersea boat (Dean 1985) belongs to this important period, probably being built after the middle of the eighteenth century. Like the Blackfriars barge, it was clinker built and flat bottomed, but is thought of as a poorly constructed example of a purely local tradition of double-ended inshore lighter or oyster-dredging boat. The recent find at Newbridge-on-Usk is a significant addition. Initial examination suggests that this vessel, 18m in length, was of post-medieval date, yet traditional in its details of construction (Marvell 1988); the full examination and conservation of a river-boat of this size will add significant data for this little-known class of vessels. Even less is known of the smaller inland river boats of the sixteenth and seventeenth centuries. The only fragment even provisionally published (*PMA* 1983: 203) is the bow end of a boat found during excavation of the mill channel at Caldecotte, Bucks. For this there is a carbon-14 date which suggests construction in the first half of the seventeenth century.

Chapter 6

Sources of power before the invention of the steam engine

Little apology need be made for treating this subject in some detail, and for paying particular attention to the archaeology of water power. Whereas certain subjects in this book possess adequate bibliographies, the material available in print for the archaeology of power sources is limited, despite the enthusiasm which the study of wind and water mills can attract.

Horse power

The use of horses to provide stationary rotative power in agriculture and industry was common before the middle of the nineteenth century. However, the physical evidence is largely limited to the farm wheel houses of the period 1770–1870 and to those mining areas where winding and ore crushing were carried out by horse power. Such survivals are certainly significant, but should be placed in a wider context, drawn from more fragmentary sources, both physical and documentary.

The earlier use of animal power has received scant treatment. Bloch assembled thirteenth-century documentary references from the Continent and from England (1967: 149, 156, 171); Faull and Moorhouse have found references to fourteenth and fifteenth-century horse-mills in Yorkshire (1981, 708), and a horse mill was recorded at Portsmouth dockyard early in the sixteenth century (Colvin 1982: 493). The best guide to the technology available in the sixteenth century is provided by Agricola (1556: 1950 edn,165–7, 193, 211) who described central-European mining practice: he showed two types of horse gin in which the central shaft was turned by cross-trees from which animal yokes were hung. In one, the shaft itself acted as a winding drum; in the other, it carried a bevel gear below ground level, meshing with a gear on a horizontal shaft which, in turn, drove a winding drum or a pump. The technology therefore existed, but the physical evidence for its use in Britain is sparse until the eighteenth century.

Winding gins of the type illustrated by Agricola were in regular use at mines in Britain by 1700. There are numerous eighteenth-century illustrations, and it appears that in the latter part of the eighteenth century, when atmospheric and expansion steam engines were adapted to provide rotative motion, they superseded a well-established technology of the use of animal power. The lack of information about earlier horse gins is due to their slight physical remains. The overhead frame of the typical mine gin was constructed of timber, and the earthworks, comprising a

Fig. 6.1 Horse ring for mine haulage, adjacent to lead-mine shaft. Longstone Moor, Derbyshire. See also fig. 8.1.

circular track and a mounting for the central post, are easily overlooked, particularly if the central bearing has been removed. In coalmining, these earthwork remains of haulage gins have been hard to find due to the successive reconstruction of surface works, and the search should be concentrated near the outcrops of the poorer seams which were not exploited on a large scale in the nineteenth century. Gin-rings survive in the Pennine leadfields, near shafts which have remained free from later disturbance. There are good examples in Derbyshire, on Bonsall and Longstone moors, with the characteristic flat circle adjacent to the capped shaft (fig. 6.1) There has been museum interest in the reconstruction of gins: a complete reproduction has been set up at Wollaton Park, Nottingham, and a frame and drum have been erected at Magpie Mine near Bakewell.

It is likely that gins were also in use for mine pumping, for this technology was certainly used for water supply (Brunner and Major 1972): some of the smaller installations were powered by tread-wheels, 'donkey wheels' with horizontal spindles, as in the example at Carisbrooke Castle, rebuilt in 1587 over a medieval well, and the pump at Godmersham, Kent, contemporary with a Jacobean house. However, a pump at Owslebury, Hampshire, built about 1650, has a surviving horse-walk of conventional pattern.

Early horse mills appear to have worked in the open rather than within permanent cover-structures, and in some parts of the country this practice continued into the period when wheelhouses were being built at model farmsteads. Bedfordshire was a county where the open gin was commonly seen in the nineteenth-century farmyard (T.P. Smith 1975). Staffordshire is also an area where the practice appears to have survived, and an undated example was noted during land reclamation in Bagots Park, on the edge of Needwood Forest. In the north and

Fig. 6.2   Farm horse-engine house near Rawcliffe, Humberside.

west, the open horse-walk was also used: Wiliam (1986: 174) has found that they were common in Wales, and Emery (1985) has recorded an example in the Isle of Man, citing parallels in the northern isles: an example on Islay using relatively modern gearing has been published by Hay and Stell (1986: 12).

Much more attention has been given to farm wheelhouses, structures which survive in remarkable numbers: at least 1300 have been recorded over England, Scotland and Wales (Hutton 1976). Their construction is known from the second half of the eighteenth century, and it has been argued (Hellen 1972) that they accompanied the spread from Scotland of the threshing machine patented by Meikle in the 1770s. Many wheelhouses were indeed built in southern Scotland about this time, and a large number have been recorded in the north-east of England (A. and J.K. Harrison 1973). In fact, as discussed in Chapter 1, this was just the period when radical improvement of farm buildings was in full swing, so it would not be surprising if open gins were incorporated in more weatherproof structures, and the connection with the introduction of the threshing machine, although likely to be influential, need not be the sole reason for construction: there were many examples in northern England and in Scotland of horse-powered turnip mills and chaff cutters, and horse mills were used in the Isle of Man for crushing gorse for animal feed. The horse-mill house was commonly built against the wall of a barn in which machinery was housed (fig. 6.2). Many had open sides, to assist the harnessing of horses to the driving arms of the gin, so few traces remain after demolition, particularly if the shaft-drive into the barn were overhead. When the pillars of an open-sided example have been robbed, only the track will remain, as was found when a ring was excavated at Baginton, Warwickshire (*PMA* 1983: 196).

Farm horse-engine houses contained alternative types of mechanism. One had a gear fixed at the top of the spindle, with the horizontal shaft taken through the roof-space and into the barn. The other system used a bevel beneath the central bearing, the horizontal shaft occupying a culvert beneath the horse track. This mechanism was increasingly constructed of cast iron, and small rural foundries were producing parts for such devices into the present century. It would, however, be unwise to dismiss the underground type as a nineteenth-century development, for it bears a strong resemblance to one of the sixteenth-century gins illustrated by Agricola.

The construction of gin-houses became less frequent after the middle of the nineteenth century, and it is probable that the introduction of the portable steam engine, forerunner of the traction engine, was responsible, enabling wheeled threshing machines to be taken to the stackyard or into the fields. But this is only one consideration, for wider economic factors were at work. It was soon after mid-century that depression in British agriculture put a stop to the new construction which had marked boom conditions in farming after 1750.

Horse-driven equipment which seems to have been common in Britain was the edge-runner mill, in which the horse was harnessed to a radial arm which served as a spindle for a circular crushing stone; the latter ran on an inner track concentric with the horse walk (Atkinson 1960–1). By the eighteenth century these mills were widespread, but it is difficult to be certain in what numbers they had previously been used: so far no earlier archaeological evidence has been forthcoming. Raistrick (1972: 111) has listed industries which employed edge-runner mills: in tanning, for the crushing of bark, in dyeing, for the crushing of woad, and as mortar mills. To these can be added pug mills in the pottery industry (Brears 1971: 88–94; Oswald 1975: 13), clay mills in brickworks (*PMA* 1982: 223–4), and mills for preparing gunpowder. These devices were particularly common in the crushing of ores, notably in areas where the water-powered stamp mill was not employed. The horse tracks for crushing-circles have been obscured when discarded waste, dumped around the circle, has been picked over for other minerals, commonly the case in the lead fields. However, significant examples do survive, as at Wanlockhead in Scotland (*PMA* 1977: 97) and in Derbyshire at the Odin mine, Castleton and at Eldon: at the last two mines there are edge-runner stones, the Odin example complete with an iron tyre as well as the cast-iron track on which it ran, but lacking the central bearing.

Edge-runner mills appear to have been less used in Britain for agricultural products than on the Continent, where there are districts where they are very common indeed. In the Mediterranean lands, notably Italy, they have been used for olive crushing, and many can be seen in the cider districts of Normandy. Indeed it is in the cider-making area of south-west England that the edge-runner was much used. Elsewhere, an example of a whin crusher, for animal feed, has been recorded at Lumphanan in Aberdeenshire, where a granite stone, wedged to a radial arm, ran in a stone-lined channel (Hay and Stell 1986: 18). This kind of provender mill was once common in north-east Scotland, and would be worth seeking elsewhere.

Windmills

The study of windmills has remained undeservedly apart from the mainstream of post-medieval archaeology: the ubiquity of the windmill, with its advantages in areas where water power was either scarce or in demand for other purposes, calls for a review not only of the excavated evidence, but of key steps in the evolution of the superstructures to which the below-ground features must be related.

The best-known earthwork feature is the mill mound, often medieval in origin, but frequently re-used. Often a nineteenth-century tower-mill shell can be found on such a mound, as recorded at Aberford, Yorkshire (Faull and Moorhouse 1981: 717) or by Addyman and Leigh (1973) in their study of the landscape of Chalton, Hampshire. The mill mound as a key element in the early landscape deserves further attention, as a feature in itself, and in relation to field names. Posnasky (1956) listed references to mill mounds in the early literature, and attention should be given to Mortimer's interest in these features during his nineteenth-century exploration of East Yorkshire earthworks. Nevertheless, this remains a topic which has had no more than sporadic treatment and requires a more comprehensive archaeological study.

The earliest windmill type, the post mill, had medieval origins, recently discussed by Kealey (1987) and Holt (1988). The operating principles can be illustrated from surviving examples: the machinery and stones are mounted in the elevated mill or buck, and the entire structure is set on a main post. The mill can be turned to face the wind, pivoting on a bearing on the top of the post. It is the post-mounting which leaves traces on and in the ground. It was normal practice to set the post on a pair of horizontal cross-trees, in rare cases, such as Moreton, Essex, over three members rather than two. The post was braced by quarter bars, set at 45 degrees between the post and the cross-trees. In some surviving examples, the main post is not only braced but also entirely supported by the securely tenoned quarter bars: in such cases the post may not actually rest on the centre of the cross-trees, for an air gap is left to prevent the cross-tree joint from rotting. Even the cross-tree half-joint may contain air spaces for the same reason. This preoccupation with prolonging the life of the timbers may be a post-medieval development, for early mills had their cross-trees buried.

Excavations of medieval and some post-medieval mill-sites have illustrated this practice of burying the cross-trees. One of the medieval examples was at Great Linford, Bucks, whose cross-trees were dated by carbon 14 to 1220 ±80. Quarter bars had been used, but it is not clear if they had taken the weight of the mill rather than acting only as braces (Zeepvat 1980). Of the dated post-medieval post-mill sites, a mound at Bridlington contained traces of cross-tree foundations for two successive mills (fig. 6.3). In the first, the centre post of the mill, originally a tree trunk 90cm in diameter, had been set in a hole dug 1m into the original ground surface; four beams radiated from the post in cruciform plan, but although no quarter bars are reported, the structure would make no sense without their use. The nearest documented parallel is at Patrington, Yorkshire, where the post was set in a pit, but apparently without cross-trees (Faull and Moorhouse 1981: 708). At the Bridlington mill the horizontal timbers had been set in trenches cut in an old surface, and were weighted with stones and chalk and covered with a clay mound. The associated pottery indicated a date of c.1500. This mill was succeeded by a second, whose cross trenches were cut into the mound, but whose timbers had not

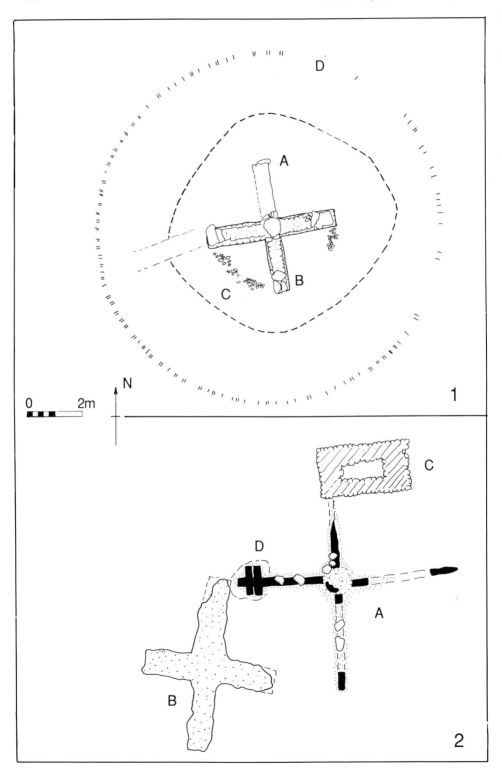

0 ▮▮▮▮ 2m   ↑N

1

2

Fig. 6.4 Shelford, Nottinghamshire: windmill mound with crop-mark of cross-trees (Cambridge University Collection).

survived. For this mill a late-sixteenth-century date was suggested (Earnshaw 1973). A possible cross-tree foundation was recorded in the top of a medieval motte at Lodsbridge, Sussex, with sixteenth and seventeenth-century pottery, but identification of the site as that of a mill remains tentative (Holden 1967). Robbed cross-tree foundations can leave a characteristic surface pattern: the undated mound at Shelford, Nottinghamshire (fig. 6.4), is a useful example, showing well from the air.

Trench mounting of mill foundation timbers appears to have died out in the sixteenth or seventeenth centuries, and none of the surviving post mills have this feature. In every case, the cross-trees are mounted clear of the ground on brick or stone walls. This practice had medieval origins, shown by the results of an excavation at Lamport, Northamptonshire (Posnasky 1956). The Lamport mill mound contained structures of two periods, one late medieval, the other probably

Fig. 6.3 Windmill mounds: (1) Lamport, Northamptonshire. Late-medieval mill rebuilt in the sixteenth century. (A) original wall to support cross-trees; (B) secondary wall to support later cross-trees; (C) scatter of nails from mill-sails; (D) ring of foot-holds (after Posnasky). (2) Bridlington, Yorkshire. Cross-tree trenches for mills. (A) first mill trenches containing traces of timbers (early sixteenth century); (B) second mill (late sixteenth century); (C) chalk ramp; (D) prehistoric pit beneath end of cross-tree (after Earnshaw).

Fig. 6.5 Bourn, Cambridgeshire: seventeenth-century post-mill cross-trees on brick plinths.

built late in the sixteenth century (fig. 6.3). In the first phase, brick walls had been built in cruciform plan, with limestone blocks mounted on the ends. The timbers would have been placed on the walls, much as in surviving mills, but the walls were hidden by a mound formed to the level of the bases of the timbers. The mill appears to have been removed from this base structure and a replacement was mounted on the walls, rebuilt but robbed of their best stonework. Clay pipes showed that this must have taken place at the end of the sixteenth century at the earliest. There are documentary references to the mill early in the seventeenth century, and other excavated clay pipes suggest that it remained in use until about 1700.

Several surviving post mills are mounted on cross-walls similar to those at Lamport, but it is usual for these to be exposed. Pitstone, Buckinghamshire, is thought to be the earliest example: it bears a carved date of 1627 on an internal timber, which is cautiously accepted as original. Another is Bourn Mill, Cambridgeshire, suggested as dating from 1636 (fig. 6.5). The design continues through to the early part of the nineteenth century, and the post mill at Great Chishill, Cambridgeshire, built in 1810, is set on cross-walls, although these appear to be partially buried by the mound (fig. 6.6).

The other characteristic sign that a mound has been used for a post mill is the track formed when turning the buck into the wind. This was done by using either a tail-pole or an access ladder, its end clear of the ground, as a lever. Some mills, Pitstone being a good example, had a wheel attached to the ladder, and there were late mills, of which Great Chishill is one, where a fan tail-drive propelled wheels on the circular track, providing automatic control, as for the cap of a smock or tower mill. Where wheels were used, the circular track was often paved, but this has been found to be the case elsewhere, for at Lamport the circular path used during the seventeenth-century phase was formed of stone slabs. The distribution of finds from deposits around the track at Lamport was significant: in the eastern sector there was a concentration of clay-pipe fragments, dropped from the ladder and thus corresponding with a mill facing the westerly wind, while to the west there

Fig. 6.6   Great Chishill, Cambridgeshire: post mill of c. 1800. Although the mill is archaic in having no roundhouse, it is unusual in having a fan of nineteenth-century pattern to turn the buck to the wind. The fan turns wheels on a track on the rim of the mill mound.

Fig. 6.7   Kibworth Harcourt, Leicestershire: post mill with brick roundhouse.

were scatters of nails which had fallen from the sails. At Great Linford there were also traces of the path marking the foot of the ladder or the end of a tail-pole, but at Bridlington this feature was not reported.

Few post mills now have exposed sub-frames. It became common in the eighteenth century to build roundhouses beneath the bodies of mills, protecting the cross-trees from the weather (fig. 6.7). Only occasionally can an archaic nineteenth-century example with exposed cross-trees be found, as at Great Chishill. Roundhouses were commonly of brick, although there are timber examples in Sussex. In addition to weather protection, they were useful as stores, and trapdoors in the floors of some mills allow sacks to be lowered into the roundhouse. It was also possible to use the roof to give additional support to the mill above, and in the Midlands mills turned on castors on a track built into the roof of the roundhouse, as well as on the central bearing.

The post mill was a fragile structure, which required constant attention. Timbers in the box-frame of the mill were frequently renewed and strengthened, in order to maintain the alignment of the shafts on which the sails and stones were set, ensuring that the gears between them ran true; yet the more weight that was added, the more vulnerable was the whole structure to storm damage. There have been many attempts to improve the stability of mills, and the smock and tower designs illustrate this theme. In passing, it should be noted that one modification, seen on the Continent, found little favour in Britain. This was to retain the form of the post mill, but to move the stones down into the roundhouse. To do this, a hollow post was used, through which a drive-shaft was taken. Only one British example has survived, at Wimbledon, dating from 1817. The portability of the post-mill should also be emphasized, for it is important to realize that not every abandoned mill mound will have seen the dereliction and collapse of a mill. Like any timber-framed building, it could be taken apart, moved and reassembled, or carried bodily. There are nineteenth-century descriptions of the transportation of post mills, in which the buck was supported, the foundations and post dismantled, and the structure carried away on a close-coupled set of wagons. Even the largest of post-mills were moved thus, a notable case being the survivor at Cross-in-Hand, Sussex, carried the 9km from Uckfield in 1855.

Smock and tower mills were designed to minimize the proportion of the mill which had to be turned to face the wind, their sails being mounted in rotating caps. Both types appear to have originated on the Continent in the Middle Ages, but it is not known when the first were built in this country. The smock mill has a distribution in the east of England, perhaps corresponding with its common use in the Low Countries. The first documented English reference is to a mill at Holbeach in 1588 (Reynolds 1970: 107), and possibly the earliest survivor is at Lacey Green, Buckinghamshire; if, as is claimed, this dates from 1650, it would be contemporary with Walter Blith's illustration in his *English Improver Improved* (1652). Tower mills were used in the Middle Ages, a well-known illustration appearing on a window in the church at Stoke-by-Clare, Suffolk. The survivor at Burton Dasset, Warwickshire (fig. 6.10), has been suggested as fitting a late-fifteenth-century documentary reference (Wailes 1954: 66; Turner and Watts 1977). Tower and smock mills lent themselves to the powering of drainage pumps, to which the post mill was unsuited. The earthworks are characteristic: the approach drains and reservoirs for dismantled mills along Bottisham Lode in Swaffham Fen have been described by Taylor (1973: 201; see also RCHM 1972a: lxiv), and similar formations can be seen along the Trent (fig. 1.5).

No excavations are known to have taken place on sites of tower or smock mills. At first sight there could be some difficulty in distinguishing between them, as well as from post-mill roundhouse foundations. However, smock mills were normally built of timber on a polyangular base, which varied in height from a few courses to a complete storey or more (fig. 6.8). This base was usually of brick, and the plan, six-, eight-or twelve-sided, distinguishes smock mill remains from those of other types. To a timber wall plate on the brickwork were fixed the cant-posts which formed the outer frame of the mill and supported the cap. The weakness in the design was the joint between cant-post and wall plate, which required strengthening with iron straps or the mounting of the posts in iron shoes. Not only might the outward thrust of the tapering upper structure break this joint, but it could also force the brickwork outwards. Even so, the smock mill was a more stable structure

Fig. 6.8   Swaffham Prior, Cambridgeshire: smock mill on brick base; the cap is missing.

than the post mill, and it continued to be built into the nineteenth century: its stones could be mounted at a low level, aiding not only stability but the handling of grain and flour. Height was needed only to ensure good exposure to the wind and to allow sails of large diameter. The surviving examples cover a range of types and sizes: the resited pump now at Wicken Fen, Cambridgeshire (fig. 6.9), is one of the smallest, while others range up to the massive mill at Cranbrook, Kent, built on a brick base that raises the smock to a height which dominates the town.

The tower mill is by far the most common type to survive. Whereas post and smock mills deteriorated or were dismantled, the tall conical tower mill (fig. 6.12) was a more durable structure, surviving as a shell or put to other uses. In western areas of Britain it has always been the dominant type, favoured for its strength in exposed places. It might be thought that there could be some confusion between the excavated traces of demolished tower mills and of post-mill roundhouses. In fact, inspection of most surviving structures shows that tower mills' walls are much

Fig. 6.9   Small smock mill for drainage; re-erected at Wicken Fen, Cambridgeshire.

more massive, having to support great weight. Indeed the ground loading of a large tower mill can be excessive for 13-in. brick foundations, and in many cases footings are thicker than this. In Scotland and very occasionally in England an answer to this problem was the massive vaulted substructure, providing both storage and strength (Douglas *et al.* 1984: 11–18).

There is also a smaller type of tower mill, of cylindrical form, which is less well known. It may well be that this is the original type, for the late-medieval stained-glass window in the church at Stoke-by-Clare shows a mill of this shape. In the south-west of England there are a number of such towers, typical of which are the pair of shells at Easton, on Portland (fig. 6.11), which could well fit a documented date of 1626. Landewednack mill, Cornwall, is another probable seventeenth-century example, and later mills of this type have been listed, the concentration in Somerset being particularly marked (Turner and Watts 1977). In Scotland there are also examples of compact stone tower mills: some are vaulted, as referred to earlier, others have simple bases. Among examples with cylindrical towers similar to those of south-west England are, over vaulted chambers, mills at Ballantrae, Ayrshire, and Hillhouse, Fife, and, un-vaulted, at Caverton, Roxburgh, and Stoneykirk, Wigtown.

Fig. 6.10 Burton Dassett, Warwickshire: tower mill suggested as late medieval.

Fig. 6.11 Easton, Dorset: tower mill of parallel-sided profile, one of two on Portland. Probably early seventeenth century.

Fig. 6.12 The fully developed tower mill: Wicklewood, Norfolk; early nineteenth century. See also fig. 1.5.

Water power

There can be few valleys in Britain where water power has not been used in the post-medieval centuries. The density of mill-sites in industrial upland areas is confirmed by eighteenth-century maps, whether of the Derbyshire lead field, the Yorkshire textile and metal-working districts (fig. 6.13), or the Cotswolds. Even in the lowlands the numbers of mills are remarkable, whether on the rivers of the

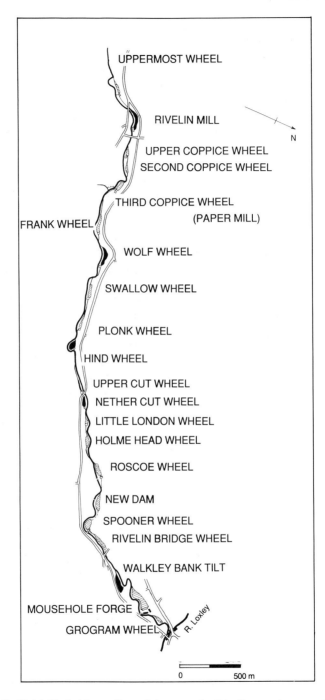

Fig. 6.13 Sheffield, Yorkshire: mills and dams on the Rivelin, a tributary of the Don. The marked sites all appear in a list of 1794, apart from New Dam.

Home Counties, formerly grinding corn or making paper for the London market, or on the rivers of Cheshire, where Burdett mapped 140 mills in 1777 (Norris 1965–6). Yet as little has been published on the archaeology of the harnessing of water power, the information deserves to be set out in some detail. This should be placed in topographical context, as seen from field surveys, for even these have received scant systematic publication apart from local studies such as those for Gloucestershire (Tann 1967) and Sheffield (Crossley *et al.* 1989). A recent book by Reynolds (1983) makes extensive use of continental and North American material, but only summarizes that from Britain.

Water power was used by a growing number of industries over the centuries after 1500, although in many cases adaptation of a process to the use of power had medieval origins, due in part to the increased cost of labour after the epidemics of the fourteenth century. In the iron industry the water-powered bloomery had evolved during the fourteenth and fifteenth centuries, and in non-ferrous smelting the tinners' blowing houses were using water-wheels before 1500. Over the sixteenth century, paper mills, lead-smelts, gunpowder mills and sawmills were among those adapted to water power, allowing industries to increase their volume of production without a proportionate rise in costs. In the seventeenth century the water-wheel was used for the drainage of land and of mines, and increasingly for agricultural purposes other than grain milling, including the production of oil, the crushing of apples for cider and of bark for tanning. Late in the eighteenth century the introduction of the threshing machine offered a further use for water power, and the farm water-wheel, long known in Scotland (J. Shaw 1984: 155–170) and the north-east of England, is being recognized elsewhere. There are particular problems in the juxtaposition of archival and archaeological evidence for water mills: notable is the frequency with which uses have changed, many mills having been operated for a series of different purposes. A further problem can arise in the case of double mills: for example, on the Don, Wadsley Bridge paper mill was in part used as a forge early in the eighteenth century, probably with a separate wheel, while in Gloucestershire, at Dursley, one wheel was used to drive both a corn mill and a fulling mill.

Archaeological attention to the use of water power has been uneven. Despite the numerical dominance of corn mills, these have received less consideration than mills used for other purposes. Only at Caldecotte, Buckinghamshire, has a substantial post-medieval corn-mill plan been recovered, in this case most of a seventeenth-century double mill in a lowland setting (Petchey and Giggins 1983). At others, Laleston in Glamorgan (*PMA* 1974: 132), Gomeldon, Wiltshire (Musty 1968), and Daws Mill, Dorset (Hodges 1974), the structures of the mills were not found, although at Laleston the wheel-pit was discovered in the present stream bed. In many such cases the frames of mills would be of timber, and the excavation of the medieval corn mill at Batsford, Sussex has shown a frame of a form and quality which could well have lent itself to dismantling and re-use elsewhere (Bedwin 1980a). There has, however, been much interest in standing corn mills, generally of eighteenth and nineteenth-century date, and several valuable area surveys have been published. Much has been learned of the archaeology of the early-post-medieval water mill from work on the metal industries: several blast-furnace sites have now been excavated, and the Wealden examples have provided a corpus of data on water-wheels. Information has also come from excavations and detailed field examination of water-powered tin mills, in Cornwall and Devon, and lead-smelts in Derbyshire, and from field surveys of blade mills in the Sheffield area. Uneven though this coverage of specialized mills may have been, the ways in which water power was harnessed, and hence the surface remains, do not vary greatly between uses.

THE TOPOGRAPHY OF THE SUPPLY OF WATER TO MILLS

Bypass systems

The simplest form of bypass was used on lowland rivers where an undershot wheel was operated in a short diversion from the main stream. Indeed occasionally the wheel was set in the stream itself, despite the risk of flood damage. Mills of this kind are mentioned by Fitzherbert in his *Book of Surveying* (1523; 1767 edn: 21, 91–5), and occasional examples, such as Inchbrook Mill at Nailsworth, Gloucestershire, have survived (Tann 1965, q.v. for other Gloucestershire mills referred to later). Even a short diversion could protect the wheel from storm water, for it was possible to insert a shuttle at the head of the channel, as may be seen at Malin Bridge corn mill, Sheffield, in a layout unusual in an upland context.

In a bypass system the key feature is the weir, set across a stream to divert water into a channel (leat or goit), and which in effect forms a dam over which surplus water can flow (fig. 6.14). Many weirs survive, often in positions used since the Middle Ages, and they are frequently the only means of locating mills shown on maps and surveys, particularly in urban areas where ponds and channels have been filled in and mill buildings demolished. Weirs, as Fitzherbert shows, were made of timber or stone or of both. The most durable are of pitched stonework set between kerbs of stone or timber, and often strengthened by division into bays. The upper kerb is generally of stone, often with iron fittings for washboards, planks set on edge to adjust the effective height of the weir. Washboard installations reached a high degree of sophistication in the eighteenth and nineteenth centuries, tilting to vary the depth of water, sometimes by means of winches on the bank, as was done at Thwaite Mills, Leeds (Faull and Moorhouse 1981: 715). Observation of deteriorating weirs has emphasized the maintenance costs which mill-owners faced. The force of floodwater and debris has torn away the stone kerbs, despite being held together with iron staples fixed into the masonry with lead. The risks were reduced by building a weir on a diagonal line across the river: an excellent example can be seen at Cheddleton flint mill in Staffordshire, and there are several on the Don, such as Sandbed Wheel and the great weir above Kelham Island. This layout also directed water towards the headrace, sited at the downstream end of the weir.

Many weirs and entrances to leats have disappeared from lowland rivers in the course of improvement of navigation and drainage, but their position can sometimes be inferred from old channels later used as drains. The risk of erosion made it necessary to strengthen the banks of races, and revetments have often survived: dry-stone walling can be seen in Derbyshire and Yorkshire examples, and the excavated corn-mill site at Caldecotte had a leat lined with brick and stone. In narrow valleys, headraces built along the contour gained considerable elevation and, to reduce seepage, channels had to be lined with puddled clay. Some long

Fig. 6.14   Weir at Shepherd Wheel, Sheffield.

headraces needed considerable ingenuity in surveying and construction; indeed on occasion they take lines so unexpected as to require equally imaginative fieldwork. An example is the leat built for Ashburnham furnace, Sussex, probably in the eighteenth century: a stream was intercepted in a neighbouring valley and the water carried around a series of spurs by dug channels and embanked or bridged aqueducts (Cleere and Crossley 1985: 231, q.v. for other Weald examples). A later and spectacular case is the feed to the Laxey wheel in the Isle of Man, where water collected in one valley is led to its neighbour.

The ponds in many bypass systems appear to have originated in a widening of the headrace. The method of construction can be seen from eroded sections: to prevent seepage to the river, a strong wall or embankment was built on the valley side of the pond. More material was dug from the hillside, increasing the space for impounding. It was vital that vegetation should not take possession, for root action broke up the puddled-clay bottom of the pond. Therefore sluices had to be provided, not only to control the level in the reservoir and to prevent flooding, but with deep shuttles to drain water to allow maintenance of the clay floor. Where ponds have been abandoned, the stonework of these sluices has often been robbed, and breaks in banks indicate where they were once sited. Where sluices survive, slots show how planks were used to regulate the water level, in combination with the weir washboards; plots of elevations of board heights survive, made by surveyors when neighbouring mill owners were in dispute about interference with each others' water.

In some narrow valleys, ponds were set in tandem. In the Cotswolds, successive ponds can be found at different levels in steep valleys, as at Days Mill, Nailsworth and Broadbridge Mill, Alderley. On occasion a cluster of ponds will be found overlapping on a stretch of hillside, feeding different mills. Ebley Mills in the Cotswolds were built thus, while on the Yorkshire Loxley the ponds for Green Wheel (cutlery) and Glass Tilt (forge) overlapped, constructed on steps on the hillside. A sophisticated variant of the bypass system was the provision of water for several mills from a single weir and race, particularly where common ownership made it possible for leasehold conditions to ensure co-operation in the use of what otherwise might be a disputed supply. What in the eastern United States would be called a 'power canal' can be seen in less developed form in the Cotswolds: Bliss Mills, in Gloucestershire comprise four mills taking water from a leat, while on the Don a leat at Wadsley originally built to supply a sixteenth-century blast furnace was in use in the second half of the eighteenth century for a paper mill, a corn mill and a forge.

Cross-valley dams

It was common practice in areas of low rainfall for water to be impounded by a dam stretching across the valley. In the north this arrangement was uncommon: of about 120 mill sites on the streams in the Sheffield district, only three had cross-valley dams, and the layout is also unusual in Derbyshire, where only two ore-hearth lead smelts appear to have been so supplied, out of about 40 where there are surviving traces. In the Lake District bypass dams are, again, virtually universal. In the Cotswolds the picture is mixed, for although bypass dams are in the majority, there are significant exceptions, such as Edgworth Mill on the Frome, Upper Steanbridge Mill on the Slad Brook, and Strange's Mill at Wootton-under-Edge. The extreme use of the cross-valley dam was in the iron-making region of the Weald, where the system was virtually universal in the relatively narrow valleys, across which short dams could be built.

Most ponds of this type were drained after mills went out of use, and the area originally flooded can only be traced from field boundaries. Where they have survived, it is generally because of the use of dams for roads, and many of the surviving ponds in the Weald have been protected in this way: St Leonards furnace and forge, west of Crawley, and Cowden furnace on the Kent-Sussex border are excellent examples. In the Weald the rate of disappearance of dams has been particularly high because so many were built for iron furnaces and forges; after the disappearance of the industry only a small proportion found other uses.

The disadvantage of the cross-valley dam was its need to withstand the flow of winter streams. To enable surplus water to pass, overflows and sluices had to be incorporated in dam structures, and it is at these points that failure has usually occurred. In addition, the flow of water through the pond set up patterns of silting and scouring; regular dredging was required to maintain capacity, a task made difficult by the problem of excluding water from the pond while work went on. It is instructive to examine ponds of this type where water is still impounded, and to note the deposit of silt and the growth of weed over a number of seasons: this can aid the interpretation of what can appear to be earthworks within former ponds, as well as leading to the appreciation of maintenance as an important cost of using water for power.

The methods of building earth dams have received scant archaeological attention in Britain, and there is little documentary material. For America Reynolds has demonstrated that a good deal of interest was being shown in construction methods in the first half of the nineteenth century when many small impounding schemes were being undertaken for the first time; hence published diagrams exist in some quantity. In Britain, by contrast, many dams dated from the Middle Ages, and in areas of later expansion of water power such as the Lake District or the Pennines, the peak of building had passed by the end of the eighteenth century, before illustrated publications on engineering topics became common. There have been few excavations where it has been possible to cut sections through dams, and still fewer where foundations could be recorded. A limited examination was possible at Panningridge furnace, Sussex (Crossley 1972), where it was found that logs had been laid on the surface of the marshy valley before the earth bank was begun. At Maynards Gate, another sixteenth-century Sussex furnace, a full section through the dam was possible, and it was shown that the old topsoil had been stripped and a bank of clay and sand laid without a foundation (Bedwin 1977–8). Field observation has supplemented the record in the Weald: for example, during pipe-laying operations at Sheffield Park it was found that the furnace dam had a stone-built core, probably dating from the sixteenth century. It became common in the Weald to raise dams, when silting had reduced storage capacity. To contain the extra material, stone or timber revetments were built, and these have been recorded at several sites: the stains of timbers could be seen in the sectioned dam at Maynards Gate, supporting deposits of furnace slag, and at Westfield Forge timber piles had been set on both sides of the dam.

RETURNING WATER TO THE RIVER

Tail races

An efficient outflow from a mill was of crucial importance to prevent a wheel being impeded by 'back-water'. For the archaeologist, the tail race is significant, often surviving as a drainage channel when little else remains of the mill. To prevent silting, not only a good outflow was necessary, but the banks of the race needed to be stable. At Caldecotte corn mill the excavations showed how vulnerable to erosion the tail-race banks had been, and at Chingley Forge (Crossley 1975b) the tail-race had been strengthened with large lumps of cinder, the slag 'bottoms' from the finery hearth.

Some mills had tail races of remarkable length, at first sight hard to explain.

Some examples in Sussex are hundreds of metres long, notable being Bibleham and Kitchenham forges. Surveys have shown that it was not unusual to gain extra head of water by setting wheels at a low level relative to the river adjacent to the mill. To ensure an adequate outflow, it was then necessary to dig a long channel, with a gradient rather less steep than that of the river itself. Styal Mill, Cheshire has a tail-race tunnel designed in this way, and there are some excellent examples on Yorkshire streams where river and tail-race can still be seen with water flowing towards the point where the levels are equal. An extreme case has been found on the Porter, where a snuff mill, developed in the eighteenth century on a former cutlery-wheel site, has a wheel-pit set so low that the tail race is culverted beneath the river, joining downstream where the levels are compatible.

THE WATER-WHEEL AND ITS HOUSING

It was noted earlier how ephemeral some mill structures have turned out to be, leaving key information to be derived from the deeper features associated with water-wheels. The wheel-pit is a focal point, frequently found by plotting back from the alignment of the tail-race. Once it has been located, traces of mill buildings are more easily identified.

It was common but not universal to place the water-wheel as near to the dam as possible. A mill building whose upstream wall forms part of the dam structure is a familiar sight, and this layout permits a short supply channel from the dam to the wheel, reducing risks of leakage, saving cost and easing the problem of controlling the flow of water and hence the speed of the wheel. There appear to have been different local traditions as to how water was brought to the wheel, and how it was controlled. The essential for overshot or pitch-back wheels was a trough laid in the top of the dam. At Chingley furnace, excavation showed a beam-slot which crossed the dam in the direction of the wheel-pit: this would carry a trough of the kind found at Pippingford furnace, reused in the floor of the tail-race (Crossley 1975c). The Pippingford trough had been hollowed from a length of oak trunk, 5.5m long. The Flemish landscape painters, notably Henri Bles at the beginning of the sixteenth century, portray simple open shoots of this kind, with the water regulated at the pond end. These contrast with the structures illustrated by Agricola, showing central-European practice, in which shuttles were set at the wheel end of the trough, in systems similar to those surviving in Britain today. The advantage of the latter is that the flow of water can be regulated from within the mill. It requires a heavily built pentrough, and some sixteenth-century English installations suggest that these were in use. For example, the timberwork at the back of the wheel-pit of the late-sixteenth-century phase at Chingley forge, although cut down for a later use of the site, was sufficient to have supported a pentrough, and was unnecessarily robust for a simple shoot. The details of such structures must remain speculative, for elevated timberwork of the sixteenth or seventeenth centuries has not survived, and no precise contemporary description of English practice has been found. Where an undershot wheel was used, the feed was through a culvert in the dam. The only excavated example published is at Ardingly forge, Sussex (fig. 10.2), dating from the end of the sixteenth century (Bedwin 1976).

Occasionally, the dam lay at some distance from the wheel, making it difficult to decide how the flow of water was controlled. A striking early example is at

Socknersh, Sussex, where a furnace, in operation from the 1520s, was 200m from the pond; there is no sign of any channel or culvert, which suggests the use of an elevated trough. Another example is at Rockley, Yorkshire, where a furnace was built about 1700, 100m from its dam: part of the linking channel ran in an open leat, part in a culvert under the ore and charcoal stacks. A spectacular survivor is the channel to the lead-smelt at Froggatt, Derbyshire, where water passes down the hillside from the pond to the wheel-pit in a trough over 30m long, formed of shaped stones laid end to end.

From these examples, a pattern has emerged of wheels set in pits at right angles to their dams, but layout became more adventurous in the seventeenth and eighteenth centuries, in ways which can cause difficulties of interpretation on the ground. The second furnace at Pippingford is a good example, where it has been deduced that the wheel was placed parallel with the dam rather than at right angles to it, occupying a position between the dam and the furnace. At the seventeenth-century furnace at Sharpley Pool, Worcestershire, the tail-water escaped through a channel set at right angles to the axis of the pit (Brown 1982); a similar arrangement has recently been found at the late-eighteenth-century blast furnace at Low Mill, Yorkshire. Complexities of this kind would raise problems at mills requiring large volumes of water for undershot or breast wheels, but where smaller amounts sufficed, for overshot wheels, such flexibility was attractive and increasingly adopted.

The installation of water wheels

Although the excavated fragments of water wheels have attracted a good deal of attention, the emplacements in which they ran can be impressive structures in their own right. Wheel-pits required skill in design and construction if the wheels which they contained were to be efficiently run, although the standard of some of the excavated examples suggests a measure of compromise, due perhaps to sites being let on leases so short that a tenant might economize on the quality of construction or maintenance.

Box-frame wheel-pit frames, designed to house overshot wheels, have been found at sixteenth-century ironworks, the earliest being at Panningridge furnace, built in 1542. There was a generally similar structure housing the wheel at Chingley furnace (fig. 6.15), dating from later in the century, the frame extended to form a culverted tail race beneath the casting floor. At Chingley the pit also differed by having a planked floor, creating a smoother outflow for the water. A double-chamber wheel-pit, designed for two wheels, was excavated in the sixteenth-century phase at Chingley forge. Although there is a tradition of double mills, with separate wheels and machinery, illustrated by the excavated corn mill at Caldecotte, at Chingley there were indications of heavy forge equipment only on one side of the pit, so the suggestion is that two wheels on a single shaft were used to drive the forge hammer.

A late example of a wooden wheel-pit structure was built in the last phase at Chingley forge, in use by the eighteenth century. It is important for two reasons: the first is the use of a timber floor curving upwards at the back of the pit, to provide a close fit with a breast-or pitch-back wheel. This is a technique usually found in stone pits in mid-to late eighteenth-century contexts, and the Chingley example

Fig. 6.15 Chingley furnace, Kent: excavated sixteenth-century timber wheel pit with fragment of wheel in situ.

raises the possibility that such features were in use before 1700. The other point of interest is that the pit frame and casing was built in the form of a trough mounted on cross-sleepers. It was found that the entire unit could be removed, leaving virtually no trace.

Stone-lined wheel-pits have also been found at furnaces and forges. In the north, the sixteenth/seventeenth-century bloomery at Rockley had three such pits, built into the dam face. The later blast furnace at Rockley, dating from about 1700, also had a stone pit, with a stone-flagged floor. In Kent, at Chingley forge, a pit dating from the early seventeenth century, between the two timber phases outlined earlier, was particularly well built in stone, suggesting a long lease which made more durable construction worth while. In addition to pits entirely built in timber or stone, hybrid examples have been found, with stone walls and timber floors. In one case, the first furnace at Pippingford, built about 1696, it was clear that a timber box-frame had originally been used, but that the side members had been removed from their mortices and stone side walls built overlapping the original timber base. It is possible that the latter relates to a forge known to have operated in the vicinity during the sixteenth century. At Maynards Gate furnace and Scarlets furnace (Crossley 1979), better-quality composite construction (fig. 6.16) showed provision for the replacement of floorboards.

Fig. 6.16 Scarlets furnace, Cowden, Kent: excavated seventeenth-century masonry wheel-pit with timber floor.

The archaeology of the post-medieval water-wheel

An important group of water-wheel fragments have been found during excavations in Britain over the last 20 years. All are from vertical wheels, and the evidence points to their having been overshot. They belong to a common tradition of mill-wrighting in which the favoured material was oak, little iron was used, and compass-arm rather than clasp-arm construction was employed. All but two come from south-east England: the exceptions are from a single Yorkshire forge (fig. 6.17). Many features of these wheels resemble those in Flemish landscape paintings of the sixteenth century, but the artists show that clasp-arm construction was also in use in the Low Countries.

The wheel shaft, as Fitzherbert wrote in 1523 (1767 edn: 93), was a costly item. It was normally shaped from a trunk of oak, and was supported on bearings at

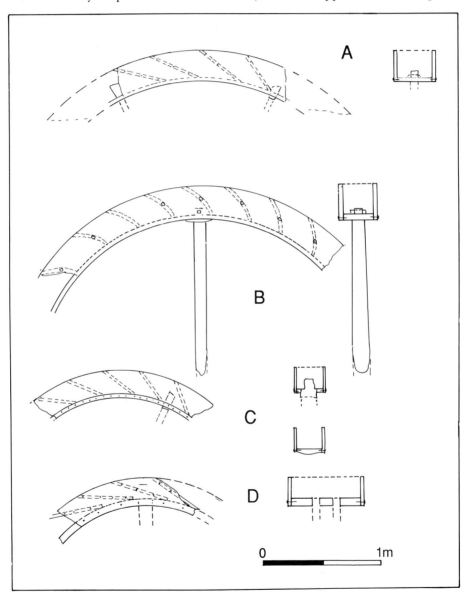

Fig. 6.17 Diagrams of excavated overshot wooden water wheels (A) Rockley Smithies, Yorkshire; early seventeenth century; (B) Chingley Furnace, Kent, sixteenth century (see fig. 6.15); (C) Batsford Furnace, Sussex, sixteenth century (after Bedwin 1980b); (D) Chingley Forge, Kent, seventeenth/eighteenth century.

either end. The only fragment of wheel-shaft so far excavated was found at Chingley furnace, a length from near the bellows end of the shaft, recognizable by the cam-mortices. Fitzherbert describes the way in which shafts were supported. He refers to bearing-journals as gudgeons, running in bearings of bell metal or stone. Gudgeons are illustrated in eighteenth-century sources, and their design is reviewed by Reynolds (1983: 159–60). Iron pins were used, driven into holes in the centres of the ends of the shaft, and prevented from turning by winged extensions fitting into mortices cut across the shaft end. Cutting the shaft in this way weakened the timber, so it was necessary to bind the end with iron hoops. Entries in the accounts for the sixteenth-century Sussex ironworks of the Sidneys confirm these methods, for there are several references to the replacement of gudgeons and hoops on wheel shafts. The importance of bearing maintenance was well understood, for Fitzherbert warns of the danger of overheating, even the burning of the shaft if bearings were allowed to run loose. He does not refer to the lubricants used, but Reynolds has shown that tallow was a favoured material, and that some millers maintained a feed of water on to the bearing, sufficient to cool the metal but not strong enough to wash the lubricant away. Bearings were mounted on blocks of wood or stone: at Chingley furnace there was a fine example of a timber bearing-block whose complex housing suggests the fitting of a cast-metal rather than a stone bearing.

There were two methods of fitting a wheel to the shaft. The clasp wheel, as illustrated by Agricola (1950 edn: 284), employed pairs of parallel spokes set at right angles, clasping the squared shaft, which was secured with wedges. This type of wheel was rare in Britain until the eighteenth century, and no excavated fragments have been found. It had the advantage of not requiring mortices to be cut in the wheel shaft, but needed constant attention to the securing wedges. The compass wheel used spokes radiating from the hub, and it is this type for which we now have a body of archaeological evidence. A varying number of spokes, probably up to eight, were morticed into the hub. In the case of wider wheels, two rows of spokes could be used, a practice which could also enable the millwright to support a wheel on lighter spokes, less deeply morticed and hence allowing a lighter shaft to be used. Of the wheels so far excavated, all but one have had single rows of spokes, the exception being the chafery wheel at Chingley forge. The best-preserved spoke fragments to survive were at Panningridge and Chingley furnaces. In each case only one spoke remained, fixed to the outer part of the wheel, with the inner tenon rotted away. Measurement of the sole boards of these wheels showed that neither could have had more than six spokes, whereas at Rockley forge there had been eight.

The sole boards on these excavated wheels had been shaped by adze to form curved members up to 2m long. There have so far been no examples of the cross-planked soles illustrated by Agricola. The tenons of the spokes were set in mortices cut through the soles, whose timber was left thicker around the mortice, strengthening the joint. It was normal for the tenon to pass right through the sole, and for a peg to be driven through a hole close to the end of the tenon. The Chingley furnace wheel had a particularly well preserved example of this kind of fixing. The shrouds, or sideboards, termed compost boards by Fitzherbert, were nailed to the sides of the soles. Only on the chafery wheel at Chingley forge was caulking found.

The greatest variation among the excavated wheel fragments has been in the design of the buckets. It was common for these to be butted against the sideboards and nailed, although at Batsford furnace the millwright had cut grooves in the sideboards to improve their location. In some cases dowels were used, instead of or in addition to nails. At Chingley furnace each bucket board had been drilled with precision from edge to edge, and a dowel passed through the board, its ends projecting through the shrouds. This wheel also showed the greatest attention to the shape of the buckets, for the boards were curved along their length, rather than straight, as was the case with every other pre-eighteenth-century wheel yet excavated. This is an important indication of the attention which millwrights were beginning to give both to filling the buckets and to delaying the point at which they emptied. Fitzherbert comments on this: 'for the longer that they holde the water the better they be'.

Efficiency was certainly important to Fitzherbert, but calculations of the power of water-wheels are not seen until the eighteenth century, at a time when there were changes to traditional designs. After 1700, iron was increasingly used, at first merely as wrought-iron parts incorporated into wooden wheels, but towards the end of the century there were new designs of cast-iron parts, notably hubs and shafts. The all-iron wheel, with cast-iron hub, spokes and shrouds was to appear early in the nineteenth century. Despite the changes seen in the new wheels installed at textile mills and ironworks during the industrial revolution, alteration was slow to spread in the traditional water-powered trades. Old wheels were patched and repaired, and even well into the nineteenth century country millwrights were building wheels with few iron parts. But the days of the traditional wheel were numbered, as local foundries equipped themselves with patterns from which sets of wheel parts could be cast.

This chapter has so far reflected the concentration of archaeological work on the overshot water-wheel. Other types, notably the undershot wheel, were numerous, but no examples have so far been excavated, rendering the archaeological record a somewhat misleading guide to the mills of post-medieval Britain. Examination of surviving mills shows the whole range of wheel types, many apparently the iron successors of wooden wheels of similar configuration. In many circumstances, where the terrain made the provision of sufficient head of water for an overshot wheel too costly, its near relation, the pitch-back wheel was used. With this design, water was discharged on to the wheel short of the highest point on the rim. At first sight, the system appears less efficient, with water being held in the buckets for a smaller proportion of the circumference than on an overshot wheel. However, a well-designed pitch-back wheel could be most effective, due to advances in wheel-pit design. If the back of the pit, as at Chingley forge, were shaped to a radius close to that of the wheel, buckets would empty less rapidly, and the weight of water acting through the spokes could virtually equal that in an overshot wheel. This type of installation is readily identifiable in the field, the masonry 'breast' at the rear of the wheel-pit being unmistakable.

Although no undershot wheels have been excavated, at many sites they would have been the only choice. Caldecotte falls into this category. The structure where the wheels had been mounted was satisfactorily identified during excavation, and even allowing for modern changes in levels, there could have been no more than 0.8m of fall between the entry to the headrace and the exit of the tail-race to the river. Undershot mills were always regarded as inferior in terms of water consumption, but because in so many cases there was no alternative, a good deal of attention was given to their improvement. In the eighteenth century, curved vanes

A)

B)

Fig. 6.18 Horizontal mills in Shetland (A) Huxter: mill, headrace (centre) and bypass (left); (B) Troswick: mill-wheel (Faith Cleverdon).

replaced straight paddles, and every effort was made to create even the slightest head of water to increase efficiency.

The other distinct tradition of hydraulic power, the horizontal wheel, deserves brief mention. Sometimes thought to be confined in the post-medieval period to the Mediterranean region, there were, and still are, survivors in northern Britain. Research in the Isle of Man shows that horizontal wheels were in use in the nineteenth century, for example in the Ballasayle mill, used for grinding gorse for cattle feed (Garrad 1978–80). There is a well-preserved example kept as a guardianship monument at Dounby, Orkney (Cruden 1946–7), and a notable concentration of mill sites in Shetland (J. Shaw 1984: 3). In Shetland mills survive at Dunrossness, Huxter, South Voe and Troswick (fig. 6.18); at Huxter there are two shells, and a roofed mill last used in the 1940s, and on the Clumlie burn at Troswick there is a fine preserved mill among a series of nine sites. Two less well known mill-sites survive on Lewis in the Hebrides, at Barvas and Bragar. Despite relatively high consumption of water, due to relying on impulse on the blade, the horizontal wheel has practical advantages for the miller whose capital is limited but whose water supply is adequate. The vertical shaft drives the millstone without the need for gearing, and the mill can be built with the minimum of materials on a compact site. Detailed variations in design can be seen in the northern survivors: at Dounby there are two rows of blades on the wheel-shaft, whereas the best-preserved of the Shetland mills has only one row. At neither is there any indication of shrouding, nor is there archaeological or documentary evidence to suggest that British horizontal mills shared the changes which in Mediterranean Europe were to develop into the early-nineteenth-century water turbine.

Chapter 7

The archaeology of ferrous metals

The iron industry: bloomeries, furnaces and forges

The archaeological indications of the principal changes in the iron industry between 1500 and 1800 have become clear over the past 25 years, as a result of excavation and field survey which exceeds, in its scale, the attention paid to other industries. The extent of work is reflected in the quantity of material reviewed in this section.

Over the post-medieval centuries there was a response to demands for iron in building, agriculture, shipping and the arms trades, and the industry reacted both by changes in method and by expansion in the number of ironworks. The change took place from the bloomery process, in which wrought iron was produced on a small scale direct from the ore, to the production of cast iron in the blast furnace, introduced from c.1500: some iron was cast in the form of artefacts, but most left the furnace as pig iron, to be converted to wrought-iron bar in the finery forge. The timing of the change to the new process varied between regions: where the market for iron was strong, as in the south-east in the sixteenth century and the west Midlands in the seventeenth, the blast furnace became universal, whereas in the north west some bloomeries still survived in 1700.

Early in the eighteenth century there began the change to the use of mineral fuel, which was to break the association of the industry with the management of coppice woodlands. This had profound implications for the contemporary landscape: it is clear that far from being a destroyer of woodlands, the industry had relied on efficient large-scale coppicing for its existence. Hammersley's calculations (1973), based on material from the Forest of Dean, show that a large blast furnace, with its forge, required about 13,000 acres of coppice for perpetual operation, and from this it can be estimated that even the smaller Wealden ironworks would require 4,000–5,000 acres for each furnace-forge combination. The end of reliance on such extensive tracts of coppice either freed ground for agriculture, at a time of growing markets for food, or released woodlands to other consumers. Hence the present-day landscape bears the evidence for the exploitation of woodland by the industry at second hand, in field-boundaries derived from former woodland divisions, ploughed-out charcoal-burning areas, or woods which survived because of alternative markets for their products.

Field surveys have disclosed many ironworking sites whose existence was once unknown, and excavations have clarified changes in technology and served as a focus for new documentary research. Evidence for ore mining has frequently been found, but as the methods differ little from those of early coal miners, the field evidence is considered in Chapter 9.

THE POST-MEDIEVAL BLOOMERY

The essentials of the bloomery process can be traced back to the beginning of the smelting of iron. The reduction of ore to metallic iron, using the carbon in charcoal at temperatures of 1100–1300°C, was a satisfactory method for the smith who required small quantities of wrought iron and who had accessible supplies of good-quality ore. Both the quality and the quantity of iron produced by the bloomsmith had improved during the Middle Ages: larger amounts of semi-liquid slag were tapped from the furnace during smelting, reducing the amount which had to be hammered out of the bloom on the anvil. Quantities of iron produced had been increased by the use of water power for bellows and hammers.

Water-powered bloomeries are known in this country from the fourteenth century, but their importance has been overshadowed by the introduction of the blast furnace, with its imposing structure and the attraction which the more spectacular aspects of its operation held for contemporary observers. The powered bloomery was nevertheless important in many parts of England as late as the middle of the seventeenth century: as a discontinuous process, producing iron as and when necessary, it suited the needs of smaller communities. Regular operation would yield 20–30 tons of iron in a year. This phase of the industry is underrepresented in the archaeological record. Some powered bloomeries were converted to other forms of mill when they ceased smelting, and others were modified as finery forges, to convert pig iron from the blast furnace. This leaves few bloomeries abandoned without reuse, and only three water-powered examples have been excavated, all of which pose problems of interpretation. The earliest is Rockley Smithies, Yorkshire (fig. 7.1), which went out of use about 1640 (Crossley and Ashurst 1968): the earliest dating evidence was provided by pottery of about 1500, in deposits of waste from ore roasting. The surviving smelting hearth was dated to the first half of the seventeenth century, and was a low-shaft furnace typical of English medieval practice. The bellows had been operated by water power, and a fragment of the water-wheel remained in its stone-lined wheel-pit alongside the bellows house. A similar assemblage, of wheel fragment, bellows house and hearth survived for the secondary stage of working, where the bloom was reheated in the string hearth during forging. What was less certain was whether water power had been used for the hammer. The foundation for an anvil was excavated, but its location suggested use with a treadle-powered hammer, perhaps working blooms which had been cut up prior to forging.

The two other excavated sites are both in Cumbria. Muncaster Head lies on the lower reaches of the Esk, and was built in 1637 (Tylecote and Cherry 1970). Although the hearths and hammer had been removed, the survival of slag, together with the location of the watercourses, showed that this was the bloomery referred to in written sources. In southern Lakeland, close to Rusland, Stoney Hazel forge was built in 1718 and probably abandoned about 1729. The shell of the forge building survives, set against the earth dam and alongside a wheel-race (*PMA* 1986: 355). Within the building the base of a hearth survives, but the problem is

(A)

(B)

Fig. 7.1 Rockley, Yorkshire: the early-seventeenth-century phase of the water-powered bloomery. (A) The base of the smelting furnace (Plan: A1) from the west, showing the slag-tapping area, foreground. The purpose of the prominent barrel set in the platform is uncertain. (B) Plan showing the smelting furnace (A1), bellows house (A2) and water-wheel (A3). The string hearth (B1) for reheating blooms of iron also had bellows (B2) blown by a water-wheel (B3). The purpose of the third wheel-pit (C) is uncertain, being too far from the anvil (D) to be likely to have powered a hammer. The overflow (F) took water from the pond (H) over the dam (G) to the tail-race (E).

whether this was for a bloomery or a finery. During the latest series of excavations at Stoney Hazel iron ore has been found in the building, which suggests that the hearth was used for smelting. There is a second building, downstream, whose function is not yet known, but which deserves examination in view of the lack of evidence for a hammer in the upstream structure.

THE CHARCOAL BLAST FURNACE

In the last 20 years many aspects of early blast-furnace design and operation have been clarified by excavation and field survey. Work has rather concentrated on the early period, the sixteenth century, and on the Weald, although there is a substantial and more widespread sample from the eighteenth century. Fewer seventeenth-century sites have been excavated, and particular questions remain about the reasons for the technological leadership which contemporaries suggest was held by furnaces in the Forest of Dean at this time.

The early furnaces in the Weald

The most intensive fieldwork on the British charcoal–iron industry has taken place in the ore-bearing areas of Sussex, Kent and Surrey, where the majority of streams, particularly on the Wadhurst clay, drove furnaces and forges, and where the iron industry was the key to a prosperous woodland economy.

The industry developed rapidly in the 50 years after the first English blast furnace was built at Newbridge, in Ashdown Forest, in 1496. The earliest furnaces were designed to supply the Crown with arms, but the general trade grew rapidly, and some existing bloomeries were soon rebuilt as finery forges, to convert pig iron into bar for the markets of London and the south-east. Important in this growth was the migration of French ironworkers to the Weald from the 1490s onwards, and there is documentary evidence for their presence at most of the first-generation furnaces (Awty 1981). For the archaeologist this relationship is of importance. It enables comparisons to be made between the sites of the Weald and those of the Pays de Bray in north-east France whence the ironworkers came, and in turn with southern Flanders, where their forebears had developed their skills during the fifteenth century. In that direction, it is valuable to examine the details of Flemish landscape paintings, notably those of Henri Bles and the Brueghels, to enlarge our archaeologically derived impressions of structures and methods. On the ground, comparisons are now becoming possible as a result of fieldwork in the Belgian and French Ardennes.

Excavations at Wealden blast-furnace sites have confirmed and amplified the details suggested by the Flemish landscape artists. The early blast furnace was a stone tower with an ashlar outer facing, rubble-cored walls and a stone-faced inner chamber (fig. 7.2). The towers were generally square in plan, with sides varying between 5.2m long in the first phase at Panningridge and 6.5m at Maynards Gate (Bedwin 1977–8). The second phase at Batsford, built late in the sixteenth century, had a rectangular plan, 8m by 5.5m (Bedwin 1980b). The heights of furnaces cannot be accurately established, for no early stacks have survived, but Sir James Hope, writing of Barden, Kent, in 1646 estimated 20 ft [6.6m] (Marshall 1958:

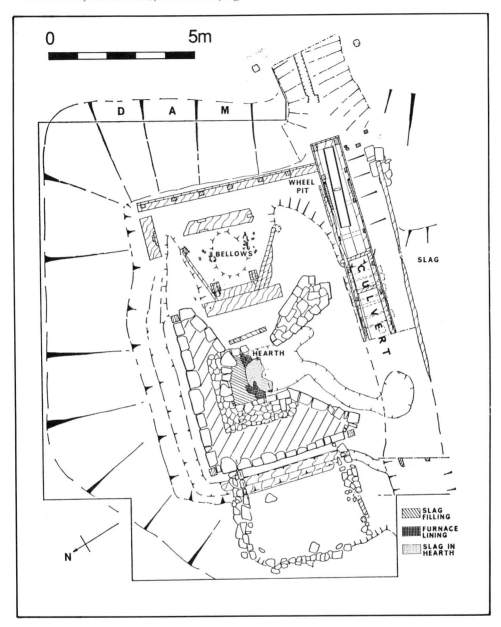

Fig. 7.2 Chingley, Kent: plan of the mid-sixteenth-century blast furnace, typical of its period and comparable with the furnaces of the southern Netherlands and north-east France whence the technology of the indirect method of iron smelting came to England.

146–53). It was normal practice to build two arches, in adjacent sides, one for blowing, the other for casting. Surviving furnaces elsewhere have cast-iron lintels to support these arches, and an archive reference to the construction of Robertsbridge furnace in 1542 (Crossley 1975a: 8) suggests that this was the practice in Sussex. Early furnaces were strengthened by external timber frames, shown on the representation of Richard Lenard's furnace at Brede, on a dated fireback of 1636. The practice is confirmed by the entry in the 1542 Panningridge building accounts for 'them that dyd help to rere the timber worke' of the furnace (*ibid.* 44); at Batsford, Chingley (Crossley 1975b: 29–30) and Maynards Gate furnaces the bases of corner posts were found in position. A similar arrangement has been recorded at the excavated late-sixteenth-century furnace at Dol-y-Clochyd, Gwynedd (fig. 7.3). Such bracing was particularly important for the integrity of the corner (pillar) of the furnace between the arches: this is shown in the Panningridge accounts to have been liable to collapse, a weakness confirmed by excavated examples.

Within the stack, construction can be divided into two parts: the lining of the hearth and the lower part of the flared bosh, which were replaced at the end of each campaign, and the lining of the upper part of the stack, which was part of the permanent structure. The hearth in the sixteenth and early seventeenth centuries was normally square in plan, measuring 0.7–1.0m across. It was constructed of refractory sandstone, and the choice of a quarry producing long-wearing material was of the greatest importance. The only furnace excavation in the Weald to produce a substantial hearth fragment was Chingley: although the side of the hearth towards the casting floor had disintegrated, a section survived which showed a substantial build-up of slag rather than erosion. This would have reduced the capacity of the hearth, in contrast to hearths of stone used by local seventeenth and eighteenth-century ironmasters which, eroding, 'grew wider and wider, so that at first it contains so much as will make a sow of six or seven hundred pound weight, at last it will contain so much as will make a sow of two thousand pound' (Walter Burrell of Cuckfield, 1672; cited in Cleere and Crossley 1985: 246). It was particularly important for ironmasters making large castings, notably guns, that the capacity of a hearth should be maintained, so that the mould could be filled with good-quality metal. By the middle of the sixteenth century guns could weigh up to 3 tons (demi-cannon) and the largest appear to have been beyond the capacity of contemporary furnaces, even if the molten metal were allowed to accumulate in the hearth. The technique in such cases was to use a 'double furnace', two hearths in the same stack, of which the best documented example was at Worth, Sussex, operating in the late 1540s. No example of such a structure has been excavated, but the form is known from furnaces still standing in France. By the seventeenth century the expedient seems no longer to have been necessary in England, for in the Forest of Dean it was possible to cast over 3.5 tons in a day, and George Browne could somehow retain up to 4 tons in a hearth at his furnaces in Kent. At the furnaces which produced pig iron, particularly in the sixteenth century, capacities appear to have been much smaller, and it was common to produce no more than a ton in a day. A feature of the hearth described by contemporaries but not yet seen on the ground was the 'fore-hearth' or 'panne', the latter the term used by Sir James Hope at Barden. This was a small extension of the hearth into the casting arch, whence metal could be ladled into small moulds.

The details of the upper part of an early Wealden stack have to be inferred from

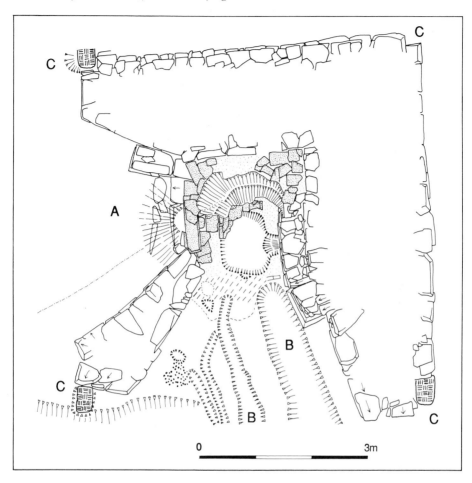

Fig. 7.3   Dol-y-Clochyd, Gwynedd: a late-sixteenth-century blast furnace, during excavations in 1986. The blowing arch (A) is to the left; the casting floor (B) retains sand beds for casting pig iron. Significant are the positions for vertical timbers at each corner of the furnace (C) (Peter Crew).

contemporary descriptions and from survivors elsewhere. The outward flaring of the bosh, the part of the shaft above the hearth, has been shown by excavations at Allensford, Northumberland (Linsley and Hetherington 1978) and at Coed Ithel, Monmouthshire (Tylecote 1966). The shaft lining, which was not changed when the hearth was rebuilt, had also to be of durable stone or brick. The latter was being used in the Weald by the 1670s, as shown by Walter Burrell, and entries in the eighteenth-century Ashburnham accounts suggest the use of high-alumina brick. At the early furnaces in the Weald it can be demonstrated from the collapsed heaps of friable brick and stone how fragile these structures became after lengthy use, how important the external timber framing must have been, and why later furnaces were so much more massively built, incorporating iron ties in their construction.

It was most important that furnaces should be adequately drained. Ground water had to be kept away from the stack, explaining the drain trenches around the furnaces at Maynards Gate and Chingley. Within the furnace, drains were built beneath the hearth: at Chingley a sizeable vaulted cavity took seepage from under the casting arch, and traces of a more sophisticated layout of brick drains were recorded at Batsford, Maynards Gate and Pippingford.

Outside the furnace, the blowing and casting houses adjoined the stack. Henri Bles shows these as lean-to structures, with tiled or, hazardously, thatched roofs. At Panningridge and Chingley the bases of the timber walls of bellows houses were found between the dam and the furnace, and at Maynards Gate tiles were scattered across this area. Bellows were sited alongside a wheel-pit: the shaft of the water wheel was extended across the bellows-house floor, and the cams with which it was fitted operated the bellows. At Chingley a fragment of the shaft survived, into which were cut sets of mortices from which cams had been salvaged (fig. 7.4). No bellows have survived, for even if parts had not been reclaimed, their position above the water-table would have led to decay. Contemporary Continental bellows design is well illustrated by Biringuccio and Agricola, and assumptions about English practice rely on these details. Biringuccio shows a simple system in which cams bear directly on the bellows bottom boards, which are hinged to expel the air. Agicola's bellows are more complicated, the cams raising and lowering the top board through a system of levers and counterweights. The arrangement at Chingley suggests hinged bottom boards as shown by Biringuccio. Bellows boards were massive, up to 4.5 m long in seventeenth-century Kent, and there are many references to the use of hides. Offcuts of leather and suitable nails were found at Chingley, and leather staining was noticeable in the floor levels there and at Panningridge. Flap valves were fitted to the bellows, referred to as vent-boards in the Panningridge accounts; the wooden hinge-pieces found at Chingley appear to have been parts of these. The iron bellows-nozzles (tuyeres) were mounted on sleepers close to the hearth: the 'tuiron' is a term appearing in the Panningridge accounts. The two tuyeres would fit into a shaped stone incorporated in the lining of the furnace, a feature so far only found at Glenkinglass, in Argyll (Lewis 1984).

Casting floors are discussed later, with reference to the products. In brief, the casting house normally covered an area in which moulding sand was spread, for the casting of pig iron and small objects, or a pit in which large moulds were placed when the furnace specialized in objects such as guns. Wealden furnaces often had very compact casting floors, particularly when confined by watercourses.

The blast furnace outside the Weald

It was more than half a century after the first blast furnace was built in Sussex before the new technology reached the Midlands and the north. In the 1560s furnaces were built at Cleobury Mortimer and Shifnal in Shropshire and in Cannock Chase, Staffordshire (Schubert 1957: 371, 387, 370), and at the same time a short-lived and probably unsuccessful furnace was built at Stocksfield, Northumberland (*HM* 1982: 74; 1983: 120). In the same decade construction began in Monmouthshire and Glamorgan, although not in the Forest of Dean, where the bloomery persisted until early in the seventeenth century. The main expansion outside the Weald began in the 1580s, and it was in the following

Fig. 7.4 Chingley furnace, Kent: details of the bellows house. Part of the shaft shows mortices for the cams which operated the bellows. The two bellows pivot posts can be seen to the left, towards the furnace.

half-century that the supremacy of the south-east in terms of total production of iron was overtaken by the rest of the country. This is a period for which disappointingly little field evidence is available. Of the Shropshire furnaces, the site at Shifnal has been located, but subsequent reuse has left little but the characteristic slags (*PMA* 1973: 115–16). In Staffordshire the site of the Cannock furnace is known, and an attempt was made to determine methods of working by examination of slags and fragments of hearth material (Morton 1964–5). Subsequently, an important report on the operation of the furnace has been found, dating from 1590 (Jones and Harrison 1978). At Stocksfield, rather more work has been possible, for the furnace survives to a height of 1.8m, with the hearth in place. Unfortunately it was partly excavated at the beginning of this century, and recent work has had to contend with this disturbance. Nevertheless, a magnetic date of 1570 ±20 corresponds with the documented attempt at operation in 1566. At the end of the sixteenth century many furnaces were built whose whereabouts are known, but the only full-scale excavation reported has been at Dol-y-clochydd, Gwynedd (*HM* 1984: 48) where the casting floor was found intact, and the drainage system beneath the hearth has been recorded (fig. 7.3).

In the seventeenth century the major development in the English iron industry was the growth in the daily output of the blast furnace from the level of one ton in a day usual in the Weald. Progress was rapid in the Forest of Dean, where, by the second quarter of the seventeenth century it was common for furnaces to cast two tons of iron in a day, and output frequently reached three tons. Unfortunately, little archaeological investigation of the causes of such improvements has been possible, for none of the furnaces actually within the Forest have been excavated. Only one survives in anything approaching complete form, Gunns Mill, built in 1635 and used into the 1640s, then rebuilt in 1682 and used for 50 years before being converted to a sawmill (fig. 7.5). It is hoped that a new survey may throw some light on the early form of this furnace.

Two excavations have taken place in neighbouring Monmouthshire which may reflect Dean practice. The furnace at Coed Ithel (Tylecote 1966) is suggested to have gone out of use before the end of the seventeenth century, and the structure was of one period. The profile was strikingly different from Wealden furnaces, not only being circular in plan but also having a smooth transition between shaft and bosh and between the bosh and the hearth. Abbey Tintern furnace (Pickin 1982, 1983) was more complete, but as it was operated until the 1820s, the circular hearth and bosh may not be an original feature of this late-seventeenth-century furnace. The circular plan, it should be pointed out, can be found elsewhere: the mid-seventeenth-century furnace at Sharpley Pool, Worcestershire, tentatively associated with Andrew Yarranton, has a similar plan and profile to Coed Ithel, and it is tempting to assume that Yarranton, an innovator in many fields, was using the best of contemporary practice (Brown 1982).

Important as they appear, the design features of furnaces such as Coed Ithel and Abbey Tintern should not be isolated as the only reasons for the apparent technical superiority of the Dean iron industry. It is also significant that the blast furnace was introduced late in the forest, after a period when the administration of the royal lands and the strength of foresters' rights seem to have stifled innovations which could only take place in combination with a radical development in woodland management, towards large-scale coppicing. Thus when change did take place, the industry had a fresh start, in comparison with the slow evolution from essentially French methods which had occurred in other areas. In addition, Dean possessed some of the finest ores in Britain, haematites, low in sulphur and phosphorus, and producing iron which commanded a high price in the emerging centres of production of metal goods in the Midlands.

The last century of the charcoal blast furnace

Long-established forms of construction have been recorded in a number of furnaces dating from the years around 1700. The furnace at Allensford, Northumberland, in use in the 1670s, was of conventional design, with a square-plan hearth and shaft. More significant is the nearby ore-roasting kiln, which is the first of its type to be excavated in Britain, and represents a break with the tradition of open-stack ore-roasting. Similar in appearance is the latest furnace excavated in the Weald: Pippingford, in Ashdown Forest, was built in 1696, and was used for casting ordnance until c.1717. The hearth is missing, but it is most probable that it was square. The third of this group is at Rockley, Yorkshire, now considered to have been built about 1700 (Crossley forthcoming). The furnace stack stands virtually complete, apart from the missing hearth, and was built with a square internal plan. The present height is 6m, and the furnace is 7m square externally (fig. 7.6). In Wales, a comparable eighteenth-century furnace, recently excavated, can

Fig. 7.5   Gunns Mill, Gloucestershire: a seventeenth-century blast furnace in the Forest of Dean whose charging level was converted to a sawmill in the eighteenth century. The wheel-pit is out of sight in the left foreground.

be seen at Dyfi, near Aberystwyth (Dinn 1988). Finally, an impressive furnace stack survives at Charlcot, Shropshire (*PMA* 1967: 120; 1968: 192). It is documented for the years 1733–79, but the actual date of building is not certain. The hearth was partially cleared, without archaeological supervision, some years ago, and the lining was found to survive: this is a significant structure which deserves further research.

Important work has taken place in recent years on furnaces in Cumbria and in the west of Scotland, built in the first half of the eighteenth century to smelt the high-quality haematites of Furness with cheap coppice wood. In Furness, where competing markets for wood were to grow during the eighteenth century, there remained the advantage of high-quality ore, explaining the expansion and profitability of an industry which clung to traditional fuel and methods. The advantages of using these deposits are shown by the feasibility of incurring the cost of carriage of ore to the Argyll furnaces and of the return of pig to England.

Fig. 7.6   Rockley, Yorkshire: the blast furnace built c.1700, from the west, looking towards the casting arch. The hearth is missing. A third arch, possibly added when the furnace was adapted to use coke at the end of the eighteenth century, can be seen beyond the hearth space.

Fig. 7.7   Bonawe, Strathclyde (Argyll): storage barn adjacent to the eighteenth-century blast furnace.

In Furness, the excavated furnace at Duddon (*PMA* 1982: 226–8; 1983: 199–200; 1984: 321) has a stack which, apart from the hearth, is intact to full height, with the unusual survival of a chimney through the side of which the charge was tipped. Such features survive at Bonawe, and contemporary Continental illustrations suggest that their use was widespread. At Duddon the arrangement of watercourses is of interest, in that the furnace appears at first to have been run from a small stream flowing down the hillside, but at the end of the eighteenth century the supply was replaced or increased by the construction of a weir on the River Duddon and a leat which is still visible. This change appears to have coincided with the installation of cylinder blowers to replace the traditional bellows. Such a change often took place when furnaces were converted to coke, but at Duddon, as elsewhere in Furness, the use of charcoal continued, in this instance until 1867. Part of the low-breast water-wheel has survived, at 8m in diameter quite exceptional in size for an ironworks. Particularly impressive are the shells of the barns where the charcoal and ore were stored. These occupy the hillside above the charging area, and demonstrate the care with which the high-grade ore and charcoal were kept.

Elsewhere in Furness, the furnace at Nibthwaite was built in 1735, part of an integrated works which included a foundry and a forge. The forge was used into the nineteenth century, but the furnace was blown out in the middle of the eighteenth century, to be succeded by a bobbin mill which was built at the charging level and over the top of the furnace. The base of the stack is in good order, and the water supply and many of the ancillary buildings can be traced (*PMA* 1985: 185). At Newland there is a complex which although complete is in a deteriorating condition. The hearth survives in part, although unstable. A charcoal or ore shed is still used as a barn, and the interesting water system can still be traced around the adjacent hillside. The earliest of the Furness sites is the most difficult to interpret, although in many ways rewarding. This is the furnace at Backbarrow, which remained in use until the 1950s, and has a remarkable assemblage of features illustrating the development of iron-smelting technology over the eighteenth and the nineteenth centuries. It was built about 1712 and continued to smelt with charcoal into the twentieth century, although from the 1920s increasing use was made of coke. The water-wheel was replaced by a steam engine in the nineteenth century and hot blast was also installed. Nevertheless, the base of the furnace is a stone structure of essentially eighteenth-century type, and the ore and charcoal storage barns are some of the finest to survive.

The Scottish furnaces are also impressive (J.H. Lewis 1984). The stack at Craleckan is substantially complete, although the water supply and storage buildings have disappeared (Hay and Stell 1986: 114–15). At Bonawe (*ibid.* 108–14) there is perhaps the best preserved ironworks complex in Britain. The furnace was built in 1752, and is complete apart from the hearth: the top is concealed in a building at charging level, and the arches are supported by dated cast-iron lintels. The earthworks of the head race can be traced, but most spectacular are the charcoal and ore barns (fig. 7.7), which are still roofed, and are connected with the furnace charging house by means of slate paths. There have been excavations at the sites of two other Scottish furnaces. At Red Smiddy the base of a furnace 5.9m square has been recorded, and the tapping and blowing arches identified. At Glenkinglass the base of the furnace was 7m square, and is particularly significant for the unique survival of a shaped stone which had accommodated the tuyeres.

THE ARCHAEOLOGY OF THE TRANSITION TO COKE

A brief comment should be included in this section on the archaeological evidence for the transition to coke in the eighteenth-century British iron industry. The earliest successful use of mineral fuel took place at Coalbrookdale in 1709. Before this date there were attempts to use coke, and archaeology has a part to play in determining how near to success these came. The early-seventeenth-century trials by Dudley have been widely noted, but the search for the slags from his furnace have not been conclusive. It is to be hoped that stratified material may be available at Cleator, Cumbria, where part of a furnace built in 1694 to use mineral fuel appears to be incorporated in later buildings (*PMA* 1982: 226). At Coalbrookdale, excavations have taken place around the Darby furnace, but these have been confined to locating the wheel-pit, and the casting and blowing areas are still unexplored. The stratification is likely to include material from the use of the furnace through the eighteenth century.

The use of coke was slow to spread beyond Shropshire, and it is not until the middle of the eighteenth century that ironmasters throughout the rest of Britain adopted the innovation. In the last years of the eighteenth century the design of furnaces changed rapidly, particularly because the strength of coke, compared with charcoal, enabled tall furnaces to be built without risk of the charge being compressed and becoming impermeable to blast. In this period there were new designs and also conversions of traditional furnaces. A case of adaptation is the furnace at Rockley, referred to earlier, which excavations have shown was re-opened and used with coke late in the eighteenth century, producing large castings in a pit cut through the pig beds. What is not clear is the extent to which this furnace was modified: an enigmatic feature is a third entry to the furnace hearth, opposite the casting arch. This differs in detail from the other arches, and has been suggested, without hard evidence, to be an insertion associated with the provision of extra blast needed when using coke instead of charcoal. Another Yorkshire example of conversion is at Low Mill, where a second tuyere arch was inserted into a furnace of traditional size, to provide extra blast. The furnace still ran on water power, but the layout suggests that cylinder blowers would be used after the conversion, replacing bellows. The date of the change is not known.

Of the furnaces which incorporated the new technology from the start, excavation or recording at three examples may be briefly noted. The earliest. Bedlam furnaces, were built alongside the Severn in 1757–8, and still stand, substantially complete. The furnaces were blown by water power, the supply being pumped by a steam engine from the Severn, to operate a water-wheel. A second preserved group are at Blaenavon, built in the 1780s and 19m tall, and demonstrating the complete change in scale which became possible with the introduction of coke. A more comprehensive programme of excavation has taken place at Moira furnace, Leicestershire, built in 1803 and used with scant success for little more than a decade (Cranstone 1985).

THE FINERY FORGE

The conversion forge was introduced into England with the blast furnace, after development on the Continent to refine brittle cast iron into a malleable material for the smith. The difficulties for the archaeologist are that the buildings were insubstantial and could be adapted for other purposes, and the residues are less easily recognizable than blast-furnace slags. Further, as only three forges have been excavated, all in the Weald, more archaeological information is needed to assess the typical layout and level of equipment over the country as a whole.

Some understanding of the process is helpful; at the forge the 3–4 per cent of carbon in pig iron was almost completely removed by re-melting in an open charcoal-fired hearth blown by water-powered bellows. Slag was released from the iron, so refining took place in a bath of molten slag, the bloom of iron being kept in motion under the oxidizing blast from the bellows. The hot bloom was taken to a water-powered tilt-hammer, where further slag was forged out as the bloom was shaped into a large bar, the ancony. During forging the iron had to be reheated, either in the finery or, as was usual in the Weald, in a second hearth, the chafery, also blown by water-powered bellows. The ancony was then forged down to the section of bar or rod in which it was sold to the wrought-iron trade.

Water was therefore needed for two if not three wheels, as used at the excavated forges in the Weald, Ardingly (fig. 10.2): Bedwin 1976); Blackwater Green (fig. 7.8); Place 1989) and Chingley (Crossley 1975b), in races running through the forge buildings. The hearths had left only slight traces, due at Ardingly to the replacement of the forge in the eighteenth century by a fulling mill, using the same dam and probably one of the races. At Chingley the forge (fig. 7.9) was left to decay in the eighteenth century, and the ground was later levelled for pasture.

By contrast, the hammer and anvil leave characteristic traces even if the forge has been demolished to ground level. Timber foundations of forge hammers have survived well in damp valley-bottom conditions: at Chingley there were foundations of hammers of two periods, while even if at Ardingly re-use of the site had left only fragmentary hammer foundations, it was still clear where they had been. In each case a length of tree trunk had been set in a pit, to support an anvil: at Ardingly the base was about 1m long, held in position by a triangle of beams at ground level, and capped by a hollow iron cylinder as a mounting for the anvil. At Chingley the base was even more massive: a length of trunk 1.7m long rested on sleepers, and was held by radial timbers which were wedged against verticals lining the pit. Examples elsewhere, at Crowborough in Sussex and in the Loxley valley in Yorkshire have shown that substructures of this kind can survive in the most adverse conditions of dereliction and re-use.

Hammers contained cast-iron parts which were worth salvaging, and it is unusual to find any substantial survival. A hammer helve kept at Batemans, Burwash, is the only example from the Wealden industry, where there are no traces of the above-ground framing seen in Yorkshire forges and well documented in Furness in the eighteenth century. At Wortley Top Forge, in use as a finery in the first half of the eighteenth century, almost the entire hammer structure survived to forge iron objects as late as 1910, and it is remarkable to note how wooden parts were replaced, piecemeal, in iron, without redesign (fig. 7.10). At Mousehole Forge, Sheffield, parts exist of a similar hammer, similarly mounted on a massive free-standing timber frame (fig. 7.11) which bears striking similarities to seventeenth and eighteenth-century descriptions of equipment used in forges in Cumbria (Awty and Phillips 1979–80).

A post-script to this section concerns attempts in the eighteenth century to overcome difficulties in the conversion forges in using mineral fuel and in refining

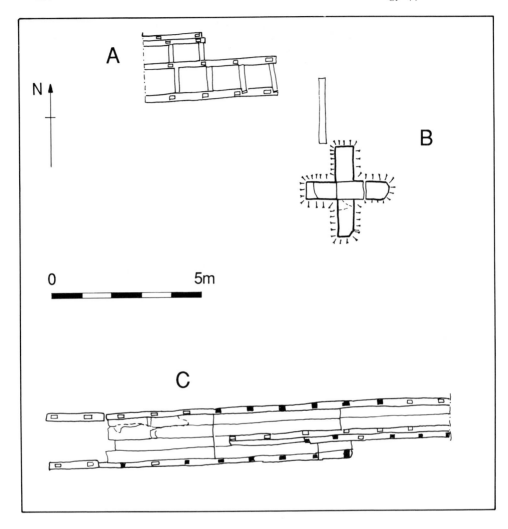

Fig. 7.8 Blackwater Green, Sussex: the fragmentary remains of a seventeenth-century finery forge recorded during rescue excavations in 1988. Of the two wheel races, (A) served the hammer, whose cruciform anvil base (B) survived. A wheel in race (C) would power the finery. Compare with the forge reused as a fulling mill at Ardingly (fig. 10.2) (Chris Place: Sussex Archaeol. Field Unit).

pig iron smelted in coke blast furnaces. These were to lead to innovations of which Henry Cort's puddling furnace was of the most lasting significance, a development outside the scope of this book. Among the documented attempts to overcome the bottleneck in forging was the potting and stamping process, in which pieces of cast iron were heated in closed crucibles containing fluxes which removed carbon and other unwanted elements. There is some potential for examination of the crucibles and their contents. One such investigation has been undertaken, at Apley Forge,

Fig. 7.9 Chingley, Kent: seventeenth/eighteenth-century finery structure with adjacent wheel-race. The slag pit is visible within the stone walls, but the hearth has been largely destroyed by a field drain. A fragment of an iron hearth-lining plate can be seen to the right of the drain trench. The timbers of the hammer base are visible at the top right.

Shropshire, where it is known that Jesson and Wright operated the potting process in the 1770s. Ceramic fragments were recovered which show that the waste has been correctly identified, and the material recovered has clarified details of the process and the extent to which it was of practical use (*PMA* 1968: 193).

STEEL

To the pre-industrial smith, steel was an important but costly commodity, but its production has left no archaeological traces in Britain from before the eighteenth century. Nevertheless, steel was of such importance for producing high-quality blades and tools that directions for research should be set out.

Fig. 7.10 Wortley Top Forge, Yorkshire: tilt-hammer of eighteenth-century design with piecemeal replacement of wooden parts in cast iron.

Steel has a carbon content ranging between approximately 0.3per cent and 1.0 per cent, compared with wrought iron at 0.1 per cent or less, and cast iron with 3–5 per cent. In the bloomery period, steel could be made direct from certain iron ores, using a high ratio of charcoal in the furnace to secure a high-carbon bloom. To identify a bloomery where this was done would be difficult unless fragments of a bloom were found. A second method was to refine cast iron, but to halt the operation before the carbon content diminished to that of wrought iron. As the element, carbon, was unknown, the process was based solely on observation of the results of variation in finery practices. The method was developed in Germany or the Netherlands at the end of the Middle Ages, and when German or Dutch workers were brought to the Weald in 1565–6, steel was made at Robertsbridge and Boxhurst forges until importers of Baltic steel undercut the operation. The exact whereabouts of the Boxhurst steel forge are uncertain, and although the forge site at Robertsbridge is well known, no excavations have taken place. Contemporary sources suggest that some of the steelmaking took place in the buildings of the former abbey at Robertsbridge, implying a very small-scale operation in which hearths were blown by hand rather than by water-powered bellows.

A large proportion of the steel used in England before the latter part of the seventeenth century was imported, some via the Baltic trade, some from Spain. But in the seventeenth century the German method of making steel from wrought iron by 'cementation' was introduced to England. It is known to have been practised in Nuremberg in the second half of the sixteenth century, and involved the heating of iron bars packed in charcoal in chests sealed with clay (Barraclough 1976). The carbon was absorbed into the surface of the iron, which, if broken and reforged at red heat, could then be formed into bars which if not thoroughly even in carbon

Fig. 7.11 Mousehole Forge, Sheffield: framework of a forge hammer similar in many details to the Wortley example, (fig. 7.10), demonstrating the free-standing construction. The cover building was demolished about 1942.

content, were adequate for many users. The principle was not new, for the medieval tradition of case-hardening iron objects by heating in a bed of charcoal had been widely used when a shell of hard metal was required. No seventeenth-century indications of cementation have survived on the ground, although there is written evidence for production on Tyneside, in Yorkshire and in the Forest of Dean, on sites yet to be discovered.

The earliest cementation furnace to survive is at Derwentcote, County Durham. This is now in guardianship and the subject of a research and excavation programme; the building was in existence by 1753, 60 years earlier than the next surviving fragment, at Bowers Spring, Sheffield. However, the actual date of construction at Derwentcote is as yet uncertain. The characteristic conical

Fig. 7.12 Derwentcote, Co. Durham: eighteenth-century cementation steel furnace. The excavation plan shows the furnace base (A); the photograph was taken, from the west, before consolidation of the structure (Plan: David Cranstone; English Heritage).

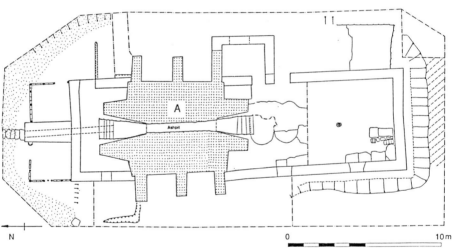

superstructure fig. 7.12), superficially resembling a bottle-kiln, survives intact, in this instance built in stone. Inside, the chests in which iron bars and charcoal were packed are also in good condition. It is part of a much larger complex, including water-powered forges, of which there are now only earthwork traces. Indeed Derwentcote is the survivor of an important industry, the Derwent powering numerous forges whose trade in high-grade iron and steel products was well known throughout the seventeenth and eighteenth centuries.

Finally, at the end of our period, an important development took place which enabled cementation steel to compete with high-grade imports. It was realized that if cementation bars were broken, placed in a crucible and melted in a furnace, ingots could be cast whose carbon content and hence hardness would be even, rather than concentrated at the surface, as in cementation bar. This development, whose key feature was the use of highly refractory clays for crucibles, took place at the end of the 1740s, and is associated with the name of Benjamin Huntsman. The process, slow to gain ground before the last decades of the eighteenth century, was principally carried on in the Sheffield area for steel used in the edge-tool trades. No eighteenth-century crucible-steel furnaces are known, but nineteenth-century survivors, along with eighteenth-century descriptions by Swedish and French observers, give a fair impression of the structures used in the Huntsman period.

Iron and steel: indications on the ground

THE BLAST FURNACE

The great majority of charcoal blast furnaces have been demolished, and when seeking sites the fieldworker often relies on earthwork indications and on slags and other waste. The frequency of destruction was partly due to the value of the ashlar stonework with which many stacks were faced, but in many cases was inevitable, given the fragile condition of a furnace after several seasons of use. Once the timbers bracing a sixteenth or seventeenth-century furnace were removed, it is doubtful whether the cracked and friable stone or brick would stand for long. Hence, a collapsed furnace is identifiable by spreads of burnt clay and weathered brick, some with glassy coatings from the inside of the stack. When the shaft has deteriorated while in use, slag can be seen in the joints in the internal stone or brickwork.

Furnaces, being reliant on water power, occupied valley-bottom sites, and were normally placed close to the dams of storage ponds, as outlined in Chapter 6. The position of a furnace can be further narrowed down by searching for the wheel-pit in an area downstream from the dam, and also by following any line of damp ground, a former tail-race, back from its confluence with the river.

Over a wider area are slags, often tipped downstream, away from the dam. These are normally glassy, by contrast with the dull surfaces of bloomery slag, but whereas bloomery tap-slag is usually black, blast furnace slag can vary from black, through shades of green, to blue and grey, depending on conditions in the furnace and on the composition of the charge. Along with the slag can be found debris cleared from the hearth at the time of relining: this is often the most useful source for a technical appraisal of the operation of the furnace. These materials can contain partly smelted ore and traces of charcoal, found trapped in slags and cinders. In the case of charcoal, prints of the cell structure of the wood can be found on the slag. Reduced metal is also found in such debris, and there is thus presented in microcosm a complete picture of the furnace process in operation, from the ore to the cast iron. Slag deposits also contain runners of cast iron. These are useful for assessment of the product, although dependent on whether the runner is typical. Normally such runners will come either from an accident in pouring or from a break-out from the hearth, when the lining has worn dangerously thin. Fieldwork based on the distribution of slag deposits is not without its dangers: Rockley is a case where remarkably little slag was found in the surrounding woods, having been used on roads and on colliery tramways in the district. Such use can lead to confusion over the location of furnace sites.

BLOOMERY AND FINERY FORGES

On the ground, bloomeries can be hard to identify, for the ponds, watercourses and dams resemble those of many small mills. If iron smelting has been the final use, or if there has been conversion to a non-metallurgical function, the characteristic bloomery tap-slag may be found: this is normally black and opaque rather than glassy in appearance, and with surfaces that show slow viscous flow. Unfortunately bloomery slags were often collected for resmelting in blast furnaces, and some bloomeries were converted to fineries, the earlier slags being covered by finery cinder. In a few cases, as at Brookland Forge in Sussex, exposed sections have been recorded which show the stratigraphical relationship of these materials (Cleere and Crossley 1985: 108, 319).

Working debris from finery forges takes many forms, and has often been wrongly identified. Slag splashed during forging could form a laminated deposit (hammer-scale) on nearby surfaces, but the quantities are rarely large. The slag from refining forms a black or rusty-brown porous cinder, occasionally with slight traces of flow on its surface. Frequently the large lumps of slag which accumulated in finery hearths were discarded, and these can be found in use as road make-up, building foundations or walls supporting the banks of watercourses. There can be confusion between cinders and hearth bottoms from fineries and from bloomeries. The important distinction is that finery material will not contain ore, as bloomery remains often do. Those finery cinders which include material which shows signs of melting and flow can resemble bloomery tap-slag, but whereas the latter usually makes up a significant proportion of waste from a water-powered bloomery, anything similar forms a small proportion of the waste from a finery. The importance of adequate sampling has thus to be stressed.

The iron industry: the products

THE MAKING OF CASTINGS

Until the eighteenth century, the production of iron castings should be regarded not as a secondary metal trade, as is the making of blades or nails, but an activity integral with the primary smelting side of the industry. Thus the archaeologist seeks evidence for casting at the blast furnace, whence the metal was fed direct to the mould, and not at the foundry.

There is now plentiful archaeological evidence for direct casting from the blast furnace. The most spectacular features are casting pits, six examples of which have now been recorded. Four timber-lined pits have been excavated in the Weald, at Batsford (Bedwin 1980b), Maynards Gate (Bedwin 1977–8), Pippingford (fig. 7.13; Crossley 1975c) and Scarlets (Crossley 1979), and there are stone-lined examples at Rockley, Yorkshire (fig. 7.14) and Dyfi furnace, Dyfed (Dinn 1988). The pits were sited close to the casting arch of the furnace, and were about 1.5m in

Fig. 7.13 Pippingford, Sussex: this overhead view of the excavated furnace shows the timber-lined casting pit to the right of the sand-covered casting floor.

Fig. 7.14 Rockley, Yorkshire: stone-lined casting pit, cut through early-eighteenth-century pig-casting beds.

diameter and up to 3.5m in depth. The wooden examples were large vertically staved barrels, bound with wooden hoops, which were prefabricated, lowered into excavated pits and rammed around with clay. Waterproofing was important to prevent any risk of steam forming around the moulds, so defects in the staves were patched and plugged, and the Pippingford pit showed how thoroughly this had to be done. The proximity of the wheel-race placed much of the casting pit below the water table, and in two cases, Pippingford and Scarlets, evidence of pumping has been found. At Pippingford a lead pipe was fixed to the side of the pit, drawing from the bottom. At Scarlets a cruder wooden fixture of channel section had been nailed and caulked to the side. In neither case were any parts of the pump found. These features explain the entries in the eighteenth-century Ashburnham furnace accounts for 'pumping the vault' for the entire time for which casting was carried out, a term not understood until the Pippingford casting pit was excavated. The Rockley casting pit, probably dating from late in the eighteenth century, was a substantial and impressive structure of shaped ashlar reminiscent of the lining of a mine shaft. No signs of any pumping equipment remained.

Deposits of mould fragments are a common sign that a blast furnace had a trade in castings. The moulds were made from loam, shaped round a model of the object to be cast. The model, whether of a gun, pipe, roller or similar object, was made on a core of wood which could be withdrawn before the clay or loam of the rest of the model was broken from within the mould formed upon it. An excellent portrayal of the method is given by the Verbruggens' series of watercolours, showing work at the Woolwich foundry in the second half of the eighteenth century (Jackson and de Beer 1973: 80–95). Although brass guns were made there, many of the methods apply to the casting of iron. Once the mould had been made, it had to be fired to give strength sufficient to stand lifting into the pit, and to bear the weight of metal poured in. At Batsford the robbed-out foundation of a hearth or kiln for this pre-firing was excavated alongside the furnace. The survival of mould material depends on local conditions and on the composition of the loam: at certain well-drained Weald sites considerable quantities have survived, notably at Ashburnham, Langleys, Maresfield and Pallingham. At Pippingford, where mould material had been scattered and buried, little was recognizable.

Moulds for large objects were placed on a table within the casting pit. At Pippingford the table remained in position, with legs which could be replaced to vary the height of the top for castings of different lengths. The space beneath served as a sump whence water could be pumped. Once lowered into the casting pit, the mould was packed around with sand, which can often be found either in the pit or scattered on adjacent floors. At Pippingford much remained above the table, where it had lain since the last large mould was removed. On occasion at Scarlets hot metal must have spilled, due either to difficulties in pouring or to a break-out from the mould: burn marks from such an accident could be seen on the wall of the pit.

Direct casting from the furnace was a risky and potentially wasteful operation. Contemporaries make the problems clear, none better than the Fullers, father and son, whose letters about casting at Heathfield, Sussex, survive in the East Sussex Record Office from the 1730s to the 1750s. The quality of the iron was hard to predict, so it was usual first to cast pig iron for the forges, then to make small objects, and to work up to the largest as the metal improved and as wear of the lining increased the capacity of the furnace. The problems have been strikingly illustrated by the gun excavated at Pippingford. This complete but faulty piece,

1.7m long, was shown by gamma radiography to contain voids in the metal, which the founder would have detected by tapping with a hammer. The gun is now displayed at Anne of Cleves House museum in Lewes: not only is it unique as a casting confirmed by modern methods as faulty, but it still retains the 'gun-head'. This was formed by extending the mould beyond the muzzle to allow gas and impurities to rise into a head which would later be sawn off and sent for refining. When a furnace produced iron of doubtful quality, heads were made large, and the quantity of metal required from the furnace was correspondingly great.

It is clear that uncertainties such as these made the development of foundries, remelting pig iron of known quality, an attractive possibility, and it is surprising that they took so long to develop in western Europe, in contrast to their early use in China. Early signs are references to 'air furnaces', used in the 1740s by London merchants who melted guns which had failed proof, and possibly also used in the Midlands soon after 1700. The form of these foundries is uncertain, for the earliest known drawings date from late in the eighteenth century. Thus indications of early foundries should be sought in urban contexts of early eighteenth-century date, to establish not only the size and details of the furnaces, but whether they were fired by charcoal or by pit coal.

So far no equipment has been found for lifting the casting and its mould from the pit. Removal was simplified by building an adjacent floor at a level below that of the main casting area, on to which the casting could be lifted before stripping the mould away. This seems to have been a seventeenth-century innovation, present at Scarlets, Pippingford and Rockley, but not at the sixteenth-century furnaces at Batsford and Maynards Gate.

Attention has been concentrated on the larger castings, but many furnaces in the Weald had a trade in small objects: in particular, cast vessels and cauldrons were made in quantity, shown by the plentiful mould fragments among furnace waste. This was a trade which developed rapidly in the Midlands in the seventeenth century, and it was the production of thin-walled pots which fostered the development of re-usable moulds in the eighteenth-century Shropshire industry, and the development of the use of mineral fuel in that region after the Darby experiments of 1709. The ability of coke-iron to flow into fine moulds was exploited by the Darbys, although it spread only slowly before the middle of the eighteenth century.

Small castings were traditionally made by ladling metal from the fore-hearth, a method which allowed the founder more control of quality than tapping in bulk. Apart from hollow-ware, the best-known products of the ladling technique were the cast-iron grave slabs and firebacks which were made in the moulding sand of the casting floor. Grave slabs are found in the Weald, excellent examples being set in the aisles of Wadhurst church. Of particular interest are those made in grey cast iron, into which it has been possible to incise additional inscriptions. Outside the Weald, the most significant assemblage is at the church at Burrington, near Ludlow (Willatts 1987). Firebacks were more widely sold, and they range from plain slabs to examples with ornate decoration relating to families in whose houses they were placed. Their distribution has been confused by the production of copies, and no systematic programme of recording has yet been completed. Their frequent survival is rather misleading, for firebacks and grave slabs must have constituted a minute proportion of the metal cast. More important was the trade in heavy goods such as anvils and hammer heads, not only for the conversion forges which the furnaces served, but for the blacksmiths. The trade is documented from the sixteenth century onwards, but the physical traces have disappeared, due to the disintegration of the clay-loam moulds in which such objects would have been cast.

The other casting trade which leaves significant remains at the furnace is the production of ammunition, often carried out by the gun-founders while furnaces were being worked up for the making of ordnance. Cannon balls were cast in moulds, themselves of cast iron: an example was excavated at Batsford, and others have appeared, unstratified, on other Wealden sites. Cannon balls themselves have been found, either failures, or scattered near the gun-casting furnaces which carried out their own proofs.

Historical evidence shows that the majority of British furnaces concentrated on casting pig iron for the conversion forges. Hot metal was run from the hearth into moulds shaped in the sand of the casting floor. Some casting floors have survived well, particularly where the local sand hardens when heated by molten metal. At Panningridge and Pippingford the beds were well preserved, but at Chingley the sand had been weathered and had washed down into the tail-race, which served as a drain beneath the casting house. Early furnaces cast large pigs, known as sows, commonly weighing 10cwt, and on occasion up to one ton. This contrasts with eighteenth-century descriptions of casting floors with numerous branching moulds, in which small pigs were produced for the foundry trade.

BORING MILLS

An important aspect of the archaeology of the casting of iron is the internal finishing, by boring or reaming, of guns or other hollow objects. Until the third quarter of the eighteenth century it was normal to cast hollow and to finish the bore by reaming, rather than to cast solid and bore out. The method of making hollow castings is known from contemporary descriptions. Inside the mould was placed a core, formed around a 'nowell bar' of iron, which had to be exactly centred. This was a difficult operation, and there was a risk of the bar and core being displaced. In the case of a gun this would lead to rejection, although objects such as pipes could be tolerated with a slight eccentricity of the bore.

Once the object had been cast, boring to a final internal finish took place on a water-powered boring mill. The field and archive evidence for these is plentiful: of the Sussex examples suggested by place-names, the mill at Mayfield was confirmed by the presence of corroded turnings. Archive references include Ashburnham forge, converted to a boring mill in 1677, Heathfield, where a new mill was built in the eighteenth century powered by tail-water from the furnace, and Lamberhurst, where a similar arrangement is shown on an eighteenth-century map. The only example so far excavated is at Pippingford, where there were deposits of turnings, the track for the gun carriage, whose four cast-iron wheels remained in position, and a hemispherical cast-iron chuck for the boring bar. In addition to the track, there was a circular brick structure which appeared to be the base for a windlass to winch the gun carriage along the track as boring took place. Nothing remained of the means for turning the bar: it is possible that a water-wheel was placed in the furnace tail-race, but Biringuccio (1540: 1958 edn: 113) shows a tread-wheel as an alternative.

A boring bar of the type illustrated by Biringuccio was found during ploughing

Fig. 7.15 Stream furnace, Chiddingly, Sussex: cutting head, for reaming the bores of guns. Two of the detachable cutters are visible (David Butler).

near Stream furnace, Chiddingly, and is now to be seen at Anne of Cleves House, Lewes (Butler and Tebbutt 1975). This fine example is 3.5m in length, and retained three out of the original four cutters (fig. 7.15). The cutters were detachable, held in position with iron shims, and had steel edges skilfully forge-welded to the wrought iron of the blades (Trent and Smart 1984). The bar illustrates the difficulties of boring with the kind of equipment used before the mid-eighteenth century: the unsupported length was so great that the head would follow irregularities in the casting.

THE SECONDARY WROUGHT-IRON AND STEEL TRADES

Over the last 20 years the methods of the medieval and post-medieval smith have become better understood through metallographic examination of excavated articles. A number of assemblages of iron objects have been recovered, and we now have an overview of objects in common use. However, in relatively few cases have comprehensive laboratory examinations been possible, and the coverage deserves to be enlarged.

It needs stressing that a large proportion of the output of sixteenth to eighteenth-century blast furnaces was refined at the forge, and found its way to the secondary trades in the form of wrought-iron bar, far outweighing the amount which was cast direct into artefacts. At a conservative estimate 10,000–12,000 tons of bar left English fineries annually in the early part of the seventeenth century, and by 1700 the quantity on the market had at least doubled, due in part to the increasing amounts of imported iron coming from Sweden and elsewhere.

Water power in the secondary trades

The secondary processes saw an increase in mechanization. In the sixteenth century the small-section bars and rods used by smiths and nailers had either been produced at the finery or reduced from larger bar by the smith himself. This was simplified by the introduction of the water-powered slitting mill from the Low Countries, probably at the end of the sixteenth century, although more research is needed into the timing and details of this development. By the second half of the seventeenth century slitting mills were becoming common in the Midlands and the north: the only example so far excavated is at Lymm, Cheshire (fig. 7.16: *PMA* 1976: 174–5), where a mill comparable in size to those documented in eighteenth-century Sheffield was recorded. The Lymm mill worked in the eighteenth century, at first using two water-wheels, later one, before being converted into a textile mill in 1800.

Wire production was mechanized towards the end of the sixteenth century, the technology being brought from Germany under the monopoly obtained by the projectors of the Mineral and Battery Works. Their objective had been to develop the production of brass wire for the wool-cards used in the textile industry, but the failure to make satisfactory brass in England led to concentration on the production of iron wire, using the ductile wrought irons produced from ores mined in Monmouthshire. The location of the early wire works in the Tintern area has been established by Paar and Tucker (1975; 1977; Tucker 1978): no excavations have taken place on wire mills in this or any other district.

Water power was also developed for blade forging. The tilt-hammer had been used in the Middle Ages in bloomeries and subsequently in finery forges, but for these the mechanisms were relatively heavy and slow-operating. In the secondary trades the makers of scythes and the other larger iron tools used hammers which were cam-operated by water wheels on traditional principles, but were lighter and faster acting. For the details of hammers in scythe forges we rely on eighteenth-century illustrations and on survivors from the eighteenth and nineteenth centuries, notably at Sticklepath, Devon, and Abbeydale, Sheffield. No such forges of sixteenth or seventeenth-century date survive or have been excavated, and it is not known how much technical development went on at this time; in particular when the faster-acting light tilt-hammers began to be driven through trains of gears, as seen at Abbeydale. The hammers illustrated by Agricola (1950 edn: 422, 425), which appear to be lightly built, are not geared; those illustrated in a representation of a sixteenth-century mill for making sheet are not sufficiently precisely drawn (Donald 1961). Nor is it certain whether anvils were mounted on massive timber blocks as in the finery forges. The impression at Abbeydale is that some form of timber block is used, but no excavation has taken place to verify its depth. Surviving documents show that tilt-forges were being built in increasing numbers on the Sheffield streams after 1750, but there are no detailed inventories. The picture is much the same in Worcestershire, and in both areas construction accelerated during the eighteenth century as the market grew for high-quality agricultural equipment, notably scythes.

Water-driven blade-grinding wheels became more numerous, and written sources suggest that construction was frequent by the end of the sixteenth century. This development is best known in the Sheffield area, where rents for cutlers' wheels appear in estate stewards' accounts. It is possible to follow expansion

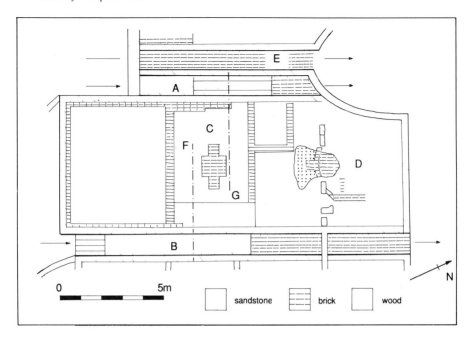

Fig. 7.16 Lymm, Cheshire: slitting mill. The races (A and B) contained wheels to drive rolls (centre lines F and G); C is the base of the mill, D the position of the reheating furnace, E is a by-pass (Barry Johnson).

through the seventeenth and eighteenth centuries, noting the particular increase in construction in the 50 years after about 1690, when numerous small grinding wheels filled the available stretches of the Don and its four tributaries (fig. 6.13). Some were conversions from other uses, others, in turn, later being converted to corn mills, paper mills and forges. A good deal is known about their construction and equipment, from eighteenth and nineteenth-century surveyors' plans which confirm that the surviving example, Shepherd Wheel, on the Porter (fig. 7.17), is typical in layout and construction. This wheel is recorded from the middle of the sixteenth century, and although it has been enlarged, the layout appears not to have radically changed. The essential below-ground features are the secondary pit for the main gear, placed in a similar manner to a pit wheel in a corn mill, and the troughs in which the grindstones ran. These cutler-wheel sites can also be identified by the scatter of discarded grindstones, distinguishable from millstones by the absence of dressing on the faces, and often by the use of sandstone rather than grit.

The hand trades

The physical evidence for secondary iron manufacture has not survived in a balanced way. Documentary sources show that water-powered establishments accommodated only a proportion of these trades, and that many were carried on in buildings without specialized features. Nevertheless, in certain districts, particularly where agriculture and metalworking provided dual sources of employment,

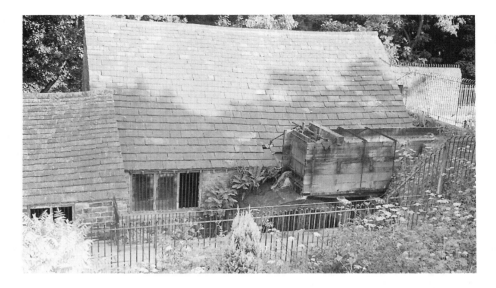

Fig. 7.17   Sheffield: Shepherd Wheel, a cutler wheel for blade grinding, first recorded in 1566. The iron water-wheel is of nineteenth-century design.

there survive buildings which were formerly used as smithies and workshops. Examples have been found in south Staffordshire, in areas overtaken by the Black Country conurbation: these date from the eighteenth century, but prolong a tradition developing 200 years earlier. In and around the Yorkshire Don valley there are several survivors: buildings can be found in and around villages west of Sheffield (fig. 7.18) which were known for the manufacture of knives and razors (Hey 1972); Grenoside, a village expanding into woodland in the eighteenth century, contains amongst its farms and house plots the largest surviving concentration of smithy buildings in the district; Ecclesfield, once famous for a variety of metal trades, now has one surviving file-workers' workshop, the remnant of numerous buildings demolished over the past 40 years (Hey 1968). Where buildings have been demolished, hand working of iron frequently defies archaeological identification. Cinders from forges had a value as road make-up or hardcore and were easily removed. Even when remaining in situ they are insufficiently distinctive to indicate the process whereby they were created. Nevertheless some examples have been found of smithy hearths and characteristic waste, as within the finery forge at Chingley and in the excavations at Oyster Street, Portsmouth (Fox and Barton 1986). The latter example underlines the problem of identification: it is thought to have been the 'Kings Forge' of the first half of the sixteenth century, and as such would be used for a wide variety of blacksmithing and metal-forming tasks, none of which could be distinguished on the ground.

Artefacts of iron and steel

A wide range of objects were made from wrought iron, and many included a proportion of steel. As with other groups of artefacts, variety and sophistication

Fig. 7.18 Dungworth, Yorkshire: smallholder's house with attached forge, used in the eighteenth century for blade making.

increased over the post-medieval period, and the specialization of metalworking communities is reflected in the more frequent occurrence of goods of high quality both in excavated assemblages and in inventories. Ironwork used in stone and timber buildings is well represented in the report on Chingley Forge, Kent, where in an early-eighteenth-century context there was a useful group, partly structural, partly scrap brought for reworking at the hand forges which were found in the finery building (fig. 7.19). Nails were present in a variety of forms dependent on function; beam stirrups, large staples, wall hooks, hinge pivots, cotter pins, eyed bars, were typical products of smiths using bar and rod of the lower qualities of wrought iron, high in phosphorus but quite adequate for use in construction and in lightly stressed machinery. All relied on the properties of wrought iron, whose slag-inclusions gave corrosion resistance and strength. A particularly important group here were the iron wedges. These are often mistaken for cold chisels, but the absence of steel on the tip indicates that they would be used for fastening joints in machinery or securing water-wheels to their axles.

The more sophisticated side of the secondary metal industry developed on the basis of medieval technologies, in which blades were made from steel and wrought iron, forge-welded together. From excavated assemblages it has been possible for sufficient metallographic examination to be carried out to show how the bladesmith worked. Tylecote (1975: 81) has shown diagramatically the various ways in which iron and steel could be forged to produce blades for knives, scissors and tools. At the top of the quality range very thin rods of iron and steel were piled alternately and forged until a virtually homogenous blade resulted. A variant was to place a bar of steel between two bars of wrought iron, and to forge a blade with a long life: the steel core would always provide an edge, despite repeated resharpening, and the technique was thus particularly suitable for scythes and sickles, which also needed the resilience offered by the wrought iron in the blade. Many blades, however, incorporated much smaller proportions of steel, in the

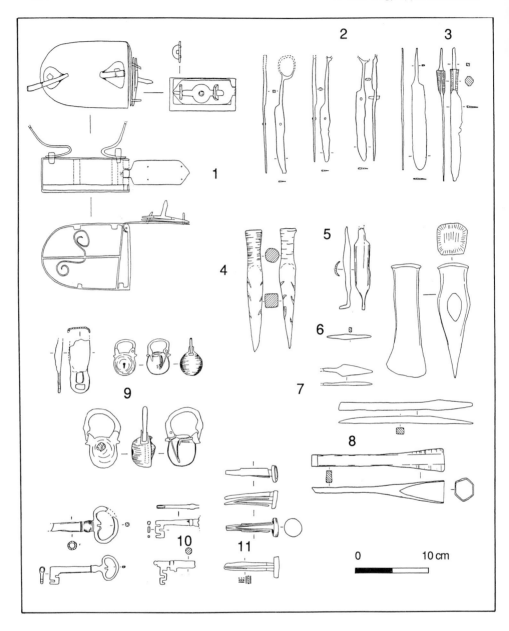

Fig. 7.19   Iron objects from Chingley Forge, Kent; a typical post-medieval assemblage from a scrap depot probably of seventeenth-century date. (1) flat iron; (2) scissors; (3) knives; (4) mason's wedge; (5) possible draw knife; (6) awl; (7) auger bit; (8) axe and chisels; (9) padlocks; (10) keys; (11) padlock bolts.

form of strips welded along the cutting edge. With these there was a limit to the number of times the blade could be resharpened, before the hard steel edge wore away. Nevertheless, with some tools there were practical advantages, apart from economy in costly steel. The chisel, for example, benefited from the strength of the wrought-iron bolster, which might be thought to compensate for the short life of the welded steel edge.

The Basing House and Chingley Forge assemblages, mostly of seventeenth-century material, give a good idea of the changes taking place in the blade industries at this time (Moorhouse 1971; Tylecote, in Crossley 1975b, 90–5). Table blades developed in characteristic ways (Goodall, in Drewett 1975): makers less frequently inlaid their marks as production increased; knives were more frequently made with bolsters, a development which had the practical advantage of allowing a wrought-iron tang and a steel blade to be joined at the thickest part of the knife. The Chingley blades include examples both of steel sandwiched between wrought iron and of the piled type which became more common by the end of the seventeenth century. It is interesting to see the number of scissors present at Chingley: these were a medieval development which became much more common by the middle of the seventeenth century. Most are of wrought iron with steeled edges, for wrought iron had the advantage of being easily forged to form a handle. It will be instructive to compare these ranges of items with the deposit, probably of scrap, excavated at Hays Wharf, Tooley Street, London, in a context dating from the first half of the sixteenth century (*PMA* 1986: 340).

Finds such as these illustrate not only the gains in quality but also the widening use of iron in the household and the workshop. Among simple household items the box iron is increasingly seen, with provision for placing hot charcoal inside. This was a time when iron appears in common locks, in addition to the more elaborate forms, although at Chingley it was found that keys and most lock parts were of ordinary wrought iron rather than steel, which was confined to springs. Firearms were important in extending precision craftsmanship from the domain of the clock and watchmaker. In firearms, swords and riding equipment, notably spurs, the need for decoration gave the skilled smith more full-time work, explaining the emergence in this period of the specialist towns and villages of the west Midlands (Rowlands 1975).

Chapter 8

Non-ferrous metals

Mining and smelting

The archaeological record of non-ferrous metal extraction is uneven both between metals and over different parts of the country. We can contrast the relatively well researched lead industry of the Derbyshire Peak with other important but less thoroughly explored or published production areas, or our ignorance of the field indications of copper smelting with the recent expansion of fieldwork in the tin-bearing districts of the south-west.

THE LEAD INDUSTRY

The lead deposits most intensively exploited in the sixteenth and seventeenth centuries were those of the Pennines and the Mendips, with some production in the Lake District, as well as in Devon and Cornwall as a mineral of importance secondary to tin. From the end of the seventeenth century production grew in the lead fields of Wanlockhead in south-west Scotland and in north and central Wales.

Lead mining

The archaeology of mining is beset by the difficulty of dating surface evidence. This problem applies to metalliferous ores over many parts of Britain, where the form of mineralization results in small areas of outcrop which have been reworked as techniques and market circumstances have changed. This is particularly clear in the Pennines, where the veins in the limestone in which minerals are concentrated are often vertical fissures in the rock: early shallow workings could be obliterated by the more substantial operations required for later mining at greater depths. This contrasts with coal mining, where, with dipping seams, some traces of early outcrop extraction were often left intact when later deep mines were sunk to the concealed coal. Difficulties of interpretation occur in most of the lead-mining areas, particularly because of the chronic instability of the lead trade in the eighteenth and nineteenth centuries: at times, boom conditions which favoured large-scale investment in structures such as engine houses and other permanent surface buildings have given way to conditions when only small-scale part-time mining has been worthwhile, using methods indistinguishable from those of earlier work. A form of extraction which is particularly difficult to date by archaeological means is 'hushing', the use of diverted streams of water to erode rock and expose ore. The method was much used in the northern Pennines, and the sites can leave spectacular remains, as in Swaledale, where the practice is thought to have died out in the eighteenth century.

There are parts of Derbyshire where the earlier phases of post-medieval mining can be distinguished: examples of early open working can be seen in the northern part of the ore field, on Longstone Moor (fig. 8.1), to the west of Hucklow and Bradwell, and in certain parts of the Sheldon, Flagg and Monyash area, and can be distinguished from the later and more concentrated deep workings, some of which are marked by remains of engine houses for steam-driven pumps and winders. The most prominent of the open workings comprise trenches up to 7m deep, visible for long distances and particularly striking from the air. Tideslow Rake is one, now weathered and grassed over, while Dirtlow Rake retains a sharp profile in a harder limestone, with visible pick-marking on the vertical sides. Small shafts can be found within these open workings, as well as galleries taken out to the sides where the main rake is intersected by others. Secondly, there are shaft mines whose small scale suggests but does not prove early working. Typically the shafts are no more than 1m in diameter, lined with dry-stone (ginging) through the topsoil to the rock, and equipped with steps (stemples), which at the top of the shaft are formed of stones projecting from the ginging. Alongside the shaft, stone-packed post-holes can sometimes be found for windlass structures. Close by the shaft, and sometimes sheltering it, there was often a small building, the coe, in which ore and tools were

Fig. 8.1 Longstone Moor, Derbyshire: lead rakes indicated by open-cast and shaft working. A horse ring similar to the example in fig. 6.1 can be seen, centre right (D.N. Riley).

stored. There are no complete surviving coes, but Bonsall Moor is an area where footings can be seen. Few shafts survive intact: in most cases the ginging has collapsed and the shaft top has fallen in, leaving a depression whose bottom hides a void covered by an often thin and unstable layer of debris.

Ore preparation

The lead industry provides good examples of equipment for ore preparation which were common to all the non-ferrous metal industries until late in the nineteenth century. There is in additon a particularly good sixteenth-century Continental source, Agricola's *De Re Metallica* (1556), illustrating methods which appear to correspond with some of those used in Britain.

Ore preparation should be divided into two stages, crushing and washing. With lead, as with other minerals, the size of ore was of importance at the smelter. As shown in the next section, the lead industry developed smelters which could accept smaller ore sizes, but preparation still remained important. Medieval lead workers appear to have broken ore by hand hammering. At an unknown date the use of the horse ring or the stamp mill was developed: in the first, a rotating stone mounted on a centrally pivoted radial arm crushed ore on a circular track. There are a number of mining sites in the Peak where such circles can be seen, but only at Odin Mine, Castleton, does the surface of a ring remain, in this case formed of cast-iron segments of early-nineteenth-century origin. Water-powered drop-stamp mills were not used in the Peak, but there were examples in the northern Pennines, of which the example under restoration at Killhope represents a nineteenth-century development of the methods illustrated by Agricola.

The washing of ore took one of two forms of flotation, using buddles. The method illustrated by Agricola employed a stream of water flowing through rectangular chambers (buddles) which were built on a descending slope, at the top of which the ore was tipped. The heavier particles would drop to the floor first, with the lighter and less pure material falling at the lower end of the buddle. This system was common in the Peak, and a good example of a buddle has been preserved on Bonsall Moor. Circular buddles, in which a horse ring was constructed outside a tank, are less common in the lead industry, by comparison, for example, with the tin-mining area of south Dartmoor. This was another use of a horse-drawn radial shaft, in this case with a paddle suspended in a circular water-filled tank, agitating the ore tipped at the centre of the buddle, on whose outward sloping floor the grading took place.

Lead smelting

From 1500 to the end of the eighteenth century, the lead industry went through two changes in smelting methods, from the bole to the ore hearth in the sixteenth century and from the ore hearth to the cupola, largely though not entirely in the eighteenth century.

Bole-hearth smelting   The archaeological evidence for the bole is controversial, for there are discrepancies between hearths which have been accepted as boles and contemporary descriptions. The boling process had evolved during the Middle

Ages (Blanchard 1981), and was used in the Mendips and the Pennines. A hearth was built within a stone-walled enclosure, on a site open to consistent winds. Ore of high grade and relatively large size was laid with brushwood over layers of more substantial wood, and as smelting took place the molten lead ran into a stone pig-mould at the side of the hearth. The bole had a poor rate of extraction, and by the sixteenth century some smelters were operating a two-stage process, wherein the bole slags were resmelted using charcoal, in a bellows-blown 'blackwork oven'. The documentary sources for Derbyshire show that by the 1530s the bole had grown in size from 1–2m up to 5m across (fig. 8.2).

The published evidence for remains of boles in the Pennine area comprises the excavation of a smelting hearth built into a Bronze Age cairn on Beeley Moor (Radley 1969), and the discovery by Raistrick (1927) of a hearth on Grassington Moor. In both cases the hearths were small, not corresponding with the sixteenth-century Derbyshire descriptions. What is not yet certain is whether these examples date from an earlier period, whether the small bole in fact remained in use into the sixteenth century, or whether they are bases of blackwork ovens rather than boles. It is unfortunate that there are no published examples from Mendip, for it will be seen later that there is evidence of technological innovation in Somerset whose origins should be explored.

Fieldwalking has resulted in the location of concentrations of boles in the Pennines, but the remains are sparse. The enclosure walls were loosely built, and the stone has disintegrated after exposure to heat and frost. Slags have been dispersed and much that was not resmelted in the blackwork ovens was collected by later smelters seeking to recover the remaining lead. Contamination patterns have provided the best guide to bole location: strips of ground with poor or lead-tolerant vegetation can be found in the lee of ridges where boles were built, and in Derbyshire soil sampling in such areas has also indicated sites whose slags are otherwise difficult to find. It has been suggested as a result of these surveys that the bole and blackwork sites can be distinguished, and on Totley Moor this has been tested on a site where the two forms of slag can be seen. But even when found, the dating of these sites is rarely possible: a particular difficulty is the relatively low temperatures needed for lead smelting (below 800°C), which leave little clay beneath the hearth sufficiently burnt to provide material for archaeomagnetic dating.

The ore hearth   During the sixteenth century the Mendip and Pennine smelters abandoned the use of the bole and adopted bellows-blown hearths. In Derbyshire these used kiln-dried wood (white-coal) as a fuel, but in the northern Pennines peat was also used. In the past there has been some confusion about the change from bole to ore hearth, largely resolved by recent documentary research (Kiernan 1988). In some areas field surveys have indicated the places where the new smelters were built, but, as no excavations have taken place, the details of the early ore-hearths are obscure and reliance must still be placed on eighteenth-century eye-witness accounts (E. Tylecote 1970).

The first stage in the change took place in the Mendips, where bellows-operated smelting hearths appear to have been in use by the middle of the sixteenth century. This is an inference drawn from the introduction of the ore hearth into Derbyshire in the 1560s by smelters from Mendip. The hearths are distinct from the medieval blackwork oven in their use of wood fuel rather than charcoal, but the essentials of

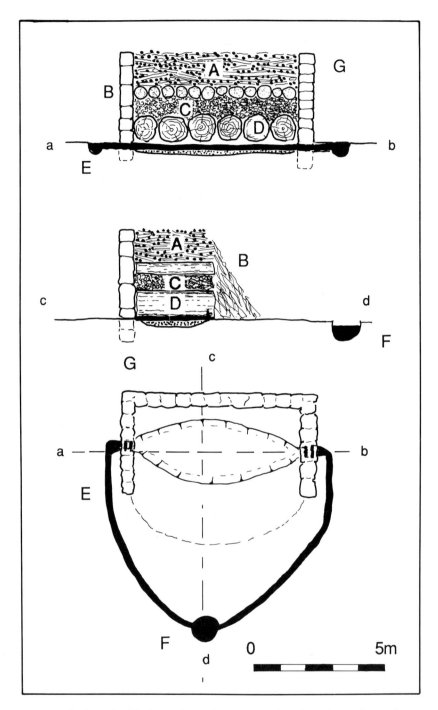

Fig. 8.2 Derbyshire lead-bole, estimated reconstruction based on sixteenth-century descriptions. In the stone enclosure (G) were placed wood (shankerds B and blocks D), with blackwork (part-smelted ore C), beneath ore and small wood (A). The smelted lead flowed by channels (E) to a mould (F) (David Kiernan).

the equipment seem similar, and the possibility is worth pursuing that one developed from the other. When introduced into Derbyshire the bellows were operated by foot, hence the term 'foot-blast'. In this they resembled the blackwork ovens.

During the last quarter of the sixteenth century the use of the ore hearth became universal in Derbyshire, but the speed of adoption further north is not yet known. It became common for bellows to be operated by water power, and the industry became concentrated in valleys where woodlands could be coppiced. This development has been confused with an attempt to introduce the Continental method of smelting, using a small water-powered blast furnace. A furnace of this type was first operated in England by Burchard Cranich at Duffield, Derbyshire in 1550. His work produced lead of unsaleable quality, but a further attempt was made by William Humphrey on the river Sheaf near Sheffield in 1567, under the protection of patents awarded to the Mineral and Battery Works, in which Humphrey was heavily involved. His process was less successful than the ore hearths to which several Derbyshire landowners were changing at this time. Nevertheless, Humphrey, whose patent embraced new methods of smelting, took action against the ore-hearth owners for infringement, the case providing an important source of information for the state of the industry and, in particular, identifying individuals involved, and assisting in the location of ore-hearth smelting-mills.

The advantages of the ore hearth were soon established. Most significant was the ability to use poorer and smaller ores, and great effort went into sifting material previously rejected at mines and boles. The location of the new smelters reduced the cost of transport, both of ore and of wood, and the use of water power allowed year-round rather than seasonal operation. By the seventeenth century the smelters had revived the tradition of two-stage working, as with blackwork ovens on bole sites. Now they built slag hearths, to smelt ore-hearth slag, extracting much of the remaining lead. There are detailed differences between the hearths (Tylecote 1976: 134–5), but the general principle of using water power to operate the bellows was similar, even though slag hearths were usually fuelled by charcoal rather than white-coal.

In Derbyshire about 40 ore-hearth sites have been located , but there remain references to smelters whose whereabouts have not been satisfactorily established. On the ground few structures remain, earthworks are on a small scale and many ponds, dams and watercourses have been obliterated by later changes in land use. The best-preserved earthworks are in woodland, particularly in the valleys descending from the gritstone ridge to the west of Chesterfield. As so few substantial earthworks remain, fieldwork has involved slag surveys and the sampling of stream silts for high lead values. The paucity of slags at some sites is due to collection in the eighteenth and nineteenth centuries for resmelting in the more efficient slag hearths of the period. Ore-hearth slag is reasonably simple to recognize, surfaces showing where the viscous semi-liquid has flowed before cooling, and the fractures have a somewhat crystalline appearance. The recognition of waste from the secondary slag hearths of the early period is still difficult, in contrast to nineteenth-century slag-hearth material which has a distinctive light grey appearance. A key indication of the Derbyshire smelting sites is the presence of white-coal kilns in nearby woodland; on occasion they can be found immediately adjacent to the smelt mill.

Other lead-producing regions also provide evidence of ore-hearth smelting. There are fine examples in the Yorkshire Dales, but here sixteenth to eighteenth-century activity is obscured by the survival of the ore hearth through the nineteenth century, when it incorporated modifications such as the condensing flues developed elsewhere for cupola smelting. Typical of this continuity are the sites visible near Greenhow, Nidderdale, Grassington, Wharfdale, and Grinton, Old Gang and Surrender, in Swaledale and Arkengathdale (Clough 1980). Further north, in the west of County Durham, towards Alston Moor, remains of the ore-hearth phase of the industry are less clear, and much work remains to be done to record sites using the methods known from the descriptions made by James Mulcaster (E. Tylecote 1970). In the Lake District lead was never extracted on a scale comparable with the Pennines, but research is under way in the Ullswater area. Although mining sites with signs of ore preparation can be seen to the south and west of the lake, there is only one clear example of an ore-hearth smelter (fig. 8.3). In the Mendips, published survey material is sparse. As already indicated, the early history of the ore hearth in Mendip is of great potential interest, with the development of methods which spread to Derbyshire. The later smelters developed in much the same way as elsewhere, although diminishing ore supplies reduced the incentive for innovation. Nevertheless there are sites around Charterhouse-on-Mendip with flues and chimneys from nineteenth-century ore hearths or cupolas.

Of the late starters in lead production, little is known about smelting in Wales before the nineteenth century, apart from in Flintshire, where the cupola was developed before 1700. In Scotland, the first smelter was built at Wanlockhead in 1682 (Downs Rose and Harvey 1979): this was definitely an ore hearth, for records survive of the supply of parts and the building of the smelt mill. Although the position of this smelter is uncertain, its successor, built by the London Lead Company in 1710, has been located, as has the headrace for the blowing house. A good deal of written detail has survived for this district, for the silver content of the ore was sufficient to make cupellation worth while.

The cupola   In the second half of the seventeenth century the widespread interest in the development of more efficient industrial furnaces began to affect methods of lead smelting. The reverberatory coal-fired furnace, the cupola, has parallels in glass and steel production: the common feature was the placing of the materials which were to be heated or melted in a chamber apart from the coal fire; the heat from the latter was drawn into the melting chamber and was reflected from a firebrick roof. The advantage was not only of fuel economy, but also the isolation of the fuel, reducing contamination by sulphur. The first application in the lead industry came about 1670, in Flintshire, but the innovation was slow to spread. It reached Derbyshire about 1730, where it was at first found difficult to operate. However, from the middle of the eighteenth century adoption was rapid, and it is from this period that numerous cupola sites survive (Willies 1969). At this time the growing demand for Peak District lead was overtaking the capacity of the ore hearths, and agricultural pressure on woodlands was preventing expansion of coppices to provide extra fuel. A further advantage was that the cupola, like the ore hearth before it, was able to smelt lower-grade ore than its predecessor.

Cupola smelting involved a change of siting, with a considerable effect on the landscape. The cupola, reliant on natural draught induced by its flues, was itself independent of water supply, and so the smelters could migrate to the high

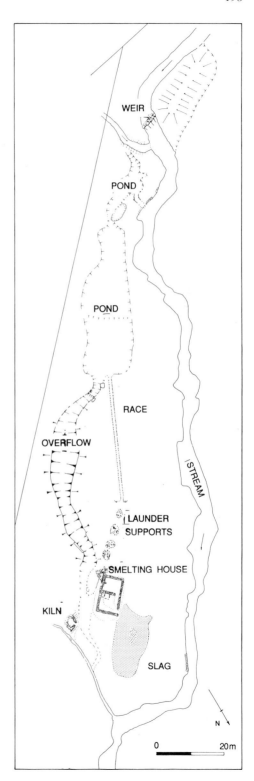

Fig. 8.3 Hoggett Gill, Cumbria: ore-hearth lead-smelting site, probably late seventeenth or early eighteenth century (see also fig. 1.8).

moorlands, where contamination from fume aroused less opposition. The change is readily apparent, with ore-hearth sites abandoned and now hard to locate, whereas the cupolas, working well into the nineteenth century on ground which has since been little used, can be found as earthwork sites, some with structural fragments. Towards the end of the eighteenth century cupola flue systems became more elaborate, with trench-built horizontal passages of considerable length and complexity, leading from the furnace to a chimney. These incorporated condensing chambers, where residues could be collected. It was normal for the passages to be built with stone and occasionally brick side walls, and floors and roofs of stone slabs. In most cases the stone, particularly the roofing slabs, has been robbed, leaving overgrown trenches. A fine complex dating from the early nineteenth century, complete with its terminal chimney, can be seen at Stone Edge, near Chesterfield, while of the earlier, simpler earthwork sites, Calow Field, Hathersage, is a good example (fig. 1.13). This kind of flue system was used elsewhere in Britain, and in some cases it was adapted to the ore hearth, which survived in areas where coal was inaccessible.

The migration to high ground eventually produced problems as well as advantages. Towards the end of the eighteenth century there was a new interest in the resmelting of slags, both from the cupolas and from earlier processes. The moorland siting of many cupolas was ill suited to the construction of water-powered slag hearths, and in Derbyshire attempts were made to build reservoirs drawing on small upland streams and springs. Both Stone Edge and Calow demonstrate the problems, with small dams and ponds created at unusually high levels.

THE TIN INDUSTRY

The archaeological evidence for tin production in Devon and Cornwall suffers even more than in the case of lead from the concealment or destruction of pre-eighteenth-century workings by later developments. The industry continued to work on some scale in west Cornwall into the present century, and thus there is some imbalance between the archaeology of the west Cornwall and the Devon and east Cornwall ore fields. The latter never developed on the same scale as the far west, so it is on the fringes of Dartmoor and Bodmin Moor that more is to be seen of the early industry.

Mining and ore preparation

There has been an increase in interest in the remains of early ore extraction in recent years over both counties, but much remains to be done, particularly in Cornwall, to identify pre-nineteenth-century mining. Tin extraction can be broadly divided between three methods: streaming was carried out where water has cut through mineral-bearing lodes, and working of this kind, in river-bed silts, leaves little physical sign. Mining on the lode itself, as in the lead fields, is visible in the form of linear open-cast workings, and these can be seen in a striking state of preservation on the southern edge of Dartmoor to the north-west of Ashburton, and on Bodmin Moor. Finally, in west Cornwall the deposits are in general deeper, and more recent operations, with engine houses and spoil generated by deep mining, have tended to obliterate anything earlier than the eighteenth century. Pre-mechanized mining certainly took place in central and west Cornwall; the sixteenth-century records of the Godolfins make this quite clear, and it would be wrong to think of extraction in this area at the end of the Middle Ages as being entirely or largely from streaming. Over the whole region, disentangling the surface remains of mining is of some priority among projects in landscape archaeology.

As in the case of other minerals, the physical remains of tin mining are to be linked with those of the preparation of ore. Pre-nineteenth-century ore-preparation sites are as yet less easily recognized in Cornwall than on Dartmoor, where there are important examples. Outstanding is the complex on the slopes of Hemerdon Moor, where a series of parallel channels can be traced, through which water was passed to separate tin ore in a series of buddles. Later circular buddles, probably dating from early in the nineteenth century, can be found further east at Challacombe Down. The relationship between the flotation stage and smelting is not altogether clear: at Hemerdon surface evidence of smelting has not yet been found, and there is a possibility that the washed and separated ore was transported for smelting. Preparation also involved stamping, and for this the recent field survey at Retallack, Cornwall, is of outstanding interest (Gerrard 1985). Here two stamping mills and four crazing mills have been located, in association with a blowing-house site considered to relate to early-sixteenth-century references (fig. 8.4). The excavation at Colliford (Austin, Gerrard and Greeves 1989) has given a detailed picture of the layout of watercourses to power a stamp mill and supply associated buddles (fig. 8.5).

Smelting

The tin industry is remarkable for its early adoption of water power for smelting, for the blowing house was well established by the end of the Middle Ages. The archaeological evidence is sparse, but an example was located in the Retallack survey. The known Dartmoor examples have been summarized by Greeves (1981), reassessing Handsford Worth's pioneer fieldwork: the plot of stamp mills, blowing houses and tinners' buildings demonstrates the importance of the industry for the south Devon economy.

The water-powered blowing house continued in use into the nineteenth century, but was superseded by reverberatory furnaces comparable with the lead-smelting cupolas. These appear in Cornwall at least by the early years of the eighteenth century, and the two methods coexisted for a period which is not easy to determine. The only example of a smelter in the west of Cornwall which has been examined in any detail is at Calenick (Tylecote 1980). This reverberatory furnace is documented from 1702, and operated until the end of the nineteenth century. There are suggestions from early-nineteenth-century documents that a blowing house was also in use: water power was certainly available, for a wheel-pit has been located. The wheel would be used for stamping ore, but might also have given sufficient power for bellows.

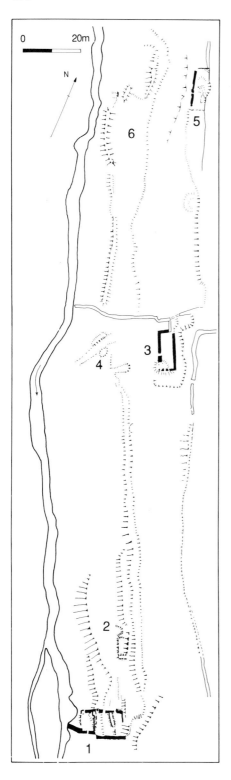

0   20m

N

6

5

3

4

2

1

Fig. 8.4   Retallack, Cornwall: sixteenth-
century tin mills. (1–2) crazing mills;
(3) stamping and crazing mill; (4) buddles;
(5) blowing house, possibly the smelting
house referred to in 1506; (6) reservoir
(Sandy Gerrard).

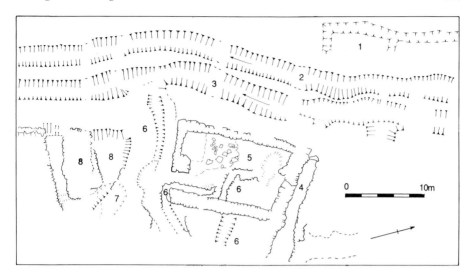

Fig. 8.5   Colliford, Cornwall: tin-stamp mill. (1) early leat to wheel; (2) leat; (3) leat; (4) wheel-pit; (5) stamp mill; (6) channels; (7) early buddle; (8) later buddles (after Austin, Gerrard and Greaves).

COPPER

To understand the paucity of physical evidence for the mining and smelting of copper in Britain it is helpful to be aware of political overtones to its extraction in the sixteenth and seventeenth centuries. The first significant attempt was made in the years following 1567, by the Company of the Mines Royal. This monopoly organization was an outcome of concern over the cost of strategic imports, and powers were given to the projectors to locate and extract metals, including copper. The company employed German workers in the Coniston area over the last decades of the sixteenth century, but was hindered by disputes over what constituted 'royal' minerals, to which the Crown had right of pre-emption. The problem arose from the presence of copper with the undoubted royal metals, gold and silver, and it was only where copper was found on its own or greatly exceeded the precious metals in value that the way to exploitation was clear. Consequently the company pursued a cautious policy, and the position did not alter until 1689, when the Mines Royal Act was repealed, and the way was opened to unfettered extraction. In addition, the demand for copper in Britain was less than had been expected in the 1560s. Significant production of brass had been planned but the efforts of the contemporary monopoly company, the Mineral and Battery Works, to make brass using calamine (zinc) from the Mendips were unsuccessful, and most brass used in England before 1700 was imported.

Sixteenth-century efforts to mine copper took place at the head of the Coniston valley, but are obscured by eighteenth and nineteenth-century mining. It is most likely that working in this period took place to the south-west of the head of the valley, but it is uncertain whether smelting was carried out in the vicinity: the ground has been repeatedly re-used for ore preparation and smelting, and no traces of early work have been recorded. It is more likely that smelting took place in the Newlands area, to the south-west of Keswick, although so far no physical evidence has appeared which can be correlated with the documentary sources. The other region where copper was mined in the sixteenth century was Cornwall, but copper extraction is hard to distinguish from that of tin, with which it was found. No workings specifically for copper are known, nor is it clear whether smelting took place in blowing houses also used for tin.

Few new copper mines were opened before the relaxation of legal restraints at the end of the seventeenth century: an exception was in Staffordshire, where mining took place at Ecton, with a smelting mill at Ellaston, not yet located on the ground (Robey and Porter 1972: 67). From the 1690s there was a major growth in copper production. The Coniston mines were increasingly active over the succeeding century, and the valley presents plentiful visual evidence which it is rewarding to follow on the ground. Of the new areas of exploitation, the Cheshire deposits at Alderley Edge are known to have been mined from 1693, and a smelt mill is mentioned in Over Alderley parish, but has not yet been located (Warrington 1981). In north Wales, there was interest in the Llanberis deposits from the 1730s (Crew 1976), although the presence of silver and lead was a complicating factor. There were no smelt mills in the district, the ore being taken to Flintshire and later to south Wales. The great copper mines of Anglesey were started during the eighteenth century, but their heyday is outside the scope of this book. Revival of interest in copper at the end of the seventeenth century coincides with the development of coal-fired reverberatory furnaces in the lead and tin industries. The copper-smelting works at Redbrook in the Forest of Dean was coal fired, and in the early years of the eighteenth century there was increasing use of coal in furnaces in Bristol, with which the brass industry was associated.

OTHER METALS

Of other minerals mined in Britain during the post-medieval period, zinc, silver and gold have left few traces on the ground, but are to be sought owing to their economic importance and their technological interest. Zinc, in the form of calamine, was found in Somerset in the sixteenth century but at that time proved unsatisfactory for use in brass production. It was not until the early part of the eighteenth century that Somerset zinc became important, closely connected with the development of the Bristol non-ferrous trades, and hence accompanying the smelting of copper in the town. There were early calamine workings on Worle Hill, Weston-super-Mare, but mining in the eighteenth century was concentrated in the Mendips, around Shipham and Rowberrow (Havinden 1981: 221).

The production of gold in any quantity was confined to Wales, but although field survey of the Carmarthenshire mines has been carried out (*PMA* 1967: 120), it is difficult to distinguish traces from different periods, as large-scale mechanized operations never developed. Silver extraction has its own problems: over the medieval and post-medieval periods most silver produced in Britain was not separately mined, but was extracted from argentiferous lead ores, primarily found in the far northern Pennines, in the Alston area, and also in north Devon around Bere Alston. No surface evidence of the cupellation of silver from lead ores has been found in either district. There has however been an important discovery of a probable seventeenth-century silver-mill site beneath the eighteenth-century Dyfi blast furnace near Aberystwyth (Dinn 1988). Waste from cupellation has been found there, and it is suggested that this was the site of the Aberystwyth mint of the Civil War period.

The secondary non-ferrous metal industries

We are dealing here with the various alloys of copper, lead, tin and zinc, which embrace a wide range of artefacts and techniques. Objects made of these metals comprise a considerable proportion of the small finds recorded on excavations, and a good deal of specialized work has been carried out on assemblages of smaller objects; thus the range of material likely to be encountered in post-medieval levels is now well known. What is less clear is the extent of survival of physical evidence for the working of these metals, both in bulk, before they reached the craftsman, and at his workshop.

THE COPPER ALLOYS

Brass

The production of copper-zinc alloys was well established in Germany and in southern Flanders by 1500. The zinc of the Aachen area was used with copper from southern Germany to make brass which was exported to Britain. To reduce this dependence, the Mineral and Battery Company was given a monopoly of brass manufacture in 1567, and in order to produce brass wire and sheet, forges were set up at Tintern, whose location has been determined (Paar and Tucker 1975; 1977; Tucker 1978). The technologies of water-powered wire drawing and 'battery' were brought from the continent by German workers, and were also used for iron wire and plate. In fact, English brass manufacture, from Coniston copper and Somerset calamine (zinc), was not successful, and the Tintern works did not produce non-ferrous wares on any scale, concentrating on iron products.

The rebirth of the English copper industry at the end of the seventeenth century led to the development of brass production in the Bristol area (Day 1973). The works at Baptist Mills were established in 1702, and recent salvage recording located the annealing furnace at what is likely to be the documented site. Rather later in origin is the brass works at Saltford (fig. 8.6), built on the site of a former fulling mill in 1721 (Day 1979, 1988). There survives a works where annealing furnaces continued in use through the nineteenth century, one still being visible in its original form. The wheel-pits for the forges have been located, and an exploratory excavation has shown where the battery hammers and rolling mills were sited. A later example of brass production is the works in the Greenfield valley at Holywell, Flintshire, where water-powered battery mills have been located, which were erected in 1765 (*PMA* 1979: 281–2).

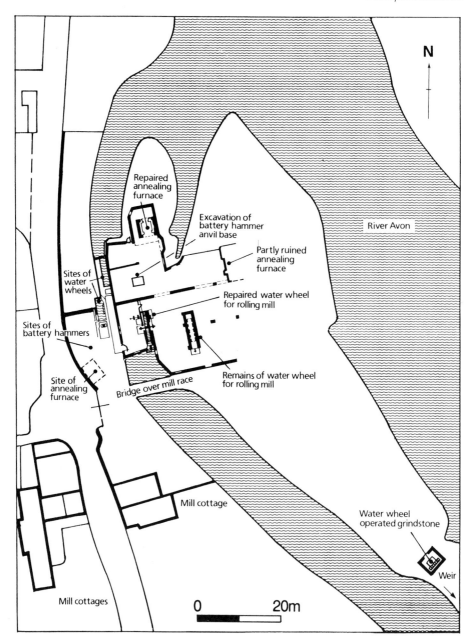

Fig. 8.6 Saltford, Avon: early-eighteenth-century brass mill, incorporating rolling and battery mills and annealing furnaces (Joan Day).

Bell and gun alloys

It had been common practice throughout the Middle Ages to cast bells using alloys largely of copper and tin. The compositions varied, dependent on the scrap carried by the bell founder and the metal of the bell which was to be recast. In many cases bell furnaces were set up in churches (see p. 101). New bells were cast in specialized urban foundries, and the most comprehensive view of such an activity comes from Exeter, in the results of two excavations which span the sixteenth and seventeenth centuries. At Cowick Street excavations have located the foundry operated by the Birdall family from about 1520 to 1625 (*PMA* 1985: 182–4). At first the main products were cauldrons and skillets, but in the 1560s, about the time of the closure of the main medieval bell foundry in the town, the Birdall works began to cast bells. Two furnaces and a bell-casting pit were excavated. The furnaces appear to have operated on a reverberatory principle, with heat reflected from the roof on to the metal, and these are dated from the late sixteenth and early seventeenth centuries. The second foundry to be excavated, at Paul Street (fig. 8.7: *PMA* 1983: 199–201), was started by Thomas Pennington on his arrival from Barnstaple in 1625, and its use follows closure of the Cowick Street foundry. Pennington also had a trade in domestic wares, made at his Paul Street foundry until mid-century, his bells probably being cast at premises outside the North Gate. Later, bells were cast in Paul Street, demonstrated by the presence of casting pits containing bell moulds, next to a reverberatory furnace. These features were accompanied by traces of workshops where domestic vessels were made. This important series of excavations indicates a trade which must have existed in most large towns, but of which the archaeological traces have so far been slight.

One of the most important uses of copper-tin alloys was the production of cast guns, but no archaeological evidence for their manufacture has yet been forthcoming. The casting of ordnance in non-ferrous alloys was contemporary with production in cast iron, beginning late in the Middle Ages. One advantage over iron was the saving in weight: at rather over half that of an equivalent iron piece, the brass gun was more suitable for maritime use, particularly on upper decks of vessels. Hence it became common practice in England for iron guns to be largely limited to shore forts, and brass pieces to be favoured by the navy at sea. On merchant ships the cost of brass guns, up to five times that of iron, meant that the latter were more commonly used. A further advantage of the brass gun was that its quality was predictable, if the composition of the foundry metal or scrap were known. This contrasts with the uncertainties of iron cast direct from the smelting furnace. There was inevitably something of a prestige element also. Brass guns were often extravagantly decorated, with a view to display.

The brass guns used in Britain came either from the continent or from a small number of foundries in England. In the sixteenth century a high proportion had been cast at Tournai, or at least purchased there. Production was developed in London, at the foundry at Moorfields, but no material associated with this gun foundry has been excavated. In the 1630s the royal gun-founder, John Browne, cast guns at a works at Brenchley, Kent. There is sound written evidence for this, not only for the production of ordnance but for carriage of scrap to the foundry (Cleere and Crossley 1985: 192). Fieldwalking and observation of service trenches have produced no characteristic debris. Perhaps the most remarkable source for the methods used by the founders of brass guns covers the work of the Verbruggens,

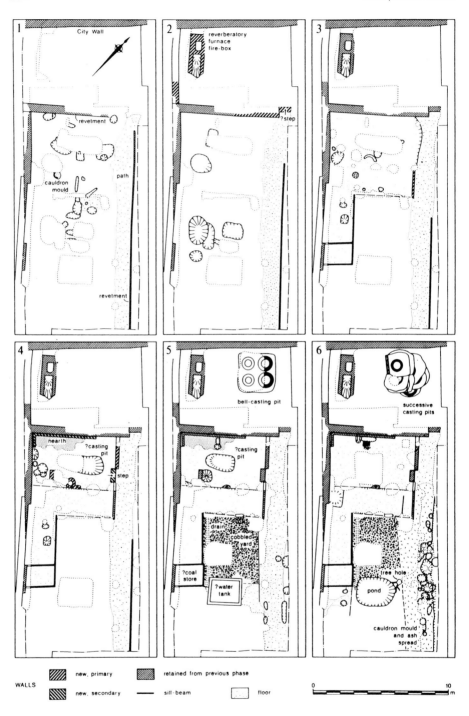

Fig. 8.7 Exeter: Paul Street. The Pennington brass foundry, c.1625–1720: phase plans of excavations, 1982-3 (Exeter Museums).

who operated the royal foundry at Woolwich in the 1770s. Jan Verbruggen produced a fine series of watercolour sketches, of which reproductions have been published (Jackson and de Beer 1973).

THE SMALLER TRADES

The Exeter foundry excavations illustrate the production of a wide variety of utility and decorative objects, present in many towns, and indicated by finds in Worcester (Carver 1980), Peterborough (*PMA* 1977: 98) and Portsmouth, where an early-sixteenth-century deposit in the Oyster Street excavations contained material from copper or brass production, in the form of furnace waste. Many workers in the non-ferrous trades operated in small urban premises and have left little trace, particularly if most of the work involved fabrication rather than casting. Towards the end of the period there was a concentration of manufacture in the Midlands, and in the eighteenth century the button trades of Birmingham (D.P. White 1977) took much of the British and export markets. Of the activities in which fabrication rather than casting took place, the most important were the makers of flat and hollow wares (for examples see Curle 1925–6; J.M. Lewis 1973). These were made in a great variety of alloys, emphasizing the importance of the scrap-metal trades. It is this which has much to do with the scarcity of metal objects on excavations: broken and discarded vessels commanded a ready market, returning to the maker of brass or latten wares to emerge recast or reshaped.

An important trade which developed in the seventeenth century was the manufacture of brass pins. The wire used was not produced in England until the middle of the seventeenth century, but thereafter, following a ban on imports in 1662, development of wire-drawing was rapid, presumably using imported brass until the increase in home production in the 1690s. Brass plates were cut into strips and then drawn, and the wire cut into pin lengths and ground. The heads were made of two turns of wire, and after annealing were fitted to the shank with a small drop stamp. The heads were finished by turning, and the whole process has been examined by Tylecote (1972).

A metal which also had an extensive scrap trade, and is hence rarely found in excavated contexts is pewter. In particular, the archaeological record is unhelpful in gauging the frequency of pewterers, for a workshop would be as easily cleared and the contents sold for scrap as would the stock of a worker in the copper alloys. References to pewterers are relatively common in London, with its well-documented company (Hatcher and Barker 1974) and, not surprisingly, there are also many documented pewterers in Cornwall (Douch 1969), the source of tin and a certain amount of lead. It is not clear what their numbers were in other towns, although a scatter of examples were referred to in attempts by the London pewterers' company to suppress provincial organizations in the trade.

The range of products of urban craftsmen working in non-ferrous metals is now well known, and reference should be made to published excavated assemblages. Those for the Middle Ages, overlapping with the post-medieval, are reviewed in Goodall 1981; examples of post-medieval assemblages are: Whitefriars, Coventry (Woodfield 1981), St Ebbes, Oxford (Goodall, in Hassall 1984) and Moulsham Street, Chelmsford (Goodall, in Cunningham and Drury 1985).

Chapter 9

Mining and quarrying

Early coal and iron-ore mining

In the sixteenth and seventeenth centuries much coal and iron ore could still be extracted at or close to the outcrop of dipping seams, to which later miners had to sink shafts or excavate drifts. Opencast outcrop extraction leaves characteristic earthworks, which can often be followed with the aid of air photographs and geological maps. Such workings are the least likely to have been obscured by modern mining, unless disturbance has taken place to gain access to deeper seams.

The progress of the early miner down the dipping seam can be followed through a series of methods of extraction. Where minerals outcropped in hilly country, it was common to dig drifts into the slope, and follow the seam down the dip. The dating of the entrances to such drifts and the spoil tipped at the exit is rarely possible, unless leases are sufficiently explicit to identify a particular working.

The alternative was to sink shafts to the seam, using bell pits. This technique involved mining to shallow coal, in practice no more than about 10m, and then excavating a bell-section chamber, the diameter depending on rock conditions and the availability of timber for shoring. In many cases no props were used, and chambers were no more than 4–5m in diameter. Bell-pit mining is often thought to be a sign of medieval extraction, but was in fact used for as long as shallow seams remained. (figs. 1.3 and 9.1) An example is the removal of coal and iron ore from under Tankersley Park, Yorkshire, in the second half of the eighteenth century, using bell pits whose remains are still prominent. These show how spoil was dumped around the shafts, forming a characteristic pattern of circular mounds which stretch across country and mark the band of coal which was accessible by this method.

Some of the best archaeological evidence for bell pits has come from examination of modern open-cast extraction. Particularly fine sections have been observed in west Yorkshire, giving characteristic profiles and illustrating how pits were partially backfilled by using the spoil from their neighbours (fig. 9.2). It can be seen that the filling was not consolidated, which explains why rings of spoil remain on the surface, despite the amount of coal, iron ore or clay extracted. Archaeological watching briefs on open-cast operations are demonstrably valuable, but illustrate the vulnerability of areas where bell-pit mining has taken place: the early miners' extraction rates were low, owing to the quantities of coal left unmined between the bell pits. Hence these seams are still attractive, and many have been reworked since

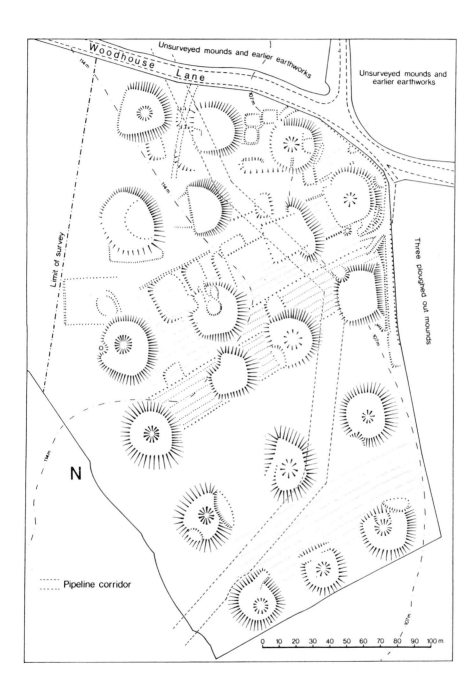

Fig. 9.1   Bentley Grange, Emley, Yorkshire: bell-pit mounds, up-cast from coal or iron-ore mining, overlying earthworks of the medieval grange (see also fig. 1.3) (West Yorkshire Archaeology Service).

Fig. 9.2   Ferry Fryston, Yorkshire: section of bell pit (right centre) in modern open-cast coal working. The up-cast from the pit is visible on the old ground surface (West Yorkshire Archaeology Service).

1945, as the capability of earth-moving equipment has developed. The best surface indications therefore survive where seams are thin and access is poor; recent field surveys in the east Lancashire uplands have recorded survivors in areas subsequently undisturbed.

To reach further down the dip of the coal seam, shafts and galleries were dug, and many of the more prolific mines were using this method in the sixteenth century. There is no sharp distinction from bell-pit to shaft mining of the more elaborate kind, for where conditions were suitable, galleries were taken out from the bell-pit chambers. In the more sophisticated workings, it was common to employ the pillar-and-stall system of mining, stalls being excavated off the galleries or roadways, but leaving large proportions of the seam in place to avoid having to prop extensive areas of roof. Consequently, workings of this kind have also been vulnerable to modern open-cast extraction, and considerable proportions of the sixteenth-eighteenth-century shallow mines on the better-quality seams have been obliterated. Nevertheless, there is more potential for the observation and recording of early mines of this kind than is often expected. The sources are varied but rewarding. In urban areas the dangers of unrecorded shallow workings have become obvious during the construction of large buildings with deep-piled foundations. Consequently in cities where there is a history of mining of seams now within the built-up area, the recording of exposures of workings is a matter of importance. For the mining engineer such knowledge is also vital, for unmapped shallow workings can store large quantities of water, dangerous to current operations. Observation of break-ins to early workings has to be linked to archive evidence: before the second quarter of the eighteenth century there were few estate plans of mineral workings, and the wording of mining leases was often imprecise. Thereafter, the rise of the mining surveyor led to more underground recording as well as the inclusion of shafts and colliery buildings on maps. Although these will not give a picture of sixteenth or seventeenth-century extraction, what they do show is how far coal owners had progressed down dipping seams, and it is between the outcrop and the shaft indicated in an eighteenth-century source that the search for workings of the previous two centuries should be made. A source which should not be overlooked is the abandonment plan, which from 1872 was legally required to be deposited whenever a working was given up. Despite the late date, some plans show mines with much earlier origins or using archaic methods.

There are several published examinations of documentary records for coal mining which illustrate their potential as a basis for fieldwork. Sources for the sixteenth-century Culross colliery on the north shore of the Firth of Forth provide a good impression of how an attractive market for coal for salt boiling fostered investment in shafts and underground workings of considerable complexity; the site of the Moat Pit sunk on the foreshore has been recognized, within an island incorporating a jetty (Bowman 1970). In north Yorkshire the Bransdale and Farndale mines, documented as operating at the beginning of the eighteenth century, have been studied from the documentary sources, and the result is useful for exploration of the physical remains (Whitaker 1969). Similarly, for Ingleton and east Cumberland there are published documentary outlines which cover areas where mining on a small scale has left surface traces never obliterated by modern working (A. Harris 1968; 1974).

Traces of early mining structures at the surface are also elusive. However, contemporary descriptions and maps indicate the features to be sought. They comprise signs of equipment for haulage and for drainage. Small shaft mines relied on windlasses for haulage, and these are described for the eighteenth-century Bransdale mines. A windlass was set up on either side of each shaft, and the corf, the sled or trolley used for underground transport, was hauled up on two ropes. Alternatively a single windlass would be used for hauling baskets or smaller corves. At larger pits horse gins were employed, as described in Sir John Clark's early-eighteenth-century account of mining on Tyneside and in west Cumberland

(Prevost 1965; Duckham 1968). Transport on the surface was commonly by cart, and in many districts was the responsibility of the purchaser buying coal at the pithead. But in the north-east, wagonways with wooden rails were being laid from the 1620s, and became the normal means of carriage from the pits to the staithes (M.J.T. Lewis 1970: 110ff.). Unfortunately most of the area where these original wagonways were laid has been built over, and the earliest of the surviving routes which can be traced for any distance is the early-eighteenth-century plateway crossing Causey Arch, built in 1727 and a fine monument to the sophistication of coal transport of the period.

The drainage problem was crucial to the early miner, and for small-scale working the cost of pumping put an effective limit on depth. An imperfect pumping technology existed, the continental forms of pump being illustrated by Agricola (1950 edn: 173ff.). Lack of precision in the machining and fitting of pump parts, many of which were of wood with leather seals, meant that attempts to power pumps by water-wheels or horse-gins were of limited use, and the preference was for the digging of drainage levels where adjacent valleys would provide an outflow. After 1700 coal-miners in many districts were encountering the limits of drainage, explaining the rapid take-up of the Newcomen atmospheric engine. The Griff engine in Warwickshire was in operation in 1714, and the first engine in Scotland, at Stevenston colliery, dated from 1719. It is worth emphasizing how quickly the atmospheric engine was adopted, although the earliest remains of the characteristic beam-engine-houses date from much later in the century.

Lime burning

A rural industry of importance was the burning of lime. Through the years between the sixteenth and the nineteenth centuries demand grew for lime for soil dressing, for use in building, as well as for tanning, which required quicklime.

In limestone areas many farmers quarried on a small scale and burned their own lime, but where fuel was plentiful and transport available, specialists developed larger quarries and built more permanent kilns. The simple sow or sod kilns have been investigated, and their basic features are now well known. Examples in Northumberland consisted either of hollows in a hill slope or small rings of stone on more level ground. In these were placed limestone packed with wood, and covered with turf: slow burning produced a lime suitable for agricultural use (Jobey 1966). In south Wales a kiln excavated in the Gower shows a similar technique, using a scoop in the hillside to hold limestone and fuel, with a cross-wall in front and a flue at the rear (fig. 9.3.1; Ward 1983). A simple lowland example has been excavated near Peterborough: a kiln probably of seventeenth-century date was indicated by a circle of red ash 3m in diameter with a stokehole linked to the kiln base by a flue (Dakin 1968).

Several permanent lime-kilns have been dated to the sixteenth and seventeenth centuries. At Clementhorpe, York, three kilns were found in a post-dissolution context, two of which were excavated. Each was double-flued with a brick and stone-built central chamber (*PMA* 1977: 99–100). Rural kilns which appear to have been intensively used have been excavated on the site of the pottery kilns at Chilvers Coton, near Nuneaton. These had been substantial structures of clay and brick, the brick vitrified in use, with a limestone lining to one of the stokeholes: one

Fig. 9.3 (1)

Fig. 9.3 (2)

Fig. 9.3 Lime kilns. (1) Sow kiln, Gower, West Glamorgan (A.H.Ward); (2) Kiln in woodland, Troutsdale, Yorkshire; (3) Farm kiln near Hawes, Yorkshire (p. 210).

Fig. 9.3 (3)

kiln was of considerable size, 8m × 3m, and there were over 20 others along the limestone outcrop, implying more than an agricultural by-employment. The dating was not precise, the excavated kilns being cut into fifteenth-century features but not producing dating evidence for the period of use (Mayes and Scott 1984: 38, 69). Location close to lime, or rather chalk, is the explanation for the documented kilns around the city of Norwich, their siting corresponding with entrances to the remarkable chalk-mine tunnels which were in use through the sixteenth and seventeenth centuries (Atkin 1983).

In most areas there evolved designs of permanent kilns, built into hillsides and charged from a high-level approach 6–7 metres above the draw hole at the base. The flare kiln, in which the charge was burnt and then raked out, became common on farms in the eighteenth century, and many survive (fig. 9.3.3). The large draw kilns in which lime was charged, burnt and discharged on a continuous basis were built on estates where limestone was easily quarried, and burning became a substantial industry. In Northumberland many were built at the small ports along the coast, and the industry became particularly important on the Scottish east coast, with examples either mapped or surviving in the Lothians and Fife (Skinner 1975). Most of the nineteenth-century kilns are massive structures, with elaborate internal drainage systems and provision for the dumping of substantial quantities of limestone and coal at the kiln head. The availability of coal was usually the key to their location, either close to mines, as in Fife, to quays, as on the Northumberland coast, or on river or canal wharves in the English Midlands. There is a danger that these survivors may give a misleading impression of the generality of eighteenth-or nineteenth-century kilns. Some of the impermanent sow or sod kilns were still used, and between the extremes some flare kilns appear to have been small and cheaply built. Those found by Harris and Spratt in North Yorkshire show the potential for seeking the less elaborate kilns, assumed to have been built by farmers for their own use (fig. 9.3.2).

Quarries

There is no extensive literature on the archaeology of quarrying, a topic with considerable potential. Quarries were an important aspect of many local economies, providing full or part-time employment, and materials either for building or for more specialized uses. As landscape features, they are apt to be accepted without investigation of their origins: the tendency has been to regard small quarries as undatable, the large quarry as modern, or the documented quarry of the sixteenth-nineteenth centuries as either unrecognizable or swallowed up by its successors. This view can be challenged. Estate maps and in particular late-eighteenth-century enclosure surveys frequently identify quarries, enabling comparison with surviving earthworks.

The best starting point is with quarries which produced specialized artefacts, particularly objects such as grindstones or millstones which were supplied to industries whose technology changed little until the nineteenth or even the twentieth centuries. With these, even late quarry remains are of value as a guide to the methods and products of their forebears. Quarries specializing in millstones have been given a preliminary listing (Tucker 1977), with more detailed attention to examples in Monmouthshire (Tucker 1971) and Derbyshire (Radley 1963–4). In Monmouthshire the Penallt quarries are referred to in an early-nineteenth-century source as producing dovetail burr stones competitive with French imports. But this area also has suitable rock for complete millstones: several found in Somerset and Dorset mills have been suggested as originating at Penallt. Examination of quarries for reject stones is frequently valuable, and Penallt illustrates this by the discovery of cider-mill stones, a specialized application which is of interest now that this farm-based industry is attracting greater attention.

At the Derbyshire gritstone quarries can be found numerous rejects, and the district has been recognized as a source for grain mills over much of England. Radley's pioneering study of these quarries, and those on the adjacent coal measures which produced stones for metal grinding, drew on the results of field surveys and references to the use of the products. Rough-outs of millstones have been noted in numerous quarries along the gritstone ridge to the west of Chesterfield and Sheffield (fig. 9.4), and correlated with references in Farey's study of Derbyshire agriculture in 1811. The trade in millstones can be traced back to the seventeenth century, with stones in use at that time in windmills in the Vale of York. The grindstone trade, from quarries in the coal-measure sandstones, and quite distinct from the millstone grit, is well known if localized, and many examples of the products of these quarries survive. Further work has been done subsequently, not only on the quarries on these outcrops, but also on the use of stones found on the surface and shaped where they lay. Some small quarries specialized in hone stones: examples have been recorded in west Yorkshire, in Gwynedd where slates were used for this purpose from the mid-eighteenth century onwards (Davies

Fig. 9.4   Hathersage, Derbyshire: Millstone quarry with abandoned edge-runner stones. The upstanding stone is 1.6m in diameter.

1976), and in Derbyshire, where quarries on Beeley Moor specialized in scythe stones (Plant 1968).

Of the great building-stone quarries, datable features are often not the quarries themselves, but associated roads, buildings and quays. In Scotland deductions have been made from survivals of this kind, particularly in association with the Argyll slate industry, where survivals can be fitted to eighteenth-and nineteenth-century documentary references. Notable are those of Easdale, where inundation by the sea late in the nineteenth century fossilized the features associated with the 'Great Quarry', the successor to activities documented from the seventeenth century (Tucker 1976). In north Wales, field survey of the Ffestiniog slate quarries has recorded features dating right through from the beginning of the large-scale trade in the 1720s to the run-down of the industry two centuries later (*PMA* 1985: 188). Portland is another area where there is considerable potential: despite the scale of nineteenth-and twentieth-century quarrying, the written evidence for early building-stone extraction, particularly from the period of Wren's use of Portland stone in the 1670s (Bettey 1971), can be correlated with surviving landscape features, notably roads and quays.

Chapter 10

Other industries

Textiles

Prior to the great changes of the eighteenth century, the post-medieval textile industry was characterized by domestic-scale working with mechanization only at the fulling stage. It is one of the ironies of medieval and post-medieval archaeology that despite the great importance of textile production in terms of employment and of wealth creation, the material remains are so few. This is particularly striking when compared with the extractive industries, whose plant and whose impact on the landscape were much more significant in proportion to their contribution to the national economy.

THE RURAL CLOTHING REGIONS

It is in rural areas that the best physical evidence for pre-industrial-revolution textile manufacture survives. It was an essential of many upland economies that income from farming had to be supplemented from industrial pursuits, a pattern which became more common in the sixteenth and seventeenth centuries as population pressed on the available land. Hence, over the Lake counties, much of the Pennines and beyond, textile manufacture was carried on at many farms (RCHM 1985b: 97ff.; 1986a: 152–5), while the towns of these regions developed as finishing and marketing centres.

Most buildings used for hand work in rural textile manufacturing districts show their function only by details, notably but not invariably by the fenestration of weaving rooms in domestic structures, the open layout of top-floor accommodation, and the presence of taking-in doors on the external walls of upper floors. The West Yorkshire survey of domestic buildings has shown how textile working was accommodated in the houses of farmers in Calderdale, some houses having loom shops within the house, others being detached from the domestic accommodation.

From the eighteenth century there survives the house with loom shop which was not part of a farm. Rows of weavers' cottages were built in Pennine villages, many of which have been submerged within subsequent urban development (RCHM 1986c: 1–8). Some were closely associated with the industry of a nearby town: an example is the linen industry of the Barnsley area, where a recent survey has identified surviving houses of outworkers in the village of Dodworth comparable with those of the woollen areas to the north and west. Less well known than the industries of the Pennines are those of the Midland lowlands. It is not always realized how far population growth brought the need to supplement farm incomes to counties such as Nottinghamshire and Leicestershire in the seventeenth and eighteenth centuries. This region became a major producer of hosiery, and knitting stockings was a frequent farmhouse occupation. Physical traces are, however, rare, except in villages where the trade grew to the extent where workshops were erected. Of these, few survive, but the fine preserved example at Ruddington, Nottinghamshire, shows the type in its most developed form.

Excavation of rural buildings used for textile manufacture might be expected to be unpromising. However, a small-scale excavation at Hound Hill, Yorkshire, has indicated the potential (Ashurst 1979). The building which was examined had been used for weaving and dyeing in the seventeenth century, an early phase producing finds relating to weaving, succeeded by the digging of pits for dyeing vats. In the eighteenth century the building was used by a maker of high-grade damasks, rather than the linens which might be expected in the Barnsley area.

URBAN CLOTH TRADES

Despite the predominantly rural location of cloth production between 1500 and 1750, specialist textile towns prospered in East Anglia and the south-west. Elsewhere the traditional town cloth trades dwindled, and urban involvement was confined to providing the middleman with facilities for finishing, sale or forwarding for export, usually through London.

In East Anglia, Norwich, Colchester and Chelmsford had medieval traditions of cloth production, Norwich still making worsteds in the first half of the sixteenth century and the Essex towns having a dwindling trade in dyed broadcloths. The declining Norwich trade was revived by the arrival of immigrants from the Netherlands from the end of the 1560s, whose skills in light and coloured cloths, the 'New Draperies', helped to revive the city's prosperity and laid the foundations for a record of innovation prolonged by French immigrants in the seventeenth century. Excavations in Norwich have shown that the physical growth of the town reflects the wealth and activity of the industry and its supporting trades. The medieval plots were infilled with dwellings and with workshops, wash houses, scouring houses and scalding houses, as well as accommodation for dyers and other finishing trades. The Alms Lane and St Georges Street site is a good example, cottages being rebuilt in flint, open halls ceiled and fireplaces installed, with other buildings being subdivided into single-cell cottages and outbuildings being equipped with dyeing vats (*PMA* 1977: 91). In Heigham Sreet there was infilling on land behind the houses fronting the street (Atkin and Carter 1977). This pattern is confirmed by a notable study of urban probate inventories: these show that by the middle of the seventeenth century Norwich was a city of contrasts: the prosperity brought by production of 'New Draperies' can be set against the overcrowding caused by the numbers needed for hand production of speciality cloths (Priestley *et al.* 1982), as demonstrated by the reconstruction in fig. 2.5.

In Essex and Suffolk, the prosperity brought by immigrants was more dispersed, affecting the small towns of the region as well as the major centres, Chelmsford and Colchester, which functioned as marketing as much as production centres. This is

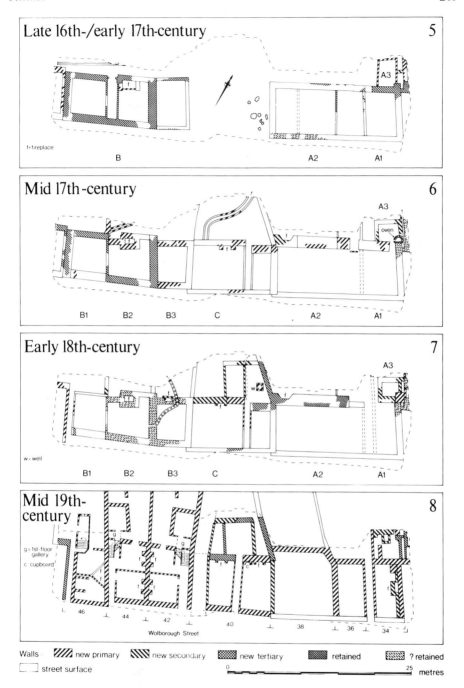

Fig. 10.1 Newton Abbot, Devon: post-medieval phases of building along the north side of Wolborough Street (Exeter Museum).

reflected by the archaeological evidence, which, so far, emphasizes the improvement of housing rather than the subdivision and congestion of plots or the
construction of workshops. In Colchester, the recording of buildings has demonstrated the pattern of improvement: hall houses had open bays replaced by
two-storey ranges, as shown in detail at Portreeve's House, but paralleled
elsewhere in the town (Crummy 1976). In Chelmsford the comprehensive
examination of the Moulsham Street site has also illustrated the practice of
building upper chambers and enlarging properties into their rear plots (Cunningham and Drury 1985). The geographical spread of the industry accounts for
contemporary improvement demonstrated by the buildings of small towns such as
Braintree, Coggeshall or Witham.

In the West Country, in general a region of rural cloth production, the
outstanding exceptions were Exeter and its neighbours. In the seventeenth century
a regional tradition of producing cloth of middling quality for local use developed
into a major industry, the making of serges. Building surveys and excavations in
Exeter have illustrated the changes which a prosperous textile industry brought
about. The improvement of housing has already been referred to (Chapter 2).
Excavations in Alphington Street, known to have been used by serge-makers in the
eighteenth century, have produced indications of a wash house which had
contained a copper or vat with a tunnelled flue to an external chimney. This is
suggested to have been used for scouring yarn (*PMA* 1985: 188–91). At another
site in the city, at Lower North Street, seventeenth-or eighteenth-century vat bases
have been found, although there is no inventory evidence from which to identify
their function (*PMA* 1983: 188).

The south Devon towns also produced and marketed cloth in the seventeenth
century, excavation and survey having thrown light on the industry and the
employment and prosperity it provided. In Totnes opportunities have arisen to
excavate central plots before redevelopment, and to record standing buildings,
giving an excellent impression of how merchant houses were enlarged from their
medieval street frontages to cover large proportions of the narrow plots in the old
town centre, and how subdivision indicates rising land values (Laithwaite 1984;
PMA 1986: 337–9). Work in Newton Abbot, on sites in Wolborough Street (fig.
10.1) has shown how seventeenth-century infilling of frontages demonstrates the
prosperity of a town in which textile production was a key source of wealth
(Weddell 1985).

The visual evidence for urban domestic textile working generally only survives
from the eighteenth century: it comprises top-floor loom shops essentially similar
to those in villages: the long rows of mullioned windows of small Pennine towns, or
the horizontal sliding sashes of shops surviving in Manchester, Macclesfield or
Leek date from late in the eighteenth century, and mark the period when domestic
hand-loom weaving took place on a large scale, using the yarn from the early water
and steam-powered spinning mills. Indeed, this combination of factory and
domestic working, using traditional styles of workshop building, lasted well into
the nineteenth century in the case of high-quality specialist wares: this was so with
silk, and the upper-floor workshops of Macclesfield are particularly good
examples.

Fulling mills

For broadcloth production, fulling was essential, creating the characteristic finish as well as cleaning the cloth prior to dyeing. It was the only stage of textile manufacture which demanded large specialized structures prior to the introduction of water-powered spinning mills late in the eighteenth century, yet the archaeological record is slight, with only one post-medieval fulling mill excavated. Even worse, it should be emphasized, is the record for the medieval period: no fulling mills dating from the Middle Ages have been excavated, despite the attention given to the historical sources for the development of water-powered fulling in the twelfth to fourteenth centuries.

The fulling mill at Ardingly, Sussex, the sole excavated example (fig. 10.2), was in use late in the seventeenth century and early in the eighteenth, a late manifestation of the rural cloth industry of the region (Bedwin 1976). This mill was housed in a brick and stone building adapted from Ardingly forge, whose hammer-scale was used as a floor level, and one of whose wheel-pits contained the water-wheel which later drove the fulling stocks. The fulling-mill evidence was confined to the uppermost levels of the excavation, and although protected by a build-up of marshland vegetation and silt, the indications were slight due to the

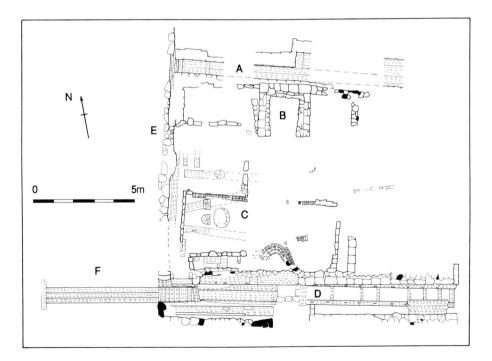

Fig. 10.2   Ardingly, Sussex: plan of sixteenth/seventeenth-century forge rebuilt as a fulling mill in the eighteenth century. (A) north channel (forge period); (B) building (possibly the finery) incorporated in the fulling mill; (C) fulling-mill structure overlying the forge anvil; (D) south channel (for forge and fulling-mill water wheels); (E) dam; (F) culvert through dam (see fig. 7.8) (after O.R. Bedwin).

demolition of the cover building. This excavation has demonstrated that once the fulling stocks and water-wheel have been removed, little may remain. Survival of identifiable fuller's earth would be exceptional, as in the case of the deposit found in a mid-seventeenth-century well at Swan Lane, London, which suggested cloth finishing nearby (*PMA* 1983: 191). At Ardingly the identification of the upper levels as belonging to a fulling mill was aided by inclusion on a map of 1724 and by place-names; without these it is doubtful whether the attribution would have been so certain.

If there are so many documented fulling-mill sites, why has so little field recording or excavation taken place? One answer is that the removal of fulling equipment left the mill free for other uses: where the textile industry was in retreat, corn milling and industrial processes adopted sites of former fulling mills, but in the thriving textile areas of the eighteenth century they were adapted first for spinning and eventually for weaving. This clearly happened in the Cotswolds where water power served the textile industry as the major source of power right through to its nineteenth and twentieth-century decline (Tann 1967), and in east Lancashire and west Yorkshire the re-use of fulling mill sites is well known from place-name and documentary sources.

OTHER ASPECTS OF THE ARCHAEOLOGY OF TEXTILES

A stage in cloth finishing for which there are archaeological indications is the stretching and drying carried out on tentering grounds. Large areas were required, often near fulling mills, as at Ardingly where the post-holes found near the mill are thought to have contained parts of the tentering frames. The urban finishing trades also needed space to stretch cloth: outside the London city wall at Houndsditch the ditch was filled in to provide the tentering grounds known from sixteenth century references (*PMA* 1979: 274), and in Bristol, excavations at Cart Lane showed where massive tentering racks were in use until about 1600 (*PMA* 1975: 243).

The archaeological study of cloth itself is restricted by poor survival. Textiles which have endured in the form of preserved garments or tapestries are usually of exceptional quality, while survival in excavated contexts is rare. The exceptions have been finds from waterlogged sites and from wrecks: the assemblage from the Cattewater wreck (Crowfoot in Redknap 1984: 75–83) is of particular import- ance, comprising a variety of the weaves in common use in late-medieval textiles. There are important parallels from Baynards Castle, London, where rubbish from garment-workers' shops appears to have been used as dockside land-fill, from Poole (Town Hall), and from the Castle Ditch, Newcastle-upon-Tyne (Walton in Harbottle and Ellison 1981: 190–228). Research into the appearance and physical characteristics of cloths of the sixteenth and seventeenth centuries should be related to the terminology used by contemporaries, in particular the new draperies and those mixture cloths which used different yarns in the weave.

Product and source identification has been aided by the study of the lead seals which were used, often for fiscal and quality-control purposes, when cloths were searched and sealed (Endrei and Egan 1982). These seals have been found all over Europe, and are a helpful archaeological confirmation of the documented direction of the textile trades. In London, specimens have been found which originated in 14 English counties. The majority are from Essex, but there have also been significant numbers from Suffolk, Norfolk, Yorkshire, Lancashire and Devon (Egan 1980). Their use on the new draperies is of particular interest in identifying varieties of cloth.

ROPE-MAKING

Of the textile-related trades, rope making is one which has left recognizable physical remains. The characteristic requirement was the lengthy walk where rope was spun, and in certain towns property boundary patterns include long strips of ground once used for this purpose. In Liverpool examples could readily be recognized until fairly recently, but the best survivors are in Bridport, Dorset, whose specialist trade in ropery was far larger than the modest size of the town might suggest. The names and boundaries of plots in the town readily illustrate this. An example in a town not usually associated with the trade is in Wantage, where a rope-walk, now a lane, runs between eighteenth-century walls bearing length marks in the brickwork (*PMA* 1968: 193). Dockyard roperies were accommodated in long buildings, and are known from documents or physical remains at Chatham, Plymouth, Portsmouth and Woolwich (Coad 1969).

Tanning and the leather trades

The making of leather was an important adjunct to livestock production for meat, and in most post-medieval towns where cattle and sheep were marketed and slaughtered tanneries were operated. The archaeological potential is good, owing to the survival of easily recognizable tanning pits: it was normal practice for hides to go through a series of immersions, hence a tannery site required numerous pits. The skins were prepared for defleshing and the removal of hair by a first immersion in a suspension of lime; after scraping they were re-limed in order to open up the grain structure; and thirdly they were de-limed by soaking in dung or vegetable liquors. After washing they underwent the lengthy tanning stage in pits containing water and oak bark, which could take up to 18 months for leather of the highest quality. The archaeology of tanning is well served by Thomson's introduction to the processes (1981), and in particular by the results of excavations in North-ampton.

The Midlands towns, notably Northampton, as well as Coventry and Leicester, were particularly known for their leather production in the sixteenth and seventeenth centuries, developing after the large-scale conversion of arable to pasture in the region in the later Middle Ages. In Northampton two tannery sites of sixteenth/seventeenth-century date have been excavated (fig. 10.3). At The Green, 46 pits have been recorded, in two or perhaps four clusters (M. Shaw 1984). Whether this was according to process stages or whether there were in fact separate small tanneries is not certain. The pits had remnants of wooden linings, surviving best where lime was still present. Some pits were circular, between 0.8m and 1.6m in diameter, with a maximum depth of 0.7m, while the rectangular pits varied in length between 0.8m and 3.6m, in breadth from 0.8m to 1.6m, with a maximum depth of 0.8m. The other Northampton site, at St Peters Street, was rather different, comprising a workshop and an adjacent open area with clay-lined pits.

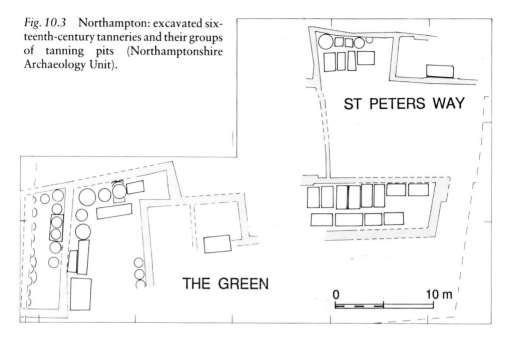

Fig. 10.3   Northampton: excavated six-teenth-century tanneries and their groups of tanning pits (Northamptonshire Archaeology Unit).

This unit is thought not to have been a tannery in the conventional sense but premises for 'tawing' small skins (J. Williams 1979: 98–103; M. Shaw 1984).

Five other excavated urban examples may be cited: in Lewes there was a tannery at Brook Street, drawing its water supply from the town brook, on which wooden sluices were recorded (Freke 1975). In Canterbury a large tanning complex of seventeenth-century date was excavated in North Lane, along the river Stour, the pits still containing bark of oak and birch (*PMA* 1985: 182). Tanning pits have been recorded associated with Tanners Hall, Gloucester (Heighway 1983). At St Albans tanning pits and accompanying timber buildings have been recorded which correspond with the documented leasing in 1538 of properties of St Albans Abbey by a family known to have had a tanning business (Saunders 1977). The tannery site at Romford also contained pits, starting with wood lining in the sixteenth century but relined in brick late in the seventeenth, demonstrating the long-term viability of a business well sited for the livestock trade from East Anglia into London (*PMA* 1985: 169).

A comprehensive review of the archaeological evidence for the post-medieval leather trades and their products has yet to appear, although there have been several reports on particular deposits, mostly of shoes. Those from Hull (Armstrong 1977), York (Goodfellow and Thornton, in Wenham 1972) and Coventry (Thomas 1980) help to provide a guide, but in other cases published drawings of excavated shoes are accompanied by the barest of descriptions, without parallels. It would be of great value, as a stimulus to the integration of leatherwork into finds-groups, to have available a study of shoe types, drawing from published and unpublished material, indicating the regional forms, the changes over the period and explaining the methods of fabrication.

Other livestock-related trades

Many craftsmen derived their materials from tanners and butchers. The most valuable waste from the tannery was horn, waste cores of which were found at the larger of the Northampton tanneries. The exterior horn was employed for many decorative purposes, but its major use was for the handles of cutlery. Horners' workshops were accompanied by soaking pits, in the manner of the fourteenth-century examples excavated at Hornpot Lane, York (Wenham 1972). Pits filled with horn cores have been found in London, at Cutler Street (*PMA* 1980: 206–7) and The Crescent (*PMA* 1986: 342), and it might be suggested that these had originally been used for soaking. Workers in bone acquired their materials from butchers, but specialist craftsmen used more exotic materials: the deposit recently found at Blackfriars illustrates this, a dump of waste of seventeenth to eighteenth-century date including bone, ivory and tortoiseshell fan parts, probably discarded from a fan-maker's workshop (*PMA* 1986: 335).

The Processing of crops

Archaeological aspects of grain milling are covered in the sections on water power (pp. 137–152) and the quarrying of millstones (pp. 211–12). Often associated with mills were malting and corn-drying kilns, the latter more common in the north. Examples are recorded in Scotland (Hay and Stell 1986: 14–15), and the Isle of Man, where survivors were noted by Cubbon and Megaw (1969) and Emery (1985). Of English examples, small kilns were incorporated into Exmoor farmhouses (E.H.D. Williams 1972, 1976), and free-standing examples have been found in Northumberland (Phillipson 1977).

Numerous examples of maltings have been recorded, mostly in towns. The essentials were threefold; a drying floor where the moisture content of the barley was reduced, a sprouting floor on which the grain was germinated, and a steeping tank for the production of the malt. Maltings varied greatly in size: at one extreme is the malt-house in Weem, Perthshire, which would have supplied the six ale-houses and two whisky houses of the town (*PMA* 1967: 118). A malting kiln which operated during the seventeenth century and perhaps earlier has been excavated in Reigate, Surrey, on a site associated with a brewery since the sixteenth century (D.W. Williams 1984). Several larger town maltings have been excavated, if only summarily published. An early post-medieval example is that in Kelso (*PMA* 1985: 181–2) where a substantial kiln had an archaeo-magnetic date late in the sixteenth century; the high temperature needed for a satisfactory dating sample of clay suggests that this is a malting rather than a corn-drying kiln. The most complete malting complex so far recorded is at Lincoln (*PMA* 1983: 198), where the north and part of the west range of the medieval hall of the guild of St Mary were certainly used as maltings in the eighteenth and nineteenth centuries, and probably in the seventeenth century. The steeping tank has been located, with underfloor drainage ducts; the germinating floor lay adjacent, and the position of the kiln has been found at first-floor level within part of the medieval hall.

The use of hops was an innovation in sixteenth-century England, and oast design underwent considerable change between then and the nineteenth century, a development which can be traced from standing buildings. Although some seventeenth-century growers employed malt kilns for hops, it became customary to use a purpose-built oast, a rectangular timber-framed building divided into three compartments. The centre housed the furnace, above which was the drying floor. Green hops were stored in one end of the ground-floor range, dried hops in the other. This was the pattern advocated by Reynold Scot in instructions printed in 1577, and one oast of this kind still survives at Cranbrook, Kent (Cronk 1978: 1979); a building recorded at Much Marcle, Herefordshire appears to be similar (*PMA* 1973: 115). The incorporation of pivoted cowls, pyramid roofs and cast-iron internal fittings was an eighteenth-century development, although it was not until the nineteenth century that the circular plan became common.

The salt industry

Salt supplies have come from three sources: brine springs in Worcestershire and Cheshire, coastal salt pans and, from the 1690s, the mining of rock salt in Cheshire.

BRINE SPRINGS

Recent work in Droitwich and Nantwich has produced impressive evidence of the scale and equipment of salt extraction. At Droitwich the Upwich 'Great Brine Pit' site has been excavated (fig. 10.4), showing that the medieval timber-lined pit remained in use until the eighteenth century (*PMA* 1984: 323–5); dating of pit timbers by dendro-chronology gives a felling date of 1281 −9 (Hillam 1985). Until the end of the Middle Ages the brine appears to have been drawn by bucket, but by the sixteenth century pumps were used, the wooden barrels having a dendro felling date of 1420–2. It has been suggested that the pump was powered by a water-wheel, in use until the cutting of the water supply by the Droitwich canal about 1770. Many brine storage pits have been recorded, and there were also indications of a boiling furnace where the brine was heated in lead pans, until the end of the seventeenth century when larger iron vessels were introduced. The Nantwich excavations have been particularly worth while for the recovery of details of brine storage tanks. Two have been excavated, formed from hollowed-out tree trunks, each 8.5m long, set in clay and with a capacity of 400 gallons.

COASTAL SALT PRODUCTION

The making of salt from sea water has a long history round most of the coasts of Britain. By the sixteenth century it was largely confined to the north and Scotland, although the discovery of eighteenth-century brine tubs and pits in the town of Chichester suggests a late local survival (*PMA* 1975: 249).

There were two methods in use, one taking salt from beach sand, the other collecting salt water in pools filled at high tide. The sand system is well documented on the Lancashire and Solway coasts (R. Taylor 1975): it involved heaping sand in wooden troughs or clay-lined trenches and allowing salt water to run out to be collected for boiling. This took place in lead pans in small buildings housing

Fig. 10.4 Droitwich, Hereford and Worcester: Upwich brine pit, showing late-medieval wooden pump frame and associated pipes (Hereford and Worcester County Museum).

peat-fired furnaces. The salt was then hung to dry in baskets, the magnesium-rich brine draining from the salt and being discarded, or in some areas used for bacon curing.

On many coasts brine was collected by impounding sea water at high tide. This was the common method in Scotland, where the correlation of the field and documentary sources for salt pans has begun to show the kinds of structures in use. In the west the evidence has been studied on Arran, where a boiling house has been identified and recorded (Whatley 1982). This was part of the expansion of coastal saltmaking which took place over much of the Scottish west coast in the second half of the seventeenth century, for saltworks are known from documentary sources on the Ayrshire, Kintyre, Skye and Islay coasts. On the east coast there is surviving information for the Tayside and south Fife industries, where salt-making and coal mining expanded together in the sixteenth and seventeenth centuries. On the Fifeshire coast recent excavations at St Monance have located a pan-house, the first to be excavated. This was 9m square, and the masonry pan-supports were found in position. Outlines of other pan-houses were recorded, as was the windmill used for pumping sea water from foreshore collecting channels to the pans (*PMA* 1986: 355–6; also Whatley 1984).

The coastal industry disappeared at the end of the eighteenth century, so there is rarely an overlay of nineteenth-century features. This is explained by the inability to compete with Cheshire salt, particularly the rock salt, mined from the end of the seventeenth century. By comparison, sea salt was poor as a preservative and bitter to taste, was often dirty in appearance and it required up to 10 times as much coal to extract a ton of sea salt as from the best of the Cheshire brines (Ellis 1980). As soon as water transport reached the Cheshire wiches, the national marketing position was transformed, and high-quality Cheshire salt, whether from brine springs or rock deposits, invaded the market and put the coastal salters out of business.

Paper and gunpowder manufacture: two water-powered industries

PAPER-MILLS

Although paper manufacture is known to have taken place in England from the end of the fifteenth century, the earliest known mill being at Hertford, from 1495, the growth of the industry became really substantial in the second half of the seventeenth century. At this time numerous French papermakers settled in England, and high prices of imports encouraged the setting up of water-powered paper mills. In fact the archaeology of the early paper mill has been little explored, and our knowledge is derived largely from inventories of equipment, contemporary descriptions of the process, and listings of mill sites based on archive sources. Regional surveys have been published for Gloucestershire (F.J.T. Harris 1976), Norfolk (Stoker 1976) and Monmouthshire (Tucker 1972), the last with field observations in some detail, and with these as a basis, wider investigation confirms that by early in the eighteenth century few rivers were without a paper mill. There was no great difficulty about adapting other types of mill for paper manufacture: blade-grinding mills were converted in Yorkshire in the eighteenth century, and at former fulling mills, as at Castle Rising, Norfolk, and on the Itchen, stocks may have been adapted for the maceration of rags for paper. The inventory of the mill at South Stoneham, Hampshire, however, shows four stamp mills, each containing between 30 and 60 hammers (Thomas 1977), suggesting equipment more akin to Cornish ore crushers. In addition, paper mills required vats for fermenting, washing and pressing, which explains the need for supplies of water greater than required to power machinery. Purity of water was also important, and papermakers appear to have favoured sites either on head-waters or where small clean tributaries could be led into the mill.

POWDER-MILLS

Gunpowder mills required water power for edge-runner stones, to crush and incorporate the constituents: charcoal, sulphur and saltpetre. Sixteenth-century works are known to have operated at Long Ditton, Rotherhithe and Faversham, and it is at Faversham that the best-preserved remains survive. These, however, had a long life, and the Chart Mills, where a restoration programme has been under way for many years represent eighteenth-century practice (Percival 1968). Nevertheless, the long history of these works, with their well-documented phases of expansion during the Dutch wars of the seventeenth century as well as in the eighteenth century, offer considerable archaeological potential. The powder mills at Bedfont, Middlesex, where excavations have recently taken place, date from the seventeenth century and, again, were in use into the nineteenth (*PMA* 1984: 319; 1985: 182). The excavations have shown two edge-runner mills, water powered, with a wheel-pit which was in use through the nineteenth century. This work awaits full publication, but so far shows that earlier deposits exist beneath the edge-runner mills, whose date of construction has yet to be verified. The seventeenth-and eighteenth-century expansion of the gunpowder industry resulted in a wide spread of works (Crocker 1988). Of those around London the sites of the mills at Waltham Abbey and Chilworth are known, but that at Battle, Sussex has yet to be firmly identified. The site of the Woolley powder works near Bath is known: built in the 1720s this was one of a number in the area (Buchanan and Tucker 1981). The mills of Lakeland, which continued in use through the nineteenth century, have also been identified, and their surface remains surveyed (Marshall and Davies-Shiel 1977).

Chapter 11

The archaeology of glass

Since the mid-1960s archaeology has contributed to our knowledge of the post-medieval glass industry by clarifying significant changes in methods and location. Between 1500 and 1750 three major technical developments took place: in the second half of the sixteenth century medieval English traditions were replaced by those of immigrant glassmakers from France, who used more efficient furnaces to make glass of better quality; in the first quarter of the seventeenth century wood was replaced by mineral fuels, and, finally, in the decades around 1700 furnaces grew more complex, particularly in their flue systems, culminating in the construction of the great conical superstructures which were to be used at many works until the end of the nineteenth century.

In the Middle Ages glass sold in Britain came mostly from abroad. Green glass, both window and vessel, was made in France and Germany, and clear crystal vessel was an Italian speciality; English producers occupied a position at the lower end of the price and quality range. There was a tradition of glass production in the west of the Weald of Sussex and Surrey, for the London market, which is documented from the thirteenth century onwards. There are also records of medieval glass manufacture in the Staffordshire forests of Needwood and Cannock Chase. By the early years of the sixteenth century the traditional industry had declined, for Continental manufacturers had further improved their methods and their competitive position. A petition of 1542 by the Glaziers' Company, referring to the price of imported glass, implies that English window glass was not available, and Thomas Charnock, writing in the 1550s, suggested that a Surrey glasshouse was the sole working remnant of the English industry.

Early-sixteenth-century furnaces

Archaeological and documentary research has shown these views to have been exaggerated, for Kenyon (1967: 117–120) found that two, possibly three families of glassmakers were still working in the Weald in the middle of the sixteenth century. There has been one excavation, at Knightons, Alfold, Surrey (Wood 1982), which illustrates methods used about 1550, before the arrival of the immigrants who came from France in and after 1567. It has a counterpart in Staffordshire where a furnace dating to approximately 1530 has been excavated in Bagots Park on the edge of Needwood Forest (Crossley 1967). To understand how

Fig. 11.1   Bagots Park, Staffordshire: early-sixteenth-century glass furnace.

these furnaces fit into the medieval tradition, brief reference should be made to the fourteenth-century furnace excavated at Blundens Wood, in the forested region of south-west Surrey (Wood 1965). Although the structures were fragmentary, they demonstrated that contemporary practice was to use separate furnaces for glass melting, the annealing of glass, and the preparation of crucibles. This excavation provided a ground plan of a melting furnace whose rectangular outline corresponds with those recorded at Bagots Park and Knightons.

The early-sixteenth-century furnaces mark the final phase of medieval glassmaking. The Bagots Park furnace (fig. 11.1), whose last firing has been magnetically dated to the 1530s, produced window glass from six crucibles, annealing being done in a small adjacent furnace of which only a fragment survived. The excavation showed weaknesses in the techniques in use: the selection of materials was poor, for the bases of crucibles contained solidified glass into which had settled partly crushed pebbles and other debris. This problem appears to have been accepted and to a degree overcome by using tall crucibles, out of whose bases it would be impossible to gather the impure material. The glass was poor in quality, being susceptible to surface weathering, although such evidence of weathering has to be used with care: glass buried near a furnace may not be typical of the material sold, and may have been affected by conditions unrelated to those encountered in normal use. However, at later furnaces there has usually been a smaller proportion of waste displaying the surface pitting so typical of the glass at Bagots Park; also, much of this weathered glass comprised centres of crowns, discarded when the diamond-shaped quarries were cut from the spun discs. These centres ought to demonstrate saleable quality more closely than discarded fragments at a vessel glass works. The furnace at Bagots Park appeared to have had a short life, for scum ('gall') had overflowed from the crucibles and choked the flue between the two sieges. Hence the remarkable number of remnants of furnaces in this part of Needwood may be due not only to movement between coppices where fuel was being cut, but because choked furnaces needed to be replaced.

The survival of the flues and the glass-coated stone sieges of melting furnaces can lead to emphasis on these rather than the annealing furnaces (lehrs) and ancillary buildings, which are more liable to damage by tree roots. At Bagots Park fragments of such structures were recorded: post-holes marked an open-sided shed, and clusters of stake-holes were interpreted as outlines of racks for the storage of crowns of glass. Drainage and roofing were important: this furnace was surrounded on three sides by a ditch, and four large post-holes had contained the upright supports for a roof to cover the furnace. This would have resembled the arrangement shown on the well-known drawing of a fifteenth-century Bohemian furnace among the illustrations to the manuscript 'Travels of Sir John Mandeville' (Kenyon 1967: pl.X).

Bagots Park best represents the last of the medieval English tradition, for although the final use of Knightons has been dated to about 1550, before the arrival of French immigrants, there are indications that methods were beginning to change. The excavation showed three phases, each marked by the base of a rectangular melting furnace of medieval type. These had all been used to produce window glass, and each had contained six crucibles. The distinctive feature was an annealing furnace, structurally linked to the last melting furnace. As only outlines had survived, it was not possible to be certain what the relationship between the upper parts of the two structures was: what is significant is that a key feature of French immigrant methods was to economize on fuel by drawing heat from the main fire for subsidiary processes, and Agricola's contemporary drawings of Continental practice show furnaces joined in a similar way (1950 edn: 588). Although Knightons does not resemble French furnaces in detail, there is a reference to an attempt by a Frenchman to set up production in the Weald in 1550, raising the possibility that Knightons may be where he worked.

The glass industry after the arrival of the French immigrants

THE ORIGINS OF THE NEW METHODS

The integration of stages of glass manufacture into fewer furnace units was common in Lorraine, whence many of the immigrants to England came. There, fieldwalking, without excavation, has shown that a typical furnace comprised a central rectangular block in which melting took place, and wings built at each corner for other stages of manufacture. Seventeenth-century descriptions, and the excavations carried out in England suggest that glassmakers might achieve some economy of fuel in such designs. The wings could be used in two ways: heat could be drawn from the main fire through channels (Godfrey 1975: 141), or separate fires could be used within the wings themselves, supplemented by the heat permeating the whole structure from the main melting furnace. In these wings several operations were possible. The mixture of sand and alkali, the frit, could be prepared for the crucibles by heating to a temperature short of the point of fusion, removing moisture and certain impurities. Secondly, newly made crucibles could be partially fired before being set on the sieges in the melting furnace. Finally, after the glass had been melted, blown and shaped, annealing could take place in a lehr built on a wing. This relieved internal stresses in the glass, and was done by heating to a temperature short of the point at which it would begin to deform, and gradually cooling by restricting the heat.

Lorraine was not the only continental centre where such furnaces were used. The fifteenth-century Bohemian furnace illustration, referred to earlier, shows annealing taking place in the same structure as the melting furnace, and excavations in Czechoslovakia have shown furnaces similar in principle if differing in detail from those in Lorraine. Unfortunately, little information is available about the methods used in glasshouses in Normandy: many of the immigrant glassmakers reaching England late in the sixteenth century came from this region, and it would be helpful to know whether the tradition on which they drew was similar to that of Lorraine.

IMMIGRANT-STYLE FURNACES IN ENGLAND

The early fieldworkers in the Weald, Winbolt and Kenyon, located furnaces with winged plans, and correctly identified them with the French glassmakers who arrived in England after 1567, when Jean Carré obtained his patent to regulate the glass industry. The surface finds of glass at these Wealden sites include vessel fragments in the forms and quality associated with the immigrants, and distinguishable from medieval glass by the relative freedom from surface weathering. Although several Wealden furnaces were uncovered and superficially planned, none from the immigrant period have been excavated to modern standards. A particular problem in the Weald is that no distinction has been sought between the furnaces of the Lorrainers and those operated by settlers from Normandy. Research into this question could well have implications for the interpretation of furnaces found in the other parts of England to which the immigrants spread.

It is from the areas to which the French glassmakers dispersed, after their initial settlement in the Weald, that more precise information about their furnaces, methods and products have come. An overview of furnace sites shows that there is considerable variation, and the four-winged plan should not be taken as a stereotype. Those at Buckholt, Hampshire (Kenyon 1967: 214–17), Woodchester, Gloucestershire (revision of Daniels 1950), and Rosedale, Yorkshire (Crossley and Aberg 1972) possessed this layout, but it is doubtful whether those at St Weonards, Herefordshire (Bridgewater 1963) or Bishops Wood, Staffordshire (Pape 1933–4) were more than simple rectangular melting furnaces. The furnace at Hutton, Yorkshire (Crossley and Aberg 1972) had only two wings rather than the full diagonal plan.

The excavation at Rosedale has provided the most complete example of a winged furnace (fig. 11.2). Nothing is known of the identity of the glassmakers, although the Netherlands-imported pottery excavated from the site of the adjacent ruined house might indicate an immigrant family. The ceramic evidence agreed with the magnetic date for the furnace to put final firing in the 1590s. The furnace was built on the edge of moorland, with outcrops of suitable sand close by, refractory clay for

Fig. 11.2   Rosedale, Yorkshire: late-sixteenth-century glass furnace.

crucibles available in coal-measure outcrops in an adjacent valley, and supplies of wood from the immediate locality. As well as suitable materials, there were markets within reasonable distance: neither the city of York nor the lowland agricultural areas of the county had yet been served by a local glasshouse, and glass sold in the area would hitherto have been carried from other parts of England or supplied by importers.

   Although the Rosedale furnace had a four-winged plan, the presence of two separate annealing furnaces shows that integration of the process stages within one structure was not complete. Vessel glass was made, using two crucibles which were smaller than those at the window-glass furnaces. The central melting furnace was conventional, having two sieges and a firing trench, roofed with clay supported by stone arches, fragments of which remained. There had originally been four wings, but one had been removed during the life of the furnace. On none of the three survivors were there indications of burning sufficient to suggest the setting of a fire, so it is assumed that heat was derived from the main flue. It was uncertain whether the annealing furnaces had been built at the same time as the main furnace or afterwards, but the removal of one of the wings may suggest that separate annealing furnaces were added, either to give more working space or for more controllable operation. This would leave the surviving wings to be used for fritting and pot-firing, but neither operation is easy to identify: so far no glasshouse excavation has yielded material positively recognizable as frit, which, being unfused, would be easily dispersed. Pot-firing would leave no trace, for even if a crucible were to break, the fragments would be removed. The stage of manufacture most readily identifiable during glasshouse excavations, and Rosedale is no exception, is the shaping of glass vessel, using heat from holes in the side of the furnace. Despite the practice of recovering glass fragments for use as cullet, charged into the crucible with the sand and alkali, there was usually a build-up of clippings, drops of glass, lumps broken from the working irons, and fragments from broken

Fig. 11.3   Hutton-le-Hole, Yorkshire: late-sixteenth-century glass furnace.

vessels. This process waste is valuable for analysis, for it indicates the composition of the glass being made, reducing the risk of confusion with cullet brought in from outside. The quality of the glass found near the furnace at Rosedale was excellent, and appears to be the product of a well-tried technology using suitable materials.

Only 10km from Rosedale, a contemporary furnace has been excavated at Hutton, where differences in methods and standards emphasize that much is still to be learned about the origins and methods of regional glassmakers at the end of the sixteenth century. At Hutton the melting furnace had been rebuilt twice. The first phase was of plain rectangular plan, but the two successors were more complex, each with two wings placed diagonally opposite each other. One of the wings had, in its final phase, been used with its own fire, shown by a thick layer of burnt clay (fig. 11.3). There was no obvious separate annealing furnace: the only fragment away from the main structure was vestigial and of uncertain purpose. It is tempting to suggest, but not proven, that this related to the earliest, plain, furnace, and that annealing had later been carried out in the wing where signs of firing were recorded. The Hutton furnace contrasted with its neighbour in the quality of its glass, for whereas at Rosedale the surfaces were bright and durable, at Hutton a high proportion were iridescent with surface weathering. It was not possible to carry out analyses on samples of glass large enough to draw conclusions about differences in batch composition between the two furnaces. Nor was it feasible to carry out environmental tests to the extent‚ which is now seen as necessary to draw conclusions about the causes of weathering. Nevertheless, the impression that the Hutton glass was distinguishable in quality from that at Rosedale prompts the question of who the glassmakers were, and why they appear to have encountered problems in the operation of their furnace.

Only at these two sites have substantial remains of immigrant-period furnaces been excavated. At St Weonards (Bridgewater 1963) little was found of the main furnace, but part of a small building with a curved outline in brick was suggested as the remains of an annealing furnace. Crucible and glass fragments were found, and the style of the product suggests that vessel was being made during the period 1580–1620. At Bickerstaffe, Lancashire, fragments of furnace material and of glass were found, corresponding with a documentary reference to French glassmakers in the Ormskirk area in 1600, but ploughing had destroyed the furnace (*PMA* 1970: 185).

Each of these furnaces produced green glass in the styles common in the northern European forest-glass industries. There is no sign that any were influenced by the other great tradition, that of the production of crystal in Italy. The manufacture of the latter material in England was confined to London, where it is assumed that the furnace used by Jacob Verselini in the former Crutched Friars building would be of the circular Venetian style illustrated by Agricola (1950 edn: 587-591).

The group of forest-glass furnace excavations is still too small to give more than an impression of change and development over the half-century from 1570. The lack of reliable archaeological evidence from the Weald, the documented centre of production nearest to London, poses a particular priority for future work. Without question, the industry changed, not just in the great increase in production by comparison with medieval levels, but in the quality of its products and the ability to sell glass at attractive prices, which rose less during the inflation of the sixteenth century than those of virtually any other industrial product. This achievement was in part due to the reduction in the cost of transport due to the foundation of glasshouses in dispersed parts of England, but increases in the efficiency of the use of fuel were also important when the price of wood was rising at a rate higher than that of most non-food goods. These changes were probably cumulative, with steady prices and good quality fostering a market for window and vessel glass which in turn led glassmakers to move to further areas where demand existed.

The change to the use of mineral fuel

The use of coal for glass manufacture came about remarkably rapidly in the decade after 1610. Shortage of fuel played a part, but the issues may have been oversimplified, partly as a result of exaggeration by rival users of wood, and also due to a genuine if often misinformed fear of denudation of English woodlands. By the beginning of the seventeenth century the glass industry had become a significant part of the woodland economy in a number of forest areas, and the popularity of its wares was leading to conflict over wood supplies with other users of coppices, such as the producers of iron or the urban firewood trade. Glass was just one of a number of industries and trades where there was a search for an alternative fuel at this time, aimed partly at escaping from the problems of competition for wood, but also at reducing costs.

The problems were in part technical. Furnaces had to be adapted to burn mineral fuels, care had to be taken that the fumes did not affect the quality of the glass, and additional supplies of alkali had to be found to replace the wood ash which the forest glassmakers had collected from their fires. Further, there were artificial restraints posed by the practice of awarding patents of monopoly not only to genuine innovators but also to speculators. For us, there is the difficulty of distinguishing the genuinely original idea from the bogus claim. In fact Godfrey, in her key study (1975) shows that the glass industry seems to have suffered less from abusive patents than some others, for despite a lack of previous connection with the industry, the major monopolist, Sir Robert Mansell, did much to foster the new technology.

The earliest coal-using furnaces were built on the south bank of the Thames in or about 1611, under the original monopoly of Sir Edward Zouch (Godfrey 1975: 64, 151). A 'wind-furnace' was in operation at Winchester House, Southwark in that year, and a new furnace at Lambeth, making window glass, followed in 1613; neither have been located on the ground. When Mansell bought out his fellow monopolists in 1615, he began a series of attempts to reduce the costs of production, for the London glassmakers, despite their access to the coastal coal trade, found that their costs and prices gave little advantage over traditional suppliers. Mansell therefore attempted to produce glass in the coalfields. He began by setting up a glasshouse at Wollaton, near Nottingham (R.S. Smith 1962), and although coal was close at hand and the furnace appears to have been technically successful, the distance from the markets of the south-east was too great. The site of the works is not known, but a useful plan of the glasshouse survives, showing the rectangular building which contained the furnace, although not the furnace itself. The second of Mansell's attempts took place at Kimmeridge, Dorset (Crossley 1987). In 1615 he made an agreement with the landowner, Sir William Clavell, to build a furnace to produce window glass, using as a fuel the oil shale which outcrops on the Purbeck coast. The site of this original furnace at Kimmeridge is not certain, although it is thought to be close to the quay which Clavell had built to ship alum mined on his estate. The venture was not a success, owing to difficulties in using the shale, so Mansell made a third brief attempt near Milford Haven, about which nothing is known. He was eventually successful on Tyneside, where his Newcastle glasshouse became a major producer, supplied with local coal and shipping glass by the coasting trade. Newcastle remained a centre of glass production through the subsequent centuries, but it has not yet been possible to excavate an early furnace site.

Mansell's patent authorized the licensing of glasshouses using coal: one was set up on the Thames at Ratcliff, another at Kimmeridge. For the latter, Sir William Clavell took as a partner Abraham Bigo, a glassmaker of French descent who had worked in Staffordshire. Bigo was licensed to produce vessel glass for sale in the south-western counties, and production began at the end of 1617, in a pre-existing furnace, no doubt that abandoned by Mansell. A new furnace was built in 1618, and continued in use until demolished in 1623 by the monopoly, after glass had been sold in London in breach of the agreement. This furnace has been excavated (fig. 11.4), and it has demonstrated the means whereby the problems of the use of coal were overcome; the close dating is also helpful in showing the types of plain vessel glass in production around 1620.

Some features of the furnace at Kimmeridge were derived from the French forest-glass tradition. Superficially, the plan was that of a winged furnace of Lorraine type, and all stages of manufacture took place in this single unit. As there were no signs of heavy burning on any of the wings, it is probable that they drew

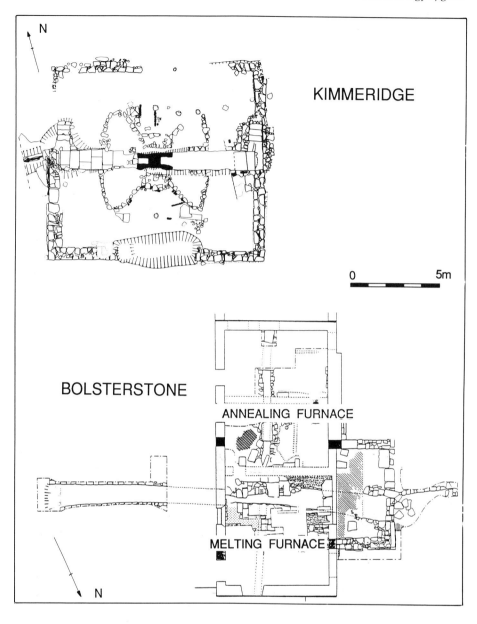

Fig. 11.4 Coal-fired glass furnaces. (1) Kimmeridge, Dorset: early-seventeenth-century furnace (fired with oil shale); (2) Bolsterstone, Yorkshire: early-eighteenth-century glass furnace in surviving building (Denis Ashurst).

heat from the main fire. This is where the resemblance ends, for instead of having two ground-level stokeholes and a central flue trench in the forest tradition, the fire was placed at the centre of the furnace above a brick plinth and probably on fire-bars. The air for the fire was drawn through the two ends of the underground passage in which the brick plinth was built. This flue passage ran from beyond each pair of wings, and at each end was accessible by a set of steps. Durably built in stone, the flues not only supplied air to the fire, but provided a means of removing ash. They had originally been roofed over with vaulted stonework, and the ground-level floor thus formed had provided the route by which the central fire could be stoked. This central location was necessary for mineral fuel, whose short flame ruled out the use of fires at each end of the furnace. Of particular importance was the location of the furnace within a rectangular building, whose footings survived. This corresponds closely in size with the plan of the Wollaton glasshouse, and gives a firmer indication of a permanent cover structure than has been seen at any furnace so far excavated.

The Kimmeridge excavation suggests that the 'wind furnace' at Winchester House, Southwark, would embody similar arrangements for draught. It also clarifies features at the other two early-seventeenth-century furnaces so far recorded. At Denton, Lancashire, excavations have revealed a furnace suggested by documents to date between c.1615 and 1653 (*PMA* 1970: 185-6; 1971: 217); this also had deep arched-over passages and access steps. A brief excavation under adverse conditions at Red Street, near Newcastle-under-Lyme (Birmingham University Excavation Unit, unpublished), also located a furnace with an underground flue approached by steps, in a district for which there are mid-seventeenth-century archive references to glassmakers.

Seventeenth-and eighteenth-century developments

A question as yet unanswered is how and when there evolved the great conical superstructures which became common in the eighteenth-century glass industry. The first record is for a cone built by Philip Roche in Dublin in 1694 (Westropp 1920: 37–8). Cones are shown on a view of Bristol dated 1710 (Witt, Weeden *et al.* 1984: 19). The first excavated example was at Gawber, Yorkshire, built in 1739–40 (Ashurst 1970). The earliest survivor stands not far distant, at Catcliffe, east of Sheffield, a cone built in 1740. It is not known whether the Dublin cone was a pioneer, or whether there were antecedents elsewhere in Britain. Continental origins are unlikely, for Diderot and D'Alembert in their *Receuil des Planches ...* of 1762–71 (Vol X, pl. III) name the cone 'Verrerie Anglaise'.

The cone was not the automatic choice at the end of the seventeenth century. We are still short of archaeological evidence for this period, but the only sites so far excavated show no sign of the new form of structure. The first was from the early period at Gawber, antedating the cone. This was a mere fragment, but a magnetic date placed the last heating of the melting furnace shortly before the end of the seventeenth century. This was probably one of the Yorkshire furnaces referred to by John Houghton in his *Letters for the Improvement of Trade and Industry* (1696). There was no indication that a cone enclosed this fragment, which appeared to be part of a furnace of archaic type without firm evidence for an underground air passage.

A more substantial survival is the recently excavated furnace at Bolsterstone (Ashurst 1987): this Yorkshire glasshouse does not appear to be recorded by Houghton in 1696, although there are documentary references to its use both before and after that year, when it may have been out of production following the death of its owner. The building is the earliest glasshouse in Britain to remain essentially complete, although the wide arched entries on either side have been blocked during use as a barn since the eighteenth century. Although the above-ground parts of the furnace have been destroyed and the substructure covered over, excavation has shown the complete plan of the flues, the sieges, and the relationship between the furnace and the standing building (fig. 11.4). These were in use from the early years of the eighteenth century until at least 1740 when the glassmakers went to Catcliffe to build the cone which survives. Whether the standing building at Bolsterstone can be traced further back is less certain. The documentary sources suggest a starting date in the 1650s, and the features of the building would not be out of place at that time. However, the break in the record after 1692 must raise the possibility of reconstruction when manufacture recommenced about 1702.

Although the Bolsterstone glasshouse was operated without a cone for the first 40 years of the eighteenth century, it incorporated innovations which show a development of the layout recorded at Kimmeridge, and it represents a step towards the complexities of cone furnaces such as Gawber, Catcliffe and similar examples in the Stourbridge area and on Tyneside. The central fire was retained, as were the long below-ground flues, bringing air from either side of the building. Three further passages entered the centre of the main flue from beneath the sieges. Two had provided extra air, and one of these also served as a drain for the entire system. A third, entering the fire area above the southern air intake, showed signs of intense heating, and it has been argued that this was part of a regenerative system in which air in the furnace was brought down into the passage and then reheated as it passed upwards through the fire zone. If this is the case, Bolsterstone is the earliest known example of heat regeneration, a technique common in numerous nineteenth-century industrial processes. However, we do not yet know whether the idea was used elsewhere in the glass industry of the eighteenth century. Despite the survival of the glasshouse building, work at Bolsterstone does nothing to solve the problem of the design of chimneys for melting furnaces of the pre-cone era: the above-ground levels within the glasshouse had been removed, and the building had been re-roofed. However, also within the glasshouse at Bolsterstone were two annealing furnaces. Although the bases had been removed, the flues remain in the west wall of the building, and are the first of the kind to be recorded.

Bolsterstone is also important in providing the earliest physical evidence for the use of domed-top crucibles with angled apertures, which could be sealed to the gathering holes in the sides of the furnace, isolating the contents of the pots from the atmosphere of the furnace interior. These were named 'English pots' by the mid-eighteenth-century French writer Bosc d'Antic (Newton 1987). This development comes after a period when our knowledge is imperfect over how or whether crucibles were sealed. Until the Kimmeridge excavation it had been assumed that lidded pots would be used in coal-fired furnaces to prevent contamination of glass by sulphur, but no evidence of this was found there, and although analysis of Kimmeridge glass showed that sulphur was present, it was not at a level which would make green glasses difficult to produce. Problems were more likely to occur when producing clear 'crystal' glasses, and Merrett (1662: 241, 246) notes a practice of 'piling' pots, where the crucible was sealed by placing another on top of it. It is not clear what form of sealing was used by Ravenscroft in the 1670s in his development of lead crystal, in which contamination with sulphur would be a serious matter.

The conical glasshouses of the eighteenth century replaced some but by no means all of the rectangular buildings which had developed over the seventeenth century. The nearest to a contemporary description comes in Diderot's *Encyclopédie*. The reasons for the development appear to be twofold. Firstly, the cone served to extract the smoke and fume which appears from contemporary illustrations to emerge from gathering and working holes in the sides of furnaces. It was also capable of inducing a massive draught, as anyone who has stood at the door of a surviving cone with an open top will have realized. Contemporary illustrations, and the surviving cone at Catcliffe (fig. 11.5), show that most cones were provided with several base arches, some of which merely led into surrounding buildings used for working and annealing or for storage, while others possessed doors opening to the exterior; the latter could be used to alter the proportion of draught passing through these arches or through the furnace air tunnels.

All the standing cones in Britain have had their interior features cleared. At Catcliffe the space where the furnace stood is concreted over, and the cone stands preserved with its side arches open. It is an impressive stone structure, about 18m in height, but showing little sign of how it operated. A brief exploratory excavation to seek the layout of its flues and to recover samples of its products remains

Fig. 11.5 Catcliffe, Yorkshire: eighteenth-century glass cone.

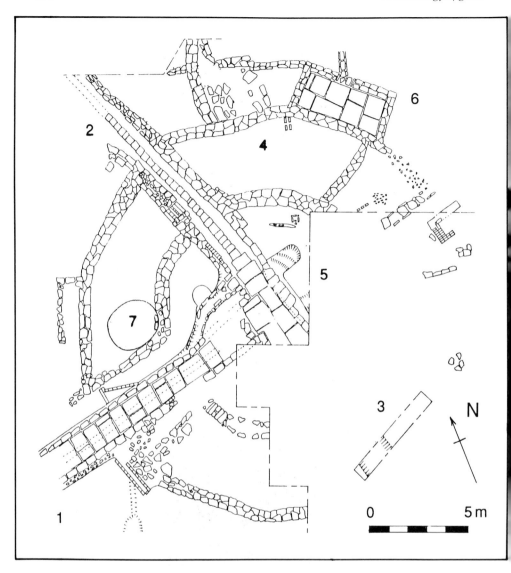

Fig. 11.6   Gawber, Yorkshire: excavated glass cone. (1), (2) and (3) flues; (4) annealing furnace; (5) melting furnace; (6) sand store; (7) earlier mine-shaft (Denis Ashurst).

unpublished. The cones at Stourbridge, Lemington (Tyneside) and Alloa have been used for many years for storage, but one of those at Stourbridge has been converted to a glassworks museum. Therefore, information about the underground air passages used in cones has had to come from excavation, namely the work carried out on the site of the Gawber cone, near Barnsley, built in 1740 (fig. 11.6). It was found that there were three passages, all of the same section. This contrasts with Bolsterstone, where one pair of flues was of more substantial size than the pair which entered the furnace beneath the sieges.

The field archaeology of the glass industry

Glass-furnace sites can be recognized by surface scatters of distinctive material. This consists not only of fragments of vessel or window, but of glass which has not been blown. This takes the form of lumps from inside the bases of crucibles removed from the furnace sieges: in these there can be great variation in colour and in the amount of impurities. Glass which has been gathered appears as lumps broken from the pontil after transfer from the blowing iron: the mark of the pontil-end is characteristic. In addition there are rings of glass which have adhered to the blowing iron when the vessel has been removed; from the process of shaping the vessel come clippings and trails, and from annealing there are fragments of vessel or flat glasses which have fractured during heating or cooling. The main product of a furnace can be deduced from examination of these latter fragments, although difficulties arise if a furnace has been abandoned leaving a large stock of intrusive cullet. Where crown window glass has been made, by spinning a blown bubble of glass into a disc, there can be characteristic thickened centres, the 'bull's-eyes' which, whatever the later fashion for their use, were generally discarded after the small quarry panes were cut. These centres are not necessarily present in quantity, for many discs were sold to glaziers who cut the glass in their own workshops. Crown glass can also be distinguished by the surviving fragments of rims of discs 30–60cm in diameter; there is a slight thickening at the edge and concentric markings and elongations of internal bubbles. The other kind of glass, broad or cylinder glass, was made by cutting and flattening a long bubble while hot, and rolling out on a flat surface. This can be recognized by the straight edges and lines of imperfections.

In addition to glass, there are frequently substantial deposits of material spilled or scraped from the tops of the crucibles. Named at different times 'sandever' or 'gall', this can take many forms, varying in density and colour. It can be particularly confusing where the gall has spilled into the fire of a coal-fired furnace, taking up some of the ash and forming a clinker-like substance: the high alumina content of the material examined from Kimmeridge was thus explained. Remains of crucibles are usually found in quantity, and are immediately identifiable in plough scatter from furnaces. It is not known how long crucibles remained in position on furnace sieges, and it must be assumed that there was considerable variation in their life, depending on the clays used and the skill of the potter. At Kimmeridge, Bagots Park and Rosedale there were prominent deposits; indeed crucible fragments were the main means of locating other furnaces in Bagots Park. The laboratory testing of crucible fragments for their heat resistance is important in determining safety-margins during operation, and the success of glassmakers in identifying the best sources of refractory clay.

The melting furnace has characteristics which make it one of the more easily located archaeological features. Although superstructures must soon have disintegrated, sieges were usually massively built, the Rosedale example being striking for its use of large boulders. The coating of spilled glass has protected the stone furnace base, either causing a characteristic mound, as at Rosedale, or obstructing the plough as at Bagots Park. In addition, the heating of the furnace and the clay beneath it can produce a substantial magnetic anomaly, important both for location and for thermo-remanent dating.

Post-medieval glass

Excavated groups of sixteenth-century glass can be divided between the crystal glasses, mostly imported, and the green forest glass, less easily attributable. The imported crystal came from Italy and the Netherlands; much was in clear glass, but there are characteristic forms with applied coloured decoration. These types, and the small amount of known sixteenth-century London crystal are summarized in the report on excavations in Southampton (Charleston 1975: 205–12 and catalogue), whose detail it is unnecessary to repeat here.

When found in early or middle-sixteenth-century contexts, most green glasses may be assumed to be from France, Germany or the Netherlands, but by the end of the century the buoyancy of the immigrant-based English industry had reduced the market for imports. It is rarely possible to distinguish between English and imported green forest glass of 1570 or later, except with the occasional second-quality item assumed to be of local origin. Northern European and hence English glass furnaces produced a fairly limited range of vessel types between 1500 and 1650: the objects most commonly found are beakers, stemmed drinking glasses, flasks and small bottles and, less commonly, urinals and items of chemical apparatus. Linen smoothers are objects whose durability probably exaggerates their original numbers. There are three common forms of beakers: those with applied prunt decoration continue a medieval continental form and although found in urban contexts, notably in Southampton, have not been seen in quantity at excavated glasshouse sites. They were present in small numbers at Rosedale, but not at Kimmeridge. Beakers with horizontally applied milled strips and applied spiral trails were found at Hutton, Rosedale and Kimmeridge; they are a common surface find at other English furnace sites and in many urban deposits. Just as common are mould-blown beakers with patterns, particularly in chequered and 'wrythen' designs. Typical ranges in furnace deposits are illustrated and discussed in the Rosedale and Kimmeridge reports (Crossley and Aberg 1972; Crossley 1987), while the Southampton material is summarized by Charleston (1975), and glasses from St Ebbes, Oxford by Haslam (in Hassall 1984, 232ff). Stemmed drinking glasses are considered by Charleston in the Rosedale report, and the occurrence of types of small bottles and flasks are covered in the discussion of the Kimmeridge material (fig. 11.7). Chemical apparatus shows little distinction between medieval and post-medieval, and is discussed by Moorhouse (1972).

In the first half of the seventeenth century, glass in circulation in Britain still owed much to the traditions of the wood-fuel period. There was still the division between green forest-glass types and the imported Italian-style crystal. The Kimmeridge glass was essentially 'waldglas' in appearance and in form . The colouring was still affected by the iron in the sand, and there seem to have been no attempts to use manganese as a decolorizer. One change was towards the production of square bottles, which appear in increasing quantities, a sign that declining costs of production were allowing glass to enter the container trade. Over the middle years of the seventeenth century, glass wine bottles became more common, and by the 1660s and 1670s the furnaces of Tyneside were producing bottles in quantity. There evolved a series of forms, moving towards the modern straight-sided bottle, in many cases bearing applied stamps denoting the customer, and increasingly useful for archaeological dating purposes (Haslam in Hassall 1984: 234–7; Oakley, *ibid*, 246–9; Haslam 1970; Ashurst 1970).

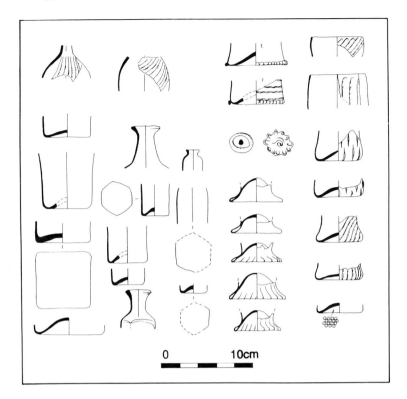

0   10cm

Fig. 11.7 Kimmeridge, Dorset: assemblage of vessel glass from a closely dated furnace (1618–23).

Our knowledge of the decorative products of the seventeenth-century English glasshouses is less certain. Italian-style crystal glass had continued to be made in London after the time of Verselini, indeed in the early years of the Mansell patent, in 1617, a new crystal works was set up in Broad Street, London. What is not certain is how much crystal glass, and of what quality, was made in this country in the middle decades of the seventeenth century, and excavated material of this kind from a furnace site is badly needed. There are also signs of innovation in colour. The Denton furnace made a black glass, a deliberate black rather than the very dark green which so many of the 'black' pieces from forest glasshouses have turned out to be.

A significant change came in the 1670s, when John Ravenscroft incorporated lead in glass. He produced a clear glass more cheaply than the traditional makers of Mediterranean-style crystal, who had relied on fine sands, decolorizers, and soda-ash alkalis. The use of lead appears to have spread fairly quickly, although there is a need for dated specimens from late in the seventeenth century for analysis. At Bolsterstone, examination shows lead in glass (Cable in Ashurst 1987), but dating of these specimens is inexact due to site disturbance.

Within the typology of glassware lies considerable variation in quality, reflecting choice of materials and competence of furnace operation. It is here that laboratory examination of furnace products is essential, directed at detecting and explaining success or difficulty in achieving consistently high standards. For discussion of objectives and methods in the scientific examination of glasses of this period, the reader is referred to the Bolsterstone and Kimmeridge reports (Ashurst 1987, and Crossley 1987).

Chapter 12
Ceramics

The pottery of the post-medieval period

The study of pottery produced between 1500 and 1750 has been central to research in post-medieval archaeology over the past 25 years. In the early 1960s it was realized that the pottery of this period possessed a potential second only to that of clay pipes for the close dating of deposits, necessary if archaeological and documentary material were to be truly complementary. It was becoming clear that certain types of pottery appeared at fairly closely definable points, established partly by the use of key documented contexts, and also by associated datable artefacts, notably clay pipes after 1600, and to a less precise degree glass. Optimism about this potential brought the Post-Medieval Ceramic Research Group into being in the early 1960s, and this in turn formed the basis for the Society for Post-Medieval Archaeology, founded in 1967.

An approach which now seems obvious, even automatic, is the emphasis on key groups of pottery excavated from particular contexts, often with other artefacts (fig. 12.1). When a group of material is found, juxtaposition of the periods when the constituent wares are known to have circulated narrows the likely date of deposit of the group as a whole. This applies at any period, but in the post-medieval the potential is considerable, due to relatively rapid changes in styles both of English and imported wares.

EARTHENWARES AND THEIR MANUFACTURE

In the sixteenth and seventeenth centuries, the pottery industry comprised numerous producers whose methods and location are reminiscent of their medieval forebears; yet the trend towards specialization meant that more potters were working full-time and for more distant markets than was possible for the medieval farmer–potter. Although this foreshadows the intense specialization of the mid-eighteenth century and beyond, the production of coarse wares was still largely a rural industry, and needs to be distinguished from the urban manufacture of finer wares which developed in the seventeenth century, based on imported prototypes of tin-glazed and stoneware pottery.

The long view of coarse-ware production, from the later Middle Ages to the industrial revolution, is one of evolution, but with certain important changes in form and decoration which extended both the utility and the attraction of pottery.

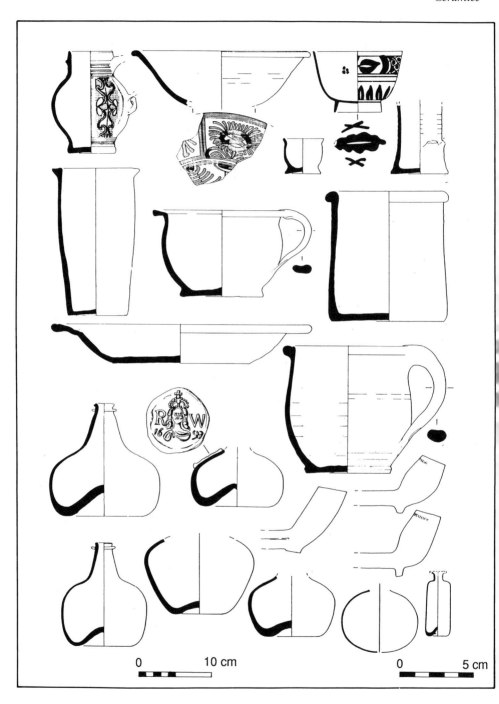

Fig. 12.1 Oxford: a group of pottery, glass and clay pipes from a pit at 16 Church Street, St Ebb
property sold to John Smart, carpenter, in 1679. The contents of the pit may have come from his househ
for the clay pipes date to 1670–1700 and the Kings Head tavern seal to 1693. Scales: 10cm – pottery
vessel-glass; 5cm – clay pipes and glass seal (Tom Hassall; Oxfordshire Architectural and Historical Soci

Expansion of the range of vessel types had begun during the fifteenth century, with traditional cooking pots, storage jars and jugs being supplemented by cups and related small forms. In the sixteenth and seventeenth centuries many new types appeared, and it is likely that the growth of production of skillets, pipkins, and in particular flat wares, parallels if not copies trends on the continent, notably in the Netherlands and in France. The following is a survey of the most important changes. It will be seen that it is difficult to set this out merely by types, or even area by area, for many kilns made changing ranges of wares.

Cistercian wares and their derivatives

This is a key range of cups and related small wares, which originated late in the fifteenth century and were produced over a wide area from Yorkshire to south-east Wales. It evolved over the sixteenth and seventeenth centuries into a variety of black-ware and slipware vessels, some of which remained in production until the eighteenth century. The true Cistercian wares, as generally defined, diminish in the middle of the sixteenth century, and their presence in a group usually points to deposit between 1475 and 1550. This explains the name, which originates from early finds in monastic dissolution contexts. The medieval origins of Cistercian ware are uncertain: it has been suggested that they formed a cheap alternative to metal drinking vessels, and also competed with those turned from wood. By 1500 the range of forms was large. Small cups, usually no more than 12cm high, were made with single handles or several; some vessels were intended to take lids; there are also bottles and flasks. The typical finish is dark brown or black, often achieved by using a nearly clear glaze over a red or brown fabric. Decoration is common, but certainly not universal. It was usual to apply a decoration in thick white slip over the body, the clear glaze giving a yellow effect. Best known are patterns of near-circular blobs, sometimes stamped, lattice designs, and zoomorphic or floral designs; for some of these, pre-shaped pieces of clay were applied to the body of the pot. Dark bodies are not universal: reversed Cistercian ware, using a light body and a clear slip, has a yellow finish with darker decoration. Some reversed-ware cups have a finish not unlike the Midlands yellow wares discussed later.

Production of Cistercian wares was until fairly recently thought to be largely in the north, particularly in Yorkshire. The distribution of kilns is now seen to stretch through the north and west Midlands as far as the Monmouth area. Nevertheless, in Yorkshire there is a remarkable concentration of kilns, in particular near Wakefield. Whatever the degree of chance in their discovery and availability for excavation, it does seem that the potters of Potovens, Silcoates and Wrenthorpe were significant in regional terms, with a market which extended over Yorkshire and along the east coast (Brears 1967; Bartlett 1971; *PMA* 1985: 180). It has been possible to trace particular decorative forms: for example recent observation of three kiln sites at Wrenthorpe disclosed high-quality sixteenth-century wares with distinctive decoration: the square notches forming the centres of applied petals and the eyes of stags have been recognized on finds in the Midlands and in London. Particular kilns in these hamlets appear to have had their own specialisms. One Wrenthorpe kiln made seven forms not previously recorded, including an ornate yellow-ware chafing dish which appears to date from the later part of the sixteenth century. To the east of Wakefield the excavated early-sixteenth-century kiln at Potterton made further variants (Mayes and Pirie 1966). Here the light-coloured reversed wares were almost as common as the dark cups, and there was also some use of green glaze over a light body, comparable with green-glazed Cistercian-type wares found in County Durham.

The emergence of the west Yorkshire industry early in the sixteenth century is an example of the need of a growing population for employment, and forms a model applicable to other districts where opportunities in agriculture were limited, but where resources of fuel and clay were plentiful. These potters had ample resources: coppiced wood and outcropping coal were present, as were clays which varied from the refractory material ideal for kiln furniture to the pot-clay used for the wares. Lead or iron was available for glazes: the lead came from Derbyshire or from the northern Pennines beyond Skipton, and the iron ore from the coal measures. These advantages were accompanied by the early development of trading links. Even though river and road improvements were yet to come, the West Riding was increasingly a trading region: its textiles and lead entered the coasting trade through the Humber, and drovers took livestock southwards by road. In return, the area formed a growing market for the farmers of the Vale of York. It is this kind of network which is important to our understanding of the distribution of pottery beyond the nearest market town, and the development of the reputation of particular kiln centres over a whole region.

Cistercian ware has been found over much of England. Although some kilns had a long-distance trade, distinctive variations in design and fabric have shown that there were also many local sources of manufacture. This applies to the north-eastern green wares mentioned earlier, and to distinctive cups found in the Manchester area, neither of whose sources have been found. The production of Cistercian wares in Staffordshire is known from the distribution of wasters around Hanley, and although little is yet known about the sixteenth-century kilns, a tradition of production has been recognized, and in the middle decades of the seventeenth century the potters of Burslem and Hanley were making slipware cups of high quality. Further south, there was early production at Chilvers Coton, Warwickshire, where the ware occurs from the end of the fourteenth century (Mayes and Scott 1984: 41). A centre which is important but which requires further investigation is Ticknall, near Burton-on-Trent. Kilns were excavated in the nineteenth century, and some of the material is in the Victoria and Albert Museum. The Ticknall Cistercian wares are distinctive for the poor mixture of iron-rich and iron-free clays, showing as white or yellow flecks through the glaze (Coppack 1972).

The manufacture of Cistercian ware in Herefordshire and Monmouth is now known to have been on some scale, explaining the amount which has been found in Gloucester. Kilns making small-wares have been sought in Herefordshire, and although a kiln-site has been located at Garway, producing black wares in the Cistercian tradition, no definitely sixteenth-century source has yet been found. More certain are the kilns near Abergavenny and Monmouth, where there was production of Cistercian wares and other types in the sixteenth and seventeenth centuries (J.M. Lewis 1980; Clarke *et al.* 1984).

In the seventeenth century the Cistercian-ware forms are encountered only as residuals. But their tradition was extended by the black wares, of which the most common forms were tygs: tall flared cups, often multi-handled, and decorative as much as useful in form. These embody so many of the features seen in the sixteenth-century dark-coloured cups that the derivation seems certain. Black-ware production started in the early part of the seventeenth century and can be found over much of England. Some potters, as at Wrotham in Kent and Ticknall, decorated a proportion of their wares with slip, but the plain black product, with a thick lustrous glaze, typifies deposits of this period. The earliest discovery of a kiln producing black wares was at the Babylon site at Ely, but the circumstances of the find are now obscure. In Norfolk, black tygs were made at Wroxham, and wares of a poorer black at Fulmodeston (Jennings 1981: 150). Near Chelmsford the kilns at Stock made black wares (Cunningham and Drury 1985: 83–5), and in Hertford-shire single-handled black mugs were made at Woodside (*PMA* 1967: 114–5). In Northamptonshire there are two known sources, Yardley Gobion and Paulersbury (*PMA* 1969: 200–202; 1974: 134) In the marches comparable wares were made at Garway, Herefordshire (*PMA* 1985, 177–9), at a kiln near Talgarth, in the Monmouth area and, in north Wales, at the Buckley kilns. In the Midlands, black wares were made at Wednesbury as well as at Ticknall (Gooder,1984), and in the north they have been found in seventeenth-century levels at one of the Wrenthorpe kilns. The dating spreads over most of the seventeenth century and into the eighteenth. Black-wares are found in many seventeenth-century groups, appearing around the 1620s, and with Staffordshire slipware plates and stoneware bellar-mines. Some kilns in the north-west, notably Buckley and Prescot, continued to make black wares until late in the eighteenth century.

The other direction in which the Cistercian-ware tradition can be traced is to the yellow wares of the Midlands. The relationship here is not so simple, for yellow wares were being produced in the region at the same time as reversed Cistercian wares further north, and both may have been striving for the same customer, who preferred light-coloured pottery. Nevertheless, production of yellow wares does increase at the beginning of the seventeenth century, and some of the former Cistercian-ware potters appear to have been involved. Yellow wares appear on sites in the Midlands over a well-defined period: they are absent from groups at the Whitefriars, Coventry, in the 1540s, but present in the town by the 1570s (Woodfield 1963-4). They are common in seventeenth-century deposits in the Midlands and the north-west, but dwindle in the face of Staffordshire yellow wares by 1700, although still present in the early-eighteenth-century deposit at Temple Balsall. The range of forms was wide: at the top end of the quality range were cups, tankards, candlesticks and pedestal bowls; for heavier use there were jars, pipkins and flat wares. Throughout, the influence of London and East Anglia can be seen, in types reminiscent of imports from the Netherlands. The problem with the yellow wares of the early seventeenth century is to know where they were made. Very few pieces of this type were found at the Nuneaton kilns, and although Ticknall has been suggested as a source, kiln wasters in any quantity have not been found.

A variant of light-coloured ware in which the Cistercian-ware tradition can also be seen appears in the south-west of the Midlands (Vince 1977: 273): in Gloucestershire and Worcestershire there is a seventeenth-century distribution of green-glazed wares, some with a white slip beneath the glaze, giving a very brightly coloured effect. These comprise two-and three-handled cups of Cistercian type, but also lobed cups and chafing dishes whose designs are similar to French and Low Countries green-glazed white wares. The interest of these is that the Cistercian-ware and the southern green tradition come together, the latter being considered in the next section.

Green wares

Green-glazed earthenwares circulated over much of England in the sixteenth and seventeenth centuries. In the south these became more popular than the red-ware pottery common at the end of the Middle Ages. Southern potteries made a great range of qualities and forms, from jugs and large coarse-ware vessels to cups, chafing dishes and flasks which are comparable in size with Cistercian wares further north, yet owe most in design and decoration to imports from the Continent. The fabrics were light in colour and the glazes cover a wide range of greens, towards yellows which approach those of the Midlands.

An important centre of production was the heathland of west Surrey and east Hampshire, whence 'border ware' was traded to London on a large scale. The capital was a traditional market for green-glazed wares in light-coloured fabrics (Matthews and Green 1969), which had been met in the fifteenth century by French imports and by the kilns at Cheam in Surrey. The market was dynamic, for London's growth, in population and in trade, marked it out as an exceptional centre of consumption, drawing goods of all kinds from the entire south-eastern region. The growth of the Surrey–Hampshire border potteries has to be seen in this light: this was an area where agriculture was hindered by poor soils, but where white clay deposits and woodland were available. Elsewhere within range of London agriculture was putting heavy pressure on woodlands, which explains the disappearance of the Cheam kilns at the end of the fifteenth century. London, however, was not the only market for the Surrey green wares, which have been found over most of the south-east, from the Thames valley where they occur in Oxford, in Winchester, and along the east coast from Dover to Newcastle. The latter was probably reached via the Thames by coastal shipping, which would also explain the presence of Surrey wares in Norwich.

The west-Surrey clays were not quite so white as those at Cheam, but at their best they gave a finer texture (Holling 1971). The range of glaze colours paralleled French output, and just as there is difficulty in telling Cheam wares from earlier imports, so some of the west-Surrey wares come close enough to the appearance of the French product to be hard to distinguish, a problem which calls for analysis of the fabrics. There has been discussion over whether the west-Surrey wares were made in the same range of colours from the fifteenth to the seventeenth century, or whether the brighter 'Tudor Green' became less common after the middle of the sixteenth century, to be replaced by the yellower greens (Holling 1977). Work at the kiln site at Farnborough Hill (*PMA* 1968–73) has suggested that production in bright green was maintained, but other potters, as at Cove, were working with yellower glazes in the seventeenth century, making wares which approach the colour of Midlands products (Haslam 1975). Forms made in the area changed in accord with market requirements and competition: at the end of the fifteenth century lobed cups become less common, being replaced by carinated profiles, and in the middle of the sixteenth century jugs appear which imitate the forms of German stoneware. Cove provides an assemblage typical of the wares saleable in the early seventeenth century, including plates, porringers, chamber-pots, candlesticks and stove tiles.

Elsewhere in rural south-east England, the east Surrey kilns at Limpsfield, which had supplied much of Surrey, west Kent and the fringe of the London area in the fourteenth century, had ceased production by 1500. Indeed, in the south-east, the density of post-medieval kilns appears to have been quite low, and a good deal of the needs of the local market came from coastal trade imports. Of the known kilns, that at Boreham Street near Herstmonceux was supplying the south-east part of the Weald with coarse wares and some finer pieces in the sixteenth century, its products being found on ironworks sites developed during the 1540s. Further into the Weald a kiln operated at Hareplain, Biddenden, in the early sixteenth century, but its products were confined to the coarser wares, with a local circulation (*PMA* 1970: 183). There is a kiln of particular interest at Parrock, near East Grinstead, which early in the sixteenth century made wares remarkably similar to imports from Beauvais (Freke 1979). The kiln was adjacent to the Parrock ironworks, which was operated by French immigrants, themselves from the Beauvaisis. The connection is a remarkable indication of how the links between the two ironworking areas involved other trades.

The green wares typical of the late sixteenth and early seventeenth centuries were made by a number of other potteries within range of urban markets in southern England. Buckinghamshire is a good example, where the best-known products are those of Brill, whose strong medieval tradition was maintained right through to the nineteenth century with wares which were sold over much of the south-east Midlands and the upper Thames valley (Farley 1979). They are common in sixteenth-century contexts in Oxford, although their sales there seem to have declined after 1600. Brill was only one among several potteries in and beyond the Chilterns: at Potter Row, Great Missenden, a variety of dishes, pipkins and bowls were made in white, yellow and red fabrics, some with unique stamped decorations, making clear that although fashions in urban markets were changing, they did not swamp local tradition or innovation (Farley *et al.* 1978). Further to the north, the kilns in Northamptonshire, at Paulersbury and Yardley Gobion, entered the trade in green-glazed wares in off-white fabrics and were in competition with the yellow wares of the Midlands.

Kilns in western Hampshire and east Dorset also made green wares, for sale in Salisbury and the coastal towns. The best-known centre was on the heathlands north of Poole, around Alderholt and Verwood (Young 1979). These potters are documented from the first decade of the sixteenth century, although the references are sparse until the 1620s. The products included a wide range of green wares, from coarse pieces to flat wares of good quality. A problem with Verwood is that no excavation has taken place, and much of our knowledge of fabrics is derived from nineteenth-century pieces in collections. Sherds from excavations in the region have been ascribed to Verwood on the basis of comparison with the fabrics of these later products, not without hazard. This was not the only centre: Dorchester and Purbeck were supplied with good-quality green-glazed dishes made close to Wareham, where a kiln site has been recognized from scatters of wasters (*ex inf.* J. Draper).

In the north of England 'reduced green wares' were widely used, the range of forms being less wide than the products of the southern kilns, but including jugs, jars and derivatives of Cistercian-ware forms. Kilns where the finer reduced green wares were made are beginning to be recognized, notably in the north-west at Silverdale and Arnside. However, despite the ubiquity of the ware, there is a lack of published information about its manufacture and a need for further research.

CHANGES IN THE PRODUCTION OF COARSE WARES

A characteristic of deposits dated to the years around 1500, particularly in the north, is the handled bung-holed storage jar. This had evolved in the fifteenth century, and examples of production can be found over much of the country, being best known at kilns in the north and Midlands. In Yorkshire, bung-holed jars formed a large proportion of the wasters found at Rawmarsh in the Don valley, and at kilns at Stearsby and Helmsley (*PMA* 1971: 216). The type is also known at southern kilns, as has been demonstrated at Woodside, Hertfordshire and by finds in Worcester. Containers of this kind, together with coarse-ware jugs, were increasingly made in the purple finishes, and a number of producers aimed at a bright, almost metallic effect which improved in quality over the sixteenth and seventeenth centuries. A great deal of coarse ware found on seventeenth-century Yorkshire sites has this finish, but the source is uncertain. In the Midlands, the tradition of purple-ware production had developed from as far back as the thirteenth century, dated by material from Derby. The kilns at Chilvers Coton, Nuneaton, made purple wares in the fifteenth century, continuing well into the sixteenth; Ticknall, a producer of Cistercian wares, developed a trade in Midland-purple jars and pancheons which had a wide circulation over the north Midlands which lasted until the eighteenth century; and to the south-west the tradition of purple wares was strong in the Malvern area.

One of the most important of the coarse-ware types of the post-medieval centuries is known as glazed red earthenware. Its ubiquity over East Anglia has increasingly been recognized, particularly as a result of excavations in Norwich (Jennings 1981: 157ff). The range of types is remarkable, from utility wares through to smaller pieces suitable for table use. There is a resemblance to wares found in the Low Countries, but the extent of imports among the pieces found in East Anglia remains a problem. Despite the low cost of return transport from the Netherlands to London in ships used to export cloth, it is unlikely that the cheaper and heavier wares would be imported and brought by coast to East Anglia. It seems certain that there must be more East Anglian kilns making plain wares than have yet been discovered: parallels are sought with Stock, in Essex, where wasters of plain glazed wares have been found (Cunningham and Drury 1985: 83–8).

A pottery form which became very common in the sixteenth and particularly the seventeenth century was the pancheon, the large shallow bowl used for household and particularly dairy purposes. Its increasing use has been noted in Norwich early in the sixteenth century, and production has been studied in Lincolnshire (A.J. White 1982), where the earliest source so far found is the kiln at Old Bolingbroke, making pancheons from about 1500. At the excavated Boston kiln they appear in an early seventeenth-century context (*PMA* 1976: 172–3) and at the Bourne kiln the dating is similar. They were used in quantity over most of the country throughout the eighteenth and nineteenth centuries and are one of the most frequent items in domestic refuse deposits over the whole period.

Slipwares

The early-sixteenth-century use of slip decoration is best known from Cistercian ware (see pp. 245–47), whose decoration is distinct from styles in use on the continent. The latter were taken up by former Cistercian-ware potters around the beginning of the seventeenth century, and were also used by those who had hitherto made plain wares at the coarser end of the quality range. It has however been suggested that potters in the London area were producing slipwares from early in the sixteenth century, for a wide range of red-ware vessels, chafing dishes, jugs, pipkins, with a white slip decoration glazing to yellow, were found on the Guy's Hospital site, and thought to be of local rather than imported origin (Dawson 1979: 44–5).

From the first quarter of the seventeenth century, the typical pottery group contains slipwares. Their use continued through the eighteenth century, and they can still be found in nineteenth-century assemblages. Slipwares were produced in large quantities over much of the country, yet the origins of this decoration are still discussed 25 years after the study became an archaeological rather than an art-historical problem.

A strong influence in enlarging the market for slipwares was the volume of imports from the Netherlands, carried cheaply into London. Those produced in south-east England in the early seventeenth century appear to be a direct response, reacting to a market developed by the importers. What is not yet clear is how far there had been a sixteenth-century London tradition of using slipwares, suggested by the finds at Guy's Hospital. Notable among the increasing quantities available are the 'metropolitan' wares, whose range of colour and pattern is easily recognizable. There is usually a white slip, clear-glazed to give a yellow finish, in a variety of floral and abstract designs. The body varies more than the decoration, with clays firing to a range of browns, almost to black, and the clear glazes giving finishes from light brown to black, the latter sometimes with a greenish effect. Important production centres appeared on the edge of Epping Forest, at Harlow and Loughton, as well as in Hertfordshire, at Woodside, and further north-west at Potterspury and Brill. Metropolitan wares are commonly found over much of southern England: apart from their ubiquity on seventeenth-century London sites they appear from Hampshire and Oxford to Norwich, and were carried on the coasting trade to Newcastle and the Northumberland coast.

The Harlow kilns are the best-known producers of metropolitan slipwares, and excavations have taken place on two kiln sites (Newton *et al.* 1960). On one, since built over, a kiln fragment was found, with, close by, a clay pit filled with sherds of metropolitan ware. This was not the only product, for black-ware tygs were also made, as well as coarse wares which included bung-hole jars, pitchers and bowls. The second site also produced metropolitan wares, found around a feature identified as a mixing floor for clay. The documentary evidence places work at these kilns in the years between about 1600 and 1670, but it is not at present certain whether there is a sixteenth-century origin or if production continued into the eighteenth century. The Loughton potters operated to the south of Harlow on the eastern fringe of Epping Forest, and are referred to in seventeenth-century documentary sources. Finds from fieldwalking and from an excavated kiln have shown that their product range was wider than at the Harlow kilns, for it included red wares and hollow wares as well as the metropolitan flat wares (*PMA* 1970: 182).

Potterspury also produced a diverse range, even if best known for its metropolitan-style flat wares (Mayes 1968). There are coarse wares and also finer products of interesting variety, including pieces with encrusted decoration. Manufacture started early in the seventeenth century, and the siting between Staffordshire and London, on Watling Street, gave access to the capital as well as a view of the improving quality of the Staffordshire wares. Despite the high standard of many of the Potterspury products and the potential of its siting, the village did not develop into a specialized community of potters on the scale found elsewhere, and production does not appear to have survived long after the 1660s.

South of the Thames, slipwares were produced at Wrotham, Kent: the majority were hollow wares, tygs and possets, rather than the flat wares of the metropolitan-ware potters. A number of dated Wrotham pieces are known, covering the period 1612 to 1709, which corresponds with the dating of contexts in which Wrotham wares have been found (Ashdown 1968). Wrotham demonstrates the influence of imported stonewares on English earthenware design: late-seventeenth-century Wrotham pieces incorporate many features reminiscent of German stoneware, one jug even bearing the mark of a Rhenish stoneware merchant (Schnitzer 1977). The coarse wares which were made at Wrotham are also of types which fit into late-seventeenth-century contexts, and have been found on sites in Kent and Surrey ranging from Dover to Croydon. Surprisingly little research has been carried out at this important centre, despite frequent references in the literature. Wasters were recovered from Borough Green, Wrotham, early this century and are now in the Fitzwilliam Museum, Cambridge, and although the source of the wasters has been re-explored, the actual kiln sites are not known.

In the north, slipware manufacture followed on from the making of Cistercian ware in Yorkshire and Staffordshire. The Staffordshire potters developed the quality and range of their wares, producing brown and yellow cups and tygs, and in the second half of the century made a speciality of the press-moulded plate. This remained in production throughout the eighteenth century and achieved a market throughout much of England. Large quantities have come from deposits in the towns of the Potteries, a notable assemblage being excavated at the site of the Hill Top pottery in Burslem (*PMA* 1967: 115–16; 1968: 187). Staffordshire specialized in the moulded plate, which was also produced at Buckley (Flints) as early as 1650 and at Midhope (Yorks) in the eighteenth century.

In Yorkshire, the change from Cistercian-style forms can be seen at the Wrenthorpe kilns. There was continuity of production in these villages through to the early part of the eighteenth century, and new designs were introduced from about 1600. Flat wares became common, and the cups and tygs were of increasing size, but echoing the sixteenth-century traditions. The quality of execution seems to have declined, with larger and thicker vessels replacing the finely potted cups of the sixteenth century. They cannot really compare in quality with the best of Staffordshire, metropolitan or Netherlands slipwares, although they found a ready market over south and west Yorkshire in the seventeenth century. After 1700 output dwindled in face of competition from Staffordshire, from Bolsterstone and Midhope in the south of the county (Kenworthy 1928), as well as from the potteries of the lower Don valley between Rotherham and Doncaster. In the West Riding new rivals appeared: the kiln at Pule Hill, Halifax was making slipwares at the end of the seventeenth century for the markets of the textile towns, and its neighbour, at Baitain, continued slipware production in the eighteenth century (*PMA* 1967: 116).

Many other potteries took up slipware manufacture, for local markets rather than to challenge the increasing dominance of Staffordshire. In north Wales the Buckley potteries turned to making slipwares of good quality from late in the seventeenth century, and sold into Cheshire and Lancashire (Davey 1975). To the south, numerous potteries in Glamorgan and Monmouthshire made slipwares, a tradition maintained at the Ewenny kilns, near Bridgend, which operated into the present century (J.M. Lewis 1982). A scatter of potteries in the south of England also made slipware dishes of general resemblance to the Staffordshire types. Of these, Bristol had a significant output (*PMA* 1986: 353), but wasters have also been found in Cornwall, at Truro (*PMA* 1969: 189–9), in Surrey, at Dorking (*PMA* 1970: 184), and in eastern Sussex there are characteristic local variants made by potteries in the Hastings area.

Sgraffito and related wares in south-west England

A different form of slipware was made in the south-west, where the sgraffito technique was used in Somerset and north Devon. The method was to apply a slip, to scratch through to the contrasting body of the pot, and to glaze over the completed design. Sgraffito is particularly associated with the kilns at Donyatt, near Yeovil (Coleman-Smith and Pearson 1989), which, although the most studied, and the subject of a series of excavations, were not the only producers, for wasters have been found near Lyme (Draper 1982). The origins of Donyatt sgrafitto have not yet been explained: the earliest context in which it has been found is at the Narrow Quay excavations in Bristol, in a deposit dated to about 1580 (Good 1987). It is not known for how long the ware had been in production at that time, or whether there are medieval prototypes in the region. Although the method was used at post-medieval kilns in Italy, France and Germany, too few of the Continental sgrafitto wares can be found in south-west England to suggest direct copying to fill a market created by the success of imports.

Wares which embodied similar techniques, but which are distinguishable from those made in Somerset, came from kilns in and near Barnstaple and Bideford (Grant 1983). These potteries emerged as suppliers for much of the Bristol Channel region in the seventeenth century, also trading in quantity to North America until displaced by the makers of Staffordshire and Buckley wares in the eighteenth century. The north-Devon potteries produced a wide range of types, of which the sgraffito slipwares were only a part. From much earlier they had produced characteristic gravel-tempered container wares whose quality and function is equivalent to coarse pottery made in other areas and referred to in preceding sections. These are dated on Lundy to early in the sixteenth century, and were being shipped to south Wales about 1600. They continued to arrive throughout the seventeenth and eighteenth centuries, but were also made by potteries such as Ewenny, Glamorgan, and material from the two sources becomes difficult to distinguish (Evans 1979). Sgraffito was also made in north Wales, at Buckley, in the second half of the seventeenth century. The range of products of the north-Devon kilns is wide, embracing flat wares, jars, cups, chamber-pots, chafing dishes and ovens, the last a type which continued to be a north-Devon speciality until late in the nineteenth century.

THE END OF THE POST-MEDIEVAL TRADITION

The great change in the scale of output of English ceramics came in the middle decades of the eighteenth century, in particular with the evolution of mass production of earthenwares in the Staffordshire industry. But to stress Stafford-shire can lead to misleading simplification. Many traditional producers continued to manufacture their wares for rural markets, and were to do so throughout the eighteenth and nineteenth centuries. Slip-decorated earthenwares for example were to remain in production and common use, owing little to the technical changes of the industrial revolution. On the other hand, increases in the scale of production were far from unique to Staffordshire: new centres, of which Leeds and the Severn Valley potteries in Shropshire are good examples, were to spring up with little or no ceramic tradition behind them.

Most of these changes are well documented, and archaeological interest in the actual production of pottery after the second quarter of the eighteenth century tends to concentrate on those few cases where the documentary record is faulty. The important aspect for the archaeologist is the recognition of the new wares and a knowledge of their dates of introduction, as a means of identifying eighteenth-century deposits.

The key innovatory types of pottery can be briefly summarized: it is outside the scope of this survey to provide a detailed account. In earthenwares, early eighteenth-century deposits are characterized by the increasing numbers of local slipwares, supplementing traditional producers and competing with the nationally traded Staffordshire wares. The Bristol, Shropshire and Yorkshire potteries are good examples of new suppliers. The beginning of mottled-glaze earthenware production in Staffordshire is also important, starting as early as 1680, and prominent in early-eighteenth-century deposits. There are also examples of locally produced mottled ware, such as from the undocumented pottery built into the remains of the Long Gallery of Sheffield Manor after its demolition in 1706 (*PMA* 1972: 219–20), and the kilns in Prescot, Lancashire where kiln wasters of mottled ware have been found in numerous sample excavations in the town (*PMA* 1985: 167). There is particular dating value in the association of these wares with white salt-glaze stoneware, which appears from about 1720 and will be referred to in the section on stoneware.

Finally, as a postscript, in the middle of the eighteenth century came the changes associated with the industrialization of the industry in the classic sense, with potteries in Staffordshire leading the transformation to mass production. The crucial change was the introduction of creamware. This first appeared in 1762 and was very quick to reach the market, being popular from 1765 and present in quantity in deposits of 1770 onwards. Pearlware, aimed at a similar level of the market, comes rather later, with experiments by Wedgwood at the end of the 1770s and significant production from about 1782. Wedgwood's green and yellow glazes were developed from 1759, and were in full production from 1764. Transfer printing comes much later, the earliest production on any scale being in the mid-1790s.

MISCELLANEOUS EARTHENWARES

In the wider field of ceramics, certain types of vessel not of a strictly domestic nature were often produced at kilns where domestic pottery was a staple. Horticultural and industrial wares can be difficult to identify, and their evolution and production deserve more attention than they have received. Horticultural wares present great difficulties, owing to the lack of stylistic development of forms which reached their utilitarian optimum at an early stage, and where changes are likely to reflect alterations in methods of manufacture or firing. They appear at the start of the period, and there are valuable references from the 1530s to the supply from kilns near Chelmsford of pans for the hothouses at Hampton Court (Musty 1977). Flowerpots of a more decorative kind were found at Basing House: these were urn-like vessels, probably made locally, in a fabric similar to the bricks of the area (Brears 1970: 87–90, offers a pre-1645 date, which recent excavations by Barton suggest may be too early). Watering pots are fairly common finds, often in fabrics and glazes similar to those of domestic wares. They were, for example, made at the west Surrey kilns, and at the Woolwich earthenware kiln soon after the middle of the seventeenth century. At the end of the century urns appear in the catalogue of the Nottingham stoneware potter, James Morley.

Little excavation has taken place on kiln sites where garden wares were made. The one example of a specialist kiln was at Brentford, where a small-scale mid-nineteenth-century pottery was excavated, showing the manufacture of flowerpots, dishes, garden urns and chimney pots (*PMA* 1975: 172–3). This illustrates that the relationship with architectural ceramics could be as close at some kilns as with domestic wares elsewhere.

A great variety of industrial ceramics have been made over the period. These embrace the refractory crucibles employed in glass and metal melting, and they are considered in relation to these industries. An interesting class, which became more common, was used in sugar refining. In this process sugar was placed to drain in a pottery cone with a hole at the tip, the cone being placed over a large jar. These two types of vessel have been found in Bristol, Exeter, London, Plymouth and Southampton (*PMA* 1986: 356), at York in particularly large quantities (Brooks 1983), at Liverpool, and at Prescot, where these forms were made. They have also been recovered from the seventeenth-century kiln site at Woolwich, well placed to supply provincial refiners by coastal shipping. The large numbers found attest to the growing market for imported sugar.

IMPORTED WARES

Our knowledge of pottery imported into Britain has developed greatly since the early 1960s, and although in terms of the total of finds of pottery on post-medieval sites the quantities are not large, they have a disproportionate importance. This lies in part in their potential for the dating of the contexts in which they are found, supplementing the information given by home-produced wares, but also in assessing the influence of Continental styles on English potters. For many years publication was confined to brief notes, but the position has been revolutionized by the appearance of the major study by Hurst, Neal and Van Beuningen (1986), upon which this section must inevitably and heavily depend, and which either supersedes or assimilates most of the earlier references.

It is not proposed to deal in any detail with wares from outside western Europe. Material from Asia Minor and the Near East is occasionally found, but the major pottery trade from outside Europe was in Chinese porcelain. This is only rarely encountered in contexts dating from before the last quarter of the sixteenth century, early imports coming by way of the Portuguese trade with the east. The situation changed as the Dutch eastern trade grew, and particularly with the foundation of the English East India Company in 1600. The latter brought the trade directly to this country, and the quantity of Chinese porcelains increases as a result. Small amounts of other wares from south-east Asia, notably celadon, also appear. Beurdeley (1962) gives a guide to the types of Chinese porcelain likely to be encountered on sites of seventeenth century date. The display in the Victoria and Albert Museum is valuable, and particularly recommended are the exhibits at the Percival David collection in Gordon Square, London.

Earthenwares

The Mediterranean   Small quantities of Italian and Spanish pottery are found in Britain, widely distributed over the country but with the more substantial deposits in London and other coastal towns. From Italy came maiolica: tin-glazed earthenware. This varied in quality over the kilns of Tuscany and Liguria, with the potters who catered for the upper levels of the market adopting the fashions of renaissance Italian art. In technique and standard they owed much to the tin-glazed pottery of the Near East, notably that known as Iznik ware, made in Anatolia, and the wares from Rakka in Persia. Iznik wares are known in Britain, but only in very small quantities.

A great range of lesser-quality Italian maiolicas were made, and those most commonly found in England came from the northern Tuscan kilns at Montelupo. Tin-glazed wares had been made there during the Middle Ages, and continued until the eighteenth century. The range of quality is wide, from fluted dishes of good quality and imitations of Chinese blue-and-white porcelain, to the polychrome wares whose varied and robust designs became increasingly crudely executed over the post-medieval period. This last type appears frequently in English deposits, and the vigour of the designs is comparable with that of the slipwares of seventeenth-century northern Europe. The importance of Italian tin glaze for Britain is not so much the limited presence here, but the indirect effect of the migration of some of the Italian potters to Flanders at the end of the fifteenth century. The foundation and development of the Netherlands maiolica potteries, and the export of the products to Britain prepared the way for the English delftware industry of the seventeenth century.

Italian slipwares reached northern Europe in small quantities and are interesting for comparison with northern methods. One type, made in the Pisa area, comprises marbled wares in red fabric, in which two or more colours of slip were mingled on the surface of the pot. Usually white was used with red, although this ranged between orange and brown; there are also examples in white with green. Tall costrels, with 'lion heads' projecting from the girth below the high neck, are the most common form, but bowls were also made. Sgraffito slipwares were also sent to northern Europe: these have similar colour ranges and fabrics to the marbled wares and were also made at Pisa in the sixteenth and seventeenth centuries. The white slip was cut through to the red body, and given a clear glaze which makes the slip yellow. These slipwares are fairly frequently found in English deposits of the first half of the seventeenth century.

Of the Iberian pottery centres, only a few sent their products to England in any quantity. The finer wares may be divided into the maiolicas, largely in blue-and-white designs, and the lustrewares. The Catalan Blue dishes with geometric designs, made in Barcelona, are only occasionally found in England, arriving in the sixteenth and early seventeenth centuries. More common are the maiolicas from Seville, which have been divided into three groups, according to designs. The earliest, the Isabela polychromes, are dishes characterized by concentric internal bands of blue and purple, often with a spiral design in the centre and dashes around the rim. These are found in early-sixteenth century contexts, and their absence from Armada wrecks indicates that production had ceased by the 1580s. These wares were replaced in the middle of the sixteenth century by simplified designs omitting most of the bands and the rim decoration, but retaining a centre motif or monogram. Known as Yayal Blue, they were made in the same Seville kilns and were traded in Europe and the Americas in the second half of the sixteenth century. The third type, known as Columbia Plain, were undecorated, apart from the uniform white tin glaze. There are a few examples of bowls half dipped in green glaze, but these are rare. This plain version of Seville ware was made and traded throughout the sixteenth century and until about the 1630s. There have also been occasional finds of Spanish costrels, probably made in the Seville area. These have a lead glaze, over the upper half of the pot only, and are characterized by a star painted in four strokes on the girth in yellow, red or blue.

Valencian lustreware is found in fifteenth and early-sixteenth-century contexts. Its production derived from medieval Islamic traditions, and the most common forms made in the fifteenth century and surviving into the sixteenth were dishes, bowls, jugs and cylindrical jars (*albarelli*). A tin glaze was used, with dense foliate designs in copper lustre and blue. Animal and human forms are occasionally found in the decoration.

Much more significant in quantity, but far less useful for dating purposes are the Iberian coarse wares. Olive jars made in Seville, some plain and some green-or yellow-glazed inside, entered Britain in large quantities as containers from late in the sixteenth until the eighteenth centuries. There are three sizes, the largest, suggested as being for wine, holding about 16 litres, a medium, globular-shaped type, of 6-litre capacity, which could have been intended for oil, and a small carrot-shaped vessel of unknown purpose. The other significant coarse pottery reaching England is known as Merida-type ware. This has a characteristic micaceous fabric, only occasionally with a white-painted decoration, and was made in southern Portugal and neighbouring parts of Spain. Although a range of jars, jugs and bowls have been found in deposits in ports, notably in Plymouth and Southampton, only the costrel-like storage jars have a wider circulation, presumably arriving as containers for a liquid too viscous to require an internally glazed container. The date range is wide, from the thirteenth to the seventeenth centuries.

France   France was a traditional source of green-glazed pottery found in southern England and it can be argued that generally comparable wares from Surrey found acceptance in a market accustomed to these imports. Some of the French green wares have been included among those described as 'Tudor Green', the brightly glazed vessels with white bodies over whose source there is still considerable doubt. The sixteenth-century material from Winchester, published over 20 years ago, was considered to resemble French rather than Surrey wares (Hurst 1964, 140). However, the term 'Tudor Green' has been used for a range of pottery wide enough to include both French and Surrey products, and now that there is potential for differentiating wares by examination of thin sections of fabric, there is a case for abandoning the term, and working towards a more precise attribution of pottery to kiln sites.

The long-standing Saintonge industry, in the neighbourhood of Saintes, produced plain and decorated wares which developed in form and complexity of decorative style in the sixteenth century. The kilns remained active until the eighteenth century, but the pottery becomes rare in English contexts after about 1650. Plain jugs and jars from the Saintonge, in off-white or buff fabric, some with splashes of green glaze, appear in English ports, particularly Southampton, in contexts of around 1500. Also to be noted are plain narrow-necked jugs in a whiter fabric with splashes of yellow glaze, which are considered to come from the Loire rather than the Saintonge. These continued to be traded throughout the seventeenth century, and are commonly found in Scotland from about 1600. Much better known are the sixteenth-century developments in the production of polychrome wares. These comprise chafing dishes, many with applied masks, as well as dishes and bowls. These pieces were normally glazed in green and brown, although some have a white slip, in imitation of white fabric. In the middle of the sixteenth century yellow and blue were added to the colours used on the standard range of wares, and these complex-coloured designs continue well into the seventeenth century. The influence behind these was Bernard Palissy, who developed his polychrome wares with moulded rustic designs in the mid-sixteenth century, for an aristocratic market.

The earthenwares produced in the Beauvais area are commonly found in sixteenth-century English deposits, particularly in those of the first half of the century. The quantity underlines the close links between south-east England and the Pays de Bray, partly a result of proximity, but also suggesting a trade fostered by the large-scale immigration of ironworkers from the forests of the Bray to the Weald between 1490 and 1540. Two types of earthenwares, plain and sgraffito, were imported, both in a fine white fabric. The plain wares were glazed in green, yellow or brown, some with one colour internally, another externally. Jugs, chafing dishes, costrels and bowls are common, flasks, whistles and jars (*albarelli*) less frequent. There is a use of relief moulding, particularly on dishes and costrels. The sgraffito wares are of high quality, in forms similar to the plain wares. Some have a red slip cut to the white fabric, which gives a yellow line when glazed. The other type was given a white slip on top of the pre-fired red. The white slip was then cut through to the red to give a brown-line design after glazing. These sgraffito wares went out of production at the beginning of the seventeenth century in favour of a trailed slipware which rarely reached England. There are a few imported examples of another slipware, made at Martincamp, near Neufchâtel-en-Bray. This has been found at Plymouth, and the source was not known until the discovery of wasters in 1974. The ware is quite distinctive, having a clear glaze over the white fabric and the green and dark brown designs. Also from the Bray come the Martincamp flasks, which are discussed under stoneware. Many, however, were of a clay fired at earthenware temperatures, although the actual forms are generally similar.

The Netherlands   This is a most important source, both for the quantity of material found in English deposits and for the influence on English potters. It is not surprising that significant quantities appeared: the shipping route between London and Antwerp, and the successor trades with other Netherlands ports after the closure of Antwerp in the mid-1560s favoured the conveyance of bulky commodities westwards, as return cargoes on a route dominated by the export of English textiles.

LEAD-GLAZED EARTHENWARE   Red and grey earthenwares, with some variants in white, represent the cheaper, bulk end of the export trade. The red wares are found in plain glazed forms and decorated with white slip. The undecorated wares strongly resemble the glazed red earthenwares of East Anglia and the London area, which have been suggested as developing to compete with the imports, or being made by immigrant potters. The red earthenwares had been gradually superseding grey wares at Netherlands kilns since the thirteenth century, and by the beginning of the sixteenth century few grey pieces were being exported. The red-ware cooking pots appear to have been exported in large numbers, and are common in English sixteenth-century contexts; they are distinguished by their three feet and two handles, a style adopted in England in the sixteenth century. They were accompanied by other forms not previously made in England: strainers, chamberpots, half-round fire covers, candlesticks and money boxes. There is a wide range of qualities of finish, from the few imported examples of unglazed grey wares, of similar fabric to the red wares but given a reduced firing, to the preponderant red wares with their varying amounts of glaze. The white-ware equivalents of the red tripod cooking pots appear in England, notably in Norwich, but are much less common.

Of the Netherlands slipwares, the most significant from the English standpoint were made in the province of North Holland and are common from late in the sixteenth century until early in the eighteenth. There was a strong slipware tradition in the Netherlands, from the medieval wares of Utrecht and the sgraffito wares made until the middle of the sixteenth century at unidentified kilns. The latter have been found in small quantities in eastern England. In terms of decoration the North Holland wares represent a new start, although the similarity of the fabric to that of the undecorated forms of red earthenware is clear. The best-known types are dishes, jugs, pipkins and fire covers. The decoration is in yellow slip trailed on the brown earthenware, with areas of green painted thinly over the yellow. The designs are often dense and complicated, not only geometric but with animals, medallions and sometimes dates incorporated. The earliest example has a date of 1573 and the latest 1711: the well-defined start in the second half of the sixteenth century is important for the dating of excavated groups.

TIN-GLAZED EARTHENWARES   The maiolica wares traded from the Netherlands in the 150 years after 1500 are one of the most important classes of pottery imported into Britain. They were widely distributed, beyond the ports and larger towns to which so many types of imported wares are restricted. Their use for dating purposes is rather less than was once hoped, not least because many types were held in sufficiently high regard to survive as ornaments or in occasional use for longer than the more utilitarian wares. The types which reached this country may be conveniently divided into three, namely the South Netherlands wares made in the Antwerp area from late in the fifteenth century until the third quarter of the sixteenth century; the North Netherlands types which date from not long before 1550 into the seventeenth century, and the wares influenced by Chinese porcelain, in blue-and-white and plain white, in production from the last quarter of the sixteenth century through the rest of the period.

South-Netherlands maiolica appears in the last years of the fifteenth century, and although a variety of bowls and jugs were made, the two-handled flower vase was the most common type to reach England. Here it is widespread, and its presence in pottery groups provides strong grounds for dating associated material to the first half of the sixteenth century. The two-handled globular form varies little in profile, but the polychrome decoration contains a variety of motifs in the two side panels. Best known is the 'IHS' monogram, but there are many zoological and floral designs. The origins are of interest: the technique of decoration is Italian, and certain forms not found in this country reflect the connection. The vase form, however, is Spanish, suggesting that examples from Valencia reached Flanders at the end of the fifteenth century and were developed by Italian potters in the Antwerp area. The other form which is tentatively attributed to Antwerp, on the basis of distribution rather than any kiln wasters, is a jug type found in England in deposits of the second half of the sixteenth century, some with silver-gilt mounts dated between 1549 and 1582. These 'Malling' jugs, once thought to have been products of unknown maiolica potters in late-sixteenth-century England have a globular profile echoing the proportions of Cologne and Frechen stoneware. The jugs are normally finished in blue or purple over tin glaze; on some the colour is mottled in imitation of stoneware, and the white tin glaze can show in patches through the blue.

The sixteenth-century north-Netherlands polychrome maiolicas are less common in England than those from the south. Nevertheless there are representative assemblages, those from Plymouth and London giving a particularly good coverage. Dishes are the most common, but *albarelli*, jugs and bowls were also imported. Botanical and zoological motifs predominate, and their execution is usually of a high quality. Imports continued into the seventeenth century, but after about 1630 they become hard to distinguish from wares made on the south bank of the Thames.

The blue-and-white and plain white wares were imported in increasing quantities at the end of the sixteenth century and after 1600, as the popularity of porcelain grew: the Delft potters adopted eastern designs to cater for such fashions at a lower price than the Chinese imports. As with the polychromes, Netherlands products began to be replaced by the Southwark wares, many of which are markedly similar to the imports. In the early years of the seventeenth century, before manufacture in England began, the import trade became far more than a marginal business. This can be judged in part by the involvement of the importers in English monopolies of the period 1590–1620, indicating the potential value to patentees of regulating the trade. It can also be measured by the solid growth of British delftware manufacture in the seventeenth century, based on the market developed by the imports.

Germany Two types of German slipware are regularly found in sixteenth-and seventeenth-century contexts in England. One came from the region of the river Werra, and has been called Wanfried ware, after a kiln site which is now known to be just one amongst many. Although hollow wares were made, the most common exports to England were dishes with hammer-headed rims which appear in late-sixteenth-century deposits and continue until about 1650. Pieces from the Werra which bear dates support this chronology, having a coverage between the 1560s and the 1650s. Werra pottery is easily recognizable, in red fabric with a wide variety of abstract, naturalistic and human elements in the designs. These are in an off-white slip which when glazed has a light-green appearance. Some dishes are partly decorated with a brown slip background to the white design, and many incorporate other colours, such as green, purple or yellow, with the use of overpainting for details.

Weser ware came from north Germany between about 1580 and 1630, overlapping with exports from the Werra. As well as plates and bowls, jugs and pots were made, but the flat wares predominate among the imports. The off-white or buff fabric is of good quality, covered with white slip, with green or brown decoration overpainted. The clear glaze gives a yellow tinge to the background white slip. The significant imports of both Weser and Werra ware are easily explained. The eastward shift of English trade after the 1560s continued through the century, culminating in the foundation of the Eastland Company and resulting in growing numbers of London vessels loading cargoes at north German ports.

In the eighteenth century slipwares were produced in large quantities in the Krefeld area. A few reached England, examples being found in Southampton, Ipswich and Kings Lynn. There does not appear to have been a regular trade and this pottery would offer little attraction in a market by then dominated by home-produced slipwares.

STONEWARES

The great majority of the stonewares imported between the late Middle Ages and the end of the seventeenth century were made in Germany and the Low Countries. A small quantity came from France: from Normandy, Beauvais and Martincamp. Made from refractory clays which were fired at high temperatures, they were impervious to liquids, and hence commanded a substantial and regular sale in Britain before home production began late in the seventeenth century (Allan 1983:37–45). The value of the trade is confirmed by its involvement in grants of patents for its regulation (Henstock 1975).

German stonewares

The stonewares which were imported to Britain in the largest quantities were made in north-west Germany, from the Rhineland in the region of Cologne westwards to the Aachen area and into modern Belgium, with a further source to the south, in the Westerwald. These wares are among the most significant imports for the archaeologist: the products of the six distinct source districts have well-established chronologies and are valuable for the dating of pottery groups (Gaimster 1988).

Siegburg Stoneware was successfully made from the end of the thirteenth century and was being exported to England by the early fourteenth. Although production continued until the 1630s, Siegburg ware becomes less frequent in English deposits after the middle of the sixteenth century, and is most common in groups dated to the fifteenth century. The usual forms are tall tankards and jugs with frilled bases and pronounced rilling round the girth. Incised and stamped ornamentation became more common during the sixteenth century. The ware is characterized by the quality of the light-grey fabric of the period around 1500. After this time a whiter fabric was achieved, and in some cases a white salt glaze was used. There is some variation from this range: ash in the kiln could give splashes of brown, and pieces with green glaze are found on the continent, although uncommon in Britain. As the firing temperature for stoneware is too high for a lead glaze, a separate low-temperature firing was used. Glazed Siegburg vessels have been found at kilns in the Netherlands, showing that glazing was an entirely separate operation from manufacture.

Langerwehe   Jugs and a few bowls from these kilns near Aachen were imported in the fifteenth and early sixteenth centuries and in many places are more common than contemporary Siegburg wares. The fabric is a darker grey than the Siegburg product, and less consistently fired. Fifteenth-century pieces often have a patchy iron wash giving a purple appearance, but in the sixteenth century salt glazing produced a finish which can be confused with Raeren products, although those with bands of rouletting are distinctive. Imports from Langerwehe diminished during the first half of the sixteenth century, although the kilns remained in production throughout the post-medieval period.

Raeren   Made to the south of Aachen, Raeren products are very common from the end of the fifteenth century, and must have been transported so cheaply that even second-grade examples could be sold in England. Until the middle of the sixteenth century the most common import was a small globular drinking jug, in grey salt glaze. The standard features are a plain rim with a single groove beneath, a cylindrical neck, a strap handle usually with a single groove, a globular body with rilling on the lower half, and a splayed frilled base. Flat plain bases became more common towards the middle of the sixteenth century. In the second half of the century the imports diminished as those from Frechen increased, and the surviving trade included decorated jugs, many in standard sizes and capacities and often glazed brown. These ranged from pieces of high quality with panelled designs to those with crude face masks. At the end of the sixteenth century blue glazes began to be incorporated in the decoration, a feature which the Raeren potters continued to develop when some moved to the Westerwald in the 1590s. It is impossible to distinguish early-seventeenth-century pieces from the two centres, and there may well be pieces from British excavations whose attribution to Westerwald is unsafe.

Frechen   Imports of Frechen tankards and jugs rapidly overtook those from Raeren in the middle of the sixteenth century, and the characteristic Bartmann (bearded face mask) jugs remained a staple trade until the development of English stoneware manufacture in the 1670s. The fabric is grey and the glaze of the earlier wares is a plain brown. This soon changed to the mottled salt glaze typical of the seventeenth century and was the prototype for many English stonewares of the eighteenth century. The mid-sixteenth-century jugs are globular, with a cordon at the base of the neck, but the profile becomes ovoid, losing the cordon. Some jugs of high quality were sufficiently regarded to be fitted with silver mounts; these bear hallmarks dated between 1560 and 1600.

Cologne   The grey-fabric wares of these kilns are easily confused with the Frechen products, because of the movement of some Cologne potters to Frechen in the mid-sixteenth century. Although the quantities of Cologne stoneware found in Britain are not large, the distribution is wide and most types are represented. In the mid-sixteenth century the typical decoration comprised friezes on the neck and a band of foliage round the girth, formed from pads and trails of clay. In the second half of the sixteenth century it became common to place a monogram band round the girth or face masks on the shoulder. The most satisfactory way to distinguish Cologne wares from those of Raeren or Frechen is by comparison of glazes. The Cologne potters achieved an even brown salt glaze, more even than at Raeren, and without the mottling which appears on Frechen wares.

Westerwald The production of export-quality stoneware east of Koblenz was begun at the end of the sixteenth century by potters from Raeren. The wares from the two potteries are indistinguishable until well into the seventeenth century, but as Raeren production declined after about 1600–20, stoneware with blue or purple glaze on the medallions in contexts dated later than the 1630s is likely to have been made in the Westerwald, where production continued throughout the entire period. The wares are in a high-quality grey fabric with a grey salt glaze. Blue and purple glazes were used to decorate medallions and panels. On the later-seventeenth and eighteenth-century wares the decorations cover the entire vessel rather than being restricted to panels, breaking away from the patterns set by the Raeren potters.

French stonewares

The Normandy stonewares are thinly distributed in deposits in southern England which date from about 1580 through to the seventeenth century. This is unexpected, for the quality is poor by comparison with the German wares, the outer surfaces being rougher and the vitrification of the interior less complete. The forms are strictly utilitarian, comprising bowls, jars and squat jugs, and this probably explains their saleability in a niche of the market not really covered by the Rhenish wares. Attribution of this fabric can be quite difficult, as there can be a similarity between the least-high-fired examples and some Midland-purple wares.

Very small amounts of Beauvais stonewares appear in England, examples being published from Norwich. They are of potential importance, in that some are difficult to distinguish from Siegburg wares. The grey fabric is of similar appearance, and although there are differences of detail, some of the forms bear sufficient resemblance for sherds to be confused. The date range of imports is similar, with a trade at its height around 1500. This is significant, for this was just the time of considerable contact, by migration as well as trade, between the Pays de Bray and south-east England, suggesting that more of this ware may have been imported than has hitherto been realized. Some of the Beauvais products are more readily distinguishable: the jugs have flat bases, in contrast to those from Siegburg with frilly bases; the flared beakers are unique, and there are no German parallels for the blue-glazed dishes and *albarelli*.

The third French type comprises unglazed globular flasks with tapering necks made at the Martincamp kilns near Neufchâtel-en-Bray, inland from Dieppe. These are distinct from the Beauvais stoneware and were made between the latter part of the fifteenth century and about 1650; they are common over much of

England, and there are documentary indications of a regular trade. Three types have been distinguished, in differing fabrics; only one, made in the sixteenth century, can be strictly regarded as a stoneware, the fifteenth and seventeenth century flasks being of a hard earthenware. Even some of the sixteenth-century flasks are marginal, and tests of porosity and firing temperatures would be helpful. The earliest type, in off-white fabric with a flattened profile, is common from about 1475 to 1550 and often accompanies Siegburg stoneware and Cistercian wares. It overlaps with the rounder brown stoneware flask, which is found throughout the sixteenth century. This in turn overlaps with the last flasks, in an orange lower-firing fabric, common in early-seventeenth-century contexts.

ENGLISH PRODUCTION OF WARES OF CONTINENTAL TYPE

Delftwares

There is still doubt about when, where and by whom tin glazed earthenwares were first made in England. The problem is whether any successful manufacture on a commercial scale took place before the seventeenth century. The argument for earlier English tin-glaze has depended on whether a successful delftware pottery was set up near Aldgate, London, by the Antwerp potters Jaspar Andries and Jacob Janson in 1571 after their arrival from Norwich (Garner 1972: 4–5). It has still to be verified whether they actually went into production in either city or, if they did, what kind of ware was made. References to their recruitment of Flemish potters and painters to London suggests that they proposed to make tin glaze, and it has been argued that Jacob Johnson, who lived near Aldgate from the 1570s until his death in 1593, was the immigrant potter Janson, and that it was at Duke's Place, Aldgate, that London delftware was made. He was described as a potter in 1583, and another six alien potters are recorded at Aldgate. In support of local manufacture are the delftware wasters found in excavations at Duke's Place (*PMA* 1978: 112), in association with a dated stoneware sherd of 1591. What is uncertain is how long after that date the group was deposited, whether the wasters indicate full-scale production of tin-glazed wares, or whether only red wares were being made in any quantity (Orton 1987).

Until the 1970s it was considered (Garner 1972: 4) that the 'Malling jugs', in dark blue over white tin glaze, were English products, but finds in the Antwerp area suggest that they were made in the southern Netherlands (Hurst *et al.* 1986: 126–7). There are also plates, bearing dates from 1600 and English wording, which have been suggested as produced in London: these also could have been made in the Low Countries for the English market.

Tin-glazed wares were involved in patents of monopoly, but the object of the early patentees appears to have been regulation of sale rather than manufacture. The first indication of an interest in manufacturing is in 1613 when Edward Bradshaw sold his share in a patent, wherein the buyers seem to have been investing in a pottery rather than merely a trading privilege.

Indisputable evidence for English manufacture comes in 1618 when Christian Wilhelm was operating a pottery at Pickleherring Quay, Southwark. He had been resident in Southwark since 1604, in his early years being described as a vinegar maker: he was described as a galley-pot (i.e. delftware) maker in 1618 (Tait 1960), but it has been argued that he began production about 1612 (Edwards 1974: 10–11). The early wares made in Southwark were of Netherlands type, but from the end of the 1620s production included distinctive mugs, posset pots and dishes, some with manganese speckling and many with imitations of Ming porcelain designs. Excavations have taken place on the site of the Pickleherring Quay pottery, which have produced wasters of tin glazed earthenware. Subsequent excavations have been carried out on the delftware site at Montague Close, Southwark, which had a long life, from early in the seventeenth century until the 1750s (Edwards 1974: 8–10). The earliest kiln to be found there was operated until about 1640, and can be associated with the potters Bradshaw and Cressey, whom documentary sources suggest as present in the second decade of the seventeenth century, contemporary with the start of Christian Wilhelm's pottery. At Montague Close, excavations showed second and third phases, with kilns built in the 1640s and about 1700 on the same site as the original. Additional confirmation of tin-glaze manufacture in Southwark comes from references to the shipment of clay suitable for light-coloured earthenware, from Yarmouth to London in 1624, and from Aldeburgh to London by John Townsend, a partner in the Montague Close pottery.

The range produced at these South Bank kilns included designs in traditional Netherlands polychrome, Chinese-influenced blue-and-white, and the plain wares which were becoming increasingly popular in the Netherlands. Numerous vessel types were made, notably polychrome cylindrical storage jars in many sizes, from the small 'drug jars' up to the large butter pots; there were jugs with polychrome decoration, and large quantities of plates with the complete range of designs: by the second half of the century these flat wares made up the bulk of production. Some types are closely datable. For example, the speckled 'manganese delft' cups, in purple on white, were made in Southwark and are found in many parts of the country in deposits dated to the 1620s or soon after. A further assemblage has recently been excavated at Rotherhithe (Norton 1988), comprising wasters and undamaged pots from a delftware pottery, built in the remains of a moated house formerly belonging to Bermondsey Priory, and documented between 1638 and 1661.

The later history of production of tin glaze in this country is bound up with the spread of manufacture to other centres (Archer, n.d: 7). The first movement from London was when Southwark potters went to Brislington about 1642, the forerunner of the Bristol industry which was set up in 1683. The major expansion took place in the first half of the eighteenth century, when Southwark potters started manufacture in Liverpool in 1710, and Bristol potters moved to Wincanton to start the short-lived manufacture which ended in 1750. Delftwares were made in Dublin from 1735 to the 1770s, in Glasgow from 1748 until the end of the eighteenth century, in Lancaster from 1754 until the 1780s and in the middle of the eighteenth century at Belfast, Limerick and Whitehaven. Excavations in Bristol, Glasgow (Denholm 1982) and Liverpool have produced kiln wasters which indicate the main types made. It is, even so, difficult to distinguish the products of these eighteenth-century potteries, due to the use of common sources of clay and the employment of potters and particularly painters trained in the same traditions.

The production of tin-glazed earthenwares declined rapidly towards the end of the eighteenth century. Sales had always been constrained at the upper end of the price range by imports of porcelain from the east, but with the production of porcelain in England in the eighteenth century that pressure grew. The appearance of rivals at the lower end of the market was crucial: creamwares and transfer-printed earthenwares offered quality and consistency at prices with which the delftware producers found it hard to compete.

Stonewares

The import of German stonewares was a trade of some importance in the late sixteenth century, involving not only inward shipments but dispersal by way of the coasting trades. It became embroiled in the grants of patents of monopoly, and on occasion patentees exploited current concern about adverse trade balances by claiming to be planning manufacture in England. Such was William Simpson, who in infringing the patent granted to Henry Noell in 1593 claimed that he planned to arrange production of stoneware, an idea that came to nothing (Henstock 1975). There are two further possibilities of manufacture: one of the patentees of the stone-bottle monopoly of 1614 may have made an attempt to produce pottery at Queenhithe, but there is no sign that this had any success, if indeed any trial was made. However there is a case for associating the stoneware-manufacture patent granted to Thomas Rous and Abraham Cullyn in 1626 (Edwards 1974: 14) with the stoneware kiln excavated at Woolwich. No building date was established from the archaeological evidence, but construction could conceivably have been as early as the 1620s. The kiln was abandoned by the period 1660–80, from evidence of clay pipes, and thus appears to predate John Dwight's Fulham stoneware pottery of 1672. The excavations (Pryor and Blockley 1978) located a short-lived kiln producing salt-glazed stonewares which included face-masked mugs and bottles. It was superseded by another kiln, which made earthenwares over the final quarter of the seventeenth century. The excavation suggested that stoneware production was not a success: the quality of the fabric was inferior to that of imports, but as the excavated material would contain a high proportion of rejects, it may not give a true impression of what was sold. There is no documentary information, but it is notable that John Dwight, in his patent case of 1695–6, made no mention of any Woolwich pottery, suggesting that the kiln had been out of use for some time. Dwight does however refer to two other attempts, for neither of which has archaeological evidence been found. Simon Wooltus was said to have made stoneware at Southampton in the 1660s, and his son to have been employed to make stoneware at Chelsea in the 1670s for a man named Killigrew. The latter reference carries some conviction, for one of Dwight's workers had also been employed by Killigrew (Oswald *et al.* 1982: 23).

Dwight himself established the Fulham pottery in 1672 after several years of experiment, and dated medallions from the Fulham excavations start at 1675 (Green forthcoming). After three years of experiment and numerous failures both with stoneware and attempts to make porcelain, Dwight perfected stoneware production and sold wares of high quality on a large scale. He used kilns based on delftware potters' designs to fire stoneware made from Purbeck pipe-clay, mixed with sand from the Isle of Wight. His wares were salt-glazed, a process which caused him most trouble to perfect. Most of his products were grey stonewares, some being acceptable copies of Westerwald and Frechen types, but he was also successful in making original designs. Excavations have located the original kilns:

six have been recorded from the period between 1674 and the middle of the eighteenth century as well as a settling tank for clay and a sand pit. The scale of Dwight's sales indicates that he was able to compete with imports from Germany, and that the problems of earlier would-be stoneware producers had been overcome.

Stoneware production spread rapidly in the 30 years after Dwight started work at Fulham. The first London rivals were south of the river in Southwark, the Bear Garden and Gravel Lane potteries being established in the 1690s (Edwards 1974: 16–18). Talbot's pottery began in Lambeth soon after, and bottles and jars were being made at Chilwell's pottery in Vauxhall from about 1697, although the better-known Vauxhall kilns of the nineteenth century did not start until the 1790s. Excavations on this site have located the nineteenth-century Vauxhall kilns and part of the pot-house.

In Nottingham James Morley was making stoneware by 1696, at the first pottery in a regional industry which grew rapidly in importance; its output reached peaks in the 1730s and the years between 1760 and 1780, declining to extinction by 1800. (Oswald *et al.* 1982: 102–38). The wares made in Nottingham are found over much of the north and the Midlands, although they are not always distinguishable from the products of the many potteries which were established to the west, in Derbyshire. Crich was the first of these, in production before 1700, and in the eighteenth century numerous potteries were set up on the coal measures, including those at Brampton near Chesterfield, and at Denby, Ilkeston and Melbourne. One of the most prolific and innovative pottery districts in the second half of the eighteenth century and through the nineteenth was Brampton, which produced a wide range of stonewares, from utility items to puzzle jugs, posset pots and characteristic mugs with handles in animal form.

In Staffordshire, there was interest in stoneware before 1700, although production on any scale appears not to have begun as early as in Nottingham. Rackham (1951: 19) accepted the possibility of experiments in the 1680s, and the probability that Aaron, Richard and Thomas Wedgwood of Burslem attempted manufacture before 1700. In the early years of the eighteenth century production of stoneware was on a regular basis; it soon accounted for a major proportion of Staffordshire output, and excavations in Burslem and Hanley have located bases of kilns where salt-glazed stoneware was being made in the 1740s or earlier (*PMA* 1976: 173–4). The closely dated innovations which followed provide important benchmarks for the archaeology of the period. White-dipped stoneware was produced from about 1710; salt-glazed wares were made from the 1720s, and scratch-blue on white salt glaze followed in the 1730s. Other eighteenth-century producers of these ranges included potteries at Bristol (Barton 1961), Jackfield, in Shropshire (*PMA* 1982: 224; 1985: 179–80), and Prescot, Lancashire (*PMA* 1985: 167), in each of which salt-glazed wasters have been found.

Pottery kilns

The technology of medieval pottery kilns is well established (Musty 1974: 41–66; the kiln typology suggested by Musty is used in this section), and many of the wares made between 1500 and late in the seventeenth century were produced in kilns which followed these earlier traditions. This does not apply to the manufacture of delftwares or, in most cases, to stonewares, for the excavated kilns in these sectors of the industry bear less relation to English traditions, resembling Continental models shown in contemporary illustrations. The great majority of kiln excavations have recovered only the bases of kilns, without substantial parts of their superstructures. The available information is summarized according to the main types of kiln.

CLAMP KILNS

There are indications that the early-medieval tradition of the clamp (Type 5) survived to the sixteenth century and beyond. The method was to stack pottery, packed with wood or peat fuel, and to cover the stack with a material such as turf, to retard combustion. There were no permanent bases or stokeholes, and firing relied upon the fuel placed in the clamp when it was set up. An example has been found in a late-fifteenth or early sixteenth-century context at Potovens, one of the Yorkshire Cistercian-ware potteries, where it has been suggested that the pottery was fired in saggars (ceramic containers) within the clamp (Bartlett 1971). By far the latest case has been recorded at Buckley, in north Wales, where the dating of associated clay tobacco pipes suggests the use of clamps at the beginning of the eighteenth century at the Brookhill potteries (Amery and Davey 1979).

Clamp kilns leave only patches of burning and ash, so this type could be under-represented in the archaeological record. As it was shown during the Leeds kiln experiments in the 1960s that clamps can provide acceptable results, the possibility of widespread use in the sixteenth and seventeenth centuries has to be taken seriously.

SINGLE-FLUE KILNS (Types 1a and b)

Small horseshoe-plan kilns, fired from a stokehole at one end, were used in the sixteenth and seventeenth centuries and were satisfactory for the potter working on a small scale with wood as a fuel. When excavated, these simple kilns often show only as an oval outline (1a): an example is the early-sixteenth-century kiln at Parrock, Sussex, probably used by a French potter from the Beauvais area, which had no internal plinth on which to load the wares (Freke 1979). A kiln similar in principle but with a paved stone floor has been excavated at Stearsby, in north Yorkshire (*PMA* 1971: 216). Although in kilns of this kind it was common for pottery to be set on the floor, at the Stearsby kiln the discovery of fired lumps of clay suggested that the load may have been raised above the paving.

The kilns with central plinths (1b) leave more substantial survivals. In these, the wares were stacked on the plinth, and the flame from the fire could pass through the surrounding channel; stone or clay fire-bars, bridging the channel, extended the area on which the load could be placed. The late-sixteenth-century kiln at Crockerton, Wiltshire (fig. 12.2), is of this type, having a stone flue lining and central plinth, and surviving stone bars, bridging the surrounding passage (*PMA* 1968: 187–9). In this example the plinth was circular, but it was common practice to incorporate a central fire channel, splitting the plinth and thus improving the distribution of heat. The two seventeenth-century kilns at Potterspury incorporated divided plinths, and one was of single-flue design (Mayes 1968).

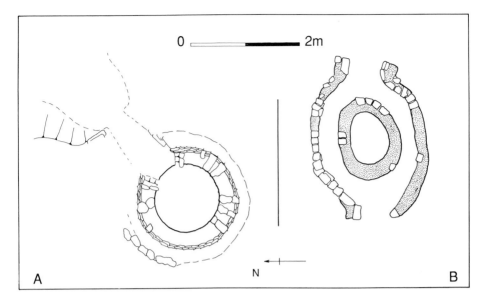

Fig. 12.2 Wood-fired pottery kilns: sixteenth and seventeenth centuries. (A) Crockerton, Wiltshire: single-flued kiln with central plinth, and stone bars bridging the flue (after David Algar). (B) Farnborough Hill, Hampshire: double-flued kiln; pottery had been stacked within the internal chamber (after Felix Holling).

OPPOSED-FLUE KILNS (Type 2)

Post-medieval kilns have been excavated which were built with two flues, one at either end. The variations in internal details correspond with those of single-flued kilns, those with plinths having either single or split pedestals, with or without surviving bars bridging the annular flue. There were two successive double-flued kilns at Farnborough Hill, Hampshire, (fig. 12.2) dating to the sixteenth century on a site where a single-flued kiln had previously been used. The first of the double-flued kilns had slight traces of a divided plinth (*PMA* 1972: 218), but was succeeded by a late-sixteenth-century kiln whose plinth was circular, walled with clay and filled with ash and discarded pottery (*PMA* 1971: 210–11). The second of the Potterspury kilns was of similar type, as was the earthenware kiln at Woolwich; this, dated to the third quarter of the seventeenth century, had a solid and durable structure of brick, and succeeded the kiln used for the attempt to make stoneware. A variation of this type was excavated in the Gower, Glamorgan, where the central plinth in the double-flue kiln at Berthlwyd Uchaf was divided across the axis of the kiln, rather than in line with the stokeholes (*PMA* 1968: 189–90).

Single and double-flued kilns remained satisfactory where wood was the available fuel, for, in both types, the long flame produced by billet wood enabled the potter to work with just one or two stokeholes. Unfortunately, little attention has been paid to the relationship between potteries, the firewood trade and coppice woodland. In certain areas, the competition for firewood was of critical importance, and the incentive to use coal was strong. It is, for example, surprising that the earthenware kiln at Woolwich was suggested (Pryor and Blockley 1978: 33–5) as being wood-burning, since, despite the similarity of its plan to those of wood-fired kilns, the high price of wood in the London area lends some significance to the coal ash found in the excavation. Elsewhere, the viability of a pottery depended on the extent of competition for coppice wood, and particularly whether rival users required wood of a different age. In the Weald, for example, the Boreham Street kiln, using billet wood, would compete with the ironworks and their need for charcoal made from younger coppice fellings. However, in the Farnborough area potters would encounter fewer competitors, being sufficiently far from the iron and glass industries of the western Weald. It must be assumed that the coppices to the south of the west-Surrey heaths would be cut at the 15–20 years' growth well suited to the kilns.

MULTI-FLUE KILNS (Type 3)

Kilns with three or more stokeholes, some with as many as six, are known from the fourteenth century onwards, and had become common by 1500. What must be regarded as the classic example of the late-medieval evolution of multi-flue kiln operation has been seen at Chilvers Coton, Warwickshire, where a development took place from double-flued kilns of thirteenth-century date to four- and five-flued kilns at the end of the Middle Ages (Mayes and Scott 1984: esp. 19–46). In the larger and more specialized pottery centres the latter appear to have become the standard type. The layout was advantageous for larger kilns, ensuring an even distribution of heat. It may also have been possible to gain greater control over the atmosphere in the kiln, even achieving some variation in different parts of the structure, by opening or closing flues or by stoking or damping individual fires. It was normal for these kilns to have flat floors, the wares being stacked in saggars placed on props or on the ground.

The multi-flue kiln had a particular advantage when coal was used as a fuel. The short flame-travel of coal made it important to place fires around the kiln in order to give even heat to the structure and the load. There is a parallel with the experience of the glassmakers, who found it necessary to place their fires in the centre of the furnace rather than rely on flames entering from an external stokehole. Coal was increasingly used in the north and Midlands at the end of the Middle Ages, and some kiln complexes appear to have been sited with local coal resources as an important consideration. At Wrenthorpe the coal outcrops were immediately adjacent to seventeenth-century potteries using multi-flued kilns, but as the coal measures, here and elsewhere, also contain suitable clays, the latter may have been the guiding factor in the first instance. At Chilvers Coton the earliest kilns, of thirteenth-century date, had been wood fired, but by the mid-fifteenth century coal firing seems to have been usual. We should not assume, however, that multi-flue layout was essential for the use of coal: the double-flued kiln in the Gower used coal, and the possibility that the Woolwich earthenware kiln did likewise has already been mentioned.

Multi-flued kilns are found at most potteries in the north and the Midlands. Besides the Chilvers Coton and Wrenthorpe examples, excavations have taken place at the late-seventeenth-century five-flued kiln at Pule Hill, Halifax (*PMA* 1967: 116–18). Other excavated examples, but in areas where wood was the

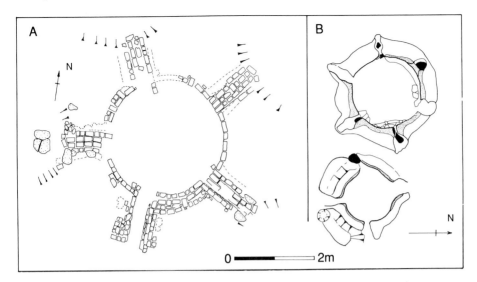

Fig. 12.3 Multi-flued pottery kilns. (A) Toynton All Saints, Lincolnshire (after Hilary Healey). (B) Potovens, Yorkshire: seventeenth-century coal-fired kilns (after K.S. Bartlett).

available fuel, are the Lincolnshire kilns at Toynton, (fig. 12.3) brick built with five flues (*PMA* 1973: 111–12), Boston, with three flues (*PMA* 1976: 172–3), and Old Bolingbroke, a kiln of c.1475–1525 with five flues (*MA* 1968: 208). Of these, it could be speculated that the Boston kiln, close to the sea-borne coal trade, might have used mineral fuel on occasion, although the composition of stokehole ashes has not been referred to in the published summary. A multi-flue kiln where there is no possibility of coal being an economic fuel is at Brill, where the most recently published excavation showed what was probably a four-flue plan, with stokeholes containing wood ash (Farley 1979).

It was essentially this type of kiln which evolved into the permanent multi-flued structure of the eighteenth and nineteenth centuries, when the kiln was contained in the bottle casing, providing added draught and a covered area for stoking and for access from surrounding workshops. The excavations carried out in the Stafford-shire potteries have shown how this form developed in the late-seventeenth and eighteenth centuries, in an area where the use of coal had become standard practice (*PMA* 1968: 187; 1976: 173–4).

THE SUPERSTRUCTURE OF TRADITIONAL KILNS

Excavated fragments show that some kilns had clay-dome roofs, good examples being recorded at Chilvers Coton. Wall bases at Chilvers Coton and at Potovens appear to be parts of such structures. Experimental firings of replica kilns have shown that clay domes can be semi-permanent and practical in use, with the kiln being loaded through walk-in entries used also as firing apertures. If the kiln dome were protected from the worst of weather by an all-over shelter as at Donyatt, it could well last for a season or more, but the worst enemy of such a structure would be frost, and it seems unlikely that, even if sheltered, a clay dome could overwinter without patching and parging.

A problem which besets the interpretation of most excavated kilns is whether any form of chimney was used. Experimental replica kilns have performed satisfactorily with careful attention to the size of vents in the top of the dome. This is a problem paralleled in the excavation of glass furnaces. Because of the mid-eighteenth-century development of large conical chimneys, in pottery kilns and glass furnaces alike, there is a temptation to seek forerunners in the smaller kilns and furnaces of 1700 and before. However, in both industries the later structures also had complex internal ducting either for the air feeding the fires or for the products of combustion, which made it necessary to develop correspondingly larger chimneys to induce sufficient draught for the fires. Late medieval pottery kilns with semi-permanent roofs appear to have had vents of two types: either a single hole, in the case of a Wrenthorpe kiln about 0.60m in diameter, estimated from excavated fragments, or, as at the Warwickshire kilns, sets of small vents spread over the dome. The latter have been suggested as giving a better control of the atmosphere in the kiln, and could be seen in use into the present century in country potteries such as Ewenny (J.M. Lewis 1982: 48ff.).

The permanent dome and walk-in entry is less easily accepted for the smaller kilns. Although experiments have shown that it is just possible to load small kilns in this way, more convincing is a technique of building permanent walls, loading through an open top, and covering the load with tiles, waste pottery and clay. This method survived in small potteries such as Ewenny until well into the nineteenth century and gave satisfactory results in the experimental firings carried out at Barton-on-Humber in 1970 (Bryant 1977).

It is not yet certain when the clay dome of the peasant pottery tradition gave way to more permanent stone or brick structures. There are signs of regular brick walls at the sixteenth-century Farnborough Hill kilns, but no clue as to what was built on them, or whether they were merely enclosing walls within which the pottery was stacked, to be covered by wasters. More convincing indications appear late in the seventeenth century. The Woolwich earthenware kiln had a well-constructed brick base, and permanent structures of this type appear in Staffordshire at this time: a kiln at the Albion site at Hanley had brickwork in the flues and plinths which appeared to have extended upwards. Brick construction has been shown to be standard practice early in the eighteenth century in the Potteries towns, and at kilns of the period excavated at Jackfield, Shropshire, and at Chester. An interesting example of this type has been excavated at Sheffield Manor, in the ruins of the long gallery of the Tudor house. This seven-flued kiln with a brick base was inserted at the beginning of the eighteenth century into a room of hexagonal plan.

CONTINENTAL-STYLE KILNS

The London delftware kilns were of an entirely different design from the English tradition (fig. 12.4). Those excavated at Southwark and Lambeth had square brick bases and they resemble illustrations of kilns on the Continent. At Montague Close, Southwark, a rectangular kiln was in use early in the seventeenth century, its first phase ending about 1640 (*PMA* 1971: 212–14). By the latter part of the

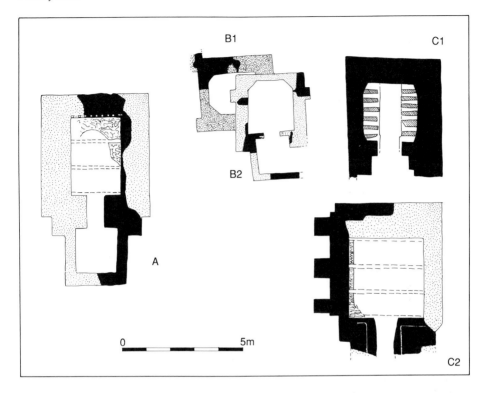

Fig. 12.4 London: seventeenth-century and later coal-fired kilns (outlines derived from structural remains shown in solid black). (A) Southwark, late-seventeenth century, for tin-glazed earthenware. (B) Fulham, salt-glazed stoneware: (1) c.1680; (2) c.1750; (C) Vauxhall, late eighteenth century – early nineteenth century (1) salt-glazed stoneware; (2) tin-glazed earthenware (after Christopher Green).

seventeenth century three kilns of this type were in use, two being built against a common wall, and forming in effect a double kiln (*PMA* 1973: 111–12). Excavations at the Norfolk House delftware pottery at Lambeth, considered to have operated between c.1680 and 1737, recorded the fireboxes of two rectangular kilns in the same tradition as at Southwark. Bloice (1971) has reviewed the parallels for kilns of this type which, apart from the Montague Close examples, are restricted to sixteenth and eighteenth-century printed sources, namely the descriptions and drawings by Piccolpasso, Diderot, Duhamel, Bolswards and Paape. These show that tin-glazed pottery was made in kilns of rectangular plan with tall arched superstructures and, in the eighteenth century, chimneys. A possible exception is an unpublished delftware kiln in Liverpool which was noted as being circular in plan; however, apart from this and a possible kiln base in Bristol of which no details survive, no excavations have been possible on delftware potteries outside London, apart from work on waster dumps, as in Glasgow (Denholm 1982).

Of the stoneware kilns excavated so far, that at Woolwich bore some resemblance to the traditional single-flue pattern, with bars between the plinth and the outer wall. However, in this case the draught appeared to have been taken horizontally through the kiln to an opposed outlet, rather than circulating upwards to a vent in the top of the dome.

At Dwight's pottery at Fulham the results from excavations of the two best-preserved kilns (fig. 12.4) show that the rectangular plan typical of the seventeenth-century delftware kiln was in use from the beginning of production in the mid-1670s through to the mid-eighteenth century (Green, forthcoming). The kiln structures comprised below-ground fireboxes approximately 2m square internally, which would be reduced by the replaceable firebrick lining to about 1.8m. The brick-lined stoking pit was built against one wall of the firebox, and appeared to have been roofed over. The load chambers of these kilns did not survive, but Dwight described the firebox as being arched at the top with vents for the smoke. The load-chamber floors would be supported on these arches.

This type of kiln may have been adopted by certain earthenware potters before 1700. A kiln excavated at Loughton, Essex, and ascribed to the second half of the seventeenth century, appears to have made metropolitan wares; it was built of brick, square in plan, with internal arches (*PMA* 1970: 182). The problem with this kiln is whether the Continental style had any influence, or whether the potters had adopted a plan similar to the form used by Essex tile makers.

Potters' workshops and houses

As with the archaeology of medieval pottery sites, the kiln itself has dominated excavation and survey. Discovery, whether as the result of fieldwalking, ploughing or construction, is usually due to the presence of characteristic kiln debris, and it is the kiln which is detected during magnetic surveys. Hence most excavations have concentrated on the kiln itself, rather than extending to workshops, storage accommodation, settling tanks and clay pits. A site as complete as the medieval example at Lyveden, Northamptonshire has yet to be found. So far, the most extensive post-medieval sites have been at Potovens, Yorkshire (fig. 12.5), where kilns have been found in association with standing cottages originally used by seventeenth-century potters, and at Bourne, Lincolnshire, where there have been excavated a workshop, two store sheds and a dwelling, suggested from written records to have been in use during the years 1550–1700 (Kerr 1973). The use of settling tanks for clay, and mixing floors built of brick, has been demonstrated: settling tanks were found at Buckley and Fulham, a sandpit at Fulham, and a brick pugging-pit at one of the Harlow kiln sites. Nevertheless, this is a small assemblage, in relation to the known pottery sites of the period, and it does no harm to re-emphasize the need to gather more physical evidence for the complete pottery, to broaden our knowledge of an industry for which the archive sources are meagre.

Clay tobacco pipes

With the introduction of tobacco smoking and the clay tobacco pipe, archaeology acquires an important means of dating. The presence or absence of pipes can be crucial in determining the date of deposits at the end of the sixteenth and the beginning of the seventeenth centuries, and, thereafter, broad dating is achieved by

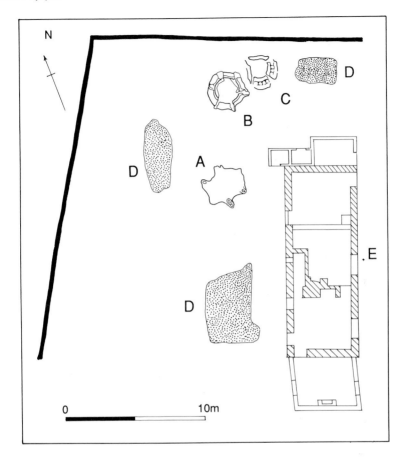

Fig. 12.5 Potovens, Yorkshire: pottery kilns and potters' housing and workshop: (A, B, C) Kilns; (D) waste dumps; (E) the potter's toft (after K.S.Bartlett).

knowledge of changes in sizes, profiles and decoration of pipe bowls and stems, refined by the increasingly detailed information about makers' marks which has been built up over the last 30 years. In the past there have been suggestions that dating might be possible by the measurement of the bores of pipe stems, on the assumption that over the seventeenth and eighteenth centuries finer wire became available to the pipemaker, with which to form stems of smaller internal diameter. More recent studies have shown that there are wide variations between trends in different parts of the country, and although such changes may be of interest in themselves, the use of stem-bore diameters for absolute dating is generally discredited.

Tobacco smoking is recorded in Britain from the last quarter of the sixteenth century. An early reference is by William Harrison who, writing in 1593, noted the appearance of the habit in the previous 20 years. Pipes, however, are rare in sixteenth-century archaeological contexts, for tobacco was still expensive and was used only by the better off. Indeed, the rarity of pipes has been noted in deposits dating well into the seventeenth century. In St Ebbes, Oxford, for example, an urban area built up to house a relatively poor population early in the seventeenth century, there are no pipes before about 1620 (Oswald 1984: 251), and excavations at Norton, Cheshire, have shown that until 1650 pipes were much more common at the great house, Norton Priory, than in the village (Davey 1985: 165–6).

There is little information about makers of clay pipes before the early years of the seventeenth century: due to the scarcity of marks on early pipes, none of the wares of sixteenth-century London manufacturers can yet be identified with any certainty. Even so, the trade of pipemaking seems to have been active in London by this date, and methods of manufacture had acquired the pattern to be familiar for several centuries: pipes were made in moulds by the 1590s, and although bowls were very small, they are of the shape which was to evolve over the next 300 years. One indication of the vigour of the trade was its attraction to potential monopolists in 1601, who attempted to profit by its regulation. The first real evidence of the size of the London industry comes in 1619, when a company of pipemakers was established, and the 36 individuals who signed the charter give a minimum size for the industry. In fact, the numbers at work appear to have been considerably greater, for the study of early London marks indicates at least 62 makers, apart from those others who were not identifying their wares (Oswald 1975: 3–10). Many pipes from seventeenth-century London makers have been found in provincial towns, particularly the ports of the east and south coasts, to which such small items as pipes could be cheaply transported as return cargo, in ships which carried supplies to the capital. As the value of pipes was high in relation to their weight, they could also be carried overland, so it is not surprising to find London pipes in Midland towns such as Coventry and Worcester.

During the first half of the seventeenth century provincial manufacture began, but it is often difficult to identify the early products of out-of-town makers who, as Atkinson has shown for Southampton, appear to have copied London styles and often did not use marks (Atkinson 1975: 344–9). The best indication that pipes were being manufactured comes from attempts by the London pipemakers' company to enforce their charter elsewhere, as was tried in Portsmouth in 1622 and in Reading in 1623. The emergence of regional styles is clear after the middle of the seventeenth century, and identification becomes simpler among the increasingly decorated pipes of the eighteenth century. Some provincial makers produced pipes of a standard sufficient to capture wide regional markets; an example is Gateshead, members of whose pipemakers' guild, chartered in 1675, sold their products over much of north-east England and into Scotland. York also had a pipemakers' guild, dating from about 1650, while in the south-west, Bristol, its guild dating from 1652, sold pipes in and beyond the Severn estuary. The vitality of the coasting trade led to overlapping distributions of pipes: the assemblage from the Durham Chapter Library is a case in point, with pipes not only from east-coast and London sources, but from as far away as Bristol (Parsons 1964). The pipemakers in the larger towns could be expected to develop trades which would spill over into their surrounding regions, but on occasion smaller communities became important sources. Such were the parishes of Broseley, Benthall and Much Wenlock in Shropshire, which, from late in the seventeenth century, supplied the west Midlands, the Severn valley and South Wales with pipes of good quality, with occasional examples reaching as far afield as London and the New World.

Most production centres made a range of qualities of pipes, the lower end of which did not travel far. The quality of a pipe depended both on the mould from which it was made and the skill with which it was manufactured. Finishing techniques, such as burnishing or milling a pipe, tended to increase its value, and pipes with longer stems were always more expensive. Many small makers, in villages or small towns, worked at the cheaper end of the market. The excavated mid-eighteenth-century kiln of William Heath at Brentford (Laws and Oswald 1981: 15ff.) fired pipes which reached no further than the western fringe of London, and kilns producing wares of similar local appeal have been excavated, or located from kiln fragments, at Aylesbury, Boston, Stamford and Wakefield. The range of quality was reflected in prices, and the results can be seen in excavated groups. At Norton, Cheshire, the pipes from the village contain a higher proportion of the cheaper locally sourced products than those found at the Priory, where the higher-quality pipes from more distant producers predominate.

The great majority of excavated pipes come from English sources. Exceptions are imports from the Netherlands, which appear from the early seventeenth century. Their distribution is largely coastal, with a particularly fine assemblage found at Plymouth (Oswald 1969). Recognition is partly by softer clays than were used for English pipes, but more by the designs, and in particular by the use of decoration on the stem as well as on the bowl. In some cases there are also characteristic marks left by the maker on the inside of the bowl during manufacture (Atkinson 1972). From the mid-nineteenth century French pipes became the most frequent imports. These were high-quality products, often with ornate decoration and embellished with enamels. They occupied a small but important niche at the top end of the market.

The changing style of pipes is indicated in outline in fig. 12.6, which illustrates how in general bowls grew in size during the seventeenth century, and how decoration appeared on the bowls during the eighteenth. Further variations involved the spurs: some traditions developed spurs at an early period, while in others the flat-based bowl was retained.

Dating by makers' marks becomes more useful with deposits of mid-seventeenth-century date, for it was then that strong regional trends developed and marks were more frequently used. Thereafter, it is in principle possible to identify a high proportion of makers by their initials and the form of the lettering of the marks. The position of marks can also be important, whether on the base, back or side of the bowl or the base or side of the spur. Marks could also be in relief or incuse. The reliability of such indications must depend on the life of any particular mould or stamp. It has been suggested that the majority of moulds would last no more than 30 years, but if a maker had numerous moulds, some, if rarely used, may well have survived for longer (Oswald 1985: 5–22). It has, for example, been shown that a maker using the mark WB in London at the beginning of the seventeenth century had 16 moulds, and such numbers are by no means uncommon throughout the history of the industry: an extreme case is Henry Bradley of Benthall in Shropshire, who has been shown by examination of wasters to have used no less than 50 different moulds and 100 different stamps for his pipes (*ex. inf.* D. Higgins). Also, pipe-kiln excavations have suggested that not all moulds were exclusively used by the makers whose initials they bear. At Brentford there were bowls with marks belonging to makers other than the documented operator of the kiln: whether he sublet to others, or whether he bought up moulds from retired pipemakers, as has often happened with marks in the cutlery trades, it is impossible to say. Similarly, at the excavated Aldgate kiln it has been noted that bowls bearing

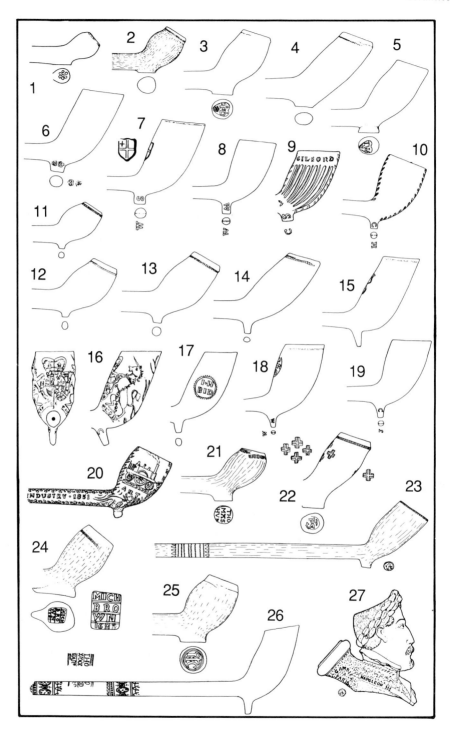

Fig. 12.6 Clay Tobacco Pipes (*Contributed by David Higgins*)

This figure illustrates the general evolution of heel (1–10) and spur (11–19) forms. Broken lines are used to indicate any surfaces which have been burnished. The bowls generally have a barrel-shaped form and milling during the seventeenth century after which they become more upright and the milling disappears. Many regional variations of these forms developed, particularly during the second half of the seventeenth century (21–25). Makers' marks were either stamped after trimming the pipe or were mould-imparted. Stamped marks could be applied to the heel (25), stem (26) or bowl (7) and show pronounced regional diversity. Moulded marks are generally confined to Scotland before *c* 1690 but become common after that. They also occur on the heel (8), stem (20) or bowl (17). Decoration was comparatively rare during the seventeenth and eighteenth centuries. Patterns of decorative stamps are found during the seventeenth century (22) while in the eighteenth century elaborate stem borders became popular (26). Moulded decoration was rarely used before the mid to late eighteenth century. Armorial pipes are found from that date (16) but the standard nineteenth-century designs, such as fluting and leaf decorated seams (9, 10), only appear from the 1780s. A great diversity of moulded designs were produced during the nineteenth century (20) together with a wide range of bowl forms. In the most elaborate examples the whole bowl was modelled in the form of an object or person (27). Imported pipes are occasionally found, the principal sources being the Netherlands during the seventeenth and eighteenth centuries and France from the mid nineteenth century (27).

1. Plymouth, Devon, *c* 1580–1610.
2. London, *c* 1610–40.
3. London, *c* 1660–80, stamped TD.
4. London, *c* 1660–90.
5. London, *c* 1680–1720, stamped TW.
6. London, *c* 1700–50, moulded mark (crowned harps).
7. London, *c* 1770–1800, moulded mark WS with stamped City Arms.
8. London, *c* 1780–1820, moulded mark WW.
9. Guildford, Surrey, *c* 1810–40, moulded mark C SWINYARD, GILFORD (sic).
10. London, *c* 1830–1900, moulded mark HC.
11. London, *c* 1610–40.
12. London, *c* 1640–60.
13. London, *c* 1660–90.
14. London, *c* 1690–1710.
15. London, *c* 1750–90, stamped with the City Arms.
16. Kingston, Surrey, *c* 1760–90, moulded mark RC.
17. Tapely, Devon, *c* 1710–50, moulded mark IH BID (Bideford).
18. London, *c* 1837–60, moulded mark WW, stamped mark WALKER (Spitalfields).
19. London, *c* 1830–80, moulded mark JC.
20. Surrey, *c* 1851, London pipe commemorating the Great Exhibition.
21. Oxford, *c* 1660–80, stamped THOMAS HUNT (Marlborough).
22. Barnstaple, Devon, *c* 1670–1700, stamped decoration and stamped PS.
23. Plymouth, *c* 1700–40, Dutch pipe with decorated stem and stamped with a chicken and letter M.
24. Stafford, *c* 1680s, Much Wenlock (Shropshire) pipe stamped MICH BROWN 168-.
25. Beverley, Humberside, *c* 1660–1700, stamped IC.
26. Leicester, *c* 1760–90, stamped THO WOODWARD.
27. Dorking, Surrey, portrait of Napoleon III (1808–73) with enamelled decoration, moulded mark GAMBIER A PARIS and stamped JG. Made by the firm of J Gambier in France. The Gambier firm had offices in London from 1865–95.

Scale: half-size, except for stamp detail of 24: full size.

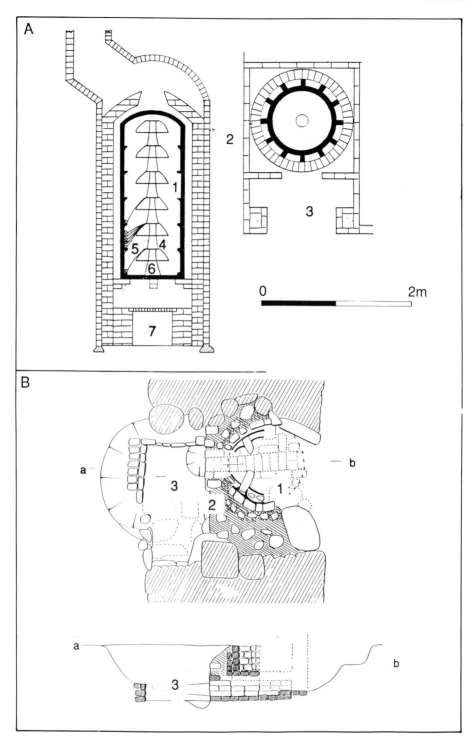

Fig. 12.7 Clay-tobacco-pipe kilns (A) Lewes, nineteenth century (N.E.S.Norris); (B) Portsmouth: Oyster Street, seventeenth century (Russell Fox). (1) lining (muffle); (2) kiln structure; (3) stokehole; (4) props; (5) pipes; (6) central pillar; (7) firebox.

the marks of several makers were present. Whilst it is likely that such moulds or stamps would not travel far, it is important that pipes should not be too readily ascribed to those who had originally used the marks they bear (Thompson *et al.* 1984: 32).

No moulds have been excavated on clay-pipe kiln-sites, but it seems that their form and principle of operation did not greatly change. Eighteenth-century sources illustrate moulds of a type which could well have been used to make the pipes which date from the earliest period of the industry: a roll of clay was placed in a two-piece mould, with a wire to form the bore already threaded most of the way through the stem. The mould halves were closed and a stopper forced down to form the inside of the bowl; the stopper was removed and the wire pushed through to complete the bore before the mould was opened. The pipe was removed from the mould, the wire withdrawn and, after drying a little, the pipe was trimmed. When fully dry it was sent for firing. One variation which is archaeologically significant is indicated by Dutch pipes: the moulds in which these were made were used with a separate plunger which, withdrawn with a twisting movement, left an identifiable mark on the inside of the bowl. Moulds appear to have been made of several materials: Oswald (1985: 5–22) has noted documentary references to seventeenth-century bronze moulds in the Netherlands, the description by John Houghton in the 1690s of brass moulds, and nineteenth-century references to the use of cast iron and wood.

White-firing clays suitable for making pipes came from numerous deposits and, where available, were used by the early makers. Such clays are particularly common in the coal measures and there are numerous references to their use in Staffordshire, Derbyshire and Nottinghamshire, as well as in Shropshire where the ready supply of clay and coal led to the establishment of the Much Wenlock/ Broseley industry. London makers used Kent clays for some of their output, but in general the favoured area was Dorset. Much pipe-clay was shipped through the port of Poole, and although the Poole district was well known for white clays, there are also sources in Purbeck and the Isle of Wight whose clays fire white at high temperatures. From the eighteenth century the Devon ball-clays, exported through Bideford and later through Teignmouth, grew in popularity with pipemakers, as they were to do with the Staffordshire potters.

CLAY-PIPE KILNS

The earliest excavated kilns date from the mid-to late-seventeenth century, the most substantial fragments from this period being the examples at Oyster Street, Portsmouth (fig. 12.7; Fox and Barton 1986: 69–71), Arcadia Buildings, Southwark (Peacey 1982: 3–12), Aldgate, London (A. Thompson 1981) and Rainford (Davey 1982b). Eighteenth-and nineteenth-century kilns have left more substantial remains, and the nineteenth-century kiln recorded at Lewes (fig. 12.7) provided an almost complete superstructure, confirming inferences drawn from kiln debris from other excavations (Norris 1970). It will be shown that over the two centuries from which these excavated examples come, changes took place in the design of pipe kilns, and it is hoped that examples from the earliest years of pipe manufacture will be found, to assess developments over the seventeenth century.

The key feature of all clay-pipe kilns so far recorded has been the separation of the pipes from the products of combustion of the fire, in order to ensure the minimum of discolouration of the white pipe-clay body. Saggers sealed with strips of clay were used in some later-nineteenth-century factories, but the traditional technique before this time had been to seal the pipes within a specially constructed muffle in the firing chamber. The pipes were usually stacked against a hollow central pillar. Hot flue gases passed through this and also through the concentric passage round the outside of the muffle. The earlier excavated kilns fail to give evidence of the height of the muffle, but the example at Lewes measured 2.25m. That this was not unusual is indicated by the estimate of 2.7m as the height of the nineteenth-century kiln at Stamford (*PMA* 1973: 114–15). These are important indications, for although the kilns are late in the history of the industry, that at Lewes having gone out of use about 1880, evidence for tall muffles should be sought on earlier sites. In most cases the muffle was constructed of pipe-clay, stiffened by the inclusion of pipe-wasters, and there are several sites where this characteristic muffle material has been found, an example being at Rainford, Lancashire, where muffles have been reconstructed from kilns of c.1650. Even where the kiln itself has not been located, as at Halesworth, Suffolk, it was probably not far away from where muffle material and nineteenth-century pipes were found (Oak-Rhind and Wade 1977). However, in large towns, as at Bristol, where waste was commonly carried away for disposal, the discovery of muffle material may be misleading.

Most of the kilns so far excavated were fuelled with coal, although at Portsmouth wood was used, and in Holland peat is documented as a fuel. The use of coal made the separation of hot gases from the pipes important, but insufficient is known about wood-fired pipe kilns to be clear whether the design of the muffle had been altered at the introduction of coal.

The firing chamber of the kiln was a permanent structure, usually built of brick. The outer plan was normally square, but the internal plan was circular and often lined with firebrick. Diameters varied from about 0.7m at Southwark to 1.5m in the nineteenth-century kiln at Boston (Wells 1970). The vertical sections of kilns appear to have varied: there were attempts to induce a flow of gases upwards through the firing chamber by reducing the cross-section of the upper space between the outer wall and the muffle: in some cases the interior of the kiln tapered towards the top, while in others the diameter of the muffle increased. The Southwark kiln possessed the first arrangement, the space between the wall and the muffle diminishing from 70mm at the base to 22mm at the top of the muffle. By contrast, the fragments from a nineteenth-century kiln found at Waverley Street, Bristol (Peacey 1982: 12–13), indicate that the muffle increased in diameter towards the top. There also appear to have been attempts to generate turbulence in the ascending gases, using baffles in the floor, and breaking the upward flow by placing supports for the muffle against the wall of the kiln.

The muffle was usually loaded from above, indicated by the shape of the top. This could be seen from muffle waste from the seventeenth-century kiln at Benthall (*PMA* 1985: 177). There are however, cases where loading was done from below, as at Boston, where access was by way of the stokehole. Pipes were stacked on internal projections from the muffle wall, those at Stamford being crescent shaped (*PMA* 1973: 114–15), and the operation was made simpler in kilns where a permanent internal pillar was used: the pipes were set bridging the space between the pillar and the muffle wall.

The relationship between the firing chamber and the firebox appears to have changed over the century from c.1670. In the Portsmouth kiln the fire appears not to have been immediately below the chamber, but to have been separated by an arched flue which transferred heat from a firebox at one side. The fragmentary kiln at Aldgate, which dates from much the same period, appears to have been laid out in a similar way, with a poorly constructed horizontal flue. The eighteenth-and nineteenth-century kilns, however, had fireboxes below the firing chamber, with the heat rising either directly or through deflectors. The fire was set on bars, for at a small kiln in Winchester iron fire-bars have been found (*PMA* 1982: 224). Beneath the fireboxes were ash pits, the ash being raked into an adjacent cellar.

The overall plan of most pipe-kiln sites is characterized by the stokehole being below ground level, often approached down steps. At Southwark this cellar was shared by two kilns used simultaneously for a time at the end of the seventeenth century. Fuel stores are found close to stoking areas: at the eighteenth-century kiln of William Heath at Brentford, the coal was stored in a cellar adjacent to the firebox. A further feature, noted at the nineteenth-century kiln at Boston was a possible drying chamber, in which the pipes could be placed before firing. In only one instance have clay pits been found: at Southwark there were two, but many kilns may only have needed small containers or stores, of which no traces need survive.

It is doubtful whether many of the buildings in which clay-pipe kilns were housed were purpose built: the kilns themselves were small and could be incorporated in pre-existing structures. In the case of Aldgate it is likely that the kiln was constructed in a cellar of a standing building, against the wall of a workshop. At the contemporary Southwark site one of the kilns was built into a brick wall, with stoking taking place from the far side. There are cases where kilns were built close to domestic accommodation: this seems likely to have been the case at Aldgate and at the seventeenth-century kiln at Castle Street, Aylesbury (Moore 1979). Photographs of several kilns at Rainford survive, all being built either partly or wholly within single-storey buildings (Davey *et al.* in Davey 1982b). Even at Broseley, where a large 'factory' unit survives, the three-storey workshop was converted from an earlier warehouse and the large kiln was built against a redundant cottage, the ground floor of which housed one of the stokeholes.

The production of bricks and tiles

Although several medieval tile kilns have been excavated in Britain, illustrating a tradition which continued through the post-medieval centuries, no medieval brick kilns have been found. Nevertheless, it has been shown that Low Countries fashions of building in brick were influencing landowners in the eastern counties before 1500 and that bricks were available in the Midland forest areas in the fifteenth century (Scott 1978–9). In the sixteenth and seventeenth centuries brick production became more common, either undertaken for specific projects or as a regular forest-fringe occupation. Examples of the latter have been derived from documentary sources in the Midlands, where mid-sixteenth-century probate inventories show farmers with goods which include bricks and unfired tiles (Whitehead 1981). Similarly, in Essex at the beginning of the eighteenth century, smallholders were still operating brick kilns (Drury 1975). The key was not just the supply of clay or brick-earth, but the availability of wood fuel. Where coppice woods were plentiful and small brickmakers were common, the price of bricks was low, and it has been shown that in the Midlands the use of brick advanced more rapidly in the wooded areas of north Warwickshire than in the 'felden' south of the county.

This reason for the growth in the use of bricks at the vernacular level needs to be stressed just as much as the change in fashions in polite building of the period. Much of the improvement of yeoman accommodation incorporated the use of brick, not for complete buildings, but in the alteration of existing structures or as features within new timber-framed houses. The most obvious use of brick was in the construction of hearths and chimney stacks, whether within a range or added to the end of a house. Examples are common over the whole of England, even where stone was available, for the heat resistance of the better bricks made them attractive for ovens, hearths and chimneys. Brick was also frequently used to replace wattle-and-daub or timber studding in timber-framed buildings and, of particular long-term value, to underpin timber houses, replacing timber sills, or stub walls of poor-quality stone.

Urban rebuilding was also an important outlet for the brickmaker. As is discussed elsewhere in this book, the seventeenth and eighteenth centuries saw not just an expansion of urban built-up areas, but a qualitative change in structures. This was particularly connected with the incidence of fire damage, and the rebuilding which took place after serious fires was generally carried out using a higher proportion of brick, under municipal regulations which sought to reduce fire hazards. Some of the changes were spectacular, as at Blandford in Dorset, where the rebuilding of the town centre in brick after the conflagration of 1731 is still an obvious feature; but there are many towns, particularly in southern England, where the increasing use of brick can be seen in the form of infilling of empty sites with brick structures, brick facades on buildings which retain timber frames behind the frontage, and insertion of brick features such as chimney stacks. In the lowlands, at least, most urban institutional buildings of the seventeenth and eighteenth centuries were built in brick: the market halls of Home-Counties towns or the Nonconformist chapels and meeting houses are frequently brick built. In and around certain towns brickworks were developed during the seventeenth century, but most have disappeared, their clay pits filled in during subsequent development. An example is the recently excavated site at Holloway Street, Exeter, where burnt clay, brick fragments and quarry pits indicate that bricks were made before the area was built over, late in the seventeenth century (*PMA* 1986: 352).

Large houses set a fashion for the use of brick, which influenced builders at all levels, although the practical advantages of brick construction in day-to-day building should not be underestimated. The large houses of the period are particularly important because their builders required bricks of high quality, predictable in size and colour. It was their needs which fostered skills among the brickmakers, and led to a greater use of permanent kilns rather than clamps. The great houses of the sixteenth century, such as Hatfield, had been supplied from kilns set up nearby, but during the seventeenth century the trends in the use of bricks emphasized high-quality work, with rubbed brickwork, fine joints, and the incorporation of special bricks: these were the products of the full-time brickmaker at a permanent kiln.

By the eighteenth century production had reached a volume which made bricks cheap enough for use in the smallest houses: it is in this period that estate cottage construction in brick became common, at a time when much of the poorest rural housing was replaced. It was during the eighteenth century that the industrialization of brickmaking took place, when the rural brickmaker found himself catering only for limited local markets; the major industrial and transport projects were increasingly served by larger-scale brickfields whose specialization brought prices down, and whose costs were still further reduced by transport over the canal network.

BRICK KILNS

Brick kilns evolved over the post-medieval period, from the clamp, with its minimum of permanent features, to kilns which were suited to long-term regular use. No kilns which can be proved to have operated in the sixteenth century have been excavated, but most of those to which a seventeenth-century date has been given are clamp kilns. The term 'clamp-brick' was certainly in use at the time, for they were used at the end of the sixteenth century in the building of Whitgift Hospital in Croydon (Lloyd 1928: 31–2), and Robert Plot, in his late-seventeenth-century description of brickmaking in Staffordshire, was still referring to clamp kilns. The excavated example which shows most clearly what can remain of such a kiln is at Shotesham St Mary, Norfolk (Wade 1980), where there was merely a fragmentary brick wall around an area of wood ash, with scatters of burnt clay and broken brick. There had been no built flues or flue-arches: bricks had been stacked leaving five channels, marked by wood ash, for the circulation of flame and heat from wood fires burning either in the base of the stack or immediately alongside the ends of the channels. It is known that bricks were valued according to the position which they had occupied in a kiln, the quality varying with the extent of firing. When a temporary outside wall was built to retain heat, this was made of wasters from previous firings: at Shotesham it was marked merely by lines of crushed brick. In most cases, such kilns have left little more than surface scatters of wasters: this was the case at Bow Brickhill, Buckinghamshire (*PMA* 1981: 230), and at South Wootton near Kings Lynn, where a kiln was dated by surface finds to the middle of the seventeenth century (*PMA* 1968: 185). In some cases, the word 'clamp' may have been too freely used, as at a kiln site at Darenth Wood, Kent, thought to date from about 1700, which consisted of an unexcavated square mound which may have concealed something more substantial than a clamp (Caiger 1964). Indeed clamp kilns, as seen at Shotesham, seem unlikely to be found from earthwork remains, rather from waster scatters and ash patches revealed during fieldwalking on ploughed ground.

The more permanent kilns had perimeter walls with flues in or beneath brick floors. Some were only different in degree from the clamps: the eighteenth-century kiln at Atherstone, Warwickshire, had narrow flue-trenches between the rows of brick which formed the floor (Scott 1978–9), and it seemed unlikely that the flues were arched over to any extent: the heat would rise from open trenches directly into

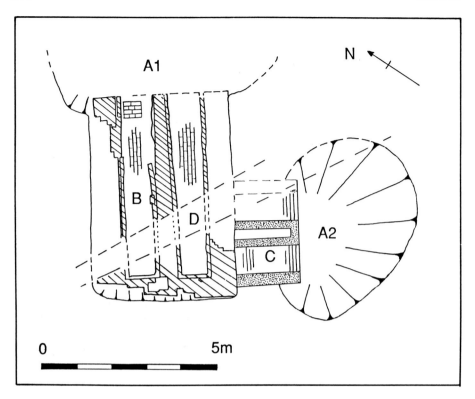

Fig. 12.8   Runsell Green, Essex: brick and tile kilns (A1, A2) stokeholes; (B) kiln 1; (C) kiln 2; (D) drain (Paul Drury).

the stacked bricks. The traces of an outside brick wall were slight, and it appears that this was a kiln only one stage away from the clamp. More sophisticated were kilns in which the flues ran beneath a full-width brick floor, the heat rising through vents in vaulted tunnels. Kilns of this kind usually had fewer flues than the Atherstone type. At the latter there were five or six passages, while at Runsell Green, Danbury, Essex (fig. 12.8; Drury 1975), there was a central spine wall between two flues, and at Little Leighs, Essex, there were two cross-walls, presumably separating three flues (*PMA* 1982: 223–4). These eighteenth-century structures had a single stokehole on one side of the kiln. A kiln excavated in Nottinghamshire, at Flintham Hall, appears to have supplied bricks for the rebuilding of the house around 1700 (Alvey 1982). Perhaps surprisingly, in view of its limited purpose, it was of the permanent type, walled, built of brick with stone facings, and with five arched flues, each with a stokehole at one end. The culmination of the development of walled kilns with firing chambers below the load-space was the 'Scotch' type, as recorded at Ebernoe, Sussex (fig. 12.9) an example which dates from the latter part of the eighteenth century when it was built to supply the Petworth estate (Aldsworth 1983). It was used until the present century, and a similar kiln, at Ashburnham, was the last in Sussex to run on wood fuel when it closed down in the 1960s.

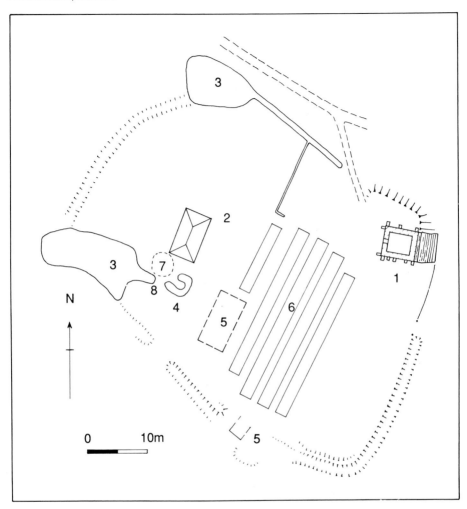

Fig. 12.9 Ebernoe, Sussex: brick kiln and associated features: (1) kiln; (2) moulding shed; (3) ponds; (4) pug mill; (5) sheds; (6) drying racks; (7) clay dump; (8) sluice (F.G Aldsworth).

As in the case of so many early industrial sites, there has been a tendency to concentrate on kilns, rather than the ancillary features and equipment which provide the complete picture of a brickworks. However, juxtaposition of excavated features, contemporary documentary records, and survivals at long-running country brickworks give an outline. The brickmaker required a building in which moulding could be done and another where bricks could be dried before firing. At Atherstone, something of the kind was indicated, but such a structure will inevitably leave little trace, an open-sided shed being the most suitable for well-ventilated drying. At Little Leighs there were signs that the clay had been prepared using a horse-powered pugging mill, for a circular feature with a central brick plinth was found, although it may date in its present form from the last period of use in the nineteenth century. A mill track of this kind was also found at Ebernoe, where there also survives much of a water-supply system, essential for brick production and perhaps to be sought at other sites.

TILE KILNS

At some kiln sites, wasters show that both bricks and tiles were fired, scatters of each being found at Darenth and South Wootton. Others, however, concentrated on roof or floor tiles. Few tile kilns have been excavated, but the published example at Bexley, Kent (Dale 1974) specialized in red roof tiles: there were two periods of construction, both kilns being of similar layout: the later kiln, built exactly above its forerunner, was rectangular, 4.5m × 3m, enclosed by walls made of tiles. The floor was of waster tiles set on edge, and beneath were two fire tunnels which were connected to a large firing pit. A small kiln or oven was set into the structure of the kiln, perhaps for firing special items. The Bexley kiln produced peg-hole roof tiles, whose use expanded greatly through the eighteenth century, despite the development of the coasting trade in slate. Many regional varieties of tiles maintained their popularity, but these are not yet reflected in the archaeological record: kilns firing, for example, the black-glazed tiles of Norfolk have yet to be recorded. A variety to whose manufacture there are documentary references is the brick-tile, the 'mathematical tile' used in south-east England from the 1720s into the nineteenth century for cladding timber-framed buildings to give the appearance of brickwork (T.P. Smith 1985). These are very common in towns such as Lewes or Faversham, and often have the characteristics of products of the local brick kilns. Manufacture is documented at the estate kilns at Holkham in Norfolk, and at Exbury in Hampshire, but brick-tile wasters are not known from kiln sites.

There also remained a market for flat tiles, either for flooring or for wall decoration. There had been a thriving medieval tradition, best expressed by the high standards of design and production of the latter part of the thirteenth century. At this time the use of tiles in ecclesiastical buildings had been at its height, and in the subsequent two centuries both this market and the skills which it fostered had declined. Nevertheless there were late-medieval potters who produced tiles of fine quality, as shown by those published from Raglan Castle (Lewis 1987) attributed to producers of the 'Malvern School'. Despite the end of the monastic requirement for tiles, makers were not without a market. Floors in parish churches were repaired, and a valuable study of church tiles in the district around the kiln at Little Brickhill, Buckinghamshire, has recorded parallels to the kiln wasters, tiles which correspond with references to building work carried out in the first half of the sixteenth century (Mynard 1975). The Little Brickhill kiln, a two-flue rectangular structure, was re-excavated in 1968 following exploration in 1930, and although it was not possible to excavate an earlier phase fully, it was clear that the tradition of the medieval Buckinghamshire kilns survived. The use of tiles in country houses provided a growing market: much of the need was for plain paving tiles, and it is at the kilns producing a wide range of bricks and utilitarian tiles that the sources should be sought. A late example is Samuel Moody of Danbury, Essex, who may have operated the excavated kiln at Runsell Green. Among the varied stock in his inventory of 1708 were 'pavements',which have been assumed to be quarry tiles.

The production of decorative tiles in the post-medieval period was divided between the traditional lead-glazed wares and tin-glazed tiles in the Low Countries fashion. It has been shown that the north-Devon potteries made lead-glazed decorative tiles in the seventeenth century, using raised relief patterns for which many parallels have been found in local churches (Keen 1969). The market for decorative tiles came to be dominated by the tin-glaze potters, providing for a fashion which grew in the middle of the sixteenth century. This was a trade in which the connection with pottery manufacture was much closer than in the case of the traditional lead-glazed products. The manufacture of maiolica tiles in England before 1600 is as doubtful as that of delftware pottery: it is not certain whether Andries and Janson, the Dutch potters, made tin-glaze tiles or pottery in London late in the sixteenth century, and it is only towards 1620 that the industry is identifiable. It is certain that the potter Christian Wilhelm or his successor Townsend made delftware tiles at Pickleherring Quay, Southwark, in the second quarter of the century, a conclusion based on excavated wasters. Much more is known about delftware tile production in England towards the end of the seventeenth century. There was an expansion of London manufacture, indicated by the warrant to the Delft potter Jan Ariens van Hamme in 1676 (Ray 1973: 35). His manufacture at Vauxhall was cut short by his death in 1680, but London output increased greatly from the 1690s. Delftware tiles were being made in Bristol from 1683 and in Liverpool from 1710. Even so, it does seem that imported Dutch tiles still held an important place in the English market in the seventeenth century, having largely monopolized it in the sixteenth. The Dutch tile was well regarded, for the Dutch makers used a softer clay, and this enabled builders to fit these tiles more easily than their harder English counterparts.

Bibliography

Abbreviations used in the bibliography and text

AA	*Archaeologia Aeliana*
ACamb	*Archaeologia Cambrensis*
ACant	*Archaeologia Cantiana*
AgHR	*Agricultural Historical Review*
AntJ	*Antiquaries Journal*
AJ	*Archaeological Journal*
BAR	*British Archaeological Reports*
CA	*Current Archaeology*
CBA	*Council for British Archaeology*
DAJ	*Derbyshire Archaeological Journal*
EAH	*Essex Archaeology and History*
EcHR	*Economic History Review*
HM	*Historical Metallurgy* (formerly *Bulletin of the Historical Metallurgy Group*)
IA	*Industrial Archaeology*
IAR	*Industrial Archaeology Review*
IJNA	*International Journal of Nautical Archaeology*
JBAA	*Journal of the British Archaeological Association*
KAR	*Kent Archaeological Review*
MA	*Medieval Archaeology*
MLPW	*Medieval and Later Pottery in Wales*
MSRG	*Moated Sites Research Group*
MVRG	*Medieval Village Research Group*
NA	*Norfolk Archaeology*
PDNHAS	*Proceedings of Dorset Natural History and Archaeological Society*
PHFCAS	*Proceedings of the Hampshire Field Club and Archaeological Society*
PMA	*Post-Medieval Archaeology*
PSAS	*Proceedings of the Society of Antiquaries of Scotland*
SxAC	*Sussex Archaeological Collections*
SyAC	*Surrey Archaeological Collections*
TBGAS	*Transactions of the Bristol and Gloucestershire Archaeological Society*
TBWAS	*Transactions of the Birmingham and Warwickshire Archaeological Society*
TCHS	*Transactions of the Caernarvonshire Historical Society*
TCWAAS	*Transactions of the Cumberland and Westmorland Archaeological and Antiquarian Society*

TDGNHAS	*Transactions of the Dumfries and Galloway Natural History and Archaeological Society*
TNS	*Transactions of the Newcomen Society*
TTS	*Transactions of the Thoroton Society*
TWAS	*Transactions of the Worcestershire Archaeological Society*
TWNHFC	*Transactions of the Woolhope Natural History and Field Club*
VA	*Vernacular Architecture*
YAJ	*Yorkshire Archaeological Journal*

Aberg, F.A., 1978, *Medieval Moated Sites* (CBA Res Rep 17).

Adams, M. and J. Reeve, 1987, 'Excavations at Christ Church Spitalfields 1984–6', *Antiquity* 61, 247–56.

Addington, S., 1978, 'The hedgerows of Tasburgh', *NA* 37, 70–83.

Addington, S., 1982, 'Landscape and settlements in south Norfolk,' *NA* 38, 97–139.

Addy, S.O., 1933, *The Evolution of the English House.*

Addyman, P.V. and S.D. Leigh, 1973, 'The Anglo-Saxon village at Chalton, Hampshire', *MA* 17, 1–15.

Addyman, P.V. and J. Marjoram, 1972, 'An 18th-century mansion, a fishpond and post-medieval finds from St Neots, Hunts', *PMA* 6, 69–106.

Agricola, G., 1556, *De Re Metallica* ed. H.C. and L.H. Hoover (New York, 1950).

Airs, M.R., 1975, *The Making of the English Country House 1500–1640.*

Alcock, N.W., 1969, 'Devon farmhouses: I, medieval and later', *Trans Devon Assoc* 100, 13–28.

Alcock, N.W., 1971–3, 'Timber-framed buildings in Warwickshire: Stoneleigh village', *TBWAS* 85, 178–202.

Alcock, N.W. and M. Laithwaite, 1973, 'Medieval houses in Devon and their modernisation', *MA* 17, 100–125.

Aldsworth, F.G., 1981, 'St Andrews Castle, Hamble, Hampshire', *PHFCAS* 37, 5–11.

Aldsworth, F.G., 1983, 'An 18th-century brick kiln on Ebernoe Common, Kirdford', *SxAC* 121, 219–24.

Allan, J., 1983, 'Some post-medieval evidence for the trade in ceramics' in Hodges, R. and P.J. Davey (eds) *Ceramics and Trade* (Sheffield) 37–45.

Allen, D., 1979, 'Excavations at Hafod y Nant Criafolen, Brenig Valley, Clwyd, 1973–4' *PMA* 13, 1–59.

Alvey, R.C., 1982, 'A post-medieval brick kiln at Flintham Hall, Notts' *TTS* 86, 118–23.

Amery, A. and P.J. Davey, 1979, 'Post-medieval pottery from Brookhill, Buckley, Clwyd (Site 1) *MLPW* 2, 49–85.

Ames, H.S., 1975, 'A note on the results of recent excavations at Camber Castle, Sussex' *PMA* 9, 233–36.

Andrews, D., 1986, 'Old Copped Hall: the site of the Tudor mansion' *EAH* 17, 96–106.

Archer, M., (n.d.), *English Delftware* (Amsterdam).

Armitage, P.L., 1982, 'Studies in the remains of domestic live-stock from Roman, medieval and early-modern London: objectives amd methods' in Hall, A. and H. Kenward (eds) *Environmental Archaeology in the Urban Context* (CBA Res Rep 43) 94–106.

Armstrong, P., 1977, *Excavations at Sewer Lane, Hull 1974* (Hull).

Ashdown, J.H., 1968, 'Seventeenth-century pottery from Wrotham, Kent' *KAR* 14, 13–17.

Ashurst, D., 1970, 'Excavations at Gawber glasshouse near Barnsley, Yorkshire' *PMA* 4, 92–140.

Ashurst, D., 1979, 'Excavations at Houndhill near Barnsley …' *PMA* 13, 227–38.

Ashurst, D., 1984, 'An 18th-century ice-house at Wentworth Castle, Stainborough, Barnsley' *PMA* 18, 304–5.

Ashurst, D., 1987, 'Excavations at the 17th–18th-century glasshouse at Bolsterstone … Yorkshire' *PMA* 21, 147–226.

Atkin, M., 1983, 'The chalk tunnels of Norwich' *NA* 38, 313–20.

Atkin, M., 1987, 'Post-medieval archaeology in Gloucester: a review' *PMA* 21, 1–24.

Atkin, M. and A. Carter, 1977, 'Excavations in Norwich 1976–7' *NA* 36, 287–304.

Atkinson, D.R., 1972, 'A brief guide for the identification of Dutch clay tobacco pipes found in England' *PMA* 6, 175–82.

Atkinson, D.R., 1975, 'The clay tobacco pipes', in Platt, C. and R. Coleman-Smith, vol. 2, 343–49.

Atkinson, F., 1960–1, 'The horse as a source of rotary power' *TNS* 33, 31–55.

Austin, D., G.A.M. Gerrard, and T.A.P. Greeves, 1989, 'Tin and agriculture: landscape archaeology in St Neot Parish' *Cornish Archaeol* 28, 1–250.

Awty, B.G., 1981, 'The continental origins of Wealden iron workers' *EcHR* 2.34, 524–39.

Awty, B.G. and C.B. Phillips, 1979–80, 'The Cumbrian bloomery forge in the 17th century and forge equipment in the charcoal iron industry' *TNS* 51, 25–40.

Baker, A.R.H. and R.A. Butlin (eds), 1973, *Studies of Field Systems in the British Isles* (Cambridge).

Barley, M.W., 1961, *The English Farmhouse and Cottage*.

Barley, M.W., 1967, 'Rural housing in Britain', in Thirsk, J. (ed.), 1967, 696–766.

Barley, M.W., 1985, 'Rural building in Britain', in Thirsk, J. (ed.), 1985, 590–685.

Barley, M.W., 1986, *Houses and History*.

Barraclough, K.C., 1976, 'The development of the cementation process for the manufacture of steel' *PMA* 10, 65–88.

Bartlett, K.S., 1971, 'Excavations at Potovens near Wakefield' *PMA* 5, 1–34.

Barton, K.J., 1961, 'Some evidence for two types of pottery manufactured in Bristol in the early 18th century' *TBGAS* 80, 160–8.

Bassett, S.R., 1982, *Saffron Walden: Excavations and Research 1972–80* (CBA Res Rep 45).

Batchelor, D., 1977, 'Excavations at Hampton Court Palace' *PMA* 11, 36–49.

Batey, M., 1968, 'Nuneham Courtenay: an Oxfordshire 18th-century deserted village' *Oxoniensia* 33, 108–24.

Bax, A. and C.J.M. Martin, 1974, '*De Liefde*, a Dutch East Indiaman lost on the Out Skerries, Shetland in 1711' *IJNA* 3, 81–90.

Beckett, J., 1989, *Laxton* (Oxford).

Bedwin, O.R., 1976, 'The excavation of Ardingly fulling mill and forge, 1975–76' *PMA* 10, 34–64.

Bedwin, O.R., 1977–8, 'The excavation of a late-16th/early-17th-century gun-casting furnace at Maynards Gate, Crowborough, East Sussex' *SxAC* 116, 163–78.

Bedwin, O.R., 1980a, 'The excavation of Batsford Mill, Warbleton, East Sussex, 1978' *MA* 24, 187–201.

Bedwin, O.R., 1980b, 'The excavation of a late-16th-century blast furnace at Batsford, Herstmonceux, East Sussex, 1978' *PMA* 14, 89–112.

Beresford, M.W., 1961, 'Habitation versus improvement: the debate on enclosure by agreement' in Fisher F.J. (ed.) *Essays in the Economic and Social History of Tudor and Stuart England*, 40–69.

Beresford, M.W., 1979, 'The Decree Rolls of Chancery as a source for economic history, 1547–c.1700' *EcHR* 2.32, 1–10.

Bettey, J.H., 1971, 'The supply of stone for rebuilding St Paul's Cathedral' *AJ* 128, 176–85.

Bettey, J.H., 1977, 'The development of water meadows in Dorset during the 17th century' *AgHR* 25, 37–43.

Bettey, J.H., 1982, 'Seventeenth-century squatters' dwellings: some documentary evidence' *VA* 13, 28–30.

Beurdeley, M., 1962, *Porcelain of the East India Companies*.

Biddle, M., 1961, 'Nonsuch Palace 1959–60: an interim report' *SyAC* 58, 1–20.

Biddle, M., 1966, 'Nicholas Bellin of Modena, *JBAA* 29, 106–21.

Biddle, M., L. Barfield and A. Millard, 1959, 'The excavation of the Manor of the More, Rickmansworth, Herts' *AJ* 116, 136–99.

Biringuccio, V., 1540, *The Pirotechnia*, Smith, C.S. and M.T. Gnudi (eds) 1959 (Cambridge Mass.).

Blanchard I.S.W., 1980, 'Lead mining and smelting in medieval England and Wales', in Crossley, D.W. (ed.) 1981, 72–84.

Bloch, M., 1967, *Land and Work in Medieval Europe*.

Bloice, B.J., 1971, 'Norfolk House, Lambeth: excavations at a delftware kiln site, 1968' *PMA* 5, 99–159.

Borne, P., T. Courtney and P. Dixon, 1978, 'The Peacock Inn, Chesterfield' *DAJ* 98, 7–58.

Bowman, A.I., 1970, 'Culross Colliery: a 16th-century mine' *IA* 7, 353–72.

Brandon, P.F., 1971, 'The origin of Newhaven and the drainage of the Lewes and Laughton Levels' *SxAC* 109, 94–106.

Brandon, V. and S. Johnson, 1986, 'The old Baptist chapel, Goodshaw Chapel, Rawtenstall, Lancs' *AntJ* 66, 330–57.

Brears, P.C.D., 1967, 'Excavations at Potovens, near Wakefield *PMA* 1, 3–43.

Brears, P.C.D., 1970, 'The horticultural wares' in Moorhouse, S. 1970, 87–90.

Brears, P.C.D., 1971, *The English Country Pottery: its History and Techniques* (Newton Abbot).

Bridgewater, N.P., 1963, 'Glasshouse Farm, St Weonards: a small glass working site' *TWNHFC* 37, 300–15.

Brooks, C.M., 1983, 'Aspects of the sugar-refining industry from the 16th to the 19th century' *PMA* 17, 1–14.

Brown, A.E. and C.C. Taylor, 1977, 'Cambridgeshire earthwork surveys' *Proc Camb Antiq Soc* 67, 85–102.

Brown, P.J., 1982, 'The early industrial complex at Astley, Worcestershire' *PMA* 16, 1–19.

Bruce-Mitford, R., 1939, 'The archaeology of the site of the Bodleian extension in Broad Street, Oxford, *Oxoniensia* 4, 89–146.

Brunner, H. and J.K. Major, 1972, 'Water-raising by animal power' *IA* 9, 117–51.

Brunskill, R.W., 1967, 'Lowther village and Robert Adam' *Trans Anc Mon Soc* 14, 57–73.

Brunskill, R.W., 1982a, *Illustrated Handbook of Vernacular Architecture*.

Brunskill, R.W., 1982b, *Traditional Farm Buildings of Britain*.

Brunskill, R.W., 1985, *Timber Building in Britain*.

Bryant, G.F., 1977, 'Experimental kiln firings at Barton-on-Humber' *MA* 21, 106–23.

Buchanan, B.J. and M.T. Tucker, 1981, 'The manufacturer of gunpowder ... the Woolley powder works near Bath' *IAR* 5.1, 185–202.

Butler, D.S. and C.F. Tebbutt, 1975, 'A Wealden cannon-boring bar' *PMA* 9, 38–41.

Butler, L.A.S., 1978, 'St Martins church, Allerton Mauleverer' *YAJ* 50, 177–88.

Butler, L.A.S., 1983, 'Church building after the Reformation' in Morris (ed.) 1983, 92–3.

Butlin, R.A., 1967, 'Enclosure and improvement in Northumberland in the 16th century' *AA* 4.45, 149–60.

Cable, M., 1987, 'Glass technology at Bolsterstone' in Ashurst 1987, 217–23.

Caffyn, L., 1983, 'A study of farm buildings in selected parishes of East Sussex' *SxAC* 121, 149–71.

Caiger, J.E.L., 1964, 'Darenth Wood: its earthworks and antiquities' *ACant* 79, 77–94.

Caiger, J.E.L., 1965, 'An ice-house at Green Street Green, Darenth' *ACant* 80, 221–26.

Carter, A., 1974, 'Excavations in Norwich ...' *NA* 36, 39–71.

Carver, M.O.H., 1980, 'Medieval Worcester: an archaeological framework' *TWAS* 7, 1–356.

Chambers, J.D., 1964, *Laxton, the Last English Open-field Village*.

Chapman, J., 1976, 'Parliamentary enclosure in the uplands: the case of the North York Moors' *AgHR* 24, 1–17.

Charles, F.W.B., 1974, 'The timber-framed buildings of Coventry' *TBWAS* 86, 113–31.

Charles, F.W.B., 1978–9, 'Timber-framed houses in Spon Street, Coventry' *ibid* 89, 91–112.

Charles, F.W.B. and K. Down, 1970–2, 'A 16th-century drawing of a town house' *TWAS* 3, 67–79.

Charleston, R.J., 1975, 'The glass' in Platt and Coleman-Smith pt 2, 203–26.

Christie, P.M. and J.G. Coad, 1980, 'Excavations at Denny Abbey' *AJ* 137, 138–279.

Clarke, H. and A. Carter, 1977, 'Excavations in Kings Lynn 1963–70' *Soc Med Archaeol* monograph 7.

Clark, P. (ed.), 1984, *The Transformation of English Provincial Towns.*

Clarke, S., R. Jackson and P. Jackson, 1984, 'Pottery from a post-medieval kiln at Dixton, Gwent' *MLPW* 7, 9–24.

Cleere, H.F. and D.W. Crossley, 1985, *The Iron Industry of the Weald* (Leicester).

Clough, R.T., 1980 (edn), *The Lead-smelting Mills of the Yorkshire Dales and Northern Pennines* (Keighley).

Coad, J.G., 1969, 'Chatham ropeyard' *PMA* 3, 143–65.

Cole, C.,1964–5, 'Carfax conduit' *Oxoniensia* 29/30, 142–66.

Coleman-Smith, R. and T. Pearson, 1988, *Excavations in the Donyatt Potteries* (Chichester).

Colvin, H.M. (ed.), 1982, *The History of the Kings Works IV 1485–1660.*

Cook, A.M., 1969, 'Oatlands Palace excavations: interim report' *SyAC* 66, 1–9.

Copeland, G.W., 1967, 'Devon dovecotes' *Trans Devon Assoc* 99, 269.

Coppack, G., 1972, 'Medieval and post-medieval pottery' in Hall, R. 'Excavations at Fall Street, Derby 1972' *DAJ* 92, 29–77 (44–76).

Couchman, C.R., 1979, 'Excavations at St Michael's church Latchingdon, 1976' *EAH* 11, 6–31.

Courtney, T., 1974, 1975, 'Excavations at the Royal dockyard, Woolwich, 1972–3 (parts 1 and 2)' *PMA* 8, 1–28; 9, 42–102.

Cowan, R. and Z. and P. Marsden, 1975, 'The Dutch East Indiaman *Hollandia* wrecked on the Isles of Scilly in 1743' *IJNA* 4, 267–300.

Crampton, C.B., 1968, '*Hafotai* platforms on the north front of Carmarthen Fan' *ACamb* 117, 121–6.

Cranstone, D., 1985, *The Moira Furnace* (Coalville).

Crew, P., 1976, 'The copper mines of Llanberis and Clogwyn Goch' *TCHS* 37, 58–79.

Crocker, G., 1988, *Gunpowder Mills Gazetteer* (Soc Protection of Anc Buildings).

Cronk, A, 1978, 1979, 'Oasts in Kent and East Sussex' *ACant* 94, 99–110; 95, 241–54.

Crossley, D.W., 1967, 'Glass making at Bagots Park, Staffordshire in the 16th century' *PMA* 1, 44–83.

Crossley, D.W., 1972, 'A 16th-century Wealden blast furnace: excavations at Panningridge, Sussex, 1964–70' *ibid* 6, 42–68.

Crossley, D.W., 1975a, *Sidney Ironworks Accounts* (Roy Hist Soc Camden 4.15).

Crossley, D.W. 1975b, *The Bewl Valley Ironworks.*

Crossley, D.W., 1975c, 'Cannon manufacture at Pippingford ...' *PMA* 9, 1–37.

Crossley, D.W., 1979, 'A gun-casting furnace at Scarlets, Cowden, Kent' *ibid* 13, 235–49.

Crossley, D.W., 1981 (ed.), *Medieval Industry* (CBA Res Rep 40).

Crossley, D.W., 1987, 'Sir William Clavell's glasshouse at Kimmeridge, Dorset: the excavations of 1980–81' *AJ* 144, 340–82.

Crossley, D.W. and F.A. Aberg, 1972, '16th-century glass making in Yorkshire: excavations at furnaces at Hutton and Rosedale, North Riding, 1968–71' *PMA* 6, 107–59.

Crossley, D.W. and D. Ashurst, 1968, 'Excavations at Rockley Smithies, a water-powered bloomery of the 16th and 17th centuries' *PMA* 2, 10–54.

Crossley, D.W., J. Cass, N. Flavell and C. Turner, 1989, *Water Power on the Sheffield Rivers* (Sheffield).

Crowfoot, E., 1984, 'The textiles', in Redknap 1984, 75–83.

Cruden, S.H., 1946–7, 'The horizontal watermill at Dounby on the mainland of Orkney' *PSAS* 81, 43–7.

Crummy, P., 1976, 'Portreeve's House, Colchester, and a method of modernising Essex houses in the 16th and 17th centuries' *PMA* 10, 89–103.

Cubbon, A.M. and B.R.S. Megaw, 1969, 'Corn-drying kilns in the Isle of Man' *Jnl Manx Mus* 7.85, 113–6.

Cunliffe, B.W., 1971, 'The Tudor store-house at Portchester Castle, Hampshire' *PMA* 5, 188–90.

Cunliffe, B.W., 1973, 'Manor Farm, Chalton, Hampshire, *PMA* 7, 31–59.

Cunningham, C.M. and P.J. Drury, 1985, *Post-Medieval Sites and their Pottery: Moulsham Street, Chelmsford* (CBA Res Rep 54).

Cunningham, C.M., 1986, 'Garden archaeology: reconstruction or destruction?' *Rescue News* 40, 5.

Curle, A.O., 1925–6, 'Domestic candlesticks from the 14th to the end of the 18th century' *PSAS* 60, 183–214.

Dakin, G.F., 1968, 'Two post-medieval industrial structures at Thorpewood near Peterborough' *PMA* 2, 164–6.

Dale, L.C., 1974, 'A post-medieval tile-kiln at Bexley' *ACant* 89, 25–32.

Daniels, J.S., 1959, *The Woodchester Glasshouse* (Gloucester).

Davey, P.J., 1975, 'Recent work on the Buckley potteries' *PMA* 9, 236–9.

Davey, P.J., 1981, *The Archaeology of the Clay Tobacco Pipe VI: Pipes and Kilns in the London Region BAR* B97 (Oxford).

Davey, P.J., 1982a, *The Archaeology of the Clay Tobacco Pipe VII: More Pipes and Kilns from England BAR* B100 (Oxford).

Davey, P.J., 1982b, 'The Rainford clay-pipe industry' in Davey, P.J. 1982a, 91–306.

Davey, P.J., 1985, *The Archaeology of the Clay Tobacco Pipe IX: More Pipes from the Midlands and Southern England BAR* B146 (Oxford).

Davey, P.J., 1987, 'The post-medieval period' in Schofield J. and R. Leach (1987), 69–80.

David, R.G., 1982, 'An ice-house experiment' *TCWAAS* 82, 191–3.

Davies, I.E., 1976, 'The manufacture of honestones in Gwynedd' *TCHS* 37, 80–6.

Davies-Shiel, M. 1972, 'The making of potash for soap in Lakeland' *TCWAAS* 72, 85–111.

Dawson, G.J., 1979, 'Excavations at Guys Hospital 1967' *Surrey Archaeol Soc Res Vol. 7*, 27–65.

Day, J.M., 1973, *Bristol Brass* (Newton Abbot).

Day, J.M., 1979, 'The Saltford brass annealing furnace' *HM* 13.1, 32–7.

Day, J.M., 1988, 'The Bristol brass industry: furnace structures and their associated remains' *HM* 22.1, 24–41.

Dean, M., 1985, 'A boat recovered from the foreshore at West Mersea, Essex' *IJNA* 14.3, 217–26.

De Boer, G., 1973, 'The two earliest maps of Hull' *PMA* 7, 79–87.

Denholm, P.C., 1982, 'Mid-18th-century tin-glazed earthenwares from the Delftfield Pottery, Glasgow: excavations at the Broomielaw, 1975' *PMA* 16, 39–84.

Dickinson, J.C., 1968, 'The buildings of the English Austin Canons after the dissolution of the monasteries' *JBAA* 31, 60–75.

Diderot, D. and J. D'Alembert, 1751–80, *Receuil de Planche sur les sciences les arts liberaux, les arts mechaniques avec leur explication* 10 vols (Paris).

Dinn, J., 1988, 'Dyfi furnace excavations 1982–7' *PMA* 22, 111–42.

Dixon, P., 1972a, 'Shielings and bastles: a reconsideration of some problems' *AA* 4.50, 249–58.

Dixon, P., 1972b, *Excavations at Greenwich Palace 1970–1* (Greenwich and Lewisham Antiq Soc.

Dixon, P., 1975, 'Excavations at Richmond Palace, Surrey' *PMA* 9, 103–16.

Donald, M.B., 1961, *Elizabethan Monopolies* (Edinburgh).

Douch, H.L., 1969, 'Cornish potters and pewterers' *Jnl Roy Inst Cornwall* 6.1, 33–80.

Douglas, G., M. Oglethorpe and J.R. Hume, 1984, *Scottish Windmills: a Survey* (Glasgow).

Downs Rose G. and W.S. Harvey, 1979, 'Lead-smelting sites at Wanlockhead 1682–1934' *TDGNHAS* 54, 75–84.

Draper, J. 1982, 'An 18th-century kiln at Hole Common, Lyme Regis, Dorset' *PDNHAS* 104, 137–42.

Drewett, P.L., 1975, 'Excavations at Hadleigh Castle, Essex, 1971–2, *JBAA* 38, 90–154.

Drury, P.J., 1975, 'Post-medieval brick and tile kilns at Runsell Green, Danbury, Essex' *PMA* 9, 203–11.

Drury, P.J., 1980, '"No other place in the kingdom will compare with it": the evolution of Audley End, 1605–1745' *Archit Hist* 23, 1–39.

Drury, P.J., 1982, 'Walden into Audley End' in Bassett 1982, 94–105.

Drury, P.J., 1983, '"A fayre house built by Sir Thomas Smith": the development of Hill Hall, Essex, 1557–1581, *JBAA* 136, 98–123.

Duckham, B.F., 1968, 'Some 18th-century coal-mining methods: the "Dissertation" of Sir John Clark' *IA* 5, 217–32.

Durant, D.N. and P.J. Riden (eds), 1980, *The Building of Hardwick Hall I: The Old Hall* (Derbyshire Rec Soc 4).

Dyer, A.D., 1981, 'Urban housing: a documentary study of four Midland towns, 1530–1700' *PMA* 15, 207–18

Dyer, C.C., 1986, 'English peasant building in the later middle Ages' *MA* 30, 19–45.

Earnshaw, J.R., 1973, 'A medieval post-mill ... at Bridlington' *YAJ* 45, 19–40.

Edwards, R., 1974, London Potters, c.1570–1710 *Jnl Ceram Hist* 6.

Egan, G., 1980, 'Leaden cloth seals and the trade of London' *PMA* 14, 185–7.

Ellis, J., 1980, 'The decline and fall of the Tyneside salt industry, 1660–1790: a re-examination' *EcHR* 2.33, 45–58.

Ellison, M. and B. Harbottle, 1983, 'The excavation of a 17th-century bastion in the castle of Newcastle upon Tyne' *AA* 5.11, 135–263.

Emery, N., 1985, 'Changing patterns of farming in an Isle of Man glen' *PMA* 19, 1–11.

Endrei, W. and G. Egan, 1982, 'The sealing of cloth in Europe, with special reference to the English evidence' *Text Hist* 13, 47–75.

Evans, D.H., 1979, 'Gravel-tempered ware: a survey of published forms' *MLPW* 2, 18–29.

Evans, D.H., 1986, 'Excavations at 18 Castle Street (Albion Court) Aberdeen' *PMA* 20, 271–95.

Everitt, A., 1967, 'The marketing of agriculture produce' in Thirsk (ed.) (1967), 466–592.

Ewart, G., 1980, 'Excavations at Stirling Castle 1977–8' *PMA* 14, 23–51.

Fairclough, G., 1976, 'Excavations of two medieval and post-medieval sites at Newark, 1975' *TTS* 80, 1–34.

Fairclough, G., 1980, 'Clifton Hall, Cumbria: excavations 1977–9' *TCWAAS* 80, 45–68.

Fairhurst, H., 1967–8, 'Rosal, a deserted township in Strath Naver, Sutherland' *PSAS* 100, 135–69.

Fairhurst, H., 1968–9, 'The deserted settlement at Lix, west Perthshire' *PSAS* 101, 160–99.

Farley, M., 1979, 'Pottery and pottery kilns of the post-medieval period at Brill, Buckinghamshire' *PMA* 13, 127–52.

Farley, M., 1978, 'A 17th-century pottery at Potter Row, Great Missenden, Buckinghamshire' *Rec of Bucks* 20.4, 586–96.

Farrant, S., 1983, 'Marchants and Hayleigh Farms in Street and Westmeston, East Sussex' *SxAC* 121, 119–27.

Fasham, P. and J. Hawkes, 1984, 'Reading', *CA* 93, 307–10.

Faull, M.L. and S.A. Moorhouse, 1981, *West Yorkshire: an Archaeological Survey to AD 1500* (Wakefield).

Fenton, A. and B. Walker, 1981, *The Rural Architecture of Scotland* (Edinburgh).

Field, J.J., 1969, 'Haselden Hall, Wakefield' *PMA* 3, 188–90.

Fitzherbert, A., 1523, *Husbandry; Surveying* (1767 edn).

Fletcher, J., M. Bridge and J. Hillam, 1981, 'Tree-ring dates for buildings with oak timber' *VA* 12, 38–40.

Fowkes, D.V. and G.R. Potter, 1988, *William Senior's Survey of the Estates of the First and Second Earls of Devonshire, c.1620–8* (Derbyshire Record Ser 13).

Fox, A., 1939, 'Early Welsh homesteads on Gelligaer Common, Glamorgan' *ACamb* 94, 162–99.

Fox, C. and Lord Raglan, 1951, 1953, 1954, *Monmouthshire Houses I, II, III* (Cardiff).

Fox, R.T. and K.J. Barton, 1986, 'Excavations at Oyster Street, Portsmouth' *PMA* 20, 31–25.

Freke, D.J., 1975, 'Excavations in Lewes 1974' *SxAC* 113, 66–84.

Freke, D.J., 1979, 'The excavation of a 16th-century pottery kiln at Lower Parrock, Hartfield, East Sussex, 1977' *PMA* 13, 79–125.

Gadd, D. and T. Dyson, 1981, 'Bridewell Palace: excavations at 9–11 Bridewell Place and 1–3 Tudor Street, City of London, 1978' *PMA* 15, 1–79.

Gaimster, D., 1987, 'The supply of Rhenish stoneware to London, 1350–1600' *London Archaeol* 5.13, 339–47.

Garner, F.H., 1972, *English Delftware.*

Garrad, L.S., 1978–80, 'Gorse mills on the Isle of Man' *Proc I of M Nat Hist and Archaeol Soc* 8.4, 385–401.

Gerrard, S., 1985, 'Retallack: a late-medieval tin-mining complex in the parish of Constantine and its Cornish context' *Cornish Archaeol* 24, 175–82.

Godfrey, E.S., 1975, *The Development of English Glass-making 1560–1640* (Oxford).

Good, G.L., 1987, 'The excavation of two docks at Narrow Quay, Bristol, 1978–9' *PMA* 21, 25–126.

Goodall, A.R., 1981, 'The medieval bronze-smith and his products' in D.W. Crossley (ed.) 1981, 63–71.

Goodall, A.R., 1984, 'Copper alloy and silver objects' in Hassall 1984, 221–24.

Goodall, A.R., 1985, Copper alloy objects and debris' in Cunningham and Drury 1985, 40–9.

Goodall, I.H., 1975, 'Metalwork' in Drewett 1975, 138–46.

Gooder, E., 1984, 'The finds from the cellar of the Old Hall, Temple Balsall, Warwickshire' *PMA* 18, 149–249.

Goodfellow, A.V. and J.H. Thornton, 1972, 'Leather shoe parts and other leather fragments' in Wenham 1972, 97–104.

Graham, A., 1966–7, 'The old harbours of Dunbar' *PSAS* 99, 173–90.

Graham, A., 1968–9, 'Archaeological notes on some harbours in eastern Scotland' *PSAS* 101, 200–85.

Grant, A., 1983, *North Devon Pottery: the 17th Century* (Exeter).

Green, C.M. (forthcoming), 'Excavations at the Fulham stoneware potteries'.

Greeves, T.A.P., 1981, 'The archaeological potential of the Devon tin industry' in Crossley (ed.) 1981, 85–95.

Hammersley, G., 1973, 'The charcoal iron industry and its fuel' *EcHR* 2.26, 593–613.

Harbottle, B., 1968, 'Excavations at the Carmelite friary, Newcastle upon Tyne, 1965, 1967' *AA* 4.46, 163–223.

Harbottle, B. and M. Ellison, 1981, 'An excavation in the Castle Ditch, Newcastle upon Tyne, 1974–6 *AA* 5.9, 75–250.

Harris, A., 1968, 'The Ingleton coalfield' *IA* 5.4, 313–26.

Harris, A., 1970, 'The rabbit warrens of East Yorkshire in the 18th and 19th centuries' *YAJ* 42, 429–43.

Harris, A., 1974, 'Colliery settlements in east Cumberland' *TCWAAS* 74, 118–46.

Harris, E.C., 1980, 'Archaeological investigations at Sandgate Castle, Kent, 1976–9' *PMA* 14, 53–88.

Harris, F.J.T., 1976, 'Paper and board mills in or near Gloucestershire' *TBGAS* 94, 124–35.

Harrison, B. and B. Hutton, 1984, 'Vernacular Houses in North Yorkshire and Cleveland (Edinburgh).

Harrison, J.R., 1984, 'The mud wall in England at the close of the vernacular era' *Trans Anc Mon Soc* 28, 154–73.

Harrison, A. and J.K., 1973, 'The horse-wheel in North Yorkshire' *IA* 10.3, 247–65.

Harvey, J.C., 1974, 'Common field and enclosure in the lower Dearne valley,' *YAJ* 46, 110–27.

Harvey, N., 1970, *A History of Farm Buildings in England and Wales* (Newton Abbot).

Haslam, J., 1970, 'Sealed bottles from All Souls College' *Oxoniensia* 35, 27–33.

Haslam, J. 1975, 'The excavation of a 17th-century pottery site at Cove, east Hampshire' *PMA* 9, 164–87.

Haslam, J., 1984, 'The glass' in Hassall 1984, 232–46.

Hassall, T.G., 1976, 'Excavations at Oxford Castle, 1965–73' *Oxoniensia* 41, 232–308.

Hassall, T.G. *et al.*, 1984, 'Excavations in St Ebbes, Oxford, 1967–76 – II: post-medieval domestic tenements and the post-dissolution site of the Greyfriars' *Oxoniensia* 49, 153–275.

Hatcher, J. and T.C. Barker, 1974, *A History of British Pewter*.

Havinden, M, 1981, *The Somerset Landscape*.

Hay, G.D. and C.P. Stell, 1986, *Monuments of Industry* (Edinburgh).

Hayes, P.A., 1967–8, 'Some cottages in the Hawarden district' *Pubs Flints Hist Soc* 23, 54–74.

Hayfield, C., 1988, 'Excavations (by T.C.M. Brewster) at the deserted village of Cowlam' *PMA* 22, 21–109.

Heighway, C.M., 1983, 'Tanners Hall, Gloucester' *TBGAS* 101, 83–109.

Hellen, J.A., 1972, 'Agricultural innovation and detectable landscape margins: the case of wheel-houses in Northumberland' *AgHR* 20, 140–54.

Henstock, A., 1975, 'The monopoly in Rhenish stoneware imports in late Elizabethan England' *PMA* 9, 219–24.

Hewett, C.A., 1969, 'Some East Anglian prototypes for early timber houses in America' *PMA* 3, 100–21.

Hewett, C.A., 1971, 'Seventeenth-century carpentry in Essex' *PMA* 5, 77–87.

Hewett, C.A., 1973, 'The development of the post-medieval house' *PMA* 7, 60–78.

Hey, D.G., 1972, *The Rural Metalworkers of the Sheffield Region* (Leicester).

Hey, D.G., 1974, *An English Rural Community: Myddle under the Tudors and Stuarts* (Leicester).

Hey, D.G., 1975, 'The parks at Tankersley and Wortley' *YAJ* 47, 109–20.

Hey, D.G. (ed.), 1981, *Richard Gough: The History of Myddle*.

Hillam, J., 1985, 'Recent tree-ring work in Sheffield' *CA* 96, 21–6.

Hillam, J. and P.F. Ryder, 1980, 'Tree-ring dating of vernacular buildings from Yorkshire' *VA* 11, 23–31.

Hodges, R., 1974, 'Excavations at Daws Mill' *PDNHAS* 95, 19–44.

Holden, E.W., 1967, 'The excavation of a motte at Lodsbridge Mill, Lodsworth' *SxAC* 105, 103–25.

Holling, F.W., 1971, 'A preliminary note on the pottery industry of the Hampshire-Surrey borders' *SyAC* 68, 57–88.

Holling, F., 1977, 'Reflections on Tudor Green' *PMA* 11, 61–6.

Holmes, N.M.M., 1975, 'Excavations within the Tron Kirk, Edinburgh, 1974' *PMA* 9, 137–63.

Holt, R., 1988, *The Mills of Medieval England* (Oxford).

Hoskins, W.G., 1953, 'The rebuilding of rural England' *Past and Present* 4, 44–59.

Hoskins, W.G., 1955 (1988), *The Making of the English Landscape*; also rev edn, C.C. Taylor (1988).

Houghton, J., 1696, *Letters for the Improvement of Trade and Industry*.

Huggins, P.J., 1969, 'Excavations at Sewardstone Street, Waltham Abbey, Essex' *PMA* 3, 47–99.

Hughes, M.F., 1982, 'Emparking and the desertion of settlements in Hampshire' *MVRG* 30, 37.

Hughes, P.M., 1980, 'Houses and property in post-reformation Worcester' TWAS 7, 269–92.

Hurst, J.G., 1964, 'Tudor Green Ware' in B. Cuncliffe Winchester Excavations 1949–60 vol. 1 (Winchester), 140–2.

Hurst, J.G., D.S. Neal and H.J.E. Van Beuningen, 1986. Pottery Produced and Traded in North-West Europe 1350–1650 (Rotterdam).

Hutton, B., 1973, 'Timber-framed houses in the Vale of York' MA 17, 87–99.

Hutton, K., 1976, 'The distribution of wheel-houses in the British Isles' AgHR 24, 30–5.

Innocent, C.F., 1916, The Development of English Building Construction (Cambridge).

Jackson, M.H. and C. De Beer, 1973, Eighteenth-century gun-founding (Newton Abbot).

Jarrett, M.G. and S. Wrathmell, 1977, 'Sixteenth and seventeenth-century farmsteads: West Whelpington, Northunberland' AgHR 25, 108–19.

Jennings, S., 1981, Eighteen Centuries of Pottery from Norwich (East Anglian Archaeology 13).

Jobey, G., 1966, 'A note on "sow" kilns' Jnl Ag Soc of Univ. of Newcastle upon Tyne (1966), 37–8.

Jobey, G., 1967, 'Excavation at Tynemouth Priory and Castle' AA 4.45, 33–104.

Johnson, W.E., 1982, 'The application of hedge-dating techniques in south Norfolk' NA 38, 182–91.

Jones, A.C. and C.J. Harrison, 1978. 'The Cannock Chase ironworks, 1590' Eng Hist Rev 93, 795–810.

Jones, E.L., 1968, 'The reduction of fire damage in southern England, 1650–1850' PMA 2, 140–9.

Jones, S.R., 1980, 'Stone houses in the vernacular tradition in South Yorkshire, 1600–1700' AJ 137, 386–93.

Kealey, E.J., 1987, Harvesting the Air (Woodbridge).

Keen, L., 1969, 'A series of 17th and 18th-century lead-glazed relief tiles from north Devon' JBAA 32, 144–70.

Kelsall, A.F., 1974, 'The London house-plan in the later 17th century' PMA 8, 80–91.

Kemp, A., 1977, 'The fortification of Oxford during the Civil War' Oxoniensia 42, 237–46.

Kenworthy J., 1928, Midhope Potteries (Sheffield).

Kenyon, G.H., 1967, The Glass Industry of the Weald (Leicester).

Kenyon, J.R., 1977, 'Wark Castle and its artillery defences in the reign of Henry VII' PMA 11, 50–60.

Kenyon, J.R., 1978, 'Two original drawings by William Stukeley …' AntJ 58, 162–4.

Kenyon, J.R., 1979, 'An aspect of the 1559 survey of the Isle of Wight' PMA 13, 61–77.

Kenyon, J.R., 1981, 'The defences of Southsea Castle and Portsmouth in 1623' PHFCAS 37, 13–21.

Kenyon, J.R., 1982, 'The Civil War earthworks around Raglan Castle, Gwent …' ACamb 131, 139–42.

Kerr, N.A., 1973, A Medieval and Post-medieval Pottery Industry: Excavations in Eastgate, Bourne, Lincs.

Kerridge, E., 1953, 'The floating of the Wiltshire watermeadows' Wilts Archaeol Mag 55, 105–18.

Kiernan, D.T., 1988, The Derbyshire Lead Industry in the Sixteenth Century (Derbys Rec Ser 14).

Laithwaite, M., 1968, 'A ship-master's house at Faversham, Kent' PMA 2, 150–62.

Laithwaite, M., 1984, 'Totnes houses, 1500–1800' in Clark 1984, 62–98.

Lambrick, G. and H. Woods, 1976, 'Excavations on the second site of the Dominican priory, Oxford' Oxoniensia 41, 168–231.

Larn, R., 1985, 'The wreck of the Dutch East Indiaman Campen on the Needles rocks, Isle of Wight, 1627: part I' IJNA 14.1, 1–31.

Laws, A. and A. Oswald, 1981, 'The kiln of William Heath, 18th-century Brentford pipe-maker' in Davey, P.J. 1981, 15–65.

Lehmann, H., 1973, 'A history of Epsom Spa' *SyAC* 69, 89–97.

Lewis, J.H., 1966, 'The charcoal-fired blast furnaces of Scotland: a review' *PSAS* 114, 433–79.

Lewis, J.M., 1966, 'The Roman fort and Civil War earthwork at Caerphilly Castle, Glamorgan' *ACamb* 115, 67–87.

Lewis, J.M., 1973, 'Some types of metal chafing dish' *AntJ* 53, 59–70.

Lewis, J.M, 1980, 'The Cistercian-ware wasters from Abergavenny, Gwent' *MLPW* 3, 56–8.

Lewis, J.M., 1982, *The Ewenny Potteries* (Cardiff).

Lewis, J.M., 1987, 'The chapel at Raglan Castle and its paving tiles' in Kenyon J.R. and R. Avent (eds) *Castles in Wales and the Marches* (Cardiff), 143–60.

Lewis, M.J.T., 1970, *Early Wooden Railways*.

Linsley, S.M. and R. Hetherington, 1978, 'A 17th-century blast furnace at Allensford, Northumberland' *HM* 12.1, 1–11.

Lloyd, G., 1967, '17th-century beacons in North Wales' *ACamb* 116, 195–7.

Lloyd, J.D.K., 1965–6, 'Flintshire dovecotes' *Flints Hist Soc Pubs* 22, 75–6.

Lloyd, N., 1928, *A History of English Brickwork*.

Loudon, J.C., 1834, *Encyclopedia of Cottage, Farm and Villa Architecture and Furniture*.

McCann, J., 1987, 'Is clay lump a traditional building material?' *VA* 18, 1–16.

Machin, R., 1977, 'The Great Rebuilding: a re-assessment' *Past and Present* 77, 33–56.

Machin, R., 1978, *The Houses of Yetminster* (Bristol).

MacIvor, I., 1965, 'The Elizabethan fortifications of Berwick-on-Tweed' *AntJ* 45, 64–96.

Magilton, J.R., 1980, The Church of St Helen on the Walls (CBA: York 10.1).

Maloney, M. and E. Howard, 1986, 'The botanical examination of hedges in east Sussex as a tool in historical research' *SxAC* 124, 129–39.

Marsden, P., 1971, 'A 17th-century boat found in London' *PMA* 5, 88–98.

Marsden, P., 1974, *The Wreck of the Amsterdam*.

Marshall, J.D. and M. Davies-Shiel, 1977, *Industrial Archaeology of the Lake Counties* (Newton Abbot).

Marshall, P. (ed.), 1958, 'The diary of Sir James Hope, 1646' *Miscellany IX*, Scot Hist Soc 3.50, 127–97.

Martin, C.J.M., 1972, '*El Gran Grifon*, an Armada wreck on Fair Isle' *IJNA* 1, 59–71.

Martin, C.J.M., 1979, '*La Trinidad Valencera*: an Armada invasion transport lost off Donegal' *IJNA* 8, 13–38.

Martin, D. and B., 1987, *A Selection of Dated Houses in Eastern Sussex* (Hastings Archaeol Papers, Robertsbridge).

Marvell, A., 1988, 'Recent excavations in Gwent' *Rescue News* 46, 6.

Matthews, L.G. and H.J.M. Green, 1969, 'Post-medieval pottery of the Inns of Court' *PMA* 3, 1–17.

Mayes, P., 1968, 'A 17th-century kiln site at Potterspury, Northants' *PMA* 2, 55–82.

Mayes, P. and L.A.S. Butler, 1983, *Sandal Castle Excavations, 1964-73* (Wakefield).

Mayes, P. and E.J.E. Pirie, 1966, 'A Cistercian ware-kiln of the early 16th century at Potterton, Yorkshire, *AntJ* 46, 255–76.

Mayes, P. and K. Scott, 1984, *Pottery Kilns at Chilvers Coton, Nuneaton* (Soc Med Arch Monograph 10).

Meeson, R., 1987, 'The timber-framed buildings of Alrewas …' in Morgan P. (ed.) *Staffordshire Studies*, (Keele), 89–104.

Mercer, E., 1975, *English Vernacular Houses*.

Merret, C., 1662, *The Art of Glass by A. Neri*, trans. with commentary.

Messenger, P., 1975, 'Lowther farmstead plans: a preliminary survey' *TCWAAS* 75, 327–51.

Miles, T.J. and A.D. Saunders, 1970, 'King Charles Castle, Tresco, Scilly' *PMA* 4, 1–30.

Miller, R., 1967a, 'Land use by summer shielings' *Scot Studies* 11, 193–221.

Miller, R., 1967b, 'Shiels in the Brecon Beacons' *Folk Life* 5, 107–10.

Milne, G., 1979, 'Medieval river-front revetment construction in London' in McGrail S. (ed.) *Medieval Ships and Harbours* (BAR Internat. Ser 66), 145–54.

Milne, G., 1981 (ed.), *Waterfront Archaeology in Britain and Northern Europe* (CBA Res Rep 41).

Milne, G., 1987, 'Waterfront archaeology in British towns' in Schofield and Leach 1987, 192–200.

Milne, G. and C., 1979, 'The making of the London waterfront' *CA* 66, 198–204.

Moore, J., 1979, 'The remains of a 17th-century clay pipe kiln at 13 Castle Street, Aylesbury ...' *Rec of Bucks* 21, 123–32.

Moorhouse, S., 1970, 1971, 'Finds from Basing House, Hampshire, I, II, *PMA* 4, 31–91; 5, 35–76.

Moorhouse, S., 1972, 'Medieval distilling apparatus of glass and pottery' *MA* 16, 79–121.

Morgan, R., 1977, 'Dendrochronological dating of a Yorkshire timber building' *VA* 8, 809–14.

Morgan, R., 1979, 'Tree-ring dating of two Georgian halls near Doncaster' *YAJ* 51, 159–61.

Morgan, R., 1980, 'Tree-ring dates for buildings' *VA* 11, 22.

Morris, R.K., 1983 (ed.), *The Church in British Archaeology* (CBA Res Rep 47).

Morris, R.K., 1987, 'Parish churches' in Schofield and Leach 1987, 177–91.

Morton, G.R., 1964–5, 'The reconstruction of an industry: the Paget ironworks, Cannock Chase, 1561' *Trans Lichfield and S Staffs Archaeol and Hist Soc* 6, 21–38.

Musty, A.E.S., 1978, 'Exploratory excavation within the monastic precinct, Waltham Abbey, 1972' *EAH* 10, 127–73.

Musty, J., 1968, 'Water mills on the River Bourne, south Wiltshire: the excavation of the site of Gomeldon Mill' *Wilts Archaeol Mag* 63, 46–53.

Musty, J., 1974, 'Medieval pottery kilns' in Evison, V.I. *et al.* (eds) *Medieval Pottery from Excavations*, 41–65.

Musty, J., 1977, 'Pots for the hot-houses at Hampton Court and Hanworth' *PMA* 11, 102–3.

Mynard, D.C., 1975, 'The Little Brickhill tile kilns and their products' *JBAA* 38, 55–80.

Newton, E.F., E. Bebbings and J.L. Fisher, 1960, '17th-century pottery sites at Harlow, Essex, *Trans Essex Archaeol Soc* 25.3, 358–77.

Newton, R.G., 1987, 'Who invented covered pots?' *Glass Technol* 29.1, 49–50.

Nicholls, P.H., 1972, 'On the evolution of a forest landscape' *Trans Inst Brit Geog* 56, 57–76.

Norris, J.H., 1965–6, 'The water-powered corn mills of Cheshire' *Trans Lancs and Ches Antiq Soc* 75–6, 33–7.

Norris, N.E.S., 1970, 'A Victorian pipe kiln in Lewes' *PMA* 4, 168–70.

Norton, E., 1988, 'The moated manor-house at Platform Wharf, Rotherhithe' *London Archaeol* 5.15, 395–401.

Oakley, G., 1984, 'Glass bottle seals' in Hassall 1984, 246–9.

Oak-Rhind, H. and K. Wade, 1977, 'A clay-pipe kiln at Chediston Street, Halesworth' *Proc Suffolk Inst of Archaeol and Hist.* 34.1, 67–70.

Orton, C., 1987, 'Delftware directions' *London Archaeol* 5.12, 335.

Orwin, C.S. and C.S., 1938, *The Open Fields* (3rd edn 1967).

Oswald, A., 1969, 'Marked clay pipes from Plymouth, Devon' *PMA* 3, 122–42.

Oswald, A., 1975, *Clay Pipes for the Archaeologist* (BAR 14).

Oswald, A., 1984, 'Clay pipes' in Hassall 1984, 251–62.

Oswald, A., 1985, 'On the life of clay-pipe moulds' in Davey P.J. 1985, 5–22.

Oswald, A., R.J.C. Hildyard and R.G. Hughes, 1982, *English Brown Stoneware*.

Paar, H.W. and D.G. Tucker, 1975, 'The old wireworks and ironworks of the Angidy Valley at Tintern, Gwent' *HM* 9.1, 1–14.

Paar, H.W. and D.G. Tucker, 1977, 'The technology of wire-making at Tintern, Gwent' *HM* 11.1, 15–24.

Palliser, D.M., 1976, *The Staffordshire Landscape*.

Palliser, D.M., 1983, *The Age of Elizabeth*.

Palmer, N., 1980, 'A beaker burial and medieval tenements in The Hamel, Oxford, *Oxoniensia* 45, 124–225.

Pantin, W.A., 1947, 'The development of domestic architecture in Oxford' *AntJ* 27, 120–50.

Pape, S., 1933–4, 'Medieval glass-workers in North Staffordshire' *Trans N Staffs Field Club* 68, 3–50.

Parker, V., 1971, *The Making of Kings Lynn* (Chichester).

Parsons, J.E., 1964, 'The archaeology of the clay tobacco pipe in north-east England' *AA* 4.42, 231–54.

Peacey, A.A., 1982, 'The structural development of clay tobacco pipe kilns in England' in Davey 1982a, 3–17.

Percival, A., 1968, 'The Faversham gunpowder industry' *IA* 5.1, 1–42.

Petchey, M. and B. Giggins, 1983, 'The excavation of a late-17th-century water mill at Caldecotte, Bow Brickhill, Bucks' *PMA* 17, 65–94.

Peters, J.E.C., 1969, *The Development of Farm Buildings in Western Lowland Staffordshire* (Manchester).

Pettit, P.A.J., 1968, *The Royal Forests of Northamptonshire* (Northants Rec Soc 23).

Phillips, A.D.M., 1972, 'The development of underdraining on a Yorkshire estate during the 19th century' *YAJ* 44, 195–206.

Phillipson, J., 1977, 'The old British round kiln in Northumberland' *AA* 5.5, 155–62.

Pickin, J, 1982, 1983, 'Excavations at Abbey Tintern furnace I; II; *HM* 16.1, 1–21; 17.1, 4–11.

Pike, H.H.M. and R.C. Combley, 1964, 'Excavations near Basing House 1962–3' *PHFCAS* 23, 11–20.

Place, C., 1989, 'Blackwater Green, Crawley' *Bull Wealden Iron Res Gp* 2.9, 10–11.

Plant, M., 1968, 'A scythe-stone industry on Beeley Moor' *DAJ* 88, 98–100.

Platt, C. and R. Coleman-Smith, 1975, *Excavations in Medieval Southampton* 2 vols (Leicester).

Pollard, E., M.D. Hooper and N.W. Moore, 1974, *Hedges*.

Porter, J., 1973, 'A forest in transition: Bowland 1500–1650' *Trans Hist Soc of Lancs and Cheshire* 125, 40–60.

Porter, J., 1974, 'Encroachment as an element in the rural landscape' *Local Historian* 11.3, 141–7.

Porter, S., 1984, 'The Oxford fire of 1644' *Oxoniensia* 49, 289–300.

Portman, D., 1966, *Exeter Houses* (Exeter).

Posnasky, M., 1956, 'The Lamport post mill' *Jnl Northants Nat Hist Soc and Field Club* 33, 66–79.

Power, M.J., 1972, 'East London housing in the 17th century' in Clark, P. and P. Slack (eds) *Crisis and Order in English Towns 1500–1700*, 237–62.

Prevost, W.A.J., 1965, 'A trip to Whitehaven to visit the coalworks there in 1739 by Sir John Clarke' *TCWAAS* 65, 305–19.

Price, R. and K. Muckelroy, 1979, 'The *Kennemerland* site … 1978 …' *IJNA* 8, 311–20.

Price, R., K. Muckelroy and L.M. Willies, 1980, 'The *Kennemerland* site: a report on the lead ingots' *IJNA* 9, 7–25.

Priestley, U., P.J. Corfield and H. Sutermeister, 1982, 'Rooms and room-use in Norwich housing, 1580–1730' *PMA* 16, 93–123.

Pryor, S. and K. Blockley, 1978, 'A 17th-century kiln site at Woolwich' *PMA* 12, 30–85.

Quiney A., 1984, 'The lobby-entrance house: its origin and distribution' *Archit Hist* 27, 456–66.

Rackham, B., 1951, *Early Staffordshire Pottery*.

Rackham, O., 1976, *Trees and Woodland in the British Landscape*.

Rackham, O., 1980, *Ancient Woodland*.

Radley, J., 1963–4, 'Peak millstones and Hallamshire grindstones' *TNS* 36, 165–73.

Radley, J., 1969, 'A triple cairn and a rectangular cairn of the Bronze Age on Beeley Moor' *DAJ* 89, 1–17.

Raistrick, A., 1926–7, 'Notes on lead mining and smelting in west Yorkshire' *TNS* 7, 81–96.

Raistrick, A., 1972, *Industrial Archaeology*.

Ramm, H.G., R.W. McDowall and E. Mercer, 1970, *Shielings and Bastles*.

Ravensdale, J.R., 1974, *Liable to Floods: Village Landscape on the Edge of the Fens* (Cambridge).

Ray, A., 1973, *English Delftware Tiles*.

RCAHM (Wales), 1988, *Glamorgan Farmhouses and Cottages: Glamorgan inventory IV, pt 2.*

RCHM (England), 1964, *Newark: the Civil War Siege Works.*

—, 1970, *Dorset ii, 2.*

—, 1972a, *Cambridgeshire ii: N E.*

—, 1972b, *City of York iii: S W of the Ouse.*

—, 1975, *Northamptonshire i: N E.*

—, 1979, *Northamptonshire ii: Central.*

—, 1981, *Northamptonshire iii: N W.*

—, 1982, *Northamptonshire iv: S W.*

—, 1985a, *Northampton.*

—, 1985b, *Rural Houses of the Lancashire Pennines.*

—, 1986a, *Rural Houses of West Yorkshire.*

—, 1986b, *Non-Conformist Chapels in Central England.*

—, 1986c, *Workers' Housing in West Yorkshire.*

—, 1987, *Houses of the North York Moors.*

Redknap, M., 1984, *The Cattewater Wreck* (BAR B131) (Oxford).

Reed, M., 1981, 'Pre-parliamentary enclosure in the east midlands, 1550–1750, and its impact upon the landscape' *Landscape History* 3, 59–68.

Reed, M., 1984, 'Enclosure in north Buckinghamshire 1500–1750' *AgHR* 32, 133–44.

Rennison, R.W., 1977, 'The supply of water to Newcastle upon Tyne and Gateshead' *AA* 5.5, 179–96.

Reynolds, J., 1970, *Windmills and Watermills.*

Reynolds, T.S., 1983, *Stronger than a Hundred Men* (Baltimore).

Rigold, S.E., 1963, 'The distribution of the Wealden House' in Foster, I. and L. Alcock (eds), *Culture and Environment*, 351–4.

Rigold, S.E., 1966, 'Some major Kentish barns' *ACant* 81, 1–30.

Rigold, S.E., 1969, 'Yardhurst, Daniels Water' *AJ* 126, 267–9.

Rigold, S.E., 1978, 'Structures within English moated sites' in Aberg 1978, 29–36.

Roberts, B.K., 1987, *The Making of the English Village.*

Roberts, D.L., 1974, 'The vernacular buildings of Lincolnshire' *AJ* 131, 298–308.

Robey, J.A. and L. Porter, 1972, *The Copper and Lead Mines of Ecton Hill, Staffordshire* (Leek).

Rodwell, K.A., 1976, 'Excavations at the site of Banbury Castle' *Oxoniensia* 41, 90–147.

Rowlands, M., 1975, *Masters and Men in the West Midlands Metal Trades before the Industrial Revolution* (Manchester).

Rowley, R.T., 1972, *The Shropshire Landscape.*

Rule, M., 1982, *The Mary Rose.*

Ryder, P.F., 1979, *Timber-framed Buildings in South Yorkshire* (Sheffield).

Sale, R.M., 1981, 'Nantwich' *CA* 77, 185–7.

Saunders, A.D., 1966, 'Hampshire coastal defences since the introduction of artillery' *AJ* 123, 136–71.

Saunders, A.D., 1969a, 'The coastal defences of the south east' *AJ* 126, 201–5.

Saunders, A.D., 1969b, 'Walmer' and 'Deal' castles *ibid* 215–19.

Saunders, A.D., 1969c, 'Upnor Castle' *ibid* 276–8.

Saunders, C., 1977, 'A 16th-century tannery at St Albans' *Hertfordshire's Past* 3, 9–12.

Schnitzer, B.K., 1977, 'Further evidence of Rhenish influence on the decorated wares of Wrotham' *PMA* 11, 103–5.

Schofield, J., 1984, *The Building of London from the Conquest to the Great Fire*.

Schofield, J. (ed.), 1987, *The London Surveys of Ralph Treswell* (London Topog Soc 135).

Schofield, J. and R Leach (eds), 1987, *Urban Archaeology in Britain* (CBA Res Rep 61).

Schofield J. and D.M. Palliser (eds), 1981, *Recent Archaeological Research in English Towns* (CBA).

Schubert, H.R., 1957, *History of the British Iron and Steel Industry ... to 1775*.

Scott, K., 1978–9, 'Brick making in north Warwickshire' *TBWAS* 89, 137–44.

Shaw, J, 1984, *Water Power in Scotland 1550–1870* (Edinburgh).

Shaw, M., 1984, 'Northampton: excavating a 16th-century tannery' *CA* 91, 241–4.

Sheail, J., 1971, 'Changes in the supply of wild rabbits, 1790–1910' *AgHR* 19, 175–7.

Shimwell, D.W., 1974, 'Sheep grazing intensity in Edale, Derbyshire, 1692–1747, and its effect on blanket-peat erosion' *DAJ* 94, 35–40.

Sills, J., 1982, 'St Peters Church, Holton-le-Clay, Lincs' *Lincs Hist and Archaeol* 17, 29–42.

Skinner, B.C., 1975, 'The archaeology of the lime industry in Scotland' *PMA* 9, 225–30.

Smith, J.T., 1985, 'Short-lived amd mobile houses in late-17th-century England' *VA* 16, 33–4.

Smith, P., 1975, *Houses of the Welsh Countryside* (1988 edn).

Smith, R.S., 1962, 'Glass-making at Wollaton in the early 17th century' *TTS* 66, 24–34.

Smith, T.P., 1975, 'A horse-engine house at Priestley Farm, Flitwick' *Beds Archaeol Jnl* 10, 77–90.

Smith, T.P., 1985, 'Brick tiles (mathematical titles) in 18th-19th-century England *JBAA* 138, 132–64.

Smith, V.T.C., 1980, 'The Milton blockhouse, Gravesend' *ACant* 96, 341–62.

Somerville, R., 1977, 'Commons and wastes in north-west Derbyshire: the High Peak "new-lands"' *DAJ* 97, 16–22.

Stell, C.F., 1965, 'Pennine houses: an introduction' *Folk Life* 3, 5–24.

Stell, C.F., 1969, 'Houses in High Street, Chalfont St Peter' *Rec of Bucks* 18.4, 277–87.

Stenuit, R., 1977, 'The wreck of the *Curacao*, a Dutch warship lost off Shetland in 1729' *IJNA* 6, 101–25.

Stoker, D., 1976, 'The early history of paper-making in Norfolk' *NA* 36.3, 241–52.

Sturdy, D., 1975, 'The Civil-War defences of London' *London Archaeol* 2.13, 334–8.

Sturdy, D. and J. Munby, 1985, 'Early domestic sites in Oxford: excavations in Cornmarket and Queen Street 1959–62' *Oxoniensia* 50, 47–94.

Tabraham, C., 1987, 'Smailholm Tower: a Scottish laird's fortified residence on the English border' *Chateau Gaillard Etudes ...* 13 (Caen), 227–38.

Tait, G.H., 1960, 1961, 'Southwark (alias Lambeth) delftware and the potter Christian Wilhelm' *Connoisseur* Aug 1960, 36–42; Feb 1961, 22–9.

Tann, J., 1965, 'Some problems of water power: a study of mill siting in Gloucestershire' *TBGAS* 84, 53–77.

Tann, J., 1967, *Gloucestershire Woollen Mills* (Newton Abbot).

Tawney, R.H. and E. Power (eds), 1924, *Tudor Economic Documents* (3 vols).

Taylor, C.C. 1970, *Dorset*.

Taylor, C.C. 1973, *The Cambridgeshire Landscape*.

Taylor, C.C., 1975, *Fields in the English landscape*.

Taylor, C.C., 1983a, *The Archaeology of Gardens* (Princes Risborough).

Taylor, C.C., 1983b, *Village and Farmstead*.

Taylor, R., 1974, 'Town houses in Taunton 1500–1700' *PMA* 8, 63–79.

Taylor, R., 1975, 'The coastal salt industry of Amounderness' *Trans Lancs and Cheshire Antiq Soc* 78, 14–21.

Taylor, R.F., 1968, 'A cob dovecot at Durleigh' *Proc Somerset Archaeol and Nat Hist Soc* 112, 101–3.

Tebbutt, C.F., 1981, 'A deserted medieval farm settlement at Faulkners Farm, Hartfield' *SxAC* 119, 107–16.

Thirsk, J., 1957, *English Peasant Farming*.

Thirsk, J. (ed.), 1967, 1985, *Agricultural History of England and Wales IV, 1560–1640; V, 1640–1750*.

Thomas, J.H., 1977, 'The Company of White Paper-makers in Hampshire: an inventory of plant' *PMA* 11, 22–35.

Thomas, S., 1980, *Medieval Footwear from Coventry: a Catalogue of the Collection of Coventry Museum* (Coventry).

Thompson, A., 1979, 'St Nicholas-in-the-Shambles' *CA* 65, 176–9.

Thompson, A., 1981, 'The Aldgate clay pipe kiln' in Davey 1981, 3–13.

Thompson, A., F. Grew and J. Schofield, 1984, 'Excavations at Aldgate' *PMA* 18, 1–148.

Thompson, D. and V. Smith, 1977, 'The excavation of the Gravesend blockhouse 1975–6' *ACant* 93, 153–77.

Thompson, M.W., 1987, *The Decline of the Castle*.

Thomson, R., 1981, 'Leather manufacture in the post-medieval period with special reference to Northamptonshire' *PMA* 15, 161–75.

Tillyard, R., 1976, 'Hedge dating in north Norfolk: the Hooper method examined' *NA* 36, 272–9.

Timmins, J.G., 1979, 'Handloom weavers' cottages in central Lancashire: some problems of recognition' *PMA* 13, 251–72.

Trent, E.M. and E.F. Smart, 1984, 'Further examination of a cutting-tip from a cannon-boring tool' *HM* 18.1, 8–12.

Trinder, B. amd J. Cox, 1980, *Yeomen and Colliers in Telford* (Chichester).

Trinder, B., 1981, *The Industrial Revolution in Shropshire* (Chichester).

Tucker, D.G., 1971, 'Millstone making at Penallt, Monmouthshire' *IA* 8, 229–39.

Tucker, D.G., 1972, 'The paper mills of Whitebrook, Monmouthshire, *ACamb* 121, 80–96.

Tucker, D.G., 1976, 'The slate quarries at Easedale, Argyllshire' *PMA* 10, 118–30.

Tucker, D.G., 1977, 'Millstones, quarries and millstone makers' *PMA* 11, 1–21.

Tucker, D.G., 1978, 'The beginning of the wireworks at Whitebrook, Gwent, in the early 17th century' *HM* 12.2, 102–3.

Turner, L. and M. Watts, 1977, 'The small tower mills of the British Isles' *Trans Internat Molinol Soc* 4, 55–74.

Turner, M., 1980, *English Parliamentary Enclosure*.

Turner, M., 1984, *Enclosure in Britain 1750–1830*.

Tylecote, E. (ed.), 1970, 'James Mulcaster's account of the method of smelting lead ore as it is practised in the northern part of England' *HM* 5.2, 45–62.

Tylecote, R.F., 1966, 'A blast furnace at Coed Ithel, Llandogo, Mon' *Jnl Iron and Steel Inst* 204, 314–19.

Tylecote, R.F., 1972, 'A contribution to the metallurgy of 18th and 19th-century brass pins' *PMA* 6, 183–90.

Tylecote, R.F., 1975, 'Metallurgical report' in Beresford G. *The Medieval Clayland Village: Excavations at Goltho and Barton Blount* (Soc Med Archaeol monograph 6), 81–2, 85, 90–1.

Tylecote, R.F., 1976, *A History of Metallurgy*.

Tylecote, R.F., 1980, 'Calenick: a Cornish tin-smelter, 1702–1891' *HM* 14.1, 1–16.

Tylecote, R.F and J. Cherry, 1970, 'The 17th-century bloomery at Muncaster Head' *TCWAAS* 70, 69–109.

Tyson, B., 1980, 'Rydal Hall farmyard: the development of a Westmorland farmstead before 1700' *TCWAAS* 80, 113–29.

Tyson, B., 1981, 'Construction schedules for some 17th-century farm buildings in Cumbria' *PMA* 15, 219–24.

Vince, A, 1977, 'The medieval and post-medieval ceramic industry of the Malvern region' in Peacock D.P.S. (ed.) *Pottery and Early Commerce* 257–305.

Wacher, J., 1966, 'Excavations at Riplingham, E. Yorks, 1956–7' *YAJ* 41, 608–69.

Wade, K., 1980, 'The excavation of a brick clamp at Shotesham St Mary, Norfolk, 1969' *PMA* 14, 187–9.

Wade Martins, S., 1977, 'The farm buildings of the agricultural revolution' *Local Historian* 12.8, 407–21.

Wadhams, M.C., 1972, 'The development of buildings in Witham from 1500 to c.1880' *PMA* 6, 1–41.

Wailes, R, 1954, *The English Windmill*.

Walker, P., 1988, 'Bee-boles in Kent', *ACant* 106, 107–27.

Walton, P., 1981, 'Textiles' in Harbottle and Ellison (1981), 190–228.

Ward, A.H., 1983, 'A sod lime-kiln on Cefn Bryn, Gower, West Glamorgan' *PMA* 17, 177–80.

Warmington, R., 1976, 'Rebuilding of "La Belle" Inn, Andover, 1534' *PMA* 10, 131–41.

Warrington, G., 1981, 'The copper mines of Alderley Edge amd Mottram St Andrew, Cheshire' *Jnl Chester Archaeol Soc* 64, 47–73.

Weddell, P.J., 1985, 'The excavation of medieval and later houses at Wolborough Street, Newton Abbot' *Trans Devon Archaeol Soc* 43, 77–109.

Wells, P.K., 1970, 'The excavation of a 19th-century clay-tobacco-pipe kiln in Boston' *Lincs Hist and Archaeol* 5, 21–7.

Wenham, L.P., 1972, 'Excavations in Low Petergate, York, 1957–8' *YAJ* 44, 65–113.

Westrop, M.S.D., 1921, *Irish Glass*.

Whatley, C.A., 1982, 'An early 18th-century Scottish saltwork: Arran c.1710–35' *IAR* 6.2, 89–101.

Whatley, C.A., 1984, *The Salt Industry and its Trade in Fife and Tayside, c.1570–1850* (Abertay Hist Soc 22).

Whiston, J.W., 1969–70, 'Bee-boles at Pipe Ridware Farm, Staffs' *Trans S. Staffs Archaeol and Hist Soc* 11, 43–5.

Whitaker, A.H., 1969, 'Coal mining in Bransdale and Farndale in the 18th century' *Rydedale Hist* 4, 55–63.

White, A.J., 1982, 'Post-medieval pancheons with name-stamps found in Lincolnshire' *PMA* 16, 29–38.

White, D.P., 1977, 'The Birmingham button industry' *PMA* 11, 67–79.

White, R.H., 1986, *Peel Castle Excavations I* (Isle of Man).

Whitehead, D., 1981, 'Brick and tile making in the woodlands of the west midlands in the 16th and 17th centuries' *VA* 12, 42–7.

Wiliam, E., 1982, *Traditional Farm Buildings in north-east Wales 1550–1900* (Cardiff).

Wiliam, E., 1986, *The Historic Farm Buildings of Wales* (Edinburgh).

Wilkinson, P.M., 1983, 'Excavations at Tilbury fort, Essex' *PMA* 17, 111–62.

Willan, T.S., 1936, *River Navigation in England* (Oxford).

Willatts, R.M., 1987, 'Iron graveslabs: a sideline of the early iron industry' *SxAC* 125, 99–113.

Williams, D.W., 1984, 'Excavations at 43 High Street, Reigate, 1981' *SyAC* 75, 111–53.

Williams, E.H.D., 1972, 'Corn-drying kilns' *Proc Somerset Archaeol and Nat Hist Soc* 116, 101–3.

Williams, E.H.D., 1976, 'Curing-chambers and domestic corn-drying kilns' *ibid* 120, 57–61.

Williams, J, 1979, *St Peters Street Northampton: Excavations* (Northampton).

Williams, M., 1972, 'The enclosure of waste land in Somerset 1700–1900' *Trans Inst Brit Geog* 57, 99–124.

Willies, L.M., 1969, 'Cupola lead smelting sites in Derbyshire, 1737–1900' *Bull Peak Dist Mines Hist Soc* 4.1, 97–115.

Witt C., C. Weeden and A.P. Schwind, 1984, *Bristol Glass* (Bristol).

Wood, E.S., 1965, 'A medieval glasshouse at Blunden's Wood, Hambledon, Surrey' *SyAC* 62, 54–79.

Wood, E.S., 1982, 'A 16th-century glasshouse at Knightons, Alfold, Surrey,' *SyAC* 73, 1–47.

Wood, P.D., 1968, 'The topography of East Grinstead borough' *SxAC* 106, 49–62.

Woodfield, C., 1981, 'Finds from the Free Grammar School at the Whitefriars, Coventry, c.1545–c.1557–8 *PMA* 15, 81–59.

Woodfield, P., 1963–4, 'Yellow-glazed wares of the 17th century' *TBWAS* 81, 78–87.

Woodward, F., 1982, *Oxfordshire Parks* (Woodstock).

Wrathmell, S. 1984, 'The vernacular threshold of northern peasant houses' *VA* 15, 29–33.

Yorke, F.W.B., 1956, 'Ice houses' *Trans Anc Mon Soc* 4, 123–32.

Young, D., 1979, 'The Verwood potters' *PDNHAS* 101, 103–20.

Zeepvat, R.J., 1980, 'Post Mills' *CA* 71, 375–7.

Index